AMERICAN NEEDLEWORK

Embroidered picture worked in silks and chenille upon satin. The use of the eagle in the decorative border of flowers would indicate the design was created during the Federal Period or Early Nineteenth Century. About 1800, by Laura Sherril, Richmond, Massachusetts.

AMERICAN NEEDLEWORK

The History of
Decorative Stitchery and Embroidery
from the Late 16th to
the 20th Century

By GEORGIANA BROWN HARBESON

Illustrated with Photographs
Drawings by the Author

BONANZA BOOKS ❦ NEW YORK

This edition published by Bonanza Books,
a division of Crown Publishers, Inc.,
by arrangement with Coward-McCann, Inc.

MANUFACTURED IN THE UNITED STATES OF AMERICA

~~~~~~

DEDICATED

TO

ALL WOMEN WHO LOVE BEAUTY

~~~~~~

CONTENTS

LIST OF STATES REPRESENTED IN NEEDLEWORK ILLUSTRATIONS

MASSACHUSETTS
CONNECTICUT
NEW YORK
OHIO
NEW HAMPSHIRE
PENNSYLVANIA
LOUISIANA
VIRGINIA
RHODE ISLAND
VERMONT
MAINE
MARYLAND
TEXAS
SOUTH DAKOTA
ILLINOIS

CALIFORNIA
NEW JERSEY
SOUTH CAROLINA
OKLAHOMA
WISCONSIN
MINNESOTA
MICHIGAN
WASHINGTON
NORTH CAROLINA
OREGON
MONTANA
ALASKA
KENTUCKY
DISTRICT OF COLUMBIA

~~~~~~

LIST OF ILLUSTRATIONS

~~~~~~

INTRODUCTION

~~~~~~

EMBROIDERY IS A PERSONAL ART AND THE POETRY OF THE NEEDLE. IN its highest sense it is an art medium comparable to painting. *American Needlework* presents an historical outline of decorative stitches used by American women in various embroidery techniques. Examples have been selected from each period in the country's development from the days before the white men came here through pioneer days to the present.

From primitive times women have embroidered their personal apparel and that of their loved ones. They have wrought embroidered decorations for their homes, whether cabin or castle, and for their sanctuaries. The style has varied from race to race and from period to period, but chiefly in the matter of the design, color, rhythm, and the materials used. Stitching has remained fundamentally the same.

With a definite vocabulary of stitch forms as a foundation, women have given expression to dominant notes in their cultural background. The uses to which their embroidery has been applied reflect the taste, the manners and the customs of their day. Needlework, too, has been the means of poetic and philosophic release for countless numbers of women who had no other outlet for their idealistic yearning. That so many fine works, notable for their beauty of design and high standard of craftsmanship, were produced even when the manner of life was crude and exacting and when dangers threatened on every side, is a great tribute not only to women's ingenuity and tireless industry, but to their nobility of soul.

It is the purpose of the author to pick up these threads which have been stitched by American women and to catch a glimpse through the needle's eye, so to speak, of the domestic life and environment of our enterprising forebears. For art students interested in research the embroideries are useful documents from which to obtain atmosphere. For the needlework artist they illustrate the traditional techniques upon which her art is founded and suggest new directions in which it may be developed.

The examples reproduced have not been selected from the point of view of art only. Some have been included because they mirror contemporary standards and modes of thought. Others have been chosen because in copying a popular pattern the embroiderer has introduced some personal touch, her own interpretation of the stitches to be used, her own idea of color harmony, the inclusion within the design of a favored flower, a bird she may have liked, or some remembered beauty of landscape or sky. These little variations are overtones that record the heart beat of the age in which the worker lived.

Much of the design used in American needlework has come from European and Asiatic sources, but a suggestion that an art of our own is emerging may be found to a greater or less degree in all the works presented. In almost every example it may be noted that though the pattern may have come from abroad, something of the simplicity of American taste has expressed itself by adaptation of or departure from the original. Either the outlines have been simplified or the color has been changed to harmonize with tones existing here. Even in the ambitious cross-stitched tapestry pictures of the middle nineteenth century there is a little less of the shading and pyrotechnics which occur in many European examples of this period.

It may be the ability to see and report only the essentials which makes much American work simpler in style. In the needlework design of today more and more emphasis is laid upon directness. It would seem that we are reverting to the purely decorative and inter-pretive effects achieved in embroideries of the early seventeenth century. There is also a hint of a throw-back to the twelfth century and early primitive work. This is, of course, in line with a similar change which is taking place in architecture, sculpture, music, painting and literary expression and like them it reflects characteristic aspects of life as it is lived in our generation.

Excellent embroideries in needlepoint and crewelwork are executed by American women today who feel the same urge which actuated women of long ago to express themselves imaginatively and to enrich their environment with work created with their own hands. May these contemporary achievements prove as interesting to the future as those of the past now are to us.

It is not generally realized how much embroidery contributes to an interpretation and understanding of the American scene, nor how much has been gathered by a discerning few for various private collections. The author owes much to these patrons of the art, many of whom have loaned items for reproduction, and to the curators and directors of museums and libraries for the time and the information which they have so generously contributed. Their co-operation has been invaluable in compiling this material which, it is hoped, will aid in the development of a better and broader understanding of the art of needlework in America.

New York, 1938.

GEORGIANA BROWN HARBESON.

PART I

NEEDLEWORK IN THE PRIMITIVE NEW WORLD

AMERICAN INDIAN PORCUPINE-QUILL EMBROIDERY

INDIAN BEAD NEEDLEWORK

INDIAN APPLIQUÉ, ALASKAN FISHSKIN NEEDLEWORK

CHAPTER I

AMERICAN INDIAN PORCUPINE-QUILL EMBROIDERY

"All thoughts that mould the age begin
Deep down within the primitive soul."
JAMES RUSSELL LOWELL.

MONG THE EARLIEST TYPES OF needlework known to exist in America was the fine art of porcupine-quill embroidery. Examples surviving in various museums are beautiful memorials to the fruitful invention of the aborigines of North America. This form of decorative art was discovered by early travelers to the continent. Hannon, in his *Journal of Voyages and Travels in the Interior of North America,* gives the following description:

The women manifest much ingenuity and taste in the work which they execute with porcupine quills. The color of these quills is various, beautiful and desirable, and the art of dyeing them is practiced only by the females.

Other accounts describe the decoration of the men's garments which were ornamented "with feathers, porcupine quills and horsehair, stained of various colors." It appears, therefore, that this art was well established among the native Indians long before the coming of the European explorers. Accumulated historical evidence would indicate that this delicate quillwork predated that of beadwork among the early inhabitants of the continent.

Although different voyagers arriving from Europe brought new materials which were readily acquired by the natives, the traditional needlework applied to skins and made from the natural resources to be found in their own environment such as quills, feathers, stones, roots, shells, and minerals, continued for a long period.

In a description written to Richard Hakluyt, Ralph Lane, who commanded Sir Walter Raleigh's second expedition to Virginia in 1585, comments on materials in use in sixteenth century America as follows:

The continent is of an huge and unknown greatness, and very well peopled and towned, though savagely, and the climate so wholesome, that we had not one sick since we touched the land here. To conclude, if Virginia had but horses and kine in some reasonable proportion, I dare assure myself, being inhabited with English, no realm in Christendom were comparable to it. For this already we find, that what commodities soever France, Spain, Italy, or the East parts do yield unto us, in wines of all sorts, in oils, in flax, in rosins, pitch, frankincense, currants, sugars, and such like, these parts do abound with the growthe of them all; but being savages that possess the land, they know no use of the same. And sundry other rich commodities, that no parts of the world, be they West or East Indies, have, here we find great abundance of. The people naturally are most courteous, and very desirous to have cloaths, but especially of coarse cloth rather than silk, coarse canvas they also like well of, but copper carrieth the price of all, as it be made red. Thus good M. Hakluyt, and M. H., I have joined you both in one letter of remembrance, as two that I love dearly well, and commending me most heartily to you both, I commit you to the tuition of the Almighty. From the new fort in Virginia, this 3rd of September, 1585.

Your most assured friend,
RALPH LANE

Although the introduction of foreign "cloath" occurs at such an early period, the new imports did not reach beyond the coast. For a long period after the coming of the white men this aboriginal American art work continued, untouched by foreign influence.

QUILLWORK ON SKIN

These embroideries were made throughout the woodland regions of the continent and among the Plains Indians, the Menominee tribe in the North, the Sioux and Chippewa tribes in the region of the Great Lakes, and the Indians along the Mackenzie River extending into Canada. The work spoke a universal language, revealing not only love of the art but the eternal desire among women to make something precious and beautiful for those dear to them. Every conceivable item of costume has been decorated with quillwork—shirts, hoods, moccasins, leggings and costume accessories of every description. Knife sheaths were popular objects for decoration. A beautiful example of Chippewa work in woven technique is shown in the collection of the Museum of the American Indian, Heye Foundation, New York City. In that collection also may be seen a deerskin mat embroidered with quills. The central design consists of figures in outline engaged in a ceremony. On the outer edge surrounding the center square are other little figures around which geometric patterns of the Otter Society are stitched. Quill-worked medicine bags of the Otter Society in which the back, head and tail of the skin have been decorated with elaborate quill embroidery may also be seen in the Heye collection.

The Menominee tribe is well represented at the American Museum of Natural History with a fine collection of medicine bags most of which are of otter skin. They are stitched with dyed quills of red, white and blue with occasional yellow-gold colors.

An early example from South Dakota, in the Berkshire Museum collection, combines bead and quillwork. This sheepskin satchel is embroidered with green, red, purple and brown, with eagle down feathers dyed green, and turquoise-blue silk ribbons probably obtained in trading with Europeans. The workmanship is a little coarse. The conventionalized animal head, a buffalo, is flanked on either side by abstract symbols of the sun representing strength and power. On the reverse side the bag is worked with coarse, native-made beads sewn in a conventionalized design as shown in the illustration facing page six.

From the same collection is a beautiful example of very fine quill embroidery applied to a European type of jacket or coat. Belonging to what is technically called the transition and later period of Indian quillwork, this frontiersman's deerskin coat is particularly exciting. The entire decoration around the collar and cuffs has been arranged with excellent restraint and selectiveness. The composition in the back panel is very graceful in its relation to the lines of the jacket.

It is an interesting question where the Indian woman who made this finely executed quill embroidery obtained her pattern. The lotus bud of Egyptian design and origin appears on the back of the jacket. The decoration is unlike most Indian ornament. The frontiersman who owned it may have belonged to the aristocratic group of Frenchmen who, with the blood of adventure flowing in their veins, broke new trails into the great forests of the Western wilderness and arrived at Indian camps by way of the Ohio or the Mississippi. The epaulets of stripped deerskin suggest, however, that he may have been an officer heading a vanguard of frontiersmen banded together to protect newly established trading posts and little log cabin communities. Inspired by the tales of Daniel Boone, a trek towards the rich country beyond the Appalachian Mountains began about the year 1770. Over the Cumberland Gap on Boone's newly blazed wilderness road they struggled, carrying the few possessions necessary for existence. The Long Hunters as they were sometimes called, like frontiersmen since the earliest days of settlement, found the Indian costume practical and warm for winter and they adopted for constant use the fringed trousers and loose shirts of buckskin. It is possible that the coat described belonged to this period.

Belonging to the same period is a deerskin waistcoat, evidently intended to complete the ensemble for it is in the same collection in the Berkshire Museum. The front is quill-worked with an allover repeat motif much like eighteenth century brocade in the spotting of the unit, but in design similar to the decoration on the frontiersman's coat. The colorings are identical and the design possesses an abstract quality approximating the Egyptian conventionalized lily and leaf motifs. The back of the waistcoat is made of woolen material, coarse but in a lovely shade of blue which still holds its color and richness.

Iroquois tribes in New York State ornamented their costumes for the war dance with striking quill embroideries. Exactness of finish combined with the neatness of the materials used gave a striking appearance during the graceful movements of the dance. In the earliest warrior dance costumes as well as in those of the squaws, the foundation material was deerskin. With the advent of the colonists deerskin gradually was replaced by broadcloth, sometimes called "English clothe" since much of it came from the English. The bearskin blanket was replaced by the woolen blanket and porcupine quillwork by bead embroidery.

An example of the combination of bead and quill embroidery may be seen in the long tobacco pouch made by a Sioux squaw of South Dakota. An elaborate white bead backing has been sewn in a square formation on the skin to silhouette two deer worked in royal-blue beads, and four American flags each four starred. Beneath this a handsome fringe has been made by sewing and wrapping red, purple and gold porcupine quills around strands of sinew, forming a conventional pattern from which hang strips of deerskin for the remaining fringe. With such a pouch for his tobacco any manly warrior could be proud to sit at peace with his world.

Quill-embroidered gloves, also made in South Dakota by a Sioux Indian, are gaily worked on skin in red, purple, jade green and white. They are fur topped and woolen lined, as gloves worn in the vicinity of the northern states should be. The moccasins illustrated, quill-embroidered by a squaw of the Gros Ventre tribe living on the Fort Bethold reservation in North Dakota, are worked in "shocking pink," bright green, bright purple, and red. Their cut is interesting; pointed tops on the tongue accent the hues of the sun-ray design on the toes. The women of this tribe were most inventive in the use of their quills, employing different methods in applying them to the skins. Dr. Clark Wissler of the American Museum of Natural History explains the various techniques explicitly in his excellent *Anthropological Papers* describing the culture of the Blackfoot Indians.

The Plains Indians made attractive use of crosshatched quillwork on their jackets. Many examples of their embroidery show both crosshatched and plain stitches. Their use of color is particularly striking. The brilliant sunlight, the intense blue of the sky and other color values of the plains country are reflected both in their quillwork and in their bead embroidery.

The foundation technique used by all Indians who found porcupine quills in their environment is as follows:

METHOD OF WORKING

There were four general methods—sewing, weaving, wrapping and, as applied to birchbark, the insertion of the ends of the quills into perforations made with an awl.

Sewing was the most common method of attaching quills to leather on a flat surface. A thin strip of sinew was used for thread, which was kept moist except at the end. The end was allowed to dry and was twisted into a stiff, sharp point with which the sewing was done. The thread did not go through the hide, but penetrated the upper surface only. In order to allow the sinew to enter and hold to the skin, little perforations were made with the sharp point of a stone chipped to resemble an awl. The "needle" was passed through these perforations carrying the sinew thread in small stitches over the quills. These in turn were lapped back and forth over the stitches as each one was taken in order to conceal them. While working the squaws would hold the quills in the mouth to soften them so that they could be easily flattened and kept flexible for bending and uniting into the desired pattern. On the reverse side no evidence of sewing is seen.

For some types of sewing bone bodkins were used. Later these were replaced by needles brought to America by the white traders. Considering the crudity of the first implements, it is all the more remarkable that such fine work was accomplished by these women. Much of it is due to clever manipulation in lapping the quills onto the surface of the skin and dexterity in catching them in place with the sinew thread. The stitch methods are similar in some instances to the "backstitch," "couching stitch," and the "chain stitch," terms used in sewing technique today.

Different skins provided the foundation according to locality. The Plains Indians obtained skins of bison, deer, elk, bear, and beaver. Hunters living a nomadic life, these Indians did not produce the basketry and weaving associated with the more settled and agricultural peoples of the Southwest and Mexico. They had skins in abundance and used them for clothing, bags and their tepee dwellings, some of which were decorated with quill embroidery.

Deerskin seems to have been used most frequently for costumes and was often embroidered with quillwork. Buckskin, which was pure white, soft and smooth as a fine cotton fabric, was particularly beautiful when decorated. Buffalo hides and deerskins, with a soft tan finish, were prepared by the Blackfoot Indians for robes and soft bags. Hundreds of these were traded at Fort Brenton as late as 1880. The tanning of skins was an additional task for the Indian women who had to soften them in preparation for sewing and embroidery.

DYES

Dyeing porcupine quills and feathers was a most important procedure. Early colors were acquired from trees and plants according to the growth in the vicinity of the tribe. The women near the Rocky Mountains produced a beautiful yellow dye from a lemon-colored moss which grows on fir trees in the mountains. A certain root provided a beautiful red. Other pigments were obtained from berries, bark, flowers and some minerals.

When the traders arrived with gay calicos, red woolens and other new fabrics, these materials were quickly boiled to provide dramatic new dyes for the later quill embroideries. With the arrival of these novelties came also new designs to be applied not only to the primitive costume, but to the new styles which Indians copied from the original settlers' jackets.

As colonial women prized their stock of dyed crewel wools for their embroidery and collected odds and ends in a large bag for future sewing work, so the Indian squaw treasured her sewing materials. Along with her sewing case, she had sacks made of gut in which were stored away the precious quills dyed in various shades and stripped ready for embroidery when the opportunity presented itself.

PATTERN TRANSFER

Outlining for quillwork on animal skins was accomplished by stretching the piece taut and tracing off a line drawing of the pattern by heavy pressure on the sharp point of an awl. The slightly scratched and indented surface was an ideal field on which to transfer the working plan for embroidery either with quills, beads, or combinations of both.

Patterns and designs were accommodated to the shape and size of the object to be adorned. They varied also according to the length of the quills. By the use of alternating colors in border arrangements and in the "wrapping" patterning on fringes interesting contrast in high light and shadow was achieved.

Since the life of the North American Indians was exceedingly primitive and full of hardship, it is remarkable that their women could find ways and means to execute the fine, exquisite work evidenced in the many beautiful specimens that remain. Their work shows skill and artistry in both technique and design. The timing, folding and twisting of the quills, as well as their application to the animal skins, was a trying and delicate procedure. In the earlier work the quills are a little larger and coarser in the sewn technique. The later work seems very much finer and more intricate, perhaps because a less primitive existence allowed the women more leisure in which to execute elaborate patterns.

DESIGN

Early designs consisted in a series of abstract units arranged geometrically. They can be di-

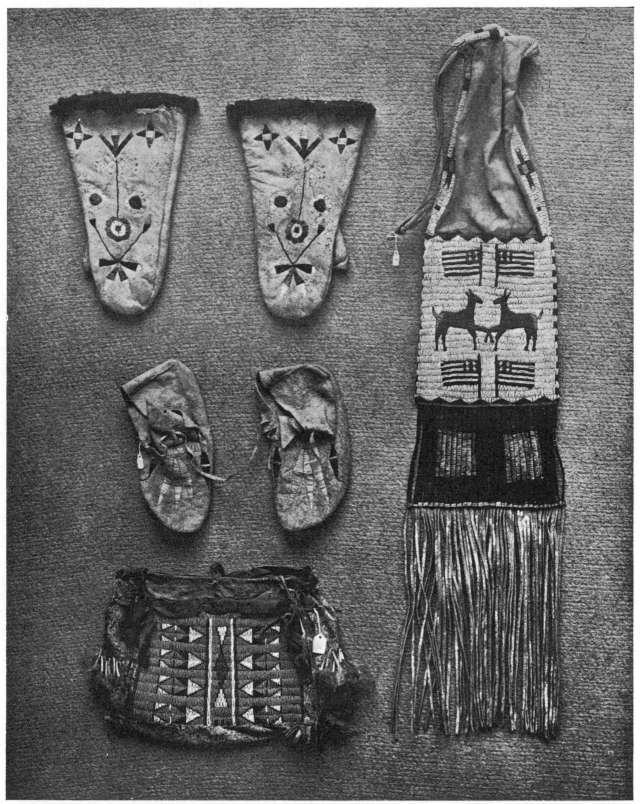

Dyed porcupine quill embroidered fur topped mittens from Sioux Indians, South Dakota.

Moccasins quill embroidered by an Indian woman of the Gros Ventre tribe, Fort Bethold reservation, North Dakota.

Satchel Cover of sheepskin porcupine quill embroidered on one side and beaded on the other, silk ribbons and dyed eagle down hangers, Indian, South Dakota.

Tobacco Pouch, long, buckskin, decorated with bead and porcupine quill embroidery. Sioux Indian Work, South Dakota.

Card Case dyed porcupine quill work on birch-bark and black cloth, sweet grass border. About 1795, Indian North West.

Reverse of Card Case Quill Embroidered on Birch-Bark.

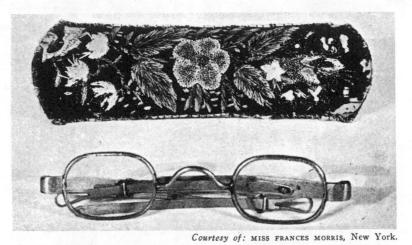

Eye glass case of porcupine quill embroidery on black cloth and birch-bark. About 1790. Eye glasses of the period, with case.

Porcupine quill embroidery on birch-bark, box top and side panels. About 1798, Indian North West.

vided into two classes, conventionalized nature forms and abstract geometrical figures entirely unrelated to nature. Gradually a series of units which had become traditional and familiar was composed into a pattern. Such patterns were given names and had either personal or general significance. A squaw might compose a pattern for her quillwork or beadwork from a pattern book of units handed down to her through her tribal association. A design might be created which would read as follows:

The "Morning Star" at the "Horizon" may be seen by the "Eye" of a "Person Standing" outside the "Tent" beside the "Lake." Beyond the "Mountain Peaks" lies the "Mythical cave of the Buffalo"; "Abundance of Buffalo" will bring "Life Prosperity." The "Arrowpoint" shows the way the "Horse Tracks" take the early morning hunter to the cave past "Lightning" over the "Valley" by the "Path going over the Hill." He brings back "Buffalo." "Buffalo horns" indicate this hunter's mighty strength which is like the "Rock." He brings "Good Luck," and the "Sun's Rays" will shine upon the "Tents" in the "Camp Circle."

Each one of these design elements has its geometric representation. The interpretation depends upon their arrangement in the pattern. In this manner records of important events were embroidered on the apparel and accessories of individual Indians in order that others might read the history of a particular occasion and be informed of the part that the wearer played in it.

Other designs had significance above specific happenings and were related to religion. These designs were composed of symbols which followed the pure geometric forms. Later they acquired a protective connotation in which a circle, spiral or some other motif represented the power which would offer magical aid or give comfort to the one for whom the needlework was made. Many examples of this early Indian embroidery have survived because of the reverence in which it was held. Considered sacred, these skins decorated with ceremonial symbols were handed down for centuries from one generation to another.

With the arrival of the white man's culture, naturalistic floral forms were introduced until finally, in work embroidered in the early eighteenth century, French floral designs and Spanish motifs began to supersede the abstract patterns. This influence passed from tribe to tribe along with the introduction of beads and woolen materials. But while the realistic forms were popular, the Indians did not lose entirely their love of symbolism and eventually the two styles became blended.

QUILLWORK ON BIRCH-BARK

In the later years of the eighteenth century, porcupine-quill embroidery was commercialized by the Chippewa Indians and the technique was then applied to birch-bark as a foundation. Sewing was omitted and the quillwork was applied to the bark through perforations made with an awl which was a little smaller than the quills used. The end of the quill was inserted and when the awl needle was withdrawn the bark would contract sufficiently to hold the quill in place. Many boxes were made to sell, the borders of which were often bands of sweet grass sewed with commercial thread.

Designs were drawn on the bark with a blunt instrument. Many of them have great charm because of their simplicity and color. Stems and leaves of the flowers give the same effect as that produced by the outline and satin stitch used in seventeenth century embroidery, but since the quills do not form a continuous line of "thread," as in embroidery, the effect was obtained by using bits of quill in a series of short insertions which simulate the appearance of outline sketches. Where cloth was applied over the birch-bark foundation, the quills were doubly protected against the possibility of being loosened from their insertion.

Many examples may be found in various collections of these black cloth and birch-bark quill embroideries, ornamented with flower forms which simulate French knots. This effect is obtained by clipping ends of the inserted quills and bending them. These short ends clustered together have a high-lighted form such as a knot gives in the doubled thread. Dyed quills in pastel tones decorating the surface of boxes, cases, holders, etc., are very attractive; the designs are eighteenth century floral forms rather than the geometric figures which were characteristic of the earlier examples of porcupine quillwork.

A unique and engaging example of this birch-bark quillwork has come to light recently in the private collection of Miss Frances Morris in New York. Miss Morris, a former curator of textiles at the Metropolitan Museum of Art and an authority on such items, places this quill-embroidered eyeglass case in the late eighteenth century; she knows definitely that it is over a hundred years old. The case was left to Miss Morris's family by her "Aunty" Caroline Hurtin. It belonged to her great-grandmother Hurtin in the South before they moved to Goshen, New York, with all their household belongings. Later, in 1850, Miss Caroline Hurtin and her sister established a young ladies' school where they taught the genteel and cultural "Arts" including needlework.

Through all these changes the delicate little eyeglass case survived. The cloth covering is a little worn about the edges where, no doubt, the glasses were slipped in and out, perhaps with the purpose of examining "samples" of the young ladies' needlework. Its stitchery remains fairly intact and colorful. The quills have been dyed in tones of rose, pink, powder blue, and deeper indigo for the flowers. The leaf tints are shaded from darker greens through a yellowish green, to an ochre yellow and deeper golden tones. Where the tightly woven black linen has chipped away from the birch-bark foundation of the case, one may see the stripes on the bark and discern the pricks of the needle which stitched the colored quills into the graceful little flowered pattern. The center flower gives the impression of being worked in very fine French knots, but upon close examination one discovers that the little quills have been clipped close to the surface, leaving tiny blunt ends which look for all the world like small loops of thread.

One wonders if some old Indian squaw on the plantation made this little present, for the technique is essentially Indian in origin employing the then "newer" materials, bark instead of deerskin for firmness, and linen to cover it instead of broadcloth. It may be that the pattern was designed by a colonial maiden in the South who then sent it to an Indian woman to be worked. Many Indian women worked upon plantations, in the North as well as in the South. There were many of them down on Cape Cod. It was there that my own great-grandmother, on her plantation near Plymouth,

Massachusetts, employed Indians from a tribe who lived at Sandwich. They used to embroider under her direction after household and plantation duties were performed. A relic left to me by my grandmother is a little beaded purse made by one of my great-grandmother's maids, Rosa Webquish, who was one of the talented members of the Sippican tribe located at what was called "Indian Village."

The long panel of birch-bark embroidered with porcupine quills, shown in the illustration, was at one time a box. The large center square was the cover, the small strips, the sides. They have been separated and framed in order to preserve this delicate work. The legend surrounding it has been noted by the owner, Mrs. Mabel Eichel, of Connecticut, who says:

> The dyed quill-embroidered birch-bark box was made by an Indian princess whose name I do not know. The tradition about it in my family is as follows: My mother's father's family was named Mix. They settled in New Haven before the Revolution. The history of the family can be found in a book in the genealogical section of the New York Public Library called "The Memoirs of Jonathan Mix."
> A member of the family was among the first to volunteer his services for naval service during the Revolution. Later the family for several generations were all in the Navy seeing much distinguished service. Some of them also served in the Army and one—so the story goes—became an Indian Commissioner and was sent to the Northwest. He is supposed to have married an Indian princess and she was the person who made the box which is now a panel. I believe that Tom Mix, the movie star, is descended from that branch of the family.

Small, flowering berrybushes or similar plant life must have been the source of design for this work. Much of the pattern has been worked in little white clipped quills, with the French-knot effect. They are combined with delicate greens, pale pinks, mauve, and deeper touches of green, against the yellow gold of the birch-bark, colors which create a lovely harmony. The floral forms are spaced and drawn with great feeling and artistry.

Belonging to the same school as the eyeglass case is the little card case worked with the "knotted" quills laid over and over in loops. This also has the foundation of birch-bark over which black cloth has been framed, the porcupine quills being embroidered over it and into the bark underneath. The case is quite substantial and is protected on the edges with the couched bandings of sweet grass.

Some later examples of the quillwork on birch-bark were made in the vicinity of Niagara. These were worked on round boxes and were less elaborate in design. Recent work attempted by a few Indians does not approach the delicacy of design or workmanship which is shown in the eighteenth and early nineteenth century pieces. The art has apparently died out and only a few scattered works remain to testify to the patient, artistic production of a people who possessed a deep appreciation of beauty.

CHAPTER II

INDIAN BEAD NEEDLEWORK

*"To him who in the love of nature holds
Communion with her visible forms,
She speaks a various language."*
WILLIAM CULLEN BRYANT.

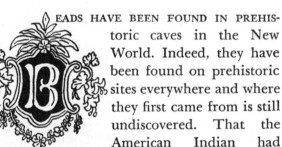

EADS HAVE BEEN FOUND IN PREHIS- toric caves in the New World. Indeed, they have been found on prehistoric sites everywhere and where they first came from is still undiscovered. That the American Indian had knowledge of and used some of the older and cruder forms along with finer beads, is shown in many examples of their exquisite workmanship. The art had evidently been practiced for some time before Europeans, coming to America, introduced the trade beads. These were highly attractive to the natives, were used in quantity, and soon took the place of beads of earlier or native make.

Records written by Columbus on his landing on Watling Island in 1492, indicate that he won the Indians with friendly gifts of "red caps and some strings of glass beads." After his time countless travelers discovered that the way to tame the "wild" Indian into docile submission was by enticing him with all manner of colored glass beads.

The Danish travelers brought glass beads to the Eskimos on the eastern coast. The whalers used such beads for exchange among the central coastal tribes. To the far western shores of

Alaska, the Russians brought shiny bits of beads with which to trade for furs. These glittering treasures were garnered by the Indian squaws everywhere on the continent. In time the new imports were translated into glowing beaded designs taken from the older porcupine quill-work patterns. Applied to their costume accessories they provided finery with which to glorify both sexes.

The beads worn by the Indians in the earlier centuries were much more crude in character, being made from native mineral substances showing pretty surfaces. Copper was preferred for its color but quartz, magnetite, slate, soapstone, turquoise, and in later periods silver were made into ornamental bead shapes.

Tribes in the southern area from the California coast to Florida found seeds a good substitute for the scarcer beads; most widely used were horns, teeth, claws, and ivory from a variety of animals. Beads made by Indians living in the vicinity of fresh water and the sea, were evolved from materials washed away by the action of the tides or racing rapids. These were ground between stones to simulate beaded effects, or cut into shapes like bugles. Much taste and skill was shown in their selection and in the grinding and polishing of the surfaces.

The tribes in the central and northern part

of the interior basin were not well supplied with bead material. Before the arrival of glass they used bits of goat and sheep horn and the perforated seeds. In Missouri tribes later melted their own glass and molded it into beads. The Mound Builders, Mississippi Valley and Gulf coast tribes found shells, pearls, seeds and rolled copper appealing for decorative sewing. The canine teeth of the elk were highly prized as ornaments.

The St. Lawrence Indians of the Atlantic area used whole shells which they cut and strung for ornament. The valves of clamshells were cut into spindles and cylinder disks for the same purpose. In Virginia oyster shells were used for beadwork ornament. Northern tribes created a money standard through the exchange medium of small white and purple clamshell beads which they termed "wampum." Pacific Indians used dentalium, abalone, and clamshells in the same way. The length of the bead established the value for the simple reason that greater time and effort were required to make the longer beads.

California coast tribes and inhabitants around the Santa Barbara Islands used quantities of little flat shell disks with which they decorated their woven baskets in a needleworked pattern. These disks were reduced to a uniform size by rolling long strings of them between or through slabs of sandstone. Sometimes the little disks were looped through the center with sinew threads and hung pendant-fashion in a geometric design applied to the baskets. They created a happy effect and were enjoyed by the Indians because they jingled.

Depending, therefore, upon materials in their immediate environment, working with claws, horn, bone, teeth and shells, which were sometimes dyed with the juices of native plants and further adorned with feathers, quills and hair decorations, the native Indians applied their findings to articles which were useful, which had commercial value, or were purely ornamental.

METHOD OF WORKING

Beads were worked in two ways: they were either sewn, embroidery fashion, to the skin, cloth or velvet, or were woven on looms. For looms they used a weaving bow in the original ancient method or a frame made to accommodate warp threads the breadth of a girdle or band.

The earliest and most universal practice was the application with a needle. Indians belonging to the Ojibway, Menominee, Sauk, Fox and Winnebago tribes, who inhabited regions around the Mississippi River, excelled in this form of the art. The Plains Indians west of the Mississippi were adept at beadwork and achieved the most dramatic and beautiful effects but their work was mostly in the woven technique. The Cheyenne, Assiniboins and Blackfoot Indians of the West combined quillwork and beadwork, employing it mostly on skins in the traditional manner.

Beads were usually strung upon short threads and sewn down upon the skin according to the pattern. They were either massed in little rows in the manner of quillwork, thus filling in a design area, or they were embroidered in outline formation. The latter was the older method. When flowers or figures were worked, beads were sewn in following the outline, each part of the design being formed separately and worked with beads of different shades. A background might be filled with beads caught down onto the skin in little horizontal rows. These often gave a ribbed effect.

Uniform spacing was accomplished by stringing an exact number of beads on the threads to be applied, and also by counting the beads on the string according to colors so that the pattern would work out in proper sequence. Sewn in close rows these strings often gave the appearance of weaving. A pattern also could be counted out in this way since the beads were almost always worked in even widths or blocks. Allowing ten or twelve to a stitch, these threadfuls could be built up to fill different forms which had previously been outlined on the material. By this method an even, harmonious surface was maintained in the composition.

Rhythmic variations were obtained by using early primitive shell beads or animal teeth. Sometimes these were radiated in semicircular patterns from a larger shell in the center, and the small ivory teeth placed around them against the dark fur looked like pearls studding the background. Such designs were used on the belts which were popular among the Northwestern Indians.

The Ojibway Indians developed the art of

working beads in outline designs with great skill and taste. Leggings, jackets, and other accessories have been finely decorated in this way.

In Montana beadwork on costumes and accessories, saddle bags, leggings, shirts, pouches, was applied by the Blackfoot and Crow Indians in the laid method, the design being blocked out in solidly massed rows of stitches. This beadwork follows the style of the ancient quillwork and is handsome.

The universal method of making moccasins calls for the beads first to be sewn in laid or outline fashion upon the skin which is fastened to the soles afterward. A handsome pair of moccasins with black velvet cuffs first embroidered with the beads and then appliquéd to deerskin, has been made by an Ojibway squaw of northern Minnesota.

Many lovely examples of beadwork on velvet in floral design may be seen in the museum collections. Tradition states that such pieces were inspired by Spanish explorers who introduced this material and style of decoration while voyaging up the Mississippi Valley. A knife sheath of black velvet embroidered with beaded floral motifs, edged with beaded fringe and wool tasseled, may be seen in the Berkshire Museum of Pittsfield, Massachusetts, among other examples of Indian needlework showing strong Spanish influence. These items came from the vicinity of Michigan. Such work also may be found at the Natural History Museum and the Museum of the American Indian, Heye Foundation, in New York City. A wide variety in design and technique is shown. The Ojibways were prolific producers of this rich type of beadwork which has provided much inspiration for modern embroidery themes.

When cloth superseded skin, beadwork was transferred to the newer foundation. Some highly decorative work was accomplished by members of the Menominee and Penobscot tribes. Both tribes eventually combined silk ribbon appliqué with their bead embroidery and the results were dramatically oriental in effect.

A coat of dark blue broadcloth worked by a Penobscot Indian in Maine is in the Natural History Museum. It is an elaborate example of costume needlework and handsomely executed. The round shawl collar top is richly embroidered with multicolored beads. A floral design circles the neckline and extends out to the shoulders. Opaque beads and large, square bugles made of silvery glass are used for the centers of the larger flowers, which are surrounded by smaller sprays embroidered with tinier beads of other hues. The yoke is finished at the edge with fringed skin.

The skirt of the coat is banded with ribbon appliqué in several colors. This style is said to have been inspired by designs made by the Naskapis, an Algonquin tribe which inhabited the interior of northern Labrador. Their decoration is quite like that of the New England Indians and others inhabiting regions near the Gulf of St. Lawrence.

In and around upper New York simple and interesting beadwork in good taste is conspicuous on the female costume of the Iroquois Indians. Colors are vigorously and harmoniously contrasted. The patterns and designs are ingeniously devised and skillfully executed. Representative work is preserved for us in the various museums. The Historical Society's collection exhibits specimens of handiwork which prove that the Iroquois squaw excelled in the art of the needle.

Beginning with the foundation garment "gise-ha," "pantalette" or "leggin," the material used would be broadcloth, ornamented with a stitched border of beadwork around the lower edge and up the side. This pantalette was secured above the knee and fell down onto the moccasin. Great variety in decorative beadwork is to be found on these items. A skirt was fastened around the waist, descending halfway to the bottom of the pantalette. This usually was made of blue broadcloth and was more elaborately decorated with bead embroidery than any other part of the squaw's costume. There was a heavy border around the lower edge and up the center front.

The Iroquois had a name, "Orenda," for the magic power, principle or force which they assumed to be inherent in every creature and involved in every operation or phenomenon of nature. To obtain his ends the Indian must gain the good will of each one of a thousand controlling minds. By prayer, sacrifice, offerings or propitiatory act, he sought to persuade them to exercise their magic power in his behalf. Therefore beadwork, like quillwork, was used to decorate objects worn or used by the medicine men or priests in their ceremonies. Much heartfelt

1. Leather coat bead embroidered; warriors, horses, moons, stars, Sioux Indians, Dakota. 2. Indian porcupine quill-embroidered vest of deerskin, cloth back, made in European style. Vicinity Michigan. 3. Saddle, bead sewn in abstract design on skin. Blackfoot and Crow Tribe, Montana. 4. Bead embroidered cloth shirt, black saddle bag, and beaded skin moccasins by Winnebago Indians, Black River Falls, Wisconsin. 5. Thimbles for jingles on stitched and beadwork cloth pieces, Menominee Indians. 6. Saddle Bag, bead embroidered velvet with naturalistic floral design. Spanish influence. Ojibway Indians, Northern Minnesota.

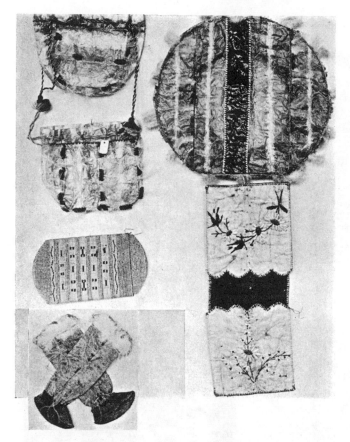

1a. Alaskan Eskimo, California, fishskin work, fur appliquéd and embroidery on skin, pouches and bags. 1b. Alaskan Eskimo fishskin, fur topped boots, hand sewn and wool tufted.

Menominee Indian appliqué work with silk ribbons.
Upper Left: Blouse, printed cotton. German silver disk ornament. Skirt cloth, silk ribbon, appliqué bands.
Right Group: Blouse, silver button pattern. Appliqué skirt. Bottom skirt, stitched block outline pattern and appliqué.

Fishskin work and fur appliqué on waterproof hunting costumes worn by Eskimo Hunters of Aleutian Islands. Hats of antique style, fishhook decoration on top.

Indian Appliqué on silk ribbons of various colors on woman's skirt of blue broadcloth. Menominee Indians, Wisconsin.

emotion was expressed in symbolic designs of infinite variety embroidered upon these tokens —pouches, medicine bags, blankets, mats, and strips.

An interesting item coming from the Sioux tribe and appealing to the same protective power is the little beaded turtle about half the size of a hand. These were made of deerskin, cut in the shape of a turtle, stuffed, sewn and worked solidly in a beaded conventionalized design to represent the shell, legs, head, and tail. They hang realistically from the breast of a beaded buckskin shirt made to be worn by a young girl. One may infer that they were meant to serve as a preventive against harm.

An amusing ceremonial and dance strip is reproduced facing page twelve. The cloth has been decoratively embroidered with symbolic designs and finally fringed at the bottom with a collection of thimbles which have been pierced and hung like little bells and which jingle and tinkle when shaken. This inventive touch was added by a woman of the Menominee tribe which inhabited the lands in Wisconsin.

Realistic "paintings" of figures in beadwork, such as eagles and horses, were combined with the abstract motifs representing the elements— triangular lines or semicircles for rain, a disk for the sun, a zigzag for lightning, arched lines for the rainbow. To the Indian these forms conveyed a message of their own which fulfilled his spiritual needs.

Both beadwork and quillwork were developed by the Indians far beyond the utilitarian stage, and embroidery as an art flourished everywhere.

INDIAN APPLIQUÉ; ALASKAN FISHSKIN NEEDLEWORK

"On my Northwest coast in the midst of the night a fisherman's group stands watching,
Out on the lake that expands before them, others are spearing salmon,
The canoe, a dim shadowy thing, moves across the black water,
Bearing a torch ablaze at the prow."

WALT WHITMAN.

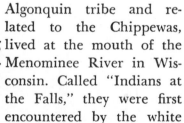

ENOMINEE INDIANS, A BRANCH OF THE Algonquin tribe and related to the Chippewas, lived at the mouth of the Menominee River in Wisconsin. Called "Indians at the Falls," they were first encountered by the white men in 1634. They made that vicinity their home until 1852. Their name translated means "Wild rice men" and they were so called because they subsisted primarily on this food. They had for their principal totems the large-tailed bear, the stag, the kilou (a sort of eagle), and in some sections, the porcupine, beaver, muskrat, mud turtle, wolf, dog, moose, and the marten. One may divine what native materials would be at hand for these Indians to apply to their decorative needs. Perhaps the fact of this abundance assisted in the creation of so many fine examples of embroidered quillwork and beadwork made by the women of this tribe. Sharing honors with them were the Winnebagos who also excelled in these arts and who likewise were adept at the later needlework expression called appliqué.

This "applied work" consists in the laying on of pieces of one kind of material so as to form a pattern upon a foundation of a different kind. The art was known in Europe in the Middle Ages before the various threads for satin stitch embroidery were obtainable. Appliqué work may be done on silk, velvet, brocade, plush, linen and leather, the applied material being intended to take the place of the needle-made embroidery. It should stand out in relief from the foundation.

The Menominee Indians did not use the ordinary onlaid technique as much as the inlaid appliqué or counterchanged method. Since this style is of Spanish origin, it is natural to assume that their understanding of this type of sewing came from the early Spanish missionaries who journeyed up the Mississippi from New Spain in Central America and from sections of Florida. Traveling northward toward the Great Lakes, they happened upon these Indian tribes and found them happily receptive to the new teachings, and in particular to working with pretty pink, yellow, purple, and other brightly colored ribbons.

Most of the Indian appliqué designs were worked on broadcloth as shown in the costume decoration facing page thirteen. Upon this foundation material, which was used for skirts, shawls, and the borders of silk ribbons were used for sewing the counterchanged appliqué work.

METHOD OF WORKING

The counterchange is effected by laying down one shade of silk ribbon with its cut-out half-design on a second ribbon of another shade which has been applied to the cloth foundation. The other half-design is cut out in reverse on a ribbon of the same shade as this second ribbon and is laid down and stitched upon a ribbon which is the color of the one first used. When worked in successive rows, the color scheme and pattern alternate. The ribbons may be counter-changed in many colors giving an effect similar to that seen in modern textiles and used in the counterchanged compositions of modern paintings. The stitches are invisible.

DESIGNS

Almost all appliquéd patterns are geometric in character, reflecting the aboriginal Indian expression rather than the naturalistic floral forms of the Spanish. It may be, however, that the general outlines of the European motifs have been simplified in adaptation, and the design influence may have trickled into this section from sources other than the Spanish. Similar ornament in the same technique may be found on the costume decoration of the Florida Seminoles and the Penobscot Indians in Old Town, Maine.

Some of the Penobscot shirts are finished around the neck with a border effect achieved by sewing a row of beads on the edges of the silk ribbon appliqué. On others the bands of red cloth appliquéd upon black broadcloth are patterned with conventional designs in white beads sewn dot fashion in outline on the surface. One Penobscot long shirt has a shawl top with a square neck heavily beaded and bordered with ribbon. Bands around the bottom are formed by elaborate ribbon appliqué worked in rows. The top row is of cerise silk ribbon cut out to allow a black pattern to show. The next is turquoise blue revealing black, then yellow cut out and applied over red silk. This is followed by bands cut in scallops, appliquéd yellow over blue, red over black, and white ribbons cut out and applied to black for the final band at the very bottom.

The women among the Potawatomi Indians, an offshoot of the Ojibways who lived in the vicinity of Milwaukee, worked their silk ribbon appliqué down the front of their skirts and shawls, with bands around the bottoms for a border. Their color schemes and designs were like those of the Penobscots. One scheme carried out in silk ribbons appliquéd on dark blue broadcloth used purple on green, red on white, with a cerise circle applied over both strips. The outside bands were in white on black and red on blue, the designs being geometrical.

The Sauk and Fox Indians who lived in the same vicinity also worked in this technique, and added the increasingly popular German silver clasps for further spot decoration on shawl collars or the front of blouses, which were usually made from percale. These circular disks are sewn on the percale blouse worn by a Menominee woman and shown in the photograph facing page thirteen. They trim the full-shirred deep shawl collar, which has been ribbon appliquéd in red. The wrap-around skirt belonging to this costume shows very elaborate counterchanged patterns banded up the center and around the hem. Another example shows the German silver disks used as button ornaments. The appliqué pattern on the bottom of the skirt is unique and amusing, being worked in outline stitch and ribbons in square block designs imitating plaids. Over the blouse and skirt ensemble a blanket "shawl" panel, banded like the skirt with silk ribbon appliqué, is wrapped or draped, and worn in the manner of the Roman togas.

Shocking pink was a popular color among the Seminoles of Florida who used cloth in this shade stitched on black and red, in conventionalized patterns, for their ceremonial coats.

One shirt from the Menominees shows a strong Chinese influence in the use of its beaded and ribbon appliqué motifs around the shoulders and sleeves. An abstract pattern of conventionalized flowers with a conventionalized butterfly at the center of the neckline is worked in the style of the Oriental embroideries and with their colors. The embroidery is stitched in a well-arranged open design, highly simplified and extremely decorative. Its spacing has been laid out with much artistic forethought.

It is claimed that inspiration for some of the designs used in Penobscot beadwork filtered down to them from the Labrador Eskimos. It may be that some of the appliqué design found its way across the northern wilds of America through the medium of the Western Eskimos and that it came originally from the land of the Tibetan lamas whose costume designs in colorful appliqué on black seem related to many of the Indian designs.

FISHSKIN NEEDLEWORK

The Eskimos spread across the North American Continent from Greenland to the Aleutian Islands. Anthropologists claim important cultural differences between those living in Alaska and those in the Hudson Bay area, with a divisional or transitional area occurring somewhere in the sections of the furthermost North between Cape Bathurst and King William Island. The clothing of the Western Eskimo is similar in plan to that worn by his Eastern relatives north of Labrador, but it varies in style of ornamentation and pattern materials. Universal use has been made by these people of animal and vegetable matter native to the Arctic Circle. Furs of the bear, seal and other animals have been converted to use, along with shells, feathers and beads of native make.

But the decoration of clothing with fishskin appliqué by the Alaskan Eskimo women is distinctive and unique. The patterns reveal a strong sense of design and a fine skill. Their men balanced this demonstration of talent with equally expressive etchings and carvings on ivory bone from which they made sewing and other implements, and on wooden masks and images, the latter strongly resembling decorative forms of the South Sea Islands.

The Western Eskimos of Northern Alaska include the groups who lived along the Arctic coast from Point Barrow down to Kotzebue Sound, around Cape Prince of Wales on the Bering Strait, south to Norton Bay and on to Vancouver and the Yukon. Their manners and customs have changed considerably since the introduction of missionary schools, which followed the influx of countless white men to this remote section during the gold-rush days. Their old beliefs and some of their native designs have fallen into disuse, but something of their craftsmanship remains in evidence and may be seen in museum collections of many examples of the early needlework in fishskin appliqué and the fascinating work in shells, teeth and beads, along with highly decorative work in other mediums.

Included among the Alaskan Eskimos proficient in appliquéd fishskin are the group known as

THE ALEUTIANS

The Aleutians, called the "People of the Foggy Seas" and referred to also by Humboldt as "People of the East" because of their supposed origin on the Asiatic continent, inhabit the Aleutian Islands, which stretch from the Alaskan Peninsula for about a thousand miles in a bow-shaped chain. Covered with high mountains of volcanic origin, some of which are extinct, they are a treeless and unapproachable archipelago dangerous to navigation. "People of the Foggy Seas" was a name given to Indians of these islands because of constant fogs and gales resulting from the mingling of two currents, a cold current from the Bering Sea and a warm current from the Kuro-Siwo of the Pacific. Because of the weather vegetation on the island is limited to low berrybushes, mosses, lichens, and alpine types of growth including some willows.

According to some authorities the original population of 30,000 inhabitants was of Russian origin. They throve on sea otters and other game. Due to a limited supply of food, however, the natives gradually diminished, and in 1910 the number was reduced to about 1,232. On the Pribilof Islands sealing is carried on under the supervision of the United States Government and the Islanders are government laborers. Almost every day during the summer seals from one rooking or another are cut off from escape by the sea and driven inland. The herd is examined, the females, old males and puppies are selected and returned to the coast. The males between two and five years are killed, and for each seal the Aleut receives two dollars credit on his account for the purchase of supplies. Sealskins and blue-fox pelts are sold in quantity.

When the hunters go down to the sea they wear waterproof rain shirts, sewn of seal intestines, which are gaily ornamented along the seams with downy feathers appliquéd to the skins, alternated with bits of a fur appliqué. Boots of fur and skins are delicately made, sewn with the greatest skill and artistry to fit the foot comfortably. These also are waterproof.

The long throwing-darts are part of the outfit. Painted wooden ceremonial hats, decorated with sea lions' whiskers, are associated with the ancient traditions and are replaced today by a type of skin hat much like a jockey's with an eye shade effect.

The Aleut women are skillful weavers, particularly with split blades of grass. Their sewing is mostly confined to making apparel out of skins ornamented with native designs.

FISHSKIN DESIGNS

Appliqué designs generally used by the Eskimo women of Alaska undoubtedly came from a combination of sources. Some designs in color and form suggest the decoration used by the coastal tribes of the South Sea Islanders. There are evident relationships to the Asiatic designs of the Far North, attributable, no doubt, to costumes worn by these early continental wanderers who came to Alaska across the short span of the northern Pacific. Possibly some ideas for designs came from Indians who migrated into that country on fishing or hunting expeditions. However they arrived at the particular themes used in this work is speculative, except in the case of accessories which have been made directly from observation of the life about them. Such examples show skill and a high form of primitive artistry in their simplicity and directness. The whales, seals, salmon, reindeer, birds, ducks, bears, and other native animals have all been adapted and applied decoratively to various objects of everyday use. While the needlework was executed principally in geometric or conventionalized forms, many little objects were sewn into images representing some of these animals, and used either as totems, amulets, dolls or toys.

Seal intestines dried and inflated by the Aleuts and other Eskimos, provided a sort of translucent parchment which was cut into strips, decorated with paint and then appliquéd to the men's waterproof costumes. Inland Eskimos substituted the intestines of bear and deer since they lacked the sea animals. The skins of salmon and losh were employed for making bags, pouches, mittens and other waterproof garments by Eskimos of the lower Yukon.

Garments worn by the Eskimos on the American shore of Bering Strait northward to Point Barrow and southward to the Yukon, including the King and Sledge Islands, were practically identical in general style and needlework design. An Eskimo doll in the American Museum of Natural History exhibits pretty accurately the type of costume generally worn. The doll has a carved wooden face and is dressed in skins which are decorated with beads on the seams. It holds a miniature bow and arrow. A top dress or shirt has been made of fur ornamented with the striped skins, and is made to be slipped over the head.

Belts of various kinds worn by the men and boys were an important decorative addition to the costume. In fact, they were a "Fashion Must" which any well dressed Eskimo, young or old, must not be without. If, for example, he were unable to possess a belt made of wolverine or wolfskin, he would lack the strength and endurance attributed to these animals. To give additional prowess, he also might carry the decoratively sewn amulet belt representing the family totem. In making these accessories the Eskimo women shared in the delight of their Indian sisters, using as much originality as possible, inventing effects from any exciting materials that came their way through intertribal exchange or the traders, and making unusual combinations of familiar sources near at hand.

Pouches made in fishskin work are of distinct interest. The designs of some in the Museum of Natural History collection in New York are exceedingly decorative. One folding case has been made of fishskin dyed in red and appliquéd in combination with white strips of fishskin on a foundation of another skin. The red band has been applied with featherstitching in navy blue thread. A series of these strips decorate the outside of the waterproof pouch and it is finished on the seams with a binding of blue and white dotted calico, giving evidence of the trader's influence in providing new materials and showing a kinship to the appliqué work of the Menominee Indians.

A large skin knapsack in the same exhibit is made of the backs of fishes pieced together. The skins are joined with skin bands, inserted and tinted in ribbon colorings of henna. Alternating bands have strips of white skin applied over each ribbon, upon which little diamond shapes have been cut out allowing the henna skin underneath to show through. These have been appliqué-stitched with a line of black thread, forming over the surface a beautiful decorative pattern. This technique bears immediate relationship to the method of counter-change appliqué previously described in the silk ribbon work of the Indians.

Fishskin appliqué has been used in various pattern arrangements, usually in striped or line effects, the changes occurring in the different combinations of color, the addition of strips of fur banded along the edges and the introduction of shells, walrus teeth or feathers.

A small purse has been made of fishskins dyed red and white and sewn together in alternate rows; the inside is lined with a patterned calico of dark blue. The edges have beads sewn in three rows for a finish, while at the bottom heavier and larger native beads have been buttonholed to the bag to form a fringe. Alternate beads have tassels of fur tufts attached to them. Skin drawstrings are tasseled with multicolored clipped wools.

An equally interesting bag about the size of a knitting bag has been made of sewn strips of all-white fishskin. Introduced into the seams are alternating tufts of red and green clipped wools, creating an effect of candlewicking. The top of the bag is finished with a handsome band of fur which looks like sable.

Other bags and pouches combine beadwork and appliqué, principally in edgings or ornamental touches sewn on the fishskin. Decorative patterns are formed with tufts of colored fur variously arranged. Occasionally a bit of clipped leather or animal skin has been introduced as a border finish. One strip, clipped in little V's, forms a border applied in silhouette over a band of dyed fishskin. This is an exceptional treatment rather than the general rule.

Objects etched with mythological figures were sometimes attached to belts as amulets. A popular symbol was the Thunderbird which was, as the legend goes, "A monstrous Eagle-man who flies out over the ocean and kills whales by throwing the Lightning Serpent." This motif has been adapted and distributed from Oregon to Bering Strait and is specially developed in Alaska and British Columbia.

SEWING IMPLEMENTS

For all this needlework the Eskimo women at first depended upon crude implements made from bones. Thimbles which they used were made differently according to locality and the accessible materials. Small oval pieces of tough sealskin were generally used for this purpose. These pieces had a slit extending across one edge which formed a loop-like strap through which the forefinger was thrust so that the strap rested across the nail and the pad of skin on the inner side of the finger. When traders brought in metal thimbles they were sewn on strips of cloth for ornamental jingling bells, a use already described in a Menominee example. These thimbles were sometimes imitated by the clever carvers in ivory, but in most instances the women preferred the traditional sealskin thimbles which they had been taught to use by their grandmothers.

Sealskin thimbles were carried on a holder at the end of a hook-shaped cord which was fastened to the workbag or else attached as a pendant to the strap of the needlecase. Designs of these holders have taken various decorative shapes. From St. Michael comes a thimble holder which has been made from a plain piece of bone taken from the leg of a bird. It is one of the earliest and crudest forms. Holders from Point Hope, Alaska, were made of ivory in different shapes. On St. Lawrence Island a simple hook has been created from a walrus tooth, and another from the hook of a deer-horn. One made in the form of a salmon came from Nunivak Island.

Needlecases exist which were made of walrus ivory inlaid with sections of beads. The needles were of bone. Vilhjalmur Stefansson describing the character of the Eskimo men and women says:

They did not beg; they did not pry into our affairs. They were hospitable, courteous and thoughtful. In Prince Albert Sound I made a present of one needle each to the forty-three married women of the tribe. Of course I kept no books, but I feel certain that every one of those women brought me something with which to pay for that needle, most of them saying that they did not want me to think that they were people who accepted gifts.

Sewing threads were made from sinew taken by the women from the legs of reindeer. Lower Yukon women found a species of tough grass which served this purpose after being beaten, dried and frayed with little ivory combs which were carved by their men.

A sewing basket or "housewife" from the lower Yukon is a decorative example of openwork, woven from grass and spruce root found in that section.

PAINTS AND DYES

The characteristic color scheme used for decorative work in painting on costumes, boxes and totems runs as follows: black, green, white, blue, red and brown. Fine shades of color were not differentiated. Additional combinations were added of black and white, russet, gray or clay color, yellow and purple.

Coloring matter was obtained from various natural sources. The dark reddish shade given to tanned sealskin is obtained by soaking the inner bark of the alder in urine for a day and washing the skin with the infusion. White was made from which clayey earth, yellow and red from ocherous earths, red from oxide of iron. Black came from plumbago, charcoal or gunpowder; the two latter were sometimes mixed with blood. Greens came from oxide of copper.

Paints and dyes when mixed were stored by the Eskimos in small boxes similar to those used for keeping fishhooks, spear or arrow points and other paraphernalia. These wooden boxes were ornamented with carvings. The square tops were fitted with covers which were raised by means of a rawhide loop on the center. A paint box from the lower Yukon was cut from a single piece of wood and represented a salmon, the eyes, mouth, nostrils and gill openings being drawn with incised lines. Another, from St. Michael, represents the figure of a seal in oval outline, the cover being in the form of a smaller seal, the projecting head and neck serving for a handle. From Norton Sound comes a box representing two seals, one on the back of the other, with their heads turned to the left, the upper seal forming the box cover. Inlaid beads have been inserted to make the eyes; the mouths and nostrils have been incised and the larger seal's fore flippers have been carved in relief on the sides. Other boxes from this section have been painted to represent seals in black, red and white. From the lower Yukon a painted pear-shaped box combines sewing with threads of spruce root in its decoration. Other handsome boxes show the use of inlaid split beads and bits of ivory to form patterns, which combined with red, blue or black painting are most effective.

All of these mediums bring forth interesting decorative results which bear witness to the talents of the aboriginal Eskimos as well as those of their descendants, and express the poetry evinced not only in their art but in their thinking. A story comes from a native of the Wanapum Village on the west bank of the Columbia River, which is a local version of similar legends circulating among the most northern Alaskans. It was told in 1884 to Major J. W. MacMurray by the son of Kamaikan, the great war chief of the Yakima:

SAGHALEE TYEE, THE GREAT SPIRIT ABOVE

The world was all water, and Saghalee Tyee was above it. He threw up out of the water at shallow places large quantities of mud, and that made land. Some was piled so high that it froze hard, and the rains that fell were made into snow and ice. Some of the earth was made hard into rocks, and anyone could see that it had not changed—it was only harder. We have no records of the past, but we have it from our Fathers from far back that Saghalee Tyee threw down many of the mountains he had made. It is all as our Fathers told us, and we can see that it is true when we are hunting for game or berries in the mountains. I did not see it done. He made trees to grow, and he made a man out of a ball of mud and instructed him what he should do. When the man grew lonesome, he made a woman as his companion, and taught her to dress skins, and to gather berries, and to make baskets of the bark of roots, which he taught her how to find.

She was asleep and dreaming of her ignorance of how to please man, and she prayed to Saghalee Tyee to help her. He breathed on her and gave her something that she could not see, or hear, or smell, or touch, and it was preserved in a little basket, and by it all the arts of design and skilled handiwork were imparted to her descendants.

And that's how Indian and Alaskan women came to sew.

Porcupine Quill Embroidery on Deerskin, Frontiersman's Coat of the Daniel Boone period, made in European style. Use of Egyptian lotus bud motif in the design exceptional. Made in eighteenth century by American Indian.

PART II
NEEDLEWORK IN THE COLONIAL PERIOD

EARLY STUMP WORK, SILK AND WOOL NEEDLEPOINT PICTURES

CREWEL EMBROIDERY IN THE COLONIES

EARLY QUILTING, CANDLEWICKING, AND TURKEY WORK

EARLY SAMPLERS

CHAPTER IV

EARLY STUMP WORK, SILK AND WOOL NEEDLEPOINT PICTURES

"My thoughts do yield me more content
Than can thy hours in pleasure spent.
Nor are they shadows which I catch,
Nor fancies vain at which I snatch,
But reach at things that are so high
Beyond thy dull capacity.
Eternal substance I do see,
With which enrichèd I would be;
Mine eye doth pierce the heavens, and see
What is invisible to thee."

ANNE BRADSTREET.

ETTERS IN THE AMERICAN ANTIquarian Society Collection written between the years 1663 and 1684 by John Hall, a London merchant, and Madame Rebekah Symonds, his mother, give revealing glimpses of life in seventeenth century England and New England. From England John Hall sent home fashion books, rich articles of dress and accounts of life in London to stimulate his mother, who was living at that time in Ipswich, Massachusetts. Her letters in reply picture the danger of invasion by the Indians who filled the forests round about them; the fears felt by the little communities because of the possibility of sudden attack and the horrible consequences of massacre; the small amount of cultivated land hewn from the wilderness; the lack of facilities for comfortable living; the denial of luxuries to many while those enjoyed by a privileged few were extreme in their richness.

Great advantages and great sacrifices went hand in hand and made living an intense experience not only in New England but in other colonies as well. Great contrasts were apparent between the manners and customs of the traveled and more prosperous colonists and those living in less privileged circles. In most sections there existed, however, the democratic bond of sympathetic understanding, generosity of spirit, and a unity of action brought about by mutual suffering.

This was the period when the colonies carried on extensive trade with the islands in the West Indies, Barbados, the Dutch Curaçao and others which in return sent to New England rum, the household standby for cold winters, which was kept in stone jugs and taken in hot punch before retiring to the chilly bedrooms for the night. No self-respecting family would be without this necessity. The desirable coffee also was imported along with sugar, whose wrapping paper contributed a dye solution for embroidery yarns.

From China, Cathay as it was then called, came "thea" and beautiful blue Canton ware which was copied in needlework. Silks and the beautiful white India mull or muslin were handsomely embroidered by the fair sex and worn for weddings, while fabrics obtained from Dutch trading posts in the Orient gave the women suggestions for all manner of designs later developed in the famous crewel embroideries on homespun linen.

When ships sailed from Boston with their cargo of Spanish gold brought up from Barbados and consigned to the mother country, they frequently carried along an extra passenger or two. Young men who had received some preliminary training in Boston were sent to English universities to complete their education. Fair young women and their mothers sometimes accompanied them to be introduced to London society and presented at the English Court. Pictures of these court presentations, embroidered in silk, are cherished in some American homes today as a glowing record of the occasion.

Offspring of the more isolated families of good English, French Huguenot, old Dutch or Moravian stock were less fortunate. Although descended from prominent families abroad, these families, many of them, had been impoverished through the confiscation of their properties for political reasons or as the result of religious intolerance. An inherited understanding belonged to these pioneers, however, many of whom became the builders of the new nation. Women who were unable, like their sisters, to buy or obtain the expensive patterns for ornamental needlework from England or France created ways to make their own decoration like the aboriginals and developed techniques from remembered European arts or learned new ones from the Indians. The art of dyeing, the making of baskets, weaving and sundry other handicrafts were learned.

It would be a misnomer to call the handwork of these settlers "folk art" since, in a general sense, it was not what one might call a peasant art. The use of oxcarts and other crude implements might belong to primitive living. That was a necessity among people who were beginning from scratch in the face of environmental difficulties. But they were not at all simple people in birth or understanding.

It must not be forgotten that this country was founded primarily by refugees who fled to America to support their many causes and beliefs and who belonged to many classes and nations. This, no doubt, accounts for the differences in needlework made during the early seventeenth century. On the one hand may be seen highly sophisticated embroidery expressing a knowledge of technique which could be learned only by contacts with privileged groups, and on the other, very naïve, simple work developed through untutored stitchery.

MATERIALS USED

Means to embroider the pictures made in New England in the seventeenth and eighteenth century seem to have been fairly well provided for so young a country. Various notices printed at the time indicate the style of materials used and are quoted in their original quaint terms. One gentlewoman shopkeeper advises that she has in stock "Silk shades, slacks, floss cruells (crewels) of all sorts, the best white chapple needles and everything for all sorts of work."

Wools for needlepoint were known as worsteds. The *Boston News Letter* of April 28, 1743, advertises "Shaded crewels, blue, red, and other colours of Worsteds." The "Canvas of many sorts," described in an earlier shop advertisement may have included "yellow canvas and canvas pictures ready drawn, a quantity of worsted slacks in shades," as mentioned in the *Boston Gazette* of 1757.

In 1742 another newspaper advises that "Simon Smith, Needlemaker from London, . . . continues to make and sell all sorts of white chapple needles and all other sorts round and square." Later on, "Imported white threads and white chapple needles" were advertised for sale in the *Boston Gazette* of July 25, 1749, as were "Sewing silks, silk and hair twist and materials; linnens and cotton of all kinds, white strip'd and check'd linnens, check shirts, oznabrigs, sail duck of all numbers, Tyke, Tartanes . . . flower'd plain and strip'd Larms." The same advertisement included guns, saddles, housewigs, sandglasses, sea compasses, mahogany telescopes, mariners' guides, and playing cards.

STUMP WORK

One of the earliest and rarest examples of stump work embroidery known to exist in America combines sophistication and naïveté in its design and stitchery. It is the work of Rebekah Wheeler who dated it "Ye month May 1664." It may be seen in the Concord, Massachusetts, Historical Society's collection and is described by Mrs. Marion E. Kent of the museum, as follows:

Miss Rebekah was the daughter of Lieut. Joseph Wheeler, one of the first group of Concord settlers, and married the Honorable Peter Bulkeley, youngest son of the Reverend

1. *Courtesy of:* THE MUSEUM OF FINE ARTS, Boston Massachusetts.

"The Lady Fishing" worked in fine needlepoint with wools. One of a series of "fishing" pictures made in this period. Worked eighteenth century about 1745, New England.

2. *Courtesy of:* THE CONCORD ANTIQUARIAN SOCIETY, Concord, Massachusetts.

Stump Work Picture; a rare embroidery, illustrating the story of Queen Esther and Ahasuerus, worked, dated and signed on the back in 1664, by Rebekah Wheeler, at the age of nineteen, one of the first settlers in Concord, Massachusetts.

Needlepoint Card Table Top; designed and made in fine stitchery by Mercy Otis (Warren), daughter of James Otis, Barnstable, Massachusetts, and sister of James Otis, well known patriot. Embroidered prior marriage, 1754, to James Warren. Needlepoint mounted on American table made in same period.

Silk Needlework; pocket book, eighteenth century, American.

Needlepoint Chair Seat Cushion; one, of set of twelve, worked at Mount Vernon, Virginia, by Martha Washington for her granddaughter, Eliza P. Custis, who left it as legacy to her daughter, Eliza Parke Custis Rogers. 1823.

Needlepoint Pocket Book; worked in colored silks with dark blue background, by Eliza Willard in 1760, Salem, Massachusetts.

Peter Bulkeley, in 1667. She was nineteen years old at the time this picture was made.

The needlework illutrates the story of Queen Esther and Ahasuerus, worked in an American girl's crude version of the "stump work" so popular in England under the Stuarts. On the back is embroidered the name of the maker.

The work resembles pictures of the Stuart period. The pattern may have been sent from abroad for Miss Wheeler to embroider, or it may have been drawn to order by one of the enterprising instructresses who made this a profession. Possibly Rebekah Wheeler drew it herself from an old print or picture. Whatever the method of approach, the result is unique. The few small crowns which rest on most of the heads have tiny beads applied to the embroidery. The panel has been shaded in true tapestry manner and while portions of it resemble stump work technique, the figures have not been padded out in quite as emphatic a manner as that shown in the original Stuart embroideries. In this respect Rebekah adds her own interpretation of the style and creates an atmosphere which is entirely personal.

METHOD OF WORKING

Stump work is a process of needlework in which the design areas are built up in bas-relief through the use of applied stuffing or wadding of wool or hair over which threads or other materials are sewn and needleworked to the background material. In England this work was popular during the time of James I; it was termed "embroidery on the stump." A complete covering of the forms with needlewoven stitches makes the work appear in some cases almost like lacework. The most elaborate pieces were said to have been made by the nuns of Little Gidding. The fashion continued until the time of Charles I, and then declined.

Faces on the figures have sometimes been constructed of carved wood and a covering worked over them with silks. English examples have been made with infinite skill, the figures being carefully costumed in complete detail like little dolls, with dresses, hats, shoes and ruffles made of real lace, silks, and satins, bits of brocade appliquéd, and shoes made with fine stitches giving a knitted effect. Gold and silver braids and bits of velvet and even small feathers were used to trim the hats. Beads, chenilles, threads, real hair, small jewels or other elements were introduced to complete the composition. The effect is often rococo, although it is ingenious and entertaining. Much invention is apparent in the style of stitches selected to express the quality of the subject represented.

Fruits, flowers, butterflies and birds are used in these compositions and are as large in proportion as the figures. Animals have been amusingly constructed with intricate stitchery, and the use of several needles at once to weave in some of the coverings required great skill and patience. That accounts in a measure for the comparatively short life of this vogue. Few women in America embroidered "on the stump," and only the one example from Concord, Massachusetts, is recorded from this period.

18TH CENTURY NEEDLEPOINT

A fascinating needlepoint card table top was designed and worked by Mercy Otis of Barnstable, Massachusetts, in the early eighteenth century. She was a daughter of the well-known patriot, James Otis. In 1754 she married James Warren who in the days preceding the Revolution, in conjunction with Samuel Adams and others, was instrumental in devising and executing measures of resistance. He was a member of the Provincial Congress and at the death of General Joseph Warren at Bunker Hill, succeeded him as president of that body.

She herself was a strenuous advocate of the principles of the Revolution and later a stanch supporter of the Jefferson administration. Besides her various and exacting duties as a hostess and homemaker and her occupation with needlework artistry, she found time to write a history of the American Revolution, in the meantime carrying on an interesting correspondence with John Adams and other political leaders of the period. Many of her letters have been included in the collection of the Warren-Adams letters which belongs to the Massachusetts Historical Society.

Her work is executed in fine tent stitch known as petit point. The colorings are fresh and pure, yet soft in their handsome blending which achieves a fine harmony of tones. The flowers are of the garden variety found in New

England gardens, many of the seeds for them, according to Richardson Wright, having been brought over to America from England with other precious possessions which were to make the new environment in the wild country as nearly like home as possible. The cards are characteristic of the period and reflect the Old World. The mother-of-pearl counters are interestingly rendered and the little pearl-colored fish also. The background color is deep jade green with a blue edge on the center border, and the lily in the very center has been worked in yellow; rose, mulberry, wine and crimson blend into a happy whole, creating a lovely mellow top for the Queen Anne card table which is of Early American cabinetmaking. It shares honors with the famous Loara Standish sampler.

Needlepoint was practiced extensively by many women in the colonies. Martha Washington continued her ardor for embroidery well into her seventies, for at sixty-nine years of age she was working twelve chair seat cushions in needlepoint as a gift for her three granddaughters. Stitched upon coarse canvas, the design consists of rows of conventionalized shells and is carried out in shades of yellow wools blended into brown with the highest color note accented by the use of golden-yellow silk floss. This introduction of silk into wool work occurs in almost all antique needlepoint and in later Berlin work as well, giving a certain vitality or sparkle to an otherwise dull-toned surface. One cushion is at present on exhibition in Mount Vernon where much interest is shown in the bits of needlework finished by this capable great lady.

Whether Madam Washington created her pattern for the chair seats is not known. Accounts suggest that some designs were imported and others were invented. The use of imported designs would depend very likely on the accessibility of the cross-country postal service or the nearness of relatives who could bring patterns from across the seas. Some notations from news sheets, published in Boston in the eighteenth century, give a sample of what the early New England housewife and her daughters found in the way of needlework suggestions when they glanced at the precious paper whenever it was brought home to them by the busy head of the family.

INSTRUCTION AND DESIGNS

Tent stitch was taught to young girls in Boston by preceptresses and other school marms who were well versed in the arts of "Embroidery on Gauze, Tent Stitch and all sorts of Colour'd Work." According to a Boston broadside published in 1716, these techniques were being taught as an essential part of the education of young ladies who aimed at culture and refinement.

Shops selling embroidery patterns existed in the early eighteenth century. Mrs. Condy, who was located near the Old North Meeting House in Boston, announced in the *Boston News Letter* of May 4, 1738, that she had "All sorts of beautiful figures on Canvas, for Tent Stick (stitch)." The patterns were from London, but drawn by her they were much cheaper than English drawings. She also advertised, "all sorts of canvas without drawings."

On December 15, 1747, the *Boston Gazette* announced

"A variety of very beautiful patterns to draw by, of the late Mrs. Susannah Condy, deceas'd, any Gentlewoman or others disposed to improve and purchase the same, which will be very much to their advantage, may inquire, of Elizabeth Russel, Daughter of the Deceas'd, near the Draw Bridge."

A widow, Mrs. Mary Sewall, let it be known through the medium of the *Boston Gazette* of October 3, 1737, that she made "All sorts of Drawing for Embroidery, Children's quilted Peaks, drawn or work'd; Caps set for Women and Children; or any sort of Needlework." It would appear that there was no lack of pattern draughting talent in early New England.

Many advertisements appear later in the eighteenth century, such as one from the *Boston Gazette* in 1757 which reads:

To be taught by Jean Day, at Mrs. Cutler's up Williams Court opposite the Brazen Head in Cornhill, vix. Dresden, Embroidery with Gold and Shell Work, Coats of Arms, Tent Stitch, and a Variety of other Work, all in the neatest and newest Fashion. N. B., The above Miss Cutler takes in young ladies to Board.

This is one of the earliest of the flock of finishing schools which later took in many young boarders to teach them embroidery "and other Works proper for young Ladies" including "Shell work and Dresden painting on Glass."

That many women were searching for ways and means to design their own needlework for costume accessories may be inferred from a notice in the *Boston Gazette* of 1767. It reads:

TO THE YOUNG LADIES OF BOSTON.

Elizabeth Courtney, as several Ladies have signified of having a desire to learn that most ingenious art of Painting on Gauze and Catgut, proposes to open a School and that her business may be a public good, designs to teach the making of all sorts of French Trimmings, Flowers, and Feather Muffs and Tippets, and those arts above mentioned (the Flowers excepted) are entirely unknown on the Continent; and more so, as every Lady may have a power of serving herself of what she is now obliged to send to England for, as the whole process is attended with little or no expense.

Other schools in "Needle-Works" in the vicinity of Boston announced their opening to "The Publick" in the years 1771, 1772, and so on. They taught "Point, Brusels, Dresden, Sprigging embroidery, Cat-gut, Diaper and all kinds of Darning, French Quilting, Marking, Plain Work and Knitting."

Ruth Hern in 1775 endeavored to "teach young Misses all the various Arts and branches of Needlework; namely, Needle Lace Work, Needlework on Lawns and Muslins, Flowering with Crewel-working, Pocket Books with Irish stitch drawing and working of Twilights, marking of Letters and Plain Sewing." Surely a large vocabulary for any needleminded young lady to master in any age!

Silk embroidery of rich character was flourishing in this eighteenth century. Barnard Andrews, Embroiderer, advertises himself as one who "Makes all sorts of embroidery for Men and Women's Ware, either Gold, Silver, or Silk; also cleans Gold and Silver Lace Work and Silk Work." Besides his needlework talents, Mr. Andrews would drive "Feathers in old Beds when matted, in four different Sorts, which makes the Bed as good as if new Feathers." Among his many trades were advertised "Tassels, Fringes, and Paper Work." The *Boston News Letter* of July 2, 1772, further adds, "If any Gentlemen and Ladies have an inclination to learn the above Businesses, they shall be waited upon in their Houses, or at Mrs. Geyer's, Flower Maker, in Pleasant Street, Boston."

From the *Boston Post* in 1748 it appears that "Embroidery with Gold and Silver, and several other sorts of Work not here enumerated" would be taught to pupils, who also "may be supplied with Patterns and all sorts of Drawings and Materials for their Work." The notice was inserted by a Mrs. Hiller who lived "in Fish Street, at the North End of Boston." Her specialty, however, was wax work, which also appealed to the "publick" in this day, and upon her removal to another part of town in 1754 Abigail Hiller advertised her new address in the *Boston Gazette*, saying that at this address she continued to teach "Embroidering, Tent Stitch &., where also may be seen Kings, Queens, &. in Wax Work as formerly." The last were evidently her masterpieces.

Silk stockings, which were worn by the elegant and which were often more costly than the coats on their backs, were frequently embroidered on the instep in elaborate florals in silk. A great-grandfather of Mrs. Alice Morse Earle, who was a Minute Man in the Revolution, used one of his silk stockings for a nightcap. Mrs. Earle describes the pair as being "of purest, whitest silk closely spun and thickly woven; they shone like silver when worn." Nightcaps were not always made of stockings, however, but were fashioned of silk and embroidered with flowers and gold lace effects.

In the Essex Institute in Salem may be seen a pair of wool hose in gray blue with flowers gracefully embroidered on the ankle in silks of rose, peach and cream. The design extends halfway up the stocking from the instep and is French of the eighteenth century. In this collection also is a quaint needlepoint pocketbook worked in gay colored silks in geometric and "modern" conventionalized flower forms against a dark blue silk background. It was made in 1760 in Salem, Massachusetts, by Eliza Willard, who has added to her design the initials of a few favored persons. Embroidered approximately in the same period is a small purse, the design in diagonals and conventionalized flowers in a stitch like fine buttonholing. The effect is rich and lacy and the colorings are appropriately soft.

Occasionally one hears of little aprons embroidered on colored silk taffeta with silks of different shades. These were a fashion during the reign of Queen Anne and a few colonial women imitated the style. The Litchfield Museum has such an apron, and while it is undated, the design and general feeling of the work strongly indicate the eighteenth century period. It is made of gray taffeta, embroidered with green and white silk flowers and leaves, and is worked so expertly on both sides, in the Chinese way, that it could be reversed.

It was at this time that the needlepoint pictures received enthusiastic support from the properly taught young ladies, and many delightful works have been left us. In most examples the designs reflect English traditions. Occasionally a departure is made along original lines but the technique and general style resemble the embroideries inspired by tapestry and made in the seventeenth century abroad. Like other fashions this particular phase reached its peak of expression later in America, during the eighteenth century.

Elegant accomplishments in pictorial needlework tapestries of this period remain in many collections. Particularly delightful is the series of panels worked in petit point, usually in fine wools, and known as "The Fishing Ladies," since this subject is the central theme of the design and is identical in each picture. "The Fishing Lady" in the Boston Museum of Fine Arts collection is a beautiful example, made approximately in 1748 on Cape Cod. According to Miss Gertrude Townsend of the museum, "This is one of a group of eight known embroideries in which there is a lady fishing while a gentleman stands behind her.... All the known embroideries come from New England families."

"The Fishing Lady" apparently was created by one designer in Boston or its vicinity who used her original model for many copies and, while retaining the figure and her pose, changed the surrounding design or combined the figure with others. Hunting scenes have been introduced in miniature, as in the Boston Museum picture. In others boats on a lake appear. The landscape is rearranged and the houses, which are of New England architecture rather than the castles frequently used in English pieces, are moved about at random. The pictures are decoratively composed in all instances, and well worked. Butterflies, birds, ducks or swans in the pond, and the flowers, plants and trees are finely shaded.

A close duplicate of this needlepoint picture came from Salem, Massachusetts, and is in the collection of Mr. Henry F. Du Pont. The date of 1743 is on one of the houses. Another panel with a single group of figures and one fishing lady is dated 1748. Another picture similar in design is in a collection on Long Island and a "Lady Fishing on Boston Common" is the title given to a similar design exhibited in New York by Mr. Israel Sacks. All are gay, delightful and unique and reflect the finest and best expression of their time.

Designed and worked along similar lines, with the exception of the hand-painted appliquéd portraits on paper, is the picture made by Abigail Parkman. Fine needlepoint has been stitched in silks on linen canvas. Fortunately her name and the date 1758 have been added. This embroidery was worked in Connecticut by Mrs. Parkman who was Miss Lloyd of Hartford before her marriage. The original is in the collection of the Cleveland Museum of Fine Arts where it tells its romantic story to many admirers, at the same time offering inspiration to needleworkers of today through its charm and able craftsmanship.

~~~~~~

CHAPTER V

CREWEL EMBROIDERY IN THE COLONIES

"Free hands and hearts are still your pride,
And duty done your honor.
Ye dare to trust, for honest fame,
The jury Time empanels,
And leave to truth each noble name
Which glorifies your annals."
JOHN GREENLEAF WHITTIER.

~~~~~~

REWEL EMBROIDERY WAS DEAR TO the pioneer women of America. In those early years they labored with the necessity of dyeing their own yarns and spinning the linens which were afterwards to be decorated with stitchery. A few of the designs had been inherited directly from English forebears and brought here by Pilgrim settlers. Later they were modified as the result of environmental observation or individual inspiration.

It appears that much of the needlework of this type originated in the New England colonies. While fine pieces from Long Island, Pennsylvania, New Jersey and other colonies on down to Virginia are shown in museum collections, the preponderance of the museum examples came from the aforementioned group. The great number of crewel embroideries which have been inherited and which may still be seen in New England homes points to the same conclusion. Frequent sailings from England to the port of Boston may have encouraged the sending of patterns to friends and relatives living in the New England district, which would account for the fact that the majority of these embroideries seem to have been made in this section.

Earlier than this work produced in closely populated communities, however, were a large number of crewel embroideries made out of the raw, so to speak, and before the larger towns had been settled. This needlework done by women who were at the same time helping their husbands to build frontiers presents a fine chapter in American needlework. The atmosphere in which these embroideries came into being was described by Ulysses S. Grant at a dinner of the New England Society on December 22, 1880.

> They (the Pilgrim Fathers), fell upon an unsympathetic climate, where there were nine months of winter and three months of cold weather and that called out the best energies of the men, and of the women, too, to get a mere subsidence out of the soil, with such a climate. In their efforts to do that, they cultivated industry and frugality at the same time, which is the real foundation of the greatness of the Pilgrims.

Such an arduous life would admit of very little in the way of home decoration, especially under the primitive conditions which surrounded them; but out of the yearnings of these women, hungry for some beauty to brighten their harsh existence, arose the crewel embroideries, worked on their homespun linens with the fine wools which many had learned to dye, throughout the long, tedious winters while they were confined to their cabins. The essentials necessary for needlework were developed from natural resources, and among them were

DYES

Dyes were something of a mystery to most early settlers who, being unable to import embroidery yarns from England, as more fortunate descendants could do, had to depend on their own inventive ability and observation to secure sewing materials. A number of colors used by them were discovered by accident or through experiment.

Many colonists raised their own indigo plants both in the North and South. Almost every New England house boasted the possession of an indigo tub in its rear kitchen. Here lamb's wool was tinted various shades of blue, from the light tints of the sky to the deepest midnight blue, depending on the length of time it was immersed. Attempts were made to match the beautiful Canton blues observed on the blue china-ware newly arrived from the Orient. These colors were finally achieved and appear in crewel embroideries identified later on as "Blue and White Work."

The yellowed taglocks of the sheep were used to obtain color variety. These wools dipped in blue added a blue green to the crewel embroidery palette. To produce colors that would be indelible was a constant study among housewives.

It may be that some early inhabitants learned dye secrets from the Indians who so successfully achieved gay colors for their porcupine quill embroideries. Going to the same sources in the immediate environment that the Indians had used for coloring matter, the early settler made a note of any stains resulting from handling berries, vegetables, or plants, or from the woods and barks of trees. During the long winters attempts were made to work out new dye formulas in these shades.

Just as the Indian squaws stored away their dyed quills in animal-skin bags, ready for their needlework, so the colonial women following the same urge to make something beautiful for their home or loved ones, began storing away their needlework stock for future decorative purposes. Their skeins of crewel in white and light tints were kept in crewel-bags tied up with the tally rags and samples of colors ready for dyeing. Such skeins were usually accompanied with the recipe for producing the shade desired. When the dyeing had been accomplished the skeins were cut into convenient lengths, listed with their color, and arranged in another bag ready to be used later for crewel embroideries.

Various experiments often resulted in new dye substances. It was found, for example, that onion skins when steeped in a copper kettle would produce one shade of yellow, and the same ingredients stewed in an iron pot would result in another tone. But the search was based primarily upon the desire for colors that would be permanent enough to endure many washings, sunnings, and constant hard usage. Discovery was made that alum combined with some of the dyes would increase their staying power, and that salt would fortify the colors.

From notes on the sources of dyes, we observe that various shades of brown were achieved from the seepings of black walnut bark. Other yellows came from the branches and leaves of the wild cherry and sumac. Maywood and goldenrod added to this range of color.

Shells of young butternuts soaked to a proper degree gave a tender spring green when the white wool was dipped in the fluid. Hemlock bark added produced an olive green shade. A touch of indigo created a deeper green, and so on. These experiments were duly recorded for future reference and must have been an entertaining occupation for the early housewife, who had little diversion from the routine of caring for the family needs.

Pinks were scarce among the early New England colonists, and were not used in their needlework for some time. It is said that one woman who had discovered the desired shade and who was envied by all her neighbors, would not reveal the secret of her color foundation, even unto death, so jealous were these ladies of their precious formulas. The particular pink discovered by the possessive lady was named after the town in which she lived and is known today as Wyndym pink.

Rose madder was raised in the Southern colonies, but gave more of a brown than a pink shade. It had to be purchased by the New Englanders who yearned, in the colder climate, for these warm rose shades to add to their embroidery palette. Some time later traders brought cochineal to these color starved women. With this new medium a great number of rose shades ranging through the reds, wine, claret, and the shade known as Wyndym pink were obtained by means of the careful introduction of extracts of logwood.

There are many legends concerning the origin of the soft mulberry violet found in the wool used on some of the early crewel-embroidered covers. One tale describes a purplish shade which was made by steeping the purple paper which came wrapped about the cones of loaf sugar brought up from the West Indies to New England. It may be true since all was grist for experiment that came to the thrifty housekeeper in those primitive days.

Modern experiments in dyes taken from the old dye books used by early colonists in America, have been tried out by several persons in different sections of the country with some success. The recipes call for local vegetables and mineral matter tried by the pioneer housewives and found to be serviceable. When followed, they have produced colors similar to nearly all those used in the early crewel wool embroideries.

A list of dyes evolved from old New England formulas and handed down from one generation to another, can be made from the tags on samples of homespun wool exhibited in the ancient Harlow House in Plymouth, Massachusetts. The samples show the colors used in most of the crewel embroideries worked prior to the eighteenth century. The basic materials used to obtain these colors are listed below. Among them are some other scattered formulas used about the same period.

Reddish Tan, Hemlock Bark
Pinkish Golden Tan, Hemlock Bark—no mordant, long boiling.
Purple Brown, Logwood
Wood Brown, Butternut
Raw Sienna Brown, Sheep Laurel B. O. Mordant.
Greenish Brown, Hemlock and Sumac
Yellow, Broome Sedge
Yellow, other dyes, Golden Rod with Alum
Lemon Yellow, Onion Skins dyed in brass kettle.

Gold Yellow, Onion Skins dyed in an iron kettle; also Lichens, Golden Rod with Alum.
Green Yellow or Chartreuse, St. John's Wort with Alum
Smoke Green, Dark & Light, Sheep Laurel and Copper
Deep Blue, Indigo
Blue Black, Logwood with Potash
Deep Black Purple, Logwood with Alum
Magenta Purple or Purple Madder, Cochineal with Alum
Deep Wine Red, Cochineal
Blue Pink or "Wyndym" Pink, Cochineal with Alum on second dyeing.
Vermillion Red, Madder with Alum and Bran.

This palette of wools is quite in contrast to the wealth of colors obtainable generally in this twentieth century! Yet with such a surfeit we have a long way to go to emulate the simple charm of the finely stitched, quaintly patterned, and beautifully colored crewel embroideries of early colonial days.

MATERIALS

Background materials were in most instances homespun. Some linens may have been imported but the heavy taxation on imports necessitated home manufacture of the majority of materials. Weaving became a part of the daily household routine and this added labor doubled the value of accessories and hangings decorated with such fond effort.

DESIGNS AND STITCHES

The designs in the beginning were, of course, descended in the main from famous Anglo-Saxon embroideries and linens with crewel-work which were used for hangings during the reign of Queen Anne. Traditional variants of the rose, the thistle, the carnation, are to be seen in the earlier examples, but the transplanting process allowed the introduction of some newer impressions in motifs and colorings inspired by fabrics which came into the colonies through the China trade. Many Dutch East Indian motifs may be found in the fantastic leaf and flower forms added to the patterns which had been derived from England. So fascinating were the new ideas that women began draughting their own designs, free hand, upon the homespun linen curtains and spreads, originating motifs from flowers and animals seen about them and adding vigorous and fresh interpretation to this art of the Old World.

STITCHES

In technique American crewel embroideries have employed the stitchery which was used in England during the seventeenth century on the Stuart proper, or as it is generally termed, the Jacobean crewelwork, with the difference that it was for the most part limited to one or two stitches in particular. One universal stitch has been called the Oriental stitch, the Roumanian stitch and sometimes the American stitch by those who associate the needlework on early examples with the environment in which they have been found. Added to this, the Kensington outline or back stitch, and the satin stitch, gave necessary variety. In other works the chain stitch, long and short stitch, chevron, stem and brick stitches may be traced.

There was a reason for the common use of the Roumanian stitch, that of long-wearing strength. Worked in very small stitchery, this method presented a far more enduring coverage than the satin stitch by reason of its little interwoven center threads. It was also economical since most of the wool remains on the surface, not passing under the linen as in the over and over satin stitch method. Wools being very precious, conservation was important. Then too this stitch, derived from ancient Oriental embroideries, was in itself beautiful and especially appropriate for rendering the fantastic shapes of flowers and leaves adapted from East Indian prints and chintz.

In some examples a colonial maiden flourished her stitch vocabulary and introduced novelties for her enjoyment and the entertainment of the family. The fishbone or herringbone stitch, various darning stitches or that variable member of the chain stitch family, the humble buttonhole stitch and its decorative relative, the featherstitch, all might find their modest but effective way into gorgeous crewel-embroidered bed curtains, or possibly a christening blanket. These needle flourishes depended entirely upon the amount of leisure allowed for such indulgence. Our earlier colonials were limited in this respect; hence the simplest and most effective method had to suffice.

That excellent craftsmanship and infinite patience attended most of their works is established by the number of embroideries fortunately preserved. A few of these extraordinary needlework heirlooms have been reproduced in the illustrations.

THE BREED BEDSPREAD

Tester beds were hung with crewel-embroidered valances and covered with matching coverlets, and windows were draped with hangings similarly embroidered, in the same fashion as were those in Elizabethan manor or farmhouses. The early examples were often worked in blue and white due to the limited dyes obtainable at the time in New England. Later they were elaborated with additional colorings. These hangings provided the most common opportunity for a display of the needleworker's skill in crewel embroidery.

From the collection at the Metropolitan Museum of Art in New York comes the Breed Bedspread, one of the most famously beautiful and finely made bedcovers of eighteenth century make in America. It was made of homespun linen by Mary Breed of Boston. Her name is embroidered on it together with the year of its completion, 1770. It is signed in the center above a cluster of crewel-embroidered flowers branching from a decoratively stitched vase beneath which is the date. Flower and grape groups on either side balance the panel design and to the left, at the end, is placed a bird embroidered in yellow and black, with a red heart within a heart stitched on his breast. In his bill he holds a branch on which a single heart is flowering. He is balanced in symbolism of particular significance to the embroideress by a similar bird at the right-hand end of the valance, worked in rose stitchery and carrying two hearts, possibly that beat as one.

This bedspread is a work of great love; poetic arrangements continue over its surface. Little embroidered birds are clustered upon sampler-like trees. Small trees like those in old Persian manuscript paintings are embroidered separately and decoratively. The vases holding the various flowers are ornamented with interesting patterns. Each flower unit is entrancing in its composition, coloring and effective stitch rhythms, the latter worked principally in but-

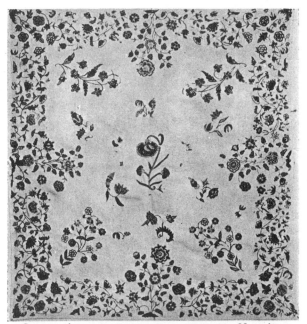

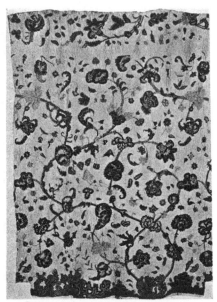

2. *Courtesy of:* THE MUSEUM OF FINE ARTS, Boston, Massachusetts.

1. *Courtesy of:* THE BOSTON MUSEUM OF FINE ARTS, Massachusetts.

Crewel embroidered christening blanket worked by Mary Fifield Adams for christening of son Samuel Adams. Early 18th century. Massachusetts.

Crewel embroidered bedspread by Mrs. Mary Fifield and her daughter (Mary Adams), Eighteenth Century American. Massachusetts.

3. *Courtesy of:* MRS. W. H. L. EDWARDS, New York.

4. *Courtesy of:* THE METROPOLITAN MUSEUM OF ART, New York.

Detail of crewel embroidery bedcover on homespun linen. Early 18th century, American. By Elizabeth Wyllis, Connecticut.

Crewel embroidered bedspread. By Mary Breed, 1770. Massachusetts.

5. *Courtesy of:* MRS. W. H. L. EDWARDS, New York.

Crewel embroidered tester valance (detail) by Elizabeth Wyllis, eighteenth century, Connecticut.

1. *Courtesy of:* THE MUSEUM OF FINE ARTS, Boston, Massachusetts.

(Top) Crewel embroidered homespun linen petticoat band, eighteenth century, American.
(Bottom) Crewel embroidered homespun linen tester bed valance, eighteenth century, American.

3. *Courtesy of:* THE MUSEUM OF FINE ARTS, Boston Mass.

Homespun linen petticoat with band crewel embroidered, eighteenth century, American. Vermont.

2. *Courtesy of:* THE OLD GAOL MUSEUM, York, Maine.

Tester bed lining with crewel embroidered hangings and valances and crewel embroidered bedcover, eighteenth century, American.

4. *Courtesy of:* THE OLD GAOL MUSEUM, York, Maine.

Detail of crewel embroidered valance for tester bed. 18th century, American, Maine.

tonhole fillings, Roumanian or Oriental stitch, couchings, surface darnings in variety, stem stitch, outline stitch, and herringbone stitch. The colors throughout the work are carried out in tones of golden yellow, light and dark browns, three shades of blue from light into the indigo of midnight intensity, rose shading out from dark pink to light peach; in greens, only a chartreuse tone has been included.

It is a splendid record of one who loved embroidery and shows it in every respect. Mary Breed has achieved a work of art, a joy to behold, and a delight forever.

Worked in the early eighteenth century is a bedcover and a set of valances of very fine homespun adorned with a design of flower groupings in sprays which display great variety in their composition and coloring and much taste in their arrangement. They were executed in fine crewelwork by Elizabeth Wyllis, the great-granddaughter of Governor George Willis of Connecticut, who came into office in 1642. Elizabeth was the great-grandmother of Henry L. Stimson. The cover and some of the tester valances have been handed down directly through the family to Mrs. W. H. L. Edwards of New York, and are still in an excellent state of preservation despite their age of three hundred years. Their wool colorings are freshly reminiscent of the rose, cream, gold, and green blue originally used.

The Old Gaol Museum in York, Maine, contains a tester bed lining with crewel-embroidered valances and curtains, and a bedspread embroidered to match the valances. The embroideries were given to Elizabeth Perkins' mother for the museum by a descendant of the woman who made them. She embroidered them in the house which stands opposite to the museum in York while her husband was with Sir William Pepperill in the siege of Louisburg, 1745.

The valances topping the tester bed include, besides trees of different species and a decoratively embroidered forground, stanzas of verse stitched into the composition on all four sides. One side contains the following lines:

BUT HENCE YE WANTON YOUNG AND FAIR
MINE IS A PURER FLAME
NO PHILLIS SHALL INFECT THE AIR
WITH HER UNHALLOWED NAME

To purify the air sweetly, gaily embroidered trees and flowers interrupt the verse which continues:

SWEET MUSE DESCEND AND BLESS THE SHADE
AND BLESS THE EVENING GROVE
BUSINESS AND NOISE AND DAY ARE FLED
AND EVERY CARE BUT LOVE.

The additional hangings and the bedcover are embroidered with graceful vines and odd foliage in an original manner.

In the Long Island Historical Society collection is a homespun bedcover or hanging, crewel-embroidered in 1776. The little soldiers worked upon it reflect the Revolutionary spirit felt by its creator.

The colonial poetess, Anne Bradstreet, was also enthusiastic with her needle. The Museum of Fine Arts in Boston is the happy possessor of beautiful crewel embroideries from her hand. It received them through a descendant, Mr. Samuel Bradstreet. The curtains are worked in soft colors with flowering vines, large flowers, carnations, tulips, and exotic forms. The background material is fustian, a twill-weave cotton which was rubbed up to give it a warp. They are said to have been made in the seventeenth century.

At Litchfield, Connecticut, in the Historical Society's collection is a section of a crewel-embroidered bedcover which was worked in 1745 by Elizabeth Taylor. She was the daughter of the Honorable Edward Taylor and Ruth Wyllys and became the third wife of Andrew Perkins of Norwich, Connecticut. The cover has been worked principally in browns and in gold and is another fine example of early American needlework. The design includes the pineapple, roses, carnations and the popular subjects of her time.

A cover in the Metropolitan Museum of Art is decorated in an unusual manner. A large heart composed of a vine and leaf arrangement encloses needleworked vines within its center. It is balanced by plant scrolls in the corners of the spread.

Bed-tester valances have received imaginative treatment in the decorative sequence running around the top of the handsomely needleworked curtains. A humorous example, beautifully worked, has little episodes tucked away in the foliage and flowing vines, such as a pair of small yellow chicks both ready to pounce upon a glamorous red cherry. The floral forms in this valance are finely worked in the Oriental stitch. It is in the Museum of Fine Arts in Boston, a new acquisition representing eighteenth century needlework, and the gift of Alice and Helen Coburn.

This museum also exhibits a lovely christening blanket made of homespun material and delicately stitched with crewel embroidery designed in the spirit of the early Persian textile motifs. The blanket was used for the christening of Samuel Adams and was worked by his mother, Mary Fifield Adams, in Massachusetts. It is a rare piece of needlework and an excellent representation of the best in crewel work during the early eighteenth century.

In the same collection is shown an elaborate crewel-embroidered bedcover, also the work of Mary Fifield Adams and made with the aid of her daughter. Fine and elaborate stitchery covers the large area with a flowing vine, flowers and leaves. It is related in composition and styling to patterns seen on Oriental fabrics, and similar, also, to Jacobean types of embroidery. The entire background material, which is cotton with linen warp, has been carefully and closely quilted. The intricately stitched crewel embroidery is superimposed on this surface. It was made in 1714 and is thought to have been used as a curtain prior to its bed covering days.

Not late enough in period to cope with these rich examples of needlework but serving in its modest capacity as a bed covering for a pioneer family, is a blanket made of homespun wool in the Harlow House in Plymouth. It has been embroidered with wool in a well-known abstract pattern which came directly from the Indians. The design is known as "The Cherokee Rose."

PETTICOAT BANDS

Costume in the colonies came in for its share of embroidery. A dominant and a strikingly odd, interesting phase in American work are the patterns which were created for borders on petticoats worn in the eighteenth century. These were costly because they carried an infinite amount of crewel embroidery. Some examples have been both quilted and embroidered.

Evidence that crewel-embroidered petticoats were worn in the early eighteenth century in New England comes from an advertisement in the *Boston Gazette* of 1749:

> On the 11th of Nov. last, was stolen out of the yard of Mr. Joseph Cort, Joiner in Boston, living in Cross Street, a Woman's Fustian Petticoat, with a large work'd Embroider'd Border, being Deer, Sheep, Houses, Forrest, &c. so worked. Whoever has taken said Petticoat, and will return it to the Owner thereof, or to the Printer, shall have 40 s. Old Tenor Reward and no Question ask'd.

This account gives some idea of the style of design and general character of these petticoats which were frequently decorated with fantastic interpretations of nature.

An early petticoat band, crewel-embroidered with flowers and landscape foreground, was made by "Grandmother Douglas," who was Olive Spalding and who married Lieutenant Colonel John Douglas in New England, January 13, 1724. This embroidery has been placed by the family of the late Mrs. Moseley of Santa Barbara, California, as having been worked in 1723 prior to the marriage of Olive Spalding.

A petticoat band, crewel-embroidered for and worn by Lady Pepperill, is exhibited in the Essex Institute in Salem, Massachusetts. It is another early eighteenth century example of floral design. A band with more intricate stitchery, showing animals, birds and flowers, is in the same collection and dates from 1750 in Salem. In 1754 a crewel-embroidered petticoat band with similar design was made in Massachusetts by a member of the family of Mrs. Lewis Bigelow of New York.

A delightful petticoat with its crewel-embroidered band intact has been acquired recently by the Museum of Fine Arts in Boston. It is the gift of Mrs. Samuel Cabot who also contributed a brief account of the circumstances under which it was made, written by Mrs. Maud Nichols to whom it was bequeathed. The account reads:

> It was my great-great-grandmother, Mrs. Kilburn, of Vermont, who made this petticoat for her wedding. She spun the flax and wove it herself. She was working on it that famous dark day of May 19, 1770. The handwork is crude but beautiful. It is one hundred and fifty-eight years old.

The design of this embroidery includes a solidly worked foreground in green wools shaded toward a yellow horizon on top of the hills. White lambs, worked in French knots, graze on the wool grass. Embroidered birds are worked in white with blue accents, cream with rose tips to the wings and are outlined in dark blue. A green polly embroidered in red sits in a brown tree not much larger than the bird itself. The bright yellow-gold leaves are filled in with dark green. Pink butterflies flit between the tree tops. There are deer worked in bright henna, orange, black and brown. Blue-green fir trees with light blue fillings in plain dot stitch are spaced at intervals around the border, completing the happy little landscape.

An odd and different band has the figure of a colonial lady sitting under a grape arbor. She is a shepherdess, shown by a tiny white sheep which sits in her lap. Birds in nests of vines are stitched upon either side of this pastoral. The lady is worked in crimson-colored crewels. The border is yellow. Blue-green leaves and a red grape-vine with violet grapes, make the arbor. A golden bird is worked in open stitches, and a blue bird is plumaged in crewel embroidery with the familiar Oriental stitch. This linen band is also a new acquisition of the Museum of Fine Arts in Boston through the gift of Mrs. Maxim Karolik.

"POCKETS" AND POCKETBOOKS

Crewel embroidery was applied to the little aprons called "Pockets" which were of homespun and often made from leftover pieces of linen from outworn skirts, bed coverings, or other accessories. The scraps were pieced together into an apron with an open pocket in the front center within whose folds sewing or other implements of household occupation might be held. Examples of these pockets are exhibited in both the Memorial Hall in Deerfield, Massachusetts, and the Essex Institute in Salem, Massachusetts. They were made in the early eighteenth century and usually embroidered in allover patterns of flowers.

Pocketbooks were an important and decoratively useful accessory to the eighteenth century costume for both men and women. A purse completely covered with crewel embroidery is worked in greens, peach, magenta, pink and a touch of gold wool. It is lined with pink satin, bound with a sage-green silk tape and has tie strings to match. It was worked by Susanna Hayward Shaw in 1768. The original is in the Museum of Fine Arts in Boston and the following letter tells its story:

Samuel Shaw, Esq.,
27 State Street,
Boston, Massachusetts.

My dear Mr. Shaw:—

The old pocketbook I gave you was worked, (as I was always told by my mother), by my Grand-mother for my Father, when he was in college, or rather the year he graduated, 1768, which date you will find on it, together with the initials of his name, and as you are in some part his namesake I am very glad to give you this relic, just a century old.

Yours very truly,

HARRIET L. WYMAN.

Boston, Nov. 23rd, 1868.

CHAIR SEATS

Chair seats also received a large amount of crewel embroidery. The needlework often disguised the patching and seams of old pieces of homespun which were converted into upholstery. They are typical of the fine crewelwork which distinguishes this period and adds a colorful chapter to the panorama of American stitchery.

CHAPTER VI

EARLY QUILTING, CANDLEWICKING AND TURKEY WORK

"Be it ours to meditate,
In these calm shades, their milder majesty,
And to the beautiful order of thy works,
Learn to conform the order of our lives."
WILLIAM CULLEN BRYANT.

ARLY SETTLERS OF NEW AMSTER-dam, New England, Virginia and the Carolinas introduced the art of quilting into America pretty much as remembered from their European homes. Quilting, particularly as used in all-white designing, became a high form of applied art in the late eighteenth century. In its purest form it has an approach to abstract art through its dependence upon line and effects of light and shade, achieving third dimensional qualities through the bas-relief "puffing" or raising of the decorative forms above the surface.

The technique has remained essentially the same as in the European examples worked in France and in England. The all-white quilting recalls the famous work of this type made during the reign of Queen Anne. In many instances the patterns created here reflect the spirit of the new country's ideals and customs, notably, throughout the colonies, the use of the pineapple, pomegranate and fern-leaf motifs, symbolizing hospitality. Plenty is represented by the cornucopia motifs and charm through the use of floral forms. These appear most frequently in a variety of arrangements. A note-worthy example of quilting including these symbols is shown in a bedcover from the collection of Mrs. Francis D. Brinton in Pennsylvania. It is a very fine all-white puffed design and has a cornucopia filled with flowers as the central motif. This is framed with a "vine" pattern and bunches of grapes. The corners of the inside square are decorated with pineapples. The design is squared off by "the princess feather" pattern worked in straight lines. Another enclosed frame of flower medallions makes a small border line with an outside square of the feather motifs. The next and outside border is composed of larger bunches of grapes on a curving vine. Another feather-patterned band forms a square border. The entire cover is finished with a handmade fringe.

The top of this cover is made of very fine white cotton and the underside, through which the holes are stretched to allow the wick to pass for the puffing of the forms, is made of homespun. It measures six by seven and a half feet and was made in Pennsylvania about 1800. The initials are M. O. The quilting is a glorious achievement treasured by the present owners and all others who are privileged to see and enjoy its beauty.

That we have so few of these fine examples of stitch design is due in a measure, according to one authority, to an economy law which existed during this period, prohibiting the buying of cotton material for this use. One might employ or decorate only what was at hand and not needed for other utilitarian purposes. Only occasionally could one find pieces of cotton which were either large enough to make a six by seven foot bedcover, or equally matched in pure whiteness to be suitable for the snowy surface which was part of its great charm.

To make one of these quilts was a work requiring the finest skill with the needle and equally great discretion and taste as a draughtsman, for these women carefully drew their own cartoons with care and study. Many such heirlooms remaining in present-day collections show fine skill, artistry and good taste in both the craftsmanship and design.

Occasionally patriotic notes appear, as in the famous "Secession Quilt" from South Carolina. This all-white quilt is in the style of eighteenth century stitchery, being exquisite in its fineness of detail, although it was made in the nineteenth century and finished in 1860. Mrs. P. D. Cook, who worked and designed it, was an ardent Secessionist and not only aimed to record her cause, but also intended that her quilts should become treasured heirlooms which would go into the dower chests of her granddaughters. Two quilts were made, but only one has been preserved. The other, according to tradition, was unfortunately cut into saddle-cloths by marauding Northern cavalrymen who invaded that section under General Sherman.

Charcoal was used for sketching the intricate pattern, composed of cornucopias filled with pomegranates, grapes and roses. These motifs are worked into the garlands which border the squares and are presided over by a spread eagle above a figure of Liberty. The arms of South Carolina appear on shields in the four corners and above them are stitched the names of the Governors who championed the State from 1830 to 1838. The name of General P. D. Cook, the husband of the needleworker, appears at the base of the centerpiece. Above the head of Liberty, General Washington's name is inscribed in a flowing hand. Below it is the inscription, "Secession—Yancey, 1860." From the beak of the spread eagle flutters a scroll on which is written, "E Pluribus Unum."

The qualities of patience and good crafts-manship are reflected in this outstanding work. Portion by portion, little areas of the large patterned cotton padding were stuffed through small stretched openings in the reverse side of the homespun to fill out the design. This method gives the raised or bas-relief effect. Each hole in the linen mesh was pulled together again and all evidence of the process obliterated. The stuffing used for the purpose was obtained by Mrs. Cook from her own cotton plants, which she picked, seeded, fluffed and carded herself on her plantation—a large task in itself. Her quilt is a work of art which will be appreciated by all lovers of good needlework and design for many years to come.

The Brooklyn Museum possesses a very fine quilted all-white bedcover worked in the same puffed or stuffed method as the preceding examples. The pattern composes the running vines, fans, and cornucopias around the center motif which consists of flowers in a basket framed with feather motifs. This work was executed by Betsey Canfield of New London, Connecticut, in 1810.

Baskets filled with flowers were universally liked and were worked by many during the eighteenth and early nineteenth century. They were generally puffed with padding through the homespun linen on the reverse side. A splendid eighteenth century example of this very fine quilting technique is in the Museum of Fine Arts collection in Boston. It is a small, circular, all-white piece. The shape and size are unusual, the pattern excellent. It may have been used for a table mat, since many table covers were quilted.

Another basket, highly conventionalized, is used for the central theme in an elaborately quilted all-white coverlet in the same museum. Flowing branches of flowers, also conventionalized, emanate from the basket and are spaced in well balanced curves over the entire area of the bedcover. Motifs well known by name are incorporated in this mid-eighteenth century design; the "Princess Plume," "The Pineapple," "The Rope" and "The Bell Flower."

A square quilt, beautifully worked and designed in feathery vines, leaves, and flowers, is in the Essex Institute collection in Salem. It was made in the eighteenth century and is an exceptional piece in both design and needlework.

Quilting patterns were applied to other articles besides counterpanes and bed coverings. Window hangings were quilted and heavy curtains for tester beds made prior to the 1800's to keep out the cold draughts at night. Chair seats and table covers were made of various left-over materials and quilted to add decorative quality to interiors. Warm clothing and coverings were needed when faring forth upon a raw winter's day, and New England women, in response to this demand, promptly applied their artistry to the creation of

COSTUME QUILTING

In the eighteenth century dresses received attention from the quilting artists. Hoods, capes and other accessories including waistcoats for the gentlemen were decorated with it.

Quilted "petti-skirts" or underskirts to be worn beneath brocaded or chintz top skirts were the height of fashion in the eighteenth century, and American women stitched their own costumes in lovely patterns. The top part of the skirt often was diapered in allover diamond or block stitching. A flower or leaf motif was spotted over the area, after the manner of the flowers scattered on brocade designs. The background of the border around the bottom was frequently worked in tiny all-over quilting with grape vines or flower scrolls in a larger puffing effect circling all around the skirt in silhouette against the smaller stitches. The result is rich and effective.

In contrast to the all-white quilted skirt, a top skirt of colored brocade was made to cover the sides and back. No doubt the double skirts provided warmth for their wearers in days when all central heating emanated from fireplaces. Mrs. De Witt Clinton Cohen owns a lovely and rare example of one of these early quilted skirts. It is in her remarkably fine collection of famous embroidery and lace.

A small piece of quilting made on a heavy brown material, a remnant of eighteenth century needlework, is in the Lighthouse Collection of Americana. It comes from the environs of Stonington, Connecticut. The curator records the strip as a bedcover section but the design and general character are strikingly like the quilted "petti-skirts" worn in that period. The patterning is identical with the treatment used in the background of upper skirt sections. The border pattern and style also are similar to other underskirts. A quilted owl sitting on a branch may be seen on the right corner of the border detail.

Another rare piece of fine American quilting worked in the eighteenth century is shown in the half-section of a white waistcoat from the Boston Museum of Fine Arts collection. The borders of the neck front, the pocket section and the lower edges, are intricately quilted in a design of tiny stitches giving a drawn work effect. It is an exquisite piece of lacy needlework and unique in craftsmanship, a work of love indeed for the favored Beau Brummel who was fortunate enough to receive it.

Some quilted flower forms look as if they were an original conception, while others bear a strong resemblance to designs found in the old India fabrics. A speaking acquaintance existed between some of the quilting designs and the designs used for the early crewel embroideries. Both may have been derived, in part, from Oriental sources. Patterns had to serve many purposes. The same design might meet itself upon a bedspread, a cloak, a border upon a cabinet, a hanging at a window or wherever else Mistress Prudence decided to transfer it in connivance with her needle, the dictates of an inventive imagination, and her ambition.

Some idea of the processes used in designing and executing quilting is given in the brief notes that follow.

METHOD OF WORKING

When the drawing had been transferred to the top of the quilt with chalk, a riding spur or, in later years, a round pricking wheel, the piece was ready to be laid on the large frame upon which the back piece of homespun or cotton, with a layer of wadding or padding laid over it, had already been mounted. The top was placed over both and fastened, ready for the design to be stitched. Running stitches were made by the needleworker with a long needle. The thread pulled through the several thicknesses of material created the quilting. After several pieces of work had been executed, the needles would bend from constant use. They then made ideal curved implements with which to make the small, curved, and intricate pat-

1. *Courtesy of:* MRS. DE WITT CLINTON COHEN, New York.

2. *Courtesy of:* THE MUSEUM OF FINE ARTS, Boston, Massachusetts.

4. *Courtesy of:* THE ESSEX INSTITUTE, Salem, Massachusetts.

3. *Courtesy of:* THE LIGHTHOUSE HISTORICAL SOCIETY, Stonington, Connecticut.

5. *Courtesy of:* THE MUSEUM OF FINE ARTS, Boston, Mass.

1. Quilted Skirt; worn under eighteenth century English chintz gown. Between 1770 and 1775, New York. 2. Half a Waistcoat; finely quilted linen American; eighteenth century. 3. Quilted Detail on Brown Cloth; from a cover or skirt. Early eighteenth century, Stonington, Connecticut. 4. "The Quilting Bee"; dolls sewn and furniture made by Mrs. Mary Cleaveland in 1850, Massachusetts. 5. Quilting Circular Piece of White Linen; eighteenth century, American.

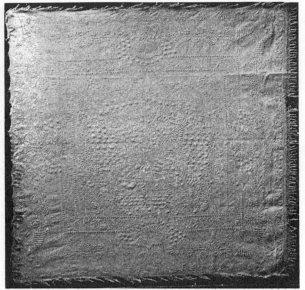

1. *Courtesy of:* MR. ALLAN NICHOLSON, Union, South Carolina.

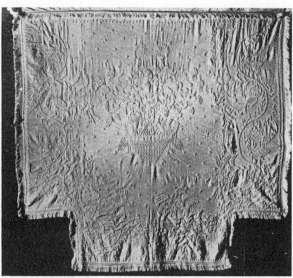

2. *Courtesy of:* THE LATE MR. HOMER EATON KEYES, New York.

3. *Courtesy of:* THE MUSEUM OF FINE ARTS, Boston, Mass.

1. Quilting, Secession Design; all white puffing; by Mrs. P. D. Cook, Union, South Carolina. 1860. 2. Candlewicked and Embroidered All White Bedspread; in a variety of stitches. New England, 1800. 3. Quilting Detail; with fine puffing. American. Second half of the eighteenth century. 4. Candlewicking, Embroidered Bedspread; designed by Mr. Anthony Thatcher, worked by his wife, Lucretia Mumford Thatcher, great-grandmother of Mrs. Junius Morgan. Connecticut, about 1800.

4. *Courtesy of:* MRS. JUNIUS MORGAN, New Jersey.

terns of feathers, small flowers and other elaborate designs.

DESIGNS

Quilts have incorporated symbolism in their design for more than two centuries. Many of the patterns were passed on from one family to another and frequently reflect the American scene.

Before the use of stencils, patterns and pricking transfers made quilting designs universally adaptable, the natural inventiveness of the colonial women turned to simple everyday things to aid them in accomplishing desired results in their needlework. Circles were carefully traced around the inverted rim of the homely tea-cup. These superimposed rings created a design lovely and effective for quilting. Those who had special talent drew their own designs free hand and sometimes turned to assist others who were less gifted.

Average geometric quilting patterns universally repeated became known as "The Diamond," "The Diagonal," "The Cross Bar," "The Horizontal," "The Basket Weave," and so forth. Among early American designs were included such names as:

"THE SPLINT": inspired by the splint weaving in early chair seats of the 1750's.

"THE TREE OF LIFE": from the Orient in theme, later becoming the "Weeping Willow" pattern.

"THE PINEAPPLE": colonial symbol of hospitality originating in the Orient and incorporated in many of the early American designs.

"THE ACANTHUS": adapted from early carvings on doorways, etc.

"THE ROPE": adapted from early carvings on mirrors, door lintels, etc.

Other quilting patterns before 1800:

"THE TIDE MILL": named for the high tides on the Atlantic coast which turned the mill wheels. The pattern was patched and laid to represent the water falling from the wheel as it turns.

"THE DOVE OF PEACE": symbol denoting a ladies' social gathering or party, often selective and elegant, later termed hen party.

"THE WEEPING WILLOW": related to the symbolism associated with the Tree of Life design from India.

Other eighteenth century designs were known as:

"THE PRINCESS FEATHER": plumes worn in eighteenth century headdresses were used as motifs in quilting patterns. The "Princess Feather" border may have been adapted from this fashion.

"THE OAK LEAF."

"THE BELL FLOWER": showing the influence of the Sandwich glass designs.

"THE INDIAN HATCHET": adapted from an object often unhappily familiar to the early settlers.

Sometimes designs took a historical turn such as:

"THE PINE TREE": a pattern made into quilts in the thirteen original states, symbolizing the spirit of North America. Many states lay claim to the lone pine tree as representative of their land.

"E PLURIBUS UNUM" and "THE EAGLE": two designs representing the United States and the preservation of the Union.

Other emblems were adapted and included in patriotic works made with love and fervor and intended to remain in families as a declaration of the worker's faith in the ideals of her country. Well-known personalities also inspired designs.

"QUEEN CHARLOTTE'S CROWN": this was made before 1770, in honor of the last Queen who governed the American colonies.

"THE DOLLY MADISON STAR": combined a personal tribute to a charming Washington hostess and also symbolized the rise of the new republic.

"MRS. CLEVELAND'S CHOICE": named for another President's wife as a tribute from her countrywomen.

A pattern which would seem to bear some relation to Biblical stories, but which in reality was christened after a plant with berries of the same shape as the design motifs, was named "Job's Tears." Later it became known as "Texas Tears" after the trials and tribulations which women suffered while this State was being settled. Some religious impulses are recorded in the following designs:

"DAVID AND GOLIATH."

"THE STARRY CROWN."

"THE STAR OF BETHLEHEM": a design of diamond-shaped patches.

Mrs. Ruth E. Finley's collection of quilts includes:

"THE BEAR'S PAW": about 1850, Ohio.

"THE SHIP'S WHEEL": Cape Cod inspiration, later becoming

"THE HARVEST SUN": according to its owner a universal pattern found in quilts from Pennsylvania and Ohio, from Kentucky and Indiana, from Kansas and the West, symbolizing the plentiful golden harvest.

From the American Desert section and the Southwest are the familiar designs named characteristically

"THE CACTUS BASKET": named "The Desert Rose" about 1800.

"THE COWBOY'S STAR": dating from the 1860's.

"THE ARKANSAS TRAVELER": suggested by a popular song of the same period.

Many other names make up a long list of traditional arrangements designed primarily for the placement of calico blocks or cut-outs of other materials to be appliquéd. In earlier years these were applied against backgrounds quilted in many fine patterns, but later the intricate quilting began to diminish until the appliquéd materials provided the main effect.

An early example of quilting combined with patchwork comes from New Jersey, about 1800, and is included in Mrs. Francis D. Brinton's collection. The patches of printed calico are presumed to have come from the mills of early Philadelphia calico manufacturers. The earliest and most famous were from the calico printer, John Hewson. Hewson came to America in 1774 under the patronage of Benjamin Franklin, who encouraged the industry.

According to Mrs. Ruth E. Finley, the quilt authority, the patches used in the "Tide Mill" quilt were made of calico manufactured in Philadelphia shortly after the Revolution and before 1800. These pieces may have come from the Hewson Mill.

Calico in greens and reds, and often browns, was applied to the linen tops in units and later quilted, providing early sewing and needlework instruction for young girls, who pieced the small blocks before learning the final intricate stitchery. Pieces of material for patches included bits cut from wedding dresses, trousseau clothing and in pioneer days scraps of homespun dyed in different hues.

Patterns were exchanged and developed and a supply of winter coverings prepared at the well known

QUILTING BEES

As popular among pioneer women as the gatherings for bridge in modern times was the institution of the quilting bee or party. Groups of women coming from distant sections of the countryside and working for hours in unison on the same frame, that the one or two spreads might be finished quickly, usually ended their labors with a grand fiesta. Husbands, brothers and sweethearts joined in the dancing and merrymaking which followed the large turkey or chicken dinner provided by the hostess in appreciation of her guests' efforts on her behalf.

These parties were immortalized in song prior to 1860. Stephen Foster, composer of American folk songs, wrote "The Quilting Party," with its well-known refrain:

'Twas from Aunt Dinah's quilting party
I was seeing Nellie home.

Another record for posterity is a quilting bee made of four little dolls dressed in colonial costumes and seated about a miniature wooden frame plying their needles on a tiny quilt. This present for a child was made in 1850 by Mrs. Mary Cleaveland in Massachusetts, and the delightful little gathering is still working assiduously in a case with other American dolls in Essex Institute at Salem.

The quilting saga is a long and beautiful episode in American needlework traditions, one that will be rediscovered and remembered in the years to come as a brave and fine and essentially American tapestry of gay patches and delicate stitchery telling symbolically the story of the States.

CANDLEWICKING

English women during the late seventeenth century embroidered white bedspreads of twilled linen with clustered flowers and fruits in small French knots, and flowing vines in fine white cord laid and couched. This knotted work traveled to America and the last years of the eighteenth century found the art practiced here. Its development through the substitution of wicking for the corded forms gave it the name candlewicking embroidery.

METHOD OF WORKING

Several strands of wicking were passed through a long, slightly large-eyed needle, and the stitches were worked through hand-woven cotton dimity or fine homespun linen. Each stitch was raised on the surface slightly by passing the loop over a small twig and making a series of small running stitches. Sometimes the knot was cut; more often in the earlier work it was left uncut, and these examples retain a certain distinction in their fine, tight wicking, graceful patterning and a generally refined, neat appearance.

DESIGNS

The early candlewicking was always in white on white, although many new designs and stitches modified the original technique. Some spreads or counterpanes were knotted in grape designs, with flowing vines and graceful grape leaves as a border theme. One such design belonging to the author employs as a central motif a basket worked in fine knotting stitches out of which long sprays of flowers, similar to the "Tree of Life" design, grow in conventionalized patterns of fine French knotting. The border scrolls are arranged in the grape design popular on spreads during the 1800's. This example bears the date of 1818 and was made in Stonington, Connecticut.

Many popular bedspreads were designed in angular abstract patterns similar to those employed in the geometric arrangement of calico patchwork on the quilts of the same period. No doubt the patterns were interchanged and tried out in different techniques. Mrs. Junius Morgan is the happy owner of an early bedspread designed and worked in this manner. An interesting description of it in her own words follows:

It was designed by my great-grandfather, Mr. Anthony Thatcher, of New London, Connecticut, and made by my great-grandmother, his wife, Lucretia Mumford Thatcher. It was made about 1800, just before or after. It is embroidered (or whatever was called that kind of tufting, beautifully knotted on the wrong side) on a hand woven heavy cotton

somewhat like madras. It is a lovely ivory white. It was made for the large four poster beds of that day.

Mr. Thatcher made an excellent design and it must have been a joy for his enthusiastic wife to embroider it, for the workmanship is exceedingly fine. Contrast in the surface of the candlewicking has been cleverly achieved by heightening some tufts or stitches and reducing others to intensify or deepen the shadows, thus emphasizing the white pattern by bringing it into sharper relief against the white of the background.

The Metropolitan Museum has a spread which also uses geometric figures. It is worked in the same technique but differs in that scroll borders and baskets are combined with the angular forms. Also a patriotic note is introduced in the form of two American eagles and stars close to the large eight-pointed star in the center. This bedspread is initialed T. C. and dated 1825.

From the late Mr. Homer Eaton Keyes' collection of fine Americana comes a most unique bedspread of this time which employs several techniques in its embroidery, fine French knotting, buttonholing, outlining and satin stitching. The design is richly handsome but not crowded, for the pattern is selective. The depth conveyed through the combination of many stitches, and the variety of lighting effects obtained by this variation in surfaces makes a lush effect which considerably enhances the flowery scrolls, basket, and small star forms. The small diamond border is unusual. Altogether this is a creative example unlike those designed by the needleworker's contemporaries, though bearing characteristic marks of the period. It was embroidered by G. A. H. of New England about 1800.

TURKEY WORK

An early type of needlework which became popular in the colonial days was called Turkey work. The idea for the style and name came by the way of England in rugs from the East imported during the seventeenth century. These Oriental carpets were a source of inspiration for the designs used. The colonists wished to emulate the patterns woven in them, only instead of weaving they substituted a cloth foundation upon which a needle was threaded with yarns of varying colors. The threads were pulled through, tied into a knot, and either cut or left uncut to achieve a pile or raised surface. Sometimes they achieved brocaded or damask effects by running the stitches parallel with the threads of the background material in contrast to others stitched at right angles.

According to Mr. C. E. C. Tattersall of the Victoria and Albert Museum in London, "a square foot of Turkey work is exactly the same technically as a square foot of hand knotted carpet." This does not refer to the type of work by this name which imitated the design and was worked with a needle on loose linen by American women, but to the work imported from England. Some of the English textiles may have been brought to America and, no doubt, were promptly reproduced.

Instruction was evidently given in stitching of this name since an advertisement appearing in the *Boston News Letter* of the year 1716 states

> That at the house of Mr. George Bronnell, late School Master in Hanover Street, Boston, are all sorts of millinary works done; ... and also young Gentlewomen and Children taught all sorts of fine Works as Quilting, Feather Work, ... Embroidering a new way, TURKEY WORK for Handkerchief ... flourishing and plain Work, and Dancing cheaper than ever was taught in Boston, Brocaded work, for Handkerchiefs and short Aprons upon Muslin, artificial Flowers work'd with a needle."

Examples of Turkey work existed in the colonies as early as 1670, according to statements and lists recording such work among household effects dated in that year. It was known in the South as well as in the New England colonies several estates in each section having left examples of such stitchery. John Carter of Virginia had several chairs upholstered with this style of needlework, dating from the seventeenth century. In South Carolina Richard Phillips in the eighteenth century used a set of chairs so upholstered. Colonel Francis Epes of Virginia also owned chairs covered in the same manner. In fact, it was a most efficient covering and was used by many housekeepers in the earlier days of colonial decoration for chairs, table covers and bedcovers. The latter sometimes were made to serve as rugs.

Exhibited in the museum at York, Maine, is an early example of Turkey work made originally for a bedspread. "It is now used as a rug, although no one must step on it," according to the statement of Miss Elizabeth Perkins. The design in this particular example is more closely related to the Queen Anne period of floral embroideries, although the technique came by way of the Mediterranean. An example at the Essex Institute in Salem follows more closely the Oriental rug design in its conventionalized geometric forms. The piece which remains measures about five by five and one-half feet. The border is gone, so the original must have been fairly large.

Perhaps because of hard usage there are few examples of this unusual needlework.

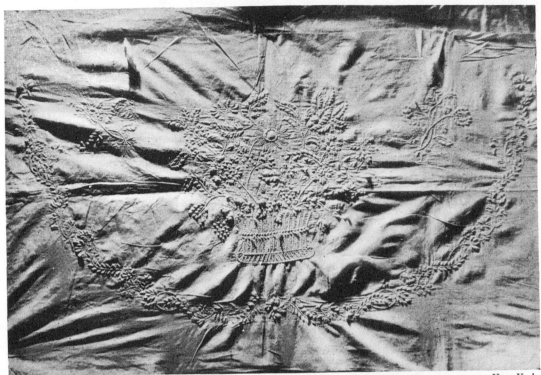

White quilting, puffed work on homespun, center of bedcover, worked by daughter of Chief Justice Swift, Julia Swift Huntington, 1830. Windham, Connecticut.

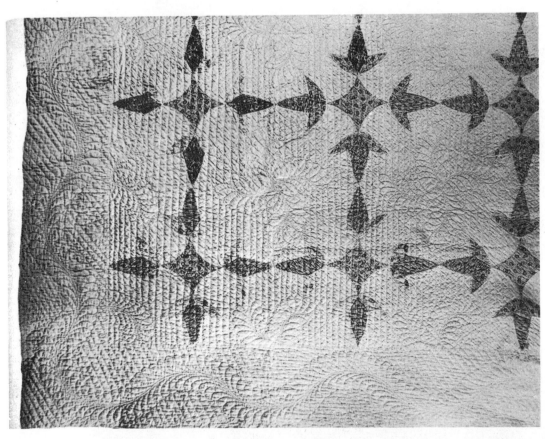

White quilting and calico applique in very fine stitchery, which distinguishes the work, about 1800, New Jersey.

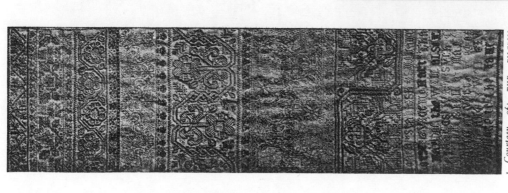

1. Sampler by Loara Standish about 1635, Plymouth, Massachusetts. 2. Early Sampler in Silks; 1795 by Patty Coggeshall, Bristol, New England. 3. Unfinished Sampler by Abigail Pinniger, made in 1730. Gift of Miss Susan B. Thurston. 4. Typical Lettering Sampler of the Early 18th Century (1718). Made by Eunice Bowditch at the age of 11 years in Salem, Massachusetts. 5. Lettering Samplers. Eighteenth century, American, on homespun linen by Salley Spofford, Sarah Weber Atkinson and Clarissa Balch. 6. Lettering Sampler of Mercy Fogg, Massachusetts. Early American, Massachusetts. 7. Sampler with Designs from which to work "Shawl Borders" by Mary Hollingsworth before 1675 and who was married July 1, 1676, to Philip English. Massachusetts.

CHAPTER VII

EARLY SAMPLERS

"Not pleasing objects which soon pass the sight,
Or richest food that highest tastes delight.
Not numbered music which captivates the ear,
Or gayest dress that pleases much the fair,
With virtue equal are, my greetings, maid,
These clog our sense, this to the mind gives aid,
This New Year's gift your sampler may adorn,
And pattern be to others yet unborn."

FROM AN AMERICAN SAMPLER IN 1738.

HERE OR WHEN THE FIRST SAMpler was made is clothed in mystery. The earliest mention of such a piece of work appears in the account of Elizabeth of York. The entry for July 10, 1502, reads: "for an elne (ell) of lynnyn (linen) cloth for a sampler for the Queen. VIIID." John Skelton, a poet who lived in Norfolk, wrote in the "Gar lande of Laurell" in 1523:

The saumpler to sowe on, the lacis to embroide.

Later on, Shakespeare mentions the art in "Titus Andronicus."

Fair Philomel, she but lost her tongue,
And in a tedious sampler sewed her mind.

The earliest sampler known to exist comes from Germany. The year is 1615. It is in the Victoria and Albert Museum. Countries that may have produced samplers which served as an inspiration for early American work are primarily England, followed by Holland and Germany. Italy, Spain and France, where samplers also were made, did not influence American work to any great degree and when inspiration

did come from these countries, it was not in sampler form but in other styles of needlework.

Samplers of the seventeenth century in Europe and in America were made on narrow strips of linen, due to the fact that the looms in those days were very narrow. Therefore many samplers were made on separate panels of homespun and seamed together afterward in graceful stitchery, much invention being shown in the joining of the strips.

The sampler grew in popularity from the sixteenth century through the eighteenth, when it reached its height. Its appeal began to diminish in the early nineteenth century. In America alone there are more than twenty-five hundred recorded examples of this type of needlework, and others exist which have not been located or listed. Not all "Exemplars," as they were called in earlier days, were utilitarian in character. The narrow strip Tudor type was purely decorative and a practice sheet for elaborate stitchery. Alphabets were introduced about 1720 along with the square type of sampler which was made possible by the fact that the linen was now loomed in wider pieces.

Little girls were taught how to embroider at the earliest age, the true beginning of a sampler being in reality a sample or "examplar" of stitches. With an increase in the number of household linens, identification became necessary and "samples" of stitchery were evolved in alphabetical forms to record various styles of letters which might be used for marking. Thus the linen strips became not only needleworked lesson books but reference plates. Numerals were added, also ornament for decorative borders or finishing. Later the sampler itself became a pictorial decoration. Figures were introduced along with houses, pets, mottoes, and other innovations dear to the embroiderer. Sentiments were expressed in verse and the design was elaborated.

Sampler construction was conditioned by the same elements in American home life that fostered the crewel embroideries and other early needlework; in fact, the different styles developed simultaneously. Homespun virtues were dominant in New World living. When the families gathered nightly in the living room or parlor, they were edified by a lesson from the Bible and dissertations from the writings of Locke, "The Spectator Papers," or works of other writers of the period. This practice was observed almost universally in towns and villages. It was usually the patriarch of the family who, seated by the high table, read aloud while the women and girls sewed, embroidered or stitched on their samplers the profound observations gleaned from this solid reading matter. Quiet, sound simplicity was in such living, and a bond of sympathetic understanding was created which contributed to family unity as well as to the betterment of the community and the strength of the country.

The wife as well as the husband was a responsible entity. Careers for American women began in the earliest days of colonial life. In the process of performing and supervising the multifarious activities of their large households, they developed executive ability and mastered techniques in many fields. The dairy industry was almost entirely in their hands, as well as the textile industry.

Weaving was not a hobby in those days. It was a necessity. In 1640 a General Court Order in Massachusetts commanded the manufacture of wool and linen cloth. In Pennsylvania the weaving of linen received the ardent support of William Penn. Later premiums were offered not only in Pennsylvania but in Rhode Island and Massachusetts, which resulted in the production of linen and woolen cloth of the highest quality. Maryland in 1731 offered premiums of tobacco for linen "Fine as to thread, white as to color." New York City in 1743 established a house on the common equipped with spinning wheels and flax for the employment of the poor, and formed a society to manufacture linen.

This period brought into being the professional traveling weaver who taught the art. At the same time, indentured servants became numerous and were bound out to spin and weave. One woman in Pennsylvania bound herself as a servant helper for a term of fifteen years to knot and spin, and when free was to be rewarded with one spinning wheel and one woolen wheel. These bound servants were sometimes very thrifty and with their savings started a business of their own upon which fortunes were builded.

Nearly every colonial homestead had its own weaving house. Benjamin Franklin had quarters especially built for weaving. A weaving house was part of the Mount Vernon homestead, in which was probably woven the material upon which Martha Washington embroidered many cross-stitched patterns. At times more than a thousand yards of fabric were woven there, including striped and plain linsey-woolsey and striped and plain woolens and cotton. All the household needs of the establishment as well as clothing for the family and help were thus provided. It is stated that one white woman was employed for this work, with five negro helpers. The Carters and the Jeffersons in Virginia also had their weaving establishments. In 1800 the Price plantation in West Virginia carded, spun and wove the material for bed coverings, tickings and other domestic necessities.

Interesting examples of early homespun are in the Litchfield Historical Society collection. Among them are linens spun, woven and cross-stitched in sampler fashion by Lucy M. Hopkins of Litchfield who marked with a cross-stitched number each item of her linen, sheets, pillow cases and towels. In most colonial households the linen supply, hand spun and hand woven and representing many hours of arduous labor, was carefully watched, and checked by name and number.

It is also recorded that Miss Hopkins' father

surprised her with a handsome present in the shape of a spinning wheel made by himself. It shows excellent craftsmanship and is evidence of the ability of men of olden days to turn their hand to any requirement from the building of a house to delicate cabinet work. Men as well as women were equal to all occasions. Versatility was the order of the day.

SAMPLER DESIGNS

The best known English pattern book was Richard Shoreleyber's, "A Schole House for the Needle," which was published in 1632. It may be well to note that before this, many of the English samplers borrowed design inspiration from German and Italian needle-pattern books. One reference book used all over Europe was a Venetian pattern book published in 1606. From this guide were obtained decorative borders and marking alphabets. The most notable German pattern books are those of the designer Hans Sibmacher of Nuremberg, which became the standard in cross-stitch patterning. Publication of these designs occurred between the years of 1591 to 1604. But his patterns were copied continuously up to the beginning of the nineteenth century and the fascinating shepherds and shepherdesses, men carrying bunches of grapes, royal lions, angels, birds, trees, elegantly costumed ladies, peacocks, castles, shrines, unicorns and all manner of sampler forms trooped over the Western World to delight, entertain and often inform the many women who found inspiration in stitching them.

In both England and America samplers made before the seventeenth century tended toward a scattered pattern arrangement. Towards the middle of the century alphabets for marking linen became more orderly and the decorative borders were worked in horizontal bands on long narrow strips in as great a variety of stitches as the needleworker could command.

The first design copied generously in the colonies came from Boston in a pattern of Adam, Eve and the Serpent. Three designs based on this theme remain, all very much alike. In Philadelphia an eighteenth century version of the same idea shows Adam and Eve properly clothed in colonial costume. This quaint, naïve sampler is one of the favorites in Mrs. Harrold Gillingham's admirable collection.

Ideas for lace and drawn work samplers originated in Italy and Spain and the technique arrived in America usually by way of France, though there were some English and Dutch interpretations. A few samplers show direct inspiration from the immediate environment. One made in the eighteenth century, for example, pictures in stitchery the life on a Southern plantation—the lady and gentleman seated in a garden, the darky servants, a house raised slightly on stilts, magnolia trees—a local scene delightfully rendered by the youthful needleworker along the traditional pattern layout for samplers, but with her own theme.

MATERIALS AND COLORS

Material upon which to embroider samplers was varied in character in the seventeenth and eighteenth centuries. Some cloth was imported but the early samplers, in particular, were generally worked on a loosely woven but firm homespun.

The coloring was usually soft and confined to simple shades of green, blue, yellow, rose, red, a soft gold and browns. Many of the wools used were from the same skeins made up for crewel embroideries. Provident families may have possessed a few silks brought from Europe, and in later sampler work imported materials were prevalent, brought in no doubt by clipper ships returning from the Orient. Occasionally the silks were produced on the home plantation as the result of experiments in silk culture.

SAMPLER STITCHES

Samplers were most generally embroidered in the following stitches: cross-stitch, stem stitch, satin stitch, eyelet, hemstitch (on borders), queen stitch, chain stitch, padded stitch, split stitch, petit point, cat stitch, tent stitch, French knot, flat stitch.

The majority were made, however, with the combination of the fundamental stitches; cross-stitch, tent stitch (needlepoint), satin stitch, and stem or outline stitch.

EARLY SAMPLERS

In the Pilgrim Museum in Plymouth, Massachusetts, rests one of our earliest named samplers. It was made by little Loara Standish, the daughter of the famous Captain Miles Standish. She was born in 1623 and died in 1656. Between these dates the little sampler was made, stitched with fine needlework in pink and green threads in an intricate pattern which included a verse which reads as follows:

LOARA STANDISH IS MY NAME
LORD GUIDE MY HEART THAT I MAY DO THY
    WILL
AND FILL MY HANDS WITH SUCH CONVENIENT
    SKILL
AS WILL CONDUCE TO VIRTUE DEVOID OF SHAME
AND I WILL GIVE GLORY TO THY NAME.

Mrs. Swan of Cambridge, Massachusetts, has the well-known Fleetwood-Quincy sampler, which has been owned by the descendants of Mrs. Henry Quincy since 1750. This example, bearing the names of Miles and Abigail Fleetwood, is dated 1654. It is an exquisite piece of needlework and is exactly alike on both sides in the tradition of ancient Chinese embroideries. That Miles Fleetwood suffered reverses in his association with England's Cromwell are referred to in the verse stitched upon it.

IN PROSPERITY FRIENDS WILL BE PLENTY
BUT IN ADVERSITY NOT ONE IN TWENTY.

Mary Hollingsworth's sampler is a very beautiful example of fine needlework in cross-stitch, outlining, seeding, fillings and backstitch, patterned after the English tradition and made by her in 1674. It registers a number of lovely motifs to be copied at a later time. With this work is the following explanation of its purpose: "Patterns to work shawl borders from, Square figures at the top of the Sampler are to work on the corners of the shawl."

None of the shawls worked with these designs have come to the author's attention, but it would be interesting to discover them if they are in existence.

The sampler of lettering in the Essex Institute in Salem, made by Eunice Bowditch at the age of eleven years, is dated the 1st of July, 1718, and shows the style of work used for marking linens, an accomplishment so important to the future housewife. It has been suggested that these lettered samplers were made by small children in order to learn the alphabet, but this theory seems inconsistent with the fact that the average age on these samplers is eight or nine years. Most girls would know their alphabets by that time. It seems more likely that the practice in lettering was for the purpose of marking the household linens, as has been said.

Made in 1730, the incomplete sampler of Abigail Pinniger somewhat resembles other early works. It contains the design elements of conventionalized tulips and carnations which are familiarly characteristic. The technique is good and the sentiment expressive of high spiritual and moral purpose to be impressed upon the mind of the young needleworker when stitching the words upon her examplar:

LOVE THOU THE LORD AND HE
WILL BE A TENDER FATHER.

Beneath a row of tulips in finer lettering is worked the supplication:

SLEEP BONNY SLEEP COME CLOSE MINE EYES
TIRED WITH BEHOLDING VANITIES SWEET.

Here a row of cross-stitched flowers intervenes encompassing within its branches her name and the year the sampler was worked. Beneath follows another inscription:

SLUMBERS COME AND CHASS A WAY THE
TOILS AND FOLLIES OF THE DAY ON YOYA

Here a row of carnations interrupts, conventionally designed and beautifully worked in fine cross-stitch. The wording continues:

SOFT BOSOM WILL I LIE FORGET THE WOR
LD AND LEARN TO DIE.

The signature of the author of the quotation which finished the line was followed by a wider and handsome grouping of flowers in excellent stitching. The design is worked on the same principle as others made in this period of narrow looming. The units are arranged in straight rows across a series of panels which compose the strip.

Showing variety in her stitching and flourishing her silks with largeness, Mary Mason Peele evidently found enjoyment in the use of these materials on her sampler, which was "Wrought in 1778" in Salem, Massachusetts, during her twelfth year. The sky above is lushly indicated in broad stitchery and likewise the grass below upon which a lady and gentleman in colonial costumes of the eighteenth century may be seen with their pets (or perhaps they were Mary's). The flowers are freely embroidered in the satin stitchery seen on French brocades of this period. They may have been derived from some such stuff imported for a gown. Then again, they may have been sketched straight from the garden. Sampler pattern convention has been adhered to in the formal balancing of the figures and the two little birds flying above the top of the lettering square.

The verse embroidered beneath the recorded name, age and date reads:

> LORD I ADDRESS THY HEAVENLY THRONE
> CALL ME A CHILD OF THINE
> SEND DOWN THE SPIRIT OF THY SON
> TO TURN MY HEART DIVINE
> IN THY FAIR BOOK OF LIFE DIVINE
> MAY GOD INSCRIBE MY NAME
> AND LET IT FILL SOME HUMBLE PLACE
> BENEATH THE SLAUGHTERED LAMB.

Occasionally needlework appears to have dropped from a "pocket" and to have been sadly missed. Advertised as lost in the *Boston Gazette* on July 25, 1749, were two breadths of white calico "drawn and partly work'd with blewish thread." This description suggests the drawn white-work type of sampler embroidered with a variety of needle lace stitches and used for practice work and decoration in the eighteenth and early nineteenth centuries.

A sampler dated 1787 is worked on a narrow loomed strip of homespun linen with an alphabet in red alternating with sage green cross-stitch and eyeleting. Then follow numerals and small border lines beneath which English royal crowns are stitched, signifying devotion to the mother country. Pale pink hearts with red centers worked in cross-stitch branch out of a flowerpot outlined in gold color. One little bird sits upon the top of a flower to brighten the composition, which is bordered with conventionalized strawberries stitched in Chinese red with sage green leaves.

Mrs. James Pendleton, who inherited this sampler, believes that the woman who made it was a Tory. The presence of the royal insignia on many American samplers may be due to the same circumstance. Some collectors, denying colonial authorship of these early works, do not realize or have forgotten the existence of this loyalty to England among some of the old American families.

An early sampler worked on linen and almost completely covered with silk stitchery introduces the pictorial aspects with an early alphabet. The elaborately embroidered design is unique. It is the work of Patty Goggeshall, dated February 15, 1780, Bristol, New England. It contains the verse:

> IF I AM RIGHT OH TEACH MY HEART
> STILL IN THE RIGHT WAY TO STAY
> IF I AM WRONG THY GRACE IMPART
> TO FIND THE BETTER WAY.

Close examination of the original in the Metropolitan Museum of Art reveals the stitches to be cross-split satin and queen stitches. The border has different flowers at the sides. At the top men and women engaged in various occupations are embroidered in costumes of the eighteenth century. It is further decorated with animals, trees, flowers and birds, and ducks in the never failing brook or pond swim happily in the traditional manner, unaware of the small boy who intends to shoot them. There is a silken pastoral scene in which a cupid in a chariot drawn by doves happens upon a lady and gentleman romantically engaged, and prepares to enslave them with his arrow, while below, to the left, another lady and her admirer discuss the birds, one of which is perched upon her hand. The background is worked in black stitchery.

Mary Fogg, when she made her lettering sampler in Massachusetts over a hundred and more years ago, little dreamed that her work would be placed in the great Fogg Art Museum of Harvard University which bears her family name. It is another typical example of the needlework required of very young maidens, worked in the transitional period between the long strip homespun samplers and those worked in square linen blocks. Other transitional lettering samplers may be found in the collection of Mrs. Lewis Bigelow. They are dated from the late eighteenth century into the nineteenth. One of them bears witness to the needlework abilities of her great-grandmother, Salley Spofford, who lived in Georgetown, Massachusetts, near Newburyport. The sampler is dated 1799, and was made when Salley was eleven years old. Another was made by Sarah Webber Atkinson,

48   AMERICAN NEEDLEWORK

New Hampshire, 1807, and a third by Clarissa Balch, born September 30, 1772, who in addition to her lettering, admonishes the world:

WHILE GOD DOTH SPARE
FOR DEATH PREPARE.

Also transitional is the sampler of Mary Belcher who dates her work March 14, 1808. She shows originality in departing from the square design used previously. The quotation has become philosophical. It is centered in a large embroidered circle, the top being festooned with a draped and tasseled curtain rising above the enclosed thought beneath:

LOVE ALL, TRUST A FEW
DO WRONG TO NONE BE ABLE FOR THINE ENEMY
RATHER IN POWER THAN IN USE KEEP THY
    FRIEND
UNDER THY OWN LIFE'S KEY BE CHECK'D FOR
    SILENCE
BUT NEVER TALK FOR SPEECH.

There are stars above the lettering and baskets of flowers beneath it; rosebuds are entwined to enclose the signature. Four trees spot the corners outside the circle, two containing busy squirrels after nuts. The alphabet forms a small square frame around the circle and outside of it is a conventionalized sampler border with more cross-stitched rosebuds.

Another transition sampler is that made by Ann Boyd of Baltimore, Maryland, dated May 4, 1804. It shows the characteristic combination of lettering and decorative embellishment. Small acorns in pots and moss roses form the border design. Its poem reads:

BY LOVE DIRECTED AND MERCY MEANT,
ARE TRIALS DIRECTED AND AFFLICTIONS SENT
AND CURB THE INSOLENCE OF PROSPEROUS
    PRIDE,
TO THAT BEST CLIME WHERE PAIN SHALL BE NO
    MORE,
WHERE WEARIED VIRTUE SHALL FOR REFUGE
    FLY,
AND EVERY TEAR BE WIPED FROM EVERY EYE.

The earliest credited example showing the introduction into sampler design of the house in which the needleworker lived comes from Margaret Ramsey of Albany in 1789. The houses pictured on the samplers usually are typical of architecture prevalent in the colonies. They range from the New England farmhouse, the "Salt Box," the dignified Georgian brick mansion to the large three-storied hip-roofed houses of later times.

A beautiful example of colonial needlework, wrought by Increase Giberson in the year 1796, is to be found in Miss Gertrude Oppenheimer's collection of American samplers. It is worked with silks upon cream homespun finely woven. Increase has stitched her house, her pets, her favorite flowers and plants, and on the opposite side of the sampler her father's and mother's initials, and those of all the children are stitched. A verse expressing her frame of mind when stitching her "sample" of needlework is as follows:

THE LORD CAN CHANGE THE DARKEST SKIES,
CAN GIVE US DAY FOR NIGHT,
MAKE FLOODS OF SACRED SORROWS RISE,
TO RIVERS OF DELIGHT.

AS ON SOME LONELY BUILDING TOP,
THE SPARROW TELLS HER MOAN,
FAR FROM THE TENTS OF JOY AND HOPE,
I SIT AND GRIEVE ALONE.

Evidently lonely, long hours were spent upon this sampler, but the work has lived these many years as a tribute to the little fingers that stitched so finely and so beautifully. Quite a variety of stitches are included, cross-stitch, satin stitch, buttonhole stitch, backstitch and lettering in very fine tent stitch. The whole design has been carefully arranged and planned, the motifs well balanced.

Most of the colors range from deep greens through yellow and olive greens for grass and leaves, to ivory tan and golden browns for flowers, house and scrolls or vines. A touch of pale pink (it was probably more deep and intense when originally worked), may be found in the center flowers and basket. All the lettering and the baskets pick up the tone of the sampler pleasantly through the introduction of antique turquoise blue. A beautiful border frames the whole, designed with the conventionalized carnation and tulip motif popular in this period.

This sampler measures nineteen by fifteen inches, quite a sizable presentation of needlework technique by this young lady of the colonies in the eighteenth century.

Needlepoint picture worked with silks in fine tent stitch on canvas. Painted appliquéd portraits. Signed and dated by Abigail Parkman, 1758, Connecticut.

~~~~~~

PART III

NEEDLEWORK IN THE EARLY NATIONAL PERIOD

~~~~~~

PHILADELPHIA TYPE SAMPLERS, QUAKER NEEDLE-WORK, AND PENNSYLVANIA DUTCH EMBROIDERY

"With gentle hand your daughters train
The housewife's various art to gain
On scenes domestic to preside
The needle, wheel and shuttle guide.

On things of use to fix the heart
And gild with every graceful art
Teach them with neatest simplest dress
A neat and lovely mind to express."
AMERICAN SAMPLER VERSE IN 1817.

ERY FEW EARLY SAMPLERS ARE recorded from the vicinity of Philadelphia, but in the eighteenth century many distinguished examples of stitchery were worked by young ladies who attended classes in needlework at the Bethlehem school of the Moravians, studied with instructresses and preceptresses at other Dame schools or practiced in samplers at the Friends schools which flourished during this period. Their samplers have become known as "the Philadelphia type," a term applied to the better examples of needlework made by cultured members of the community, and in particular to the fine needlework exhibited in the Quaker samplers.

Designs for lettering were made in the finishing schools upon samplers or in drawing books. A "poor, dear Aunt Matilda" was usually chosen not only to supervise such marking and sewing, but to coach and prepare the damosels in the social graces. A young gentlewoman in town, besides being "taught Wax Work, Transparent and Filigree, Painting on Glass, Quill Work, Feather Work, and Embroidery with Gold and Silver and several other sorts of Work," might in her spare time try a little sketching or memorize poetry to be stitched upon her sampler. Poems enumerating qualities desired in the ideal mate were popular in the later samplers. A sampler of 1821 advises:

CONVINCE THE WORLD THAT YOU ARE JUST AND
　　TRUE
BE JUST IN ALL YOU SAY AND ALL YOU DO
WHAT SOEVER BE YOUR BIRTH YOUR SURE TO BE
A MAN OF THE FIRST MAGNITUDE TO ME.

Botany also was studied and the Latin names of plants and flowers in the family garden were conscientiously learned. Reproductions of these favorites were introduced along with other motifs on the embroidered "sample." The Georgian architecture of the worker's house also appeared.

The alphabet in various styles of needlework was the beginning of the practice sheet for stitchery and after the technique was accomplished the remainder of the linen block might be embellished to display the other accomplishments and observations of the embroiderer. It was as necessary to learn the art of stitchery as to be an able cook or to appreciate the qualities in good books and music. In fact embroidery was an essential study in the young ladies' seminaries around Philadelphia as it was in the other colonies.

Many examples of these lessons on linen have

been preserved for posterity by proud descendants. A particularly fine sampler from Mrs. Henry E. Coe's collection emphasizes the patriotic note which is struck on many samplers in America in the nineteenth century. The sampler shows an American eagle bearing in his bill the inscription "E Pluribus Unum" worked in satin stitches. There are flags with nine stars. The homestead, made of bricks and three-storied, is carefully reproduced in needlepoint, tent, outline and cross-stitches. In the foreground are animals: dogs, sheep, ducks, cows, deer. The parents and the shepherd standing beside the beehive with its circle of buzzing bees are worked in tent stitch, cross-stitch, stem, satin and block stitch, the last being used in the diamond-shaped tree tops back of the house. Birds sitting in the tops of the willow and other trees are cross-stitched.

The entire "estate" is bordered with an elaborate conventionalized passion flower design. To the left of the eagle two little cross-stitched angels are flying over the encased inscription embroidered in memory of "Elizabeth Wiert, Age 80, Died 1825." Balancing this wreath to the right of the eagle and under another star and pair of flying angels, is the worker's name, Margaret Moss, aged eleven years.

An eighteenth century example in a contrasting style is a needlepoint or tent stitch sampler made by Mary Bulyn in Kensington, Pennsylvania, in 1730. It is an early type of pictorial sampler somewhat in the manner of the tapestry scenic design and similar in technique to the Fishing Lady needlepoint pictures made in Boston and its vicinity during this period. A shepherdess stands with her sheep under a full, branching tree which harbors many birds. A deer and a horse among the hills and flowers complete the composition. It is in the possession of Mrs. Frederick F. Thompson and is an excellent example of this earlier type of embroidery.

A large Philadelphia type sampler is that made by Jane Niles in 1791. It measures approximately eighteen by twenty-two inches. It was inherited by its present owner, Mrs. Henry J. Miller, through her aunt who was a granddaughter of Jane Niles. The homespun linen has become a deep brown. The lettering begins with a very small top row of block letters in cross-stitch, then numerals with a line of decoration in a conventional border, followed by two rows of large letters worked with cross-stitch and eyelet. Beneath is a stanza of verse, now almost obliterated. The sampler is finished with decorative pine trees. Some symbolic meaning may be attached to these trees by little Mistress Niles. They are five in number and are set in graduated sizes.

Underneath is the name stitched in verse, which reads:

> JANE NILES IS MY NAME
> AMERICA IS MY NATION,
> PHILADELPHIA IS MY DWELLING PLACE
> AND CHRIST IS MY SALVATION.

The date follows amidst the conventionalized strawberries, peacocks and baskets of fruit, worked in close stitches. In two corners are small lions wearing crowns on their heads which may indicate that Jane Niles still cherished a family fondness for England.

A gay sampler made in 1799 attempted architecture in a large way. Liberty Hall in Philadelphia is pictured with a frolicsome horse made in cross-stitches prancing on the lawn.

An exceedingly handsome sampler from the nineteenth century, in the collection of Mrs. Harrold Gillingham in Philadelphia, was made by her great-aunt, Lydia Lancaster, in the year 1830. The group of flowers in the center of this work is gracefully arranged and worked in fine cross-stitch in delicate pastel shades against a linen background. A butterfly adorns the upper right-hand corner, and a bow is made to the traditional sampler formulas in the two baskets of fruit on either side of the signature at the panel's base. An unusual border of squares placed cornerwise, each centered with a cross-stitched flower, encompasses the embroidery.

Another of Mrs. Gillingham's samplers was worked by a prominent Philadelphia maiden and stitched with the following information:

> RESPECTFULLY PRESENTED TO JOHN AND ANN
> HEWSON BY THEIR AFFECTIONATE DAUGHTER,
> MARTHA N. HEWSON DONE IN THE ELEVENTH
> YEAR OF HER AGE. KENSINGTON, NOVEMBER 8T.

It has been said that Ann Hewson's grandfather was responsible for the first calico printing works in Philadelphia, created at Benjamin Franklin's request at a time when not to use

Quaker sampler made in the "Westtown Boarding School"
by Elizabeth Rowland, Philadelphia.

Quaker sampler, Westtown insignia made at Pleasant Hill
Boarding School 1806 by Anna Eliza Roes, Philadelphia.

Quaker sampler, worked at Westtown Boarding School,
1809, by Eleanor Brinton, Philadelphia.

Quaker sampler, 1820, by Sarah H. James, Pennsylvania.

1. Pennsylvania Dutch embroidered towel by Anna Herr. Pennsylvania.
2. Pennsylvania Dutch embroidered sampler picture, middle 19th century, American. 3. Pennsylvania Dutch embroidered towel with drawn work, 1827. Inscribed Cadare Na Kuns. Pennsylvania.

Pennsylvania Dutch cross stitch sampler, 1896, Pennsylvania.

Pennsylvania Dutch embroidered sampler, 1851, by Elizabeth Blank, Pennsylvania.

American homemade products was considered especially unpatriotic.

The sampler is believed to have been made in 1830. It is finely cross-stitched, shades of green and blue predominating among the leaves in the basket, the latter being in cream. Flowers are worked in pale rose tones. Spiral stitches on the pineapples in the center of the basket are unique. The verse of religious character is enclosed within a trim, conventional border, and the outside finish of carnations is neatly conventionalized into a wide cross-stitched border. It is a creditable work in every way.

Space will not permit mention of many other samplers made in the vicinity of the City of Brotherly Love which are equally good and precious.

White needlework and lace samplers are the rarest of all in this class of embroidery and did not predate 1700. Besides being difficult to execute, there is a theory that the pricked ink patterns by which these designs were transferred, became worn out with frequent use. Two known examples of this style are outstanding in their dainty perfection. One made by Jane Humphreys in 1771 of white lace stitches and darned work on white linen is a gift of Miss Letitia Humphreys to the Memorial Hall in Fairmont Park, Philadelphia. For a girl of twelve years, it is an amazingly good example of intricate needlework. This sampler is almost identical in design, stitch technique and general character with another which has found a place in a collection of

QUAKER SAMPLERS

An all-white sampler inscribed "Mary Jackson Her Work, 1788" demonstrates a variety of darned lace work stitches and white work embroidery. In the four corners are inserted circles of fine needle-made lace. The design consists of a drawn- and darning-worked basket with the vines and tendrils embroidered solid in fine buttonhole stitches. The flowers show individual patternings in darned technique. This lovely work is in the collection of Mrs. Francis D. Brinton, of Pennsylvania, who has inherited other examples of Quaker needlework directly from her family antecedents who attended the Westtown Boarding School. This first Quaker school of consequence is thus described in the

State Annals of Pennsylvania, published in 1843:

THE WESTTOWN BOARDING SCHOOL

Among the most distinguished of the seminaries of learning in the country, is the old institution established by the Society of Friends in Westtown, in 1794, "with a desire, more especially for the promotion of piety, than the cultivation of science." It was to be under the patronage of the yearly meeting of Philadelphia, and to furnish, "besides the requisite portion of literary instruction; an education exempt from the contagion, of vicious example, and calculated to establish habits and principles favourable to future usefulness in religious and civil society." A farm of 600 acres was purchased of James Gibbons, and a large brick building erected for the accommodation of the students. The farm cost between $16,000 and $19,000, and the building $22,470. Pupils were first received in the 5th month, 1799, ten of a sex being admitted until the whole number amounted to nearly two hundred. In 1802, a large building of stone was erected, originally intended to be used as a hospital in case of infectious diseases, but subsequently appropriated for the use of teachers with families.

The immediate charge is intrusted to a superintendent and eight teachers—three men and five women. The superintendent attends to the finances of the institution, but has no direct oversight of the literary departments. A library and philosophical apparatus is provided and the usual branches of an English and Classical education is taught. For many years the Classics were omitted.

A fine sampler made in 1809 by Martha Heuling of Moorestown, New Jersey, has a needleworked portrait of the Westtown Boarding School centered in the linen panel. Prancing deer are stitched below and verse, undecipherable, is embroidered within a square-shaped vine at the top. A beautifully designed and worked border of fruit in baskets, flowers, and abstract motifs encloses the picture. It is owned by Hannah F. Gardiner.

One of the earliest known Quaker samplers with the name of this boarding school stitched upon it is that of Elizabeth Rowland, the grandmother of Mrs. Francis D. Brinton. Elizabeth stitched this quotation upon her sampler:

'TIS NOT THE CURIOUS, BUT THE PIOUS PATH
THAT LEADS ME TO MY POINT: LORENZOI KNOW,
WITHOUT OR STAR, OR ANGEL, FOR THEIR GUIDE,

WHO WORSHIP GOD, SHALL FIND HIM, HUMBLE
    LOVE,
AND NOT PROUD REASON, KEEPS THE DOOR OF
    HEAVEN;
LOVE FINDS ADMISSION, WHERE PROUD SCIENCE
    FAILS.

Beneath these words of wisdom, which were embroidered in black sienna silk thread in the neatest lettering, comes the full signature and date, the latter worked in Roman numerals. The quotation is enclosed in a classic vine and leaf scroll border which was used as a signature of the school. Every sampler made by a student or graduate displayed this border, in later work made a little more elaborate, but with the original foundation vine unaltered.

Finely cross-stitched within the same Westtown School signature, is the title on a Quaker sampler which reads, "Pleasant Hill Boarding School." It was made by Anna Eliza Roes according to her signature and dated in 1806. A story is connected with the adoption by a new school of the signature of the Westtown School. It is as follows:

John Comly, author of Comly's Speller and Reader and Grammar, and Rebecca Budd were students at the Westtown School where they met and fell in love, despite the fact that boys and girls were not allowed to speak to each other. They finally married at Merion Meeting and left for Byberry which was a community outside of Philadelphia. There they started their own school in the tradition of Westtown, and named it Pleasant Hill Boarding School. Anna Eliza Roes, a student, began the traditional pattern on her work, but added more decoration by filling in the corners of her sampler with garden flowers. Description of the Quaker discipline maintained at the school adds that "they were so strict that one couldn't whistle" and some harmony-hungry students "filed sleigh bells" to obtain a semblance of attractive sounds. It was the only music allowed in these austere surroundings.

Elinor Brinton contributes another interpretation of the Westtown School insignia and adds strawberry borders outside her encircled alphabet. Other flowers are spotted over the background of this design in the eighteenth century manner. At the very top traditional baskets of fruit are cross-stitched sampler fashion. One bird enters the design along with scattered initials of the family or friends. It is dated the "1st mo 12th 1809." This work which was done by an ancestor, is in Mrs. Francis Brinton's unique collection of samplers.

About 1820 Quaker maidens grew very decorative and strewed silk stitched flowers over their samplers at random. Sarah H. James performed an ambitious work in a jolly and decorative sampler on which she has immortalized the name of her instructress, E. Passmore, in a little box opposite her own signature. Birds have been duplicated. Butterflies flit among silken trees and upon the solidly stitched foreground, which is also a recent addition to the sampler patterning; little French-knotted lambs gambol upon the green silk grass while small rabbits are busy eating green silk lettuce leaves. These must have been stitched directly from fresh impressions made upon the worker's mind while watching her pets. Here the Westtown insignia has branched out into a double vine bursting with bunches of grapes. It encloses the stitched names of all the immediate family, "My Parents and Grand Parents Names" on through to Aunt James ending with an "Extract" of "six lines of philosophical admonitions."

The panel is framed with the fashionable silk ribbon quilling used in this vicinity on many needlework samplers and pictures of this period. The idea may have emanated directly from England, for quilled ribbon borders on samplers have been discovered there on examples dated 1796.

Besides these samplers Mrs. Brinton has several others of the Philadelphia type, one having an elaborate cross-stitched border in conventionalized design, worked during the early nineteenth century. For reasons best known to herself Elizabeth Rowland, who worked the sampler in 1803, has embroidered a row of crowns symbolic of the mother country, and has stitched them upside down. Greens of many shades predominate in the needlework.

Susanna Cox made her sampler at the Westtown school in 1802, with flowers spotted brocade fashion on its background and worked in fine cross-stitch. Sarah Brinton has worked the name of her teacher, Susanna Harvey. The J of the alphabet is left out on her sampler thus dating it prior to 1800, when I and J were interchangeable.

PENNSYLVANIA DUTCH NEEDLEWORK

A God-fearing sect from Germany who sought freedom of religious opinion were drawn to Pennsylvania and settled in the county of Chester, now called Lancaster, about the year 1722. Although Germans, their dialect is a mixture emanating from the upper Rhine which included Switzerland, with some fusion of English. They called themselves "Dutch folks" of Pennsylvania, possibly because their faith is related to that of the Baptist Dutch. They were of the Mennist and Amish denominations, the latter being exiles from Switzerland and Alsace who followed the teachings of a Swiss Mennonite preacher of the late seventeenth century named Jacob Amen.

Other faiths were represented among the Germans who settled in Berks and Lebanon County. They were Lutherans and members of the German Reformed Church. Later a Society of Dunkers called "River Brethren," was formed by a Mennonite near the Susquehanna. There were also sects of "New Mennists" and "Dutch Methodists." The prevailing religious denomination in 1843, however, was that of the Mennonites. German dialect was used in preaching.

The embroidery techniques traditional in the old country were reflected in their needlework, and since they lived almost completely isolated, few influences from the outside penetrated to modify their art. Homely proverbs inherited from the fatherland were used, as were favorite rhymes and quotations from the Bible along with old German hymns.

Gradual changes occurred, however, and later homely philosophy was introduced along with pictures of the animals they raised, the flowers they cultivated, and the costumes they wore. When "Dutchmen" assisted in the farming of a Quaker's land, the women might acquire a new method of stitchery as well as English ideas and customs. The Yankee trader brought further information to the section and quilting parties provided another opportunity for exchanging designs.

Unique among the embroideries of this community were the towels made by the young maidens for their dower chests. After marriage little time would be left for such elaborate work, and infinite pains were taken to make these creations endure for all time, carrying youthful enthusiasms in permanent form through the many years of hardship. How many miniature prayers, hopes and dreams were woven into their gay, stitched panels!

Due to their fine craftsmanship and intimate personal expression, Pennsylvania Dutch embroidered towels have been found worthy of museum homes. Included in the bridal or hope chests, such sampler-like linen strips were the counterpart of the familiar guest towel, and were used for company best. All good housekeepers must have their quota of such traditional treasures, and by their linens one knew the measure of their maker's ability as a housewife. The strips were hand woven before being needleworked.

DESIGN AND METHOD OF WORKING

Like samplers these towels included dates and the initials or name of the maker. Some have small alphabets, scattered motifs, animals. For example one towel pictures two racing horses at the bottom of the panel. Others include birds and conventionalized flowers or abstract symbols, pomegranate flowers having a religious significance. The peacock was important, representing in a general sense good luck or good fortune. He was also the symbol of resurrection, the emblem of opulence, and the forecaster of coming storms, farmers being warned of their approach by the bird's harsh cries. Most of the motifs were adapted from the ornamental patterns used on other articles, the painted chests identified with these people, the tinseled glass, the tole ware and other pottery ware. Fractur painting used in recording certificates of marriages, births, deaths, and other manuscript decoration was a splendid source for embroidery patterns. Some dating back to 1702 provided quaint suggestions for needlework application.

The particular peacock motif used so often in the Pennsylvania Dutch samplers may have come from some pattern book of the Nuremberg Sibmacher series which found its way across the ocean with German "Dutch" refugees. Original plates of this design emphasized the lamb and peacock motif. The crucifixion and its symbols were used generally in Catholic Bavaria and while these early Pennsylvania settlers were of Protestant faith, the designs evidently were impressed upon their minds and adopted for their significance.

A towel sampler in the Metropolitan. Museum of Art dated in 1827 bears the inscription:

CADARE/NA/ KUNS/C/K/.

It is embroidered with very fine cross-stitch, backstitch and chain stitch, and shows a pair of peacocks, floral motifs, and a large leaf motif arranged like a swastika. These designs have been worked on the hand-woven linen strip with silks in pink and blue principally. The lower end has been carried out in drawn work, which employs three figures in its all-white lacy pattern, as well as peacocks and conventionalized flowers. The drawn work is not unlike Dutch homespun needlework. The technique, originating about 1800, was called Benewaka. Drawn threads were stitched into a net upon which the pattern was darned with a linen thread. The decoration was used on the ends of pillowcases and bureau covers.

From the same collection, a towel cover of white homespun linen is designed with conventionalized birds. It is inscribed by Ann Herr, 1833. It has two large geese in one section and two small roosters, also native. A pair of peacocks stand on either side of a vase of flowers and at the very top a vase may be seen holding one tulip. This flower is exceedingly important to the Pennsylvania Dutch, having many meanings. In the single use on the sampler, and worked in groups of three, the tulip symbolized the Trinity of God. The borders and other motifs on this example may have been taken from the traditional pattern books.

Another "Dutch" towel quotes, either from the scripture or from a preacher's admonition, the following, worked in red thread:

FEAR NONE OF THOSE THINGS WHICH THOU
    SHALT SUFFER
BEHOLD THE DEVIL SHALL CAST SOME OF YOU
    INTO PRISON THAT YE MAY BE TRIED
AND YE SHALL HAVE TRIBULATION.
TEN DAYS BE THOU
FAITHFUL UNTO DEATH
AND I WILL GIVE THEE A CROWN OF LIFE.

Worked in blue thread, the admonition continues:

AND I HEARD A LOUD VOICE SAYING IN HEAVEN
NOW IS COME SALVATION AND STRENGTH AND
    THE KINGDOM OF OUR GOD
AND THE POWER OF HIS CHRIST
FOR THE ACCUSED OF OUR BRETHREN IS CAST
    DOWN
WHICH ACCUSED THEM BEFORE OUR GOD DAY
    AND NIGHT.

This linen strip was embroidered in cross-stitch on three pieces of linen, each fringed at the ends and joined to make one long towel cover. The first panel was designed with formalized flowers and wreaths enclosing the initials, M. T. and I. F. The second contained the quotation worked in red and in blue. The third section contained three rows of the drawn work in all-white darned patterning. The Metropolitan Museum of Art owns this early nineteenth century example also.

In many of the later Pennsylvania Dutch samplers we find an interesting combination of techniques. For example an embroidery owned by the author and made on a large homespun linen panel displays a huge bouquet of flaming red roses and other red flowers from a thriving garden. These flowers are broadly worked in sweeping lines with heavy, thick, "Germantown" yarns in satin stitch. Chenille has been introduced by Elizabeth Blank in "Her work 1851," for additional effect.

The unrestrained "painting" of these flowers is a spontaneous expression of the needleworker, who no doubt was filled with delight and enthusiasm for her own luxurious garden bouquet placed in a tight bunch upon her parlor table. It is the central theme in her rendering and to her mind all absorbing. However, to frame this bouquet and create the sampler feeling, she bordered the work with an Early American cross-stitched pattern of strawberries, quite English in character and no doubt seen by the worker upon a visit to another locality where there was a New England sampler. Or possibly a Quaker neighbor's design provided the new technique. The border work is carefully and finely executed in lighter wools as if to say the worker could express herself in many ways, such versatility being the objective of most early American needlewomen.

In character with the sentimental tendency characteristic of the very early nineteenth century, the large Pennsylvania Dutch sampler has appliquéd in the middle top center of the wool-embroidered bouquet of roses, a piece of material on which two purple pansies are worked in silk. Perhaps this bit of technique was introduced as a memento of some romantic moment, "Pansies for Thoughts."

The introduction of souvenirs belonging to a loved member of the family or a sweetheart, ran riot all through nineteenth century needle-work design and all manner of knickknacks were introduced into the embroidered pictures. Among wool-embroidered ship pictures made by sailors at sea, one included beneath the picture of the ship a daguerreotype of the girl left behind applied upon the canvas and encircled by a stitched wreath of flowers. Clasped hands in the center of a motif with two crossed flags above symbolized the American sailor and a sweetheart in another nation. Hands across the sea!

Following or just preceding this sampler came a pictorial expression the style of which was influenced perhaps by the silk on satin embroideries prevalent during the 1800's and up to 1860.

A large rough linen panel has been embroidered in colored silks with a number of isolated units. The worker has drawn her subjects crudely from the life about her. The house, the trees, lamp posts on the fence, the pet dog, are there, together with favorite chairs, much admired no doubt, for there are three of them including a velvet cushioned rocker. Hearts, stars, moons and anchors have symbolical significance. The deer, the potted plants are all stitched surrealistically, in the best modern art manner. The panel is a true "Primitive" in American needle-work.

Worked in 1896 this "Dutch" sampler combines all the influences of the traditional European patterns. It is an entertaining mixture worked in the most brilliant Berlin wools, which may have been sent to this little "Dutch" maiden from the Old World.

The designs generally used by the Pennsylvania Dutch in their potteryware, paintings, and needlework might be termed folk art since their motifs have been inspired by and are related to the peasant art of Swiss and German origin. Their contribution is a colorful one.

~~~~~~

CHAPTER IX

LATER SAMPLERS

"Ay, soon upon the stage of life,
Sweet, happy children, you will rise,
To mingle in its care and strife,
Or early find the peaceful skies.
Then be it yours, while you pursue
The golden moments, quick to haste
Some noble work of love to do,
Nor suffer one bright hour to waste."
DANIEL CLEMENT COLESWORTHY.

 EEDLEWORK GENERALLY DURING the early nineteenth century became a form of relaxation and an expression of mood. The sampler ceased to be primarily a pattern book for linen marking and became rather a lesson book for the development of needlework art. Experiment in other fields of stitchery, such as the silk on satin embroidery, necessitated changes in design and in technique. These new ideas in embroidery were immediately applied to the later samplers which show combinations of tent stitches worked on satin and silk stitches worked on linen. Contacts with other parts of the country made possible through the establishment of new post roads and other means of communication also account for the introduction of new patterns.

After frontiers had been pushed back toward the West, life in the East assumed more ease and calm. Families began to consider the possibility of a broader education for their daughters and numerous boarding schools, Dame schools, and female seminaries sprang up along the seaboard. The Moravian school in Bethlehem, and the Quaker school at Westtown have already been mentioned.

Other schools of that time included the Quaker or Friends School in New Jersey, Leah Meguier's School in Harrisburg, Pennsylvania (1825), the Red Bank School, Miss Sarah Stevens School, Mrs. Welcham's School at Maytown (1812), Miss Sarah Pierce's School at Litchfield, Connecticut, Miss Polly Balch's Seminary in Providence (1785), Miss Sally Hinsdale's School in New Hartford, The "Nine Partners" Friends School in New York (1800), Sarah Knight, School Dame, at Ivers Lane in Salem (1792), The Westport School (1803), Mrs. Rowson's Academy in Boston (1812), Madame Mansfield, School Mistress, in Salem (1791), The Northern Liberty School in Philadelphia (1827), The "Old Boarding School" in Wilmington, Delaware, presided over by Mr. Crips (1797), Mary Walden's School in Baltimore (1818), The Piney Grove School in Virginia (1809), The Moravian School in North Carolina (1805), Mrs. Condy's Embroidery School in Boston (1800), The Salem Female Academy in Kentucky (1803), The Waynesville School in Ohio (1807).

A larger percentage of the samplers of this period bear the name of the school where they were worked, and frequently the name of the needlework teacher. Inspiration for the verse came from those Yankee classics, the New England primers, from hymns, Psalms and chapters in the Gospel. Alexander Pope was quoted more often than any other single author with the exception of the Reverend Isaac Watts, whose works were admired above all others. Stanzas from "Divine Songs for Children" were the most popular for reproduction. Edward Young, Congreve, Goldsmith, Thompson, John Bunyan, Gay and Milton are represented in various stitched extracts. Besides these sources, lines were created by the young embroiderer. Sometimes she evolved a combination of lines from several poems.

Representative samplers made in this period and here described are to be found in well-known private collections, museums and families who have inherited them. They present an interesting commentary on the period in which they were executed.

One of these later samplers from Mrs. Henry E. Coe's famous collection presents the cross-stitched design of Margaret Barnhott who worked it in 1831 at the age of twelve years. The church is characteristic of those seen on the green in early American towns. In the center foreground are the father and mother; the pet bird is perched in a tree; on either side are a cow, a horse and a number of butterflies; above are angels and vases of cross-stitched flowers. Adam and Eve take the center left under their historic tree above which, on either side, rests a bird of paradise. Opposite is a tender mourning scene with parents and children grieving for a departed one beneath a weeping willow. More angels and birds appear, a large basket of flowers rises to meet other butterflies and to divide three rural scenes containing trees, figures, animals, and birds. The presence of the peacocks and birds of paradise as well as the name of the embroiderer suggest that Margaret Barnhott may have been influenced by the Pennsylvania Dutch or German traditions, and that she considered these feathered friends symbolic of good luck, long life and prosperity.

Margaret's verse evidently voices the thought of the lost one who is mourned in the little scene below it.

MOTHER DEAR, WEEP NOT FOR ME
WHEN IN THIS YARD MY GRAVE YOU SEE
MY TIME WAS SHORT AND BLEST WAS HE
THAT CALLED ME TO ETERNITY.

A lettering and family register sample of unusual character comes from the Louisiana State Museum's collection of Americana. This design subscribes to the traditions in its lettering and stitchery but departs in the theme. It was apparently worked in 1830 by Emilie Wiltz while attending a convent belonging to the religious order of the Ursulines in New Orleans, and studying needlework under their direction. It is lettered in French. An altar in the center foreground is balanced by devotional lamps, chalices and a cross. These are bordered by potted plants in conventional cross-stitch and at the very end a little bird and two hearts united with a single arrow speak feelingly. Almost hiding under a large needleworked plant is the most loved pet, a small dog faithfully attending his mistress, even in stitches.

South Carolina is credited with the creation in 1806 by Sarah S. Caldwell of the first sampler showing the emblematic American eagle. He flies a pennant from his beak calling for "Independence." Beneath him is a handsomely embroidered landscape.

In Miss Gertrude Oppenheimer's collection in New York another American eagle appears, stitched upon the sampler of Susan Cunning North Bovey which is dated June 27th, 1827. Her verse, embroidered in fine cross-stitch with black silk thread, reads as follows:

HAVE NOT EVE AND ADAM TAUGHT US
THEIR SAD PROFIT TO COMPUTE
TO WHAT DISMAL STATE THEY BROUGHT US
WHEN THEY STOLE FORBIDDEN FRUIT.

It is hard to tell what experiences of the day brought such reflections to Susan's mind. Cross-stitch and satin stitch are combined in the technique. The work, exceedingly fine and intricate, may account for the "dismal state" to which the young embroiderer says she has been brought.

Below the verse a man and woman cross-stitched in colonial blues tend their sheep. They are standing on a green silk foreground made with satin stitches. Beside the shepherd and shepherdess vases holding drooping acorn branches and the inevitable carnation are stitched. This motif is delightfully composed. Birds and little trees complete the bottom row. The border frames are worked with satin-stitched blue triangles. Within is a conventional pattern composed of vines, leaves and a lily. This has been worked in slightly deeper shades than the central pastel figures and accents the dark coloring of the brown eagle. Some of the little motifs may have been borrowed from a European pattern book which some refugee stowed away with other treasures for use in America.

The collection contains another Adam and Eve motif centered in the delightful sampler worked by Margaret Reid at the age of 13, in the year 1837. This sampler is unique in its combination of needlepoint, Kensington, and chain stitches worked in both fine wools and silks. The animals, as delightful in their way as those in Walt Disney's *Snow White and the Seven Dwarfs*, are arranged in and about potted flowers and trees in Adam and Eve's garden. Vain peacocks strut below and proud cocks head the sampler under the verse:

THE LOSS OF GOLD IS MUCH
THE LOSS OF TIME IS MORE
BUT THE LOSS OF CHRIST IS SUCH
AS NO MAN CAN RESTORE.

Deep observation for thirteen-year-old Margaret! Evidently to emphasize the sentiment expressed in the verse a plant is embroidered, the top branches of which have bloomed into a trinity of flower crosses.

The colors are well ranged in a variety of greens, browns, reds, powder and colonial blues and golds. A radical shade for this period occurs in the small but effective use of violet in some of the lettering.

Another sampler from this group shows the stitching of religious teaching required in the sampler curriculum of nearly every finishing school in the land. The name of the embroiderer has been included in the verse:

HENRIETTA TUTTLE IS MY NAME,
AND NEW ENGLAND IS MY NATION
FAIR HAVEN IS MY DWELLING PLACE
AND CHRIST IS MY SALVATION.

WORKED THIS IN THE 13TH YEAR OF HER AGE,
AUGUST 27TH, 1823.

Evidently Henrietta worked this sampler with deep feeling, since following on the same line are stitched several hearts. Then follows the Apostles' Creed:

I BELIEVE IN GOD THE FATHER ALMIGHTY MAKER OF HEAVEN AND EARTH AND IN JESUS CHRIST HIS ONLY SON OUR LORD WHO WAS CONCEIVED BY THE HOLY GHOST BORN OF THE VIRGIN MARY SUFFERED UNDER PONTIUS PILATE WAS CRUCIFIED DEAD AND BURIED HE DESCENDED INTO HELL THE THIRD DAY HE AROSE FROM THE DEAD AND ASCENDED INTO HEA

Here the material ends and the rest of the word had to be omitted. Two alphabets in different styles are interesting. The sampler is worked mainly in black silk on linen. A small touch of rose in the flower border furnishes the only contrasting color.

A sampler made by Elizabeth Starr Fowler, which includes an alphabet and stitch sampler of the early nineteenth century, is another example from Miss Oppenheimer's collection. It is here reproduced for the first time. Elizabeth made it in 1832 at the age of nine years and nine months. The background is fine linen scrim, the threads used are silk in shades of red and brown for some of the lettering, ivory white and dark blue-green. The weeping willows are worked in back and loop stitch in two shades of blue-green. Sad drooping little white flowers in a row under the tree are growing up out of a green foreground stitched in needlepoint, and on the opposite side a tombstone is worked in Kensington stitch. The lettering of the verse is in needlepoint which would lead one to believe that this sampler was made by a New England maiden, a conclusion which is borne out by the title

THE LITTLE PILGRIM

LITTLE PILGRIM, YOUNG IN YEARS,
HAST THOU NOT A HUNDRED FEARS
THUS TO ENTER LIFE'S NEW ROAD,
NEVER BUT WITH DANGER TROD?

PATHS ARRAY'D IN TEMPTING BLOOM,
WILL ENTICE THY STEPS TO COME,
BUT, THOUGH EVERY FRAGRANCE SWEET,
CHARM THY SENSES, SHUN THE CHEAT.

YES, KIND FRIEND, I KNOW FULL WELL,
SIN AND SORROW IN THEM DWELL,
NEVER SHALL MY STEPS BE LED
WHERE THE VIRTUOUS SHOULD NOT TREAD.

Sampler, 1830, by Lydia Lancaster, Philadelphia.

Sampler, 1830, by Martha N. Hewson, Kensington, Pennsylvania.

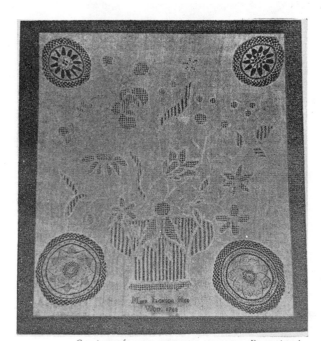

Quaker Sampler of white embroidery and darned lace work. 1788 by Mary Jackson, Reading, Pennsylvania.

Sampler of the American Scene, American Eagle bearing the inscription, "E Pluribus Unum," embroidered by Margaret Moss, aged 11 years in 1825, Philadelphia.

1. *Courtesy of:* MISS GERTRUDE OPPENHEIMER, New York.

Sampler of Susan Cuming, North Bovey, New England. June 27, 1827. American.

2. *Courtesy of:* MRS. HENRY E. COE, New York.

Sampler by Margaret Barnhott. Made at the age of twelve years. 1831, American.

3. *Courtesy of:* THE MUSEUM OF THE CITY OF NEW YORK.

Sampler, silk embroidered with satin stitches, antique Chinese style, 1809. By Amalie August Schmidt, New York.

I WILL CHOOSE ME SUCH A GUIDE,
THAT I CANNOT STEP ASIDE,
LORD, IF THOU WILL BE MY AID,
ALL THOSE GAY DECEITS SHALL FADE.

Underneath this verse Elizabeth has made another row or sample of stitchery in outline back-stitch, followed by a row of little square eyelet stitches in alternating shades of ivory and brown silk.

A tender, modest sampler included among the more sophisticated or learned examples is a mourning sampler made by Emily Silcox, aged seven, who states:

WHEN THIS WAS DONE, THIS I HAVE DONE TO LET YOU SEE WHAT CARE MY PARENTS TOOK OF ME.

So wrote Emily, and dedicated her stitches to Sister Sarah Jane Silcox, who died in 1839 at the age of thirteen years and six months. The little pets grieve also under the drooping cross-stitched willow trees. The Greek border is interesting in that it reflects the classic revival which came into being about that time. The colors are sage, green and black, in wool and silk.

Included also in Miss Oppenheimer's collection is the splendid "exemplar" or sampler worked on homespun linen in the year 1800 by Ann Gawthorn. The top row of lettering has been cross-stitched with the finest linen thread. Various styles of lettering and numerals continue down to an alphabet which is so tiny that it is completed halfway across the sampler. The letters, a quarter of an inch high, occupy approximately five inches. Below this are two alphabets in one row of even smaller scale worked in tiny cross-stitch and petit point. This is a truly remarkable feat. A larger lettering group follows worked entirely of eyelet stitches and below this is still another alphabet in which the letters are composed of tiny outlined squares. These are very beautiful in technique and effect.

Surely the household linen marked from Ann's lettering manual would be treasured by all her family and their descendants. Concluding the work and bordered with practice rows of "border" styles, the following verse is inscribed:

FOR EV'RE TRIFLE SCORN TO TAKE OFFENSE,
THAT ALWAYS SHOWS GREAT PRIDE OF LITTLE SENSE;
GOOD NATURE AND GOOD SENSE SHOULD EVER JOIN,
TO ERR IS HUMAN, TO FORGIVE DIVINE.

At seven years of age, Ann Gawthorn signs her name to these great truths under which are pets, bunnies and big and little dogs. A dainty, most finely stitched border of vines and flowers encases this treasured relic.

Samplers which registered births, marriages, deaths and other family history were prevalent in this period. The following are examples of this type.

A family register is worked upon a green homespun linen background; since ivory was the general rule in those days, the material was no doubt hand-dyed to this deep sage color. The sampler is very finely cross-stitched in cream white silk. Following the practice alphabet upon the panel is the inscription:

REGISTER OF TIMOTHY HALL'S FAMILY, WHO WAS BORN JUNE 4TH, 1758 AND MARRIED APRIL 3RD, 1783 TO EUNICE HILLS, WHO WAS BORN MARCH 25TH, 1760. DIED JUNE 24TH, 1797 AND BY HER HATH THE FOLLOWING CHILDREN: VIZ.

Then follows the list, dating from January 7, 1784, from Luke up to Sally Hall who was born May 5, 1795. It is noted that one child of the seven died.

Sally signs her name under the register and adds a philosophical note in the following praise of fond parents:

HAPPY THE YOUTH WHOSE GREEN UNPRACTISED YEARS,
THE GUIDING HAND OF PARENT FONDNESS REARS,
TO RICH INSTRUCTIONS AMPLE FIELD REMOVES,
PRUNES EVERY FAULT, EVERY WORTH IMPROVES.

Miss Oppenheimer's collection is admirably representative. The samplers, from different states and sections of the country, sensitively reflect the environment in which they were created and in this respect speak also for many others made in their vicinity under similar influences and in the same years.

A family register from an ancient and honorable Stonington family was wrought by Marcia Denison in 1833 at the age of eight. The "Sampler of Work" as she titled her panel is banked on either side with the quotation:

JESUS PERMIT THY GRACIOUS NAME TO STAND
AS THE FIRST EFFORTS OF AN INFANT'S HAND
AND WHILE HER FINGERS ON THE CANVAS MOVE
ENGAGE HER TENDER HEART TO SEEK THY LOVE.

There are daintily stitched alphabets, the first in scroll letters finely cross-stitched, the second in large block letters in Roman style, arranged in two rows and stitched in alternated eyelets and double cross-stitch. These are followed by the family register. Amid hearts enclosing various initials of persons dear to the tender maiden are stitched in script the following records:

OLIVER DENISON WAS BORN JAN. 2ND, 1787
NANCY P. NOYES WAS BORN AUGUST 7TH, 1801
AND WERE MARRIED MAY 24TH, 1825 BY THE
REVD IRA HART.

EMMA P. DENISON WAS BORN OCT. 24TH, 1826
OLIVER DENISON WAS BORN APR. 8TH, 1829
EDGAR DENISON WAS BORN JAN. 20TH, 1832

SARAH E. DENISON WAS BORN MARCH 29TH, 1835
NATHAN N. DENISON WAS BORN JAN. 9TH, 1838.

A border of roses, buds and leaves completes this sampler edged with a winding ribbon around a straight band design. Descendants in Stonington who have inherited this quaint record treasure it beyond measure.

A sampler made in Charleston by Betsy W. Davidson in 1806 is in the Metropolitan Museum of Art. It has been worked in colored silks upon fine canvas. The border is composed of conventionalized flowers. Within it are alphabets, an urn of fairly large size initialed M. D., and a verse below beginning with the humble query, "Who taught my simple heart the Way?"

Stitched reproductions of buildings were popular on these later samplers. Princeton College was worked on the sampler of Ann Watson in 1808. The college quarters at that time consisted of a two-storied brick building having three dormers in the roof, chimneys at either end, and a one-storied wing extension on either side. There is a fence in front surrounding a green crinkly silk lawn upon which numbers of finely stitched trees are growing. The sampler is owned by Miss Anna Read.

The inscription includes a statement on

EDUCATION

IT IS A COMPANION WHICH NO MISFORTUNE CAN DEPRESS, NO CLIME DESTROY, NO ENEMY ALIENATE, NO DESPOTISM ENSLAVE. AT HOME A FRIEND, ABROAD AN INTRODUCTION, IN SOLITUDE A SOLACE AND IN SOCIETY AN ORNAMENT. IT CHASTENS VICE, IT GUIDES VIRTUE, IT GIVES AT ONCE A GRACE AND GOVERNMENT TO GENIUS.

An ambitious bit of stitchery belonging to Mrs. Arthur Curtiss James shows the "Old Brick Row" of Yale College. The sampler is by Emily Clark, "wrought in the twelfth year of her age in 1832." Four dormitories and the chapel encompassed by four great elms are embroidered at the bottom of the panel. The college buildings are in the Georgian style of architecture while the chapel with its high steeple is in the traditional style of the New England meeting house.

Not to be outdone by the sampler which reproduced Philadelphia's Liberty Hall in stitchery, Elizabeth Jane Hosmer made a cross-stitch sampler of New York's City Hall in 1822. The broad walks, green lawns and handsome trees are needleworked very effectively with able technique.

A building from William and Mary College in Williamsburg, Virginia, one of the earliest in America, has been stitched on a sampler made probably in the 1800's. There are many names embroidered upon it, with emphasis upon the name of Saunders.

Houses have been reproduced frequently and faithfully, but it was left for a young lady in Crawford, New Hampshire, to stitch her home town with all the main buildings into her sampler, including a poem and other decorative embellishment.

The Main Street of North Branford, Connecticut, was recorded in separate needleworked buildings, with a neighborly farmhouse, a bridge and a passing coach included, by the busy needles of Palmyra M. Keen who stitched her architectural masterpiece in 1818.

Mrs. Henry E. Coe owns a sampler with an elaborate scene of the same town also worked in

1818 by Sophia Stevens Smith. It includes the church which recently burned down. Sophia's house is seen on the opposite side of the river. An arched bridge spans the stream, on which a stage coach with two horses is crossing. The water has boats upon it. The composition of the two scenes is similar and suggests that a pattern existed from which several copies have been made.

The use of satin backgrounds combined with the classic influence on design which began to appear in this period resulted in the production of exquisite samplers. Mrs. Coe has two especially lovely examples of this type of work in her collection. Mary Hamilton's sampler worked in cross-stitch on satin is bordered by a series of squares. Differently designed baskets of flowers ornament the top corners; flying ducks under flowering trees fill the bottom corners and flowering sprays or branches occupy the other squares. An oval center encloses a figure in Empire costume. Her face and arms are painted. She stands upon solidly stitched grass, under a spreading oak. Beneath her is the inscription embroidered in a square:

MARY HAMILTON A DAUGHTER OF JOHN AND CATHERINE HAMILTON WAS BORN IN COUNTY ANTRIM, FEBRUARY THE 1 IN THE YEAR OF OUR LORD 1794 AND MADE THIS SAMPLER IN MAY-TOWN IN MRS. WELCHAM'S SCHOOL IN THE YEAR OF OUR LORD 1812.

A silk and satin sampler made in 1825 by Ann E. Kelly, at Mrs. Meguier's in Harrisburg, Pennsylvania, follows the same general layout. The squares which form the border enclose sheaves of wheat, birds, sheep, flowers and small fruit trees. In a square central panel a woman with a garland of flowers in her hands stands beside a pilaster or column. A pitcher is at her feet. She also is in an Empire costume. Her face has been painted in water color and a fine muslin is appliquéd over it. Wheat sprays make an inner border around this lunette and the boxed-in embroidered inscription reads:

O MAY THE LORD INSTILL GOOD PRINCIPLES IN ME AND MAKE ME A GOOD AND FAITHFUL SERVANT.

The stitches used are the chain stitch and cross-stitch. Mrs. Henry E. Coe is the owner of this lovely piece of needlework.

Made prior to these two examples but stitched in the same style, is a particularly fine sampler exhibited by the Museum of the City of New York. It is a silk and satin embroidery. The needlework is exquisite, worked in the manner of old Chinese silk embroideries. The design is altogether perfect in its scattered allover patterning of separate units, nicely placed with careful regard to the whole. Daffodils, lilies of the valley, tulips, sweet peas, poppies, violets, carnations, daisies, morning glories, and lilacs, meticulously executed, are mixed like an old brocade pattern with butterflies, small birds on branches, urns and dragon flies. Pediments with shields are standing beside them. Above, realistically stitched on leaves, are a beetle and a caterpillar. A bowl of fruit is embroidered beneath scrolls and garlands which frame the name of the embroiderer, Amalie Augusta Schmidt, worked in script. It is dated 1809. A border encloses the entire design worked in the Greek key pattern with spiral scrolls and other arabesques. The needleworker was a school teacher in New York and made the embroidery while in the city. She was the great-aunt of the donor, Miss Ella Eckhart. To those rediscovering silk needlework this sampler should be a delightful and inspiring study.

A very much later sampler, in which the entire design and the background have been filled in with small cross-stitch, comes from Ohio where it was embroidered in 1830 by Mrs. John Humphrey Winterbothom, the grandmother of Mrs. Frank Burroughs Mulford of Chicago, who now owns it. This is a quaint and amusing sampler panel, with small designs and little figures scatered over it: a man and a woman, rosebuds, a fiddle, a rooster, and a lyre, a polly on a stand, a small boat, a basket of fruit, a pipe, book and racing dog, stars, a small church, a pearl silk counter in outline (upon this counter silks were wound and kept), an American flag in one corner and jug of wine with a glass in the other. A circle of leaves encloses the large initials in block letters, M. R. W. The materials used were silk floss and wool on canvas. Background coloring is in wine color. The motifs are embroidered in the brilliant colors which are characteristic of the Berlin work of that period.

A sampler class in an engraving which appeared in *Harper's Bazaar* in 1868, and which is entitled "Youthful Industry," discloses a little girl busily engaged in sewing mysterious looking words upon her sampler. Later when the plate was reversed it was discovered that a temperance message was being worked upon the sampler, reading:

FROM ALL INTOXICATING DRINK
I PROMISE TO ABSTAIN.

As interesting and as significant as the embroideries themselves are the thoughts and admonitions worked with such great patience. Deep, melancholy notes (fashionable at the time), philosophical or metaphysical deductions, the virtues of parents, the profitable value to be obtained through industrious occupation, study, and eternal vigilance, the Ten Commandments, the Lord's Prayer, all bear witness to the efforts of parents and teachers to mold the mind and morals of the little worker.

From a sampler made in 1828 comes the following, said to have been written by "nearly an idiot":

SUBLIME THOUGHT

COULD WE WITH INK THE OCEAN FILL
WERE THE WHOLE EARTH OF PARCHMENT MADE
WERE EVERY SINGLE STICK A QUILL
AND EVERY MAN A SCRIBE BY TRADE
TO WRITE THE LOVE OF GOD ABOVE
WOULD DRAIN THE OCEAN DRY.
NOR COULD THIS SCROLL CONTAIN THE WHOLE

THO STRETCHT FROM SKY TO SKY
WERE THE WHOLE REALM OF NATURE MINE
THAT WERE A PRESENT FAR TOO SMALL
LOVE SO AMAZING SO DIVINE
DEMANDS MY SOUL, MY LIFE, MY ALL.
        FROM THE CLERGYMAN'S ALMANACK
            FOR 1812.

Long hours of patient work produced on a sampler of 1822 a selection from Epistle IV of Alexander Pope's "Essay on Man." It is entitled "Happiness."

REMEMBER MAN, THE UNIVERSAL CAUSE ACTS NOT BY PARTIAL, BUT BY GENERAL LAWS AND MAKES WHAT HAPPINESS WE JUSTLY CALL, SUBSIST NOT IN THE GOOD OF ONE BUT ALL. THERE'S NOT A BLESSING INDIVIDUALS FIND, BUT SOME WAY LEANS AND HEARKENS TO THE KIND.

NO BANDIT FIERCE, NO TYRANT MAD WITH PRIDE
NO CAVERNED HERMIT REST ALL SATISFIED
WHO MOST TO SHUN OR HATE MANKIND PRETEND,
SEEK AN ADMIRER OR WOULD FIX A FRIEND,
EACH HAS HIS SHARE AND WHO WOULD MORE OBTAIN
SHALL FIND THE PLEASURE PAYS NOT HALF THE PAIN.

It is possible that such thoughts impressed upon youthful minds during the period of growth helped to lay sturdy foundations upon which to continue the building of a strong nation.

CHAPTER X

EMBROIDERED WEDDING GOWNS AND WAISTCOATS

"And now the gown of sober stuff
Has changed to fair brocade,
With broidered hem, and hanging cuff
And flower of silken braid."
OLIVER WENDELL HOLMES.

ERE COMES THE BRIDE AS SHE would be dressed in her wedding gown in the early eighteenth century in New England. The material for the gown would have been made of linen, spun, woven and crewel-embroidered by the bride herself long before the happy nuptials.

An example of this early style is the wedding dress of Miss Elizabeth Bull of Boston, who designed and embroidered it in 1731, and who wore it on the occasion of her marriage to the Reverend Roger Price on April 14, 1735. It was later worn by her eldest daughter at the coronation of King George the Third.

The flowing vines, leaves, and tendrils rise from the full hem in profusion and are embroidered in happy shades of crewel wools. They reach toward the plain small bodice and tight-fitting waist of the eighteenth century, from which small puffed sleeves droop off the shoulders and the low plain neckline. The Bostonian Society in Massachusetts owns this early treasure.

Also spun, woven and crewel-embroidered by the bride is the linen wedding gown of Miss Mary Myers who married John Johnson in Connecticut in 1732. She was the great-great-great-grandmother of Miss Emma S. Babcock who

gave the gown to the Wadsworth Atheneum in Hartford, Connecticut, in 1910, where it has attracted considerable admiration. The design is similar to the gown made in Boston the previous year, although it is not quite as fine and elaborate in pattern and general detail. The sleeves are embroidered and are less puffed than in the Boston gown.

After this period satin appeared in a wedding dress worn by a Moravian bride. It is preserved in one of their museum collections. The white satin is ornamented with ribbon work and small pieces of gauze formed into roses. Worn approximately in 1790 it belongs to the period of high waists and short puffed sleeves. In the customary fashion the bride wore over this gown a white embroidered gauze shawl of triangular shape, one corner of which is elaborately embroidered.

In 1828 a New York bride, Anne Galilee, married Buchanan Greer, and wore for the joyful occasion a handsome white taffeta wedding gown, its two full flounces profusely embroidered at the hem with white silk flowers entwined. The flounces are scalloped in small deep points finely embroidered with silk as a finish. A "V" collar on the low round neckline is also embroidered to match the hem. The high waist is tiny, the bodice closely fitted, and the sleeves are puffed. It was probably worn over many petticoats or stiffened material giving the effect of a hoop skirt. It was given by Miss Adele Faile Browning to the Museum of the City of New York.

This museum has a marvelous collection of American gowns of nearly every period since the country's inception. Among them is a wedding gown presented by Mrs. Arthur Curtiss James in 1930. It was worn by her grandmother, Helena Maria Couch, when she married Levi Curtiss in New York on March 5, 1833. It is made of cobwebby white silk mull, a material so sheer that it could be drawn through a wedding ring. Captains of clipper ships brought this lovely gossamer muslin back with them from India and happy the maiden who possessed such "stuffs." Flowers are embroidered with silk on this exquisite gown. Mull embroidery became popular in this decade and needle art climbed ecstatic heights in its rendering of Indian shawl or chintz designs. Motifs worked in white-embroidered repeats on the hems of slim gowns and matched with tinier duplicates on a gauzy mull shawl to throw over the shoulders and bust, were the essence of refinement both in design and technique.

A white embroidered wedding gown made in this style of the Empire period, was worn in 1838 by Anne Nevins of New York, the great-grandmother of its present owner, Miss Anna M. Culbert of Stonington, Connecticut. The repeat motif at the bottom of the gown is the tree. These trees are about ten inches high and are set about three inches apart. The outline of the tree is formed by eyelets. The interior is filled in with small satin-stitched feathery leaves which spring from a central stem composed of larger eyelets and making an effective curving shadow up through the tree. Miniature Persian tree motifs about an inch high and half an inch apart are embroidered on the hem which is eyeleted and scalloped. The dress is perfectly plain up to the high-waisted bodice; then embroidery rises on three shoulder straps, a series of small conventionalized flowers worked solid in satin stitches. A fichu, heavily embroidered and having an embroidered ruffle, tops the ensemble.

Made to go with the same type of gown either for the marriage or afterwards, but always worn during this period, is a beautiful white mull cap embroidered around the crown with laurel leaves and a dot pattern of white satin stitches. The crown is slightly gathered and hemstitched onto a narrow band over the forehead. It drops down over the ears and hair and is somewhat like an aviator's helmet in shape. It is bordered with a row of double leaves. Small dots are embroidered all over the intervening mull. It also is in the Empire style.

In the issue of July 1855, *Harper's Monthly Magazine* features a bridal morning gown. It is a very elaborate costume in a style resembling Dutch gowns of the seventeenth century. The bride stands beside a piano with a sheet of music in her hand. In the distance a fountain plays. Butterflies hover about. The bridegroom is nowhere to be seen. The romantically dressed young lady seems to be thinking only of her music, or perhaps she is selecting a sentimental song to sing for her beloved.

Harper's describes the details of the costume as follows:

It is composed of white mousseline de laine; stone tint, azure, or mode colors are, however equally appropriate. The first series of loops which confine the garment is left unfastened to show the chemisette, which is of lace bouillonnee crossed by narrow plaited white satin ribbon. The robe adjusts itself easily to the figure in front; the back is gathered in four reversed plaits. The skirt, folded back upon itself, displays an elaborate embroidery; an underskirt panel worked with scrolls and sprays of scattered flowers in white and an eyeleted lace effect border cut up from the hem of the skirt in "V" point which are embroidered in fine scallops. An under hem with a scalloped edge skirts the floor having one row of eyelets above it set about an inch apart all around the border. The folded back upper skirt is embroidered in a design more related to the Rennaisance in style. Scrolls, leaves and lacings may be interpreted in applied braids. Cords passing through the large eyelet holes, which form part of the ornamental design, loop the revers. The sleeves are Vandycked. They are very full, short upon the forefront, descending abruptly midway below the elbow, and are richly ornamented to match the skirt. The under-sleeves are of lace, very full, and are caught up in festoons upon the upper arm. The jupe is of nansouk, richly embroidered.

This style closely resembles early gowns worn by the Dutch in Manhattan. Just what the early Dutch brides wore for wedding gowns has been

Crewel embroidered wedding gown. The spinning of the linen, the dyeing of yarns and needlework were all done in 1732 by Mary Myers, who married John Johnson in 1732. Connecticut.

Crewel Embroidered Wedding Dress of Miss Elizabeth Bull, who designed and embroidered it on homespun linen in 1731 and who wore it at her marriage to the Rev. Roger Price on April 14, 1735, Massachusetts.

Wedding dress, white silk mull, with embroidery on skirt in white silk, worn by grandmother of Mrs. Arthur Curtiss James, Helena Maria Couch, who married Levi Curtiss in New York, March 5, 1833.

Gift of Mrs. Arthur Curtiss James, 1930.

Wedding dress of white taffeta embroidered with silk on skirt and silk braided on waist. Worn by Anne Gallilee, who married George Buchanan Greer, July 24, 1828, New York.

Gift of Miss Adele Faile Browning, 1932.

EMBROIDERED WEDDING DRESSES

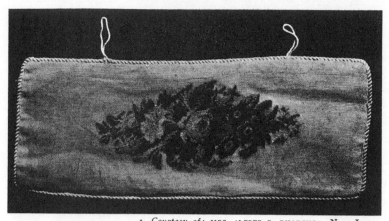

Needlepoint Case for Wedding Slippers. By Elizabeth Day. 1845.
Connecticut.

"Whispers to a Bride." Silk on
white silk moire book, containing
white mull embroidered bride's
handkerchief, carried at wedding.
About 1830, Connecticut.

White Pique Embroidered Wedding Waistcoat and White
Embroidered Wedding Shirt. 1852, Connecticut. Worn at
wedding of Joseph Moss White.

Waistcoat; silk embroidered satin, 1784. Belonged to Colonel Benjamin Talmadge,
Litchfield, Connecticut.

difficult to establish, but authorities describe their accessories, which included "many petticoats worn one over another" and the bridal crown which, in the Holland tradition, was indicative of the family wealth. In the old country it was often made of silver ornamented with jewels. The more modest version was made of pasteboard and covered with embroidered silk.

Under the elaborate wedding gown, one had to have shoes. In New England women called all shoes

SLIPPERS

The early and late eighteenth century slippers were lightly constructed. The materials most frequently used were satin or light cloth. Embroidery on these slippers was a fashion not only for the wedding day or court presentation abroad, but for other important social occasions. A young lady of Boston made a pair of satin shoes to wear at a court presentation in France and in accordance with the mode at the court of Marie Antoinette, she had them embroidered with paste "diamonds" while the back seams were stitched in outline with paste "emeralds."

Mrs. Earle, describing American costume in the period of 1740, says: "There were satinett patterns for ladies' shoes embroidered with flowers in the vamp." Wedding slippers, "needlepointed," were worn by Cornelia de Peyster, bride of Oliver Teller, in 1712. The slippers were made of yellow silk brocade like the wedding gown and were silk embroidered. A fashion note of this period says that "Silk embroidered slippers were worn by Mrs. Carroll to correspond with a brocaded silk sacque, and were embroidered with the same colors, matching the brocade."

To protect such dainty footwear embroidered cases were the rule. A needlepoint case for wedding slippers was made in 1845 by Elizabeth Day, daughter of Reverend Jeremiah Day, D.D., LLd., President of Yale College from 1817 to 1846. Elizabeth married Thomas A. Thatcher, Professor of the Latin Languages in Yale College, September 17, 1846, and Mrs. A. D. Thatcher of New Jersey has both case and slippers in her possession. The case is constructed of finest cream scrim and the small flowers are minutely worked in pastel-colored floss. The satin slippers that pattered over many a recep-

tion room when the professors and their wives entertained dignitaries at Yale University, are still freshly white, and rest quietly, well preserved, in their silk-lined covering.

Embroidered night caps were included in every bride's wardrobe. Regular "baby bonnets" in shape, they were embroidered in white with French knots or small flowers on white India muslin. Long streamers tied in a bowknot under the chin. Ruffles, often finished with finely buttonholed scallops, edged the bonnet. Such caps were worn in England during the reign of Queen Elizabeth but were more elaborately ornamented with spangles, cut work and bone lace. Martha Washington owned and wore nightcaps, lace worked and ruffled.

BRIDES' BOOKS AND POCKETS

One of the most quaintly romantic accessories is a book which was carried at the wedding ceremony and which contained important memoranda along with the neatly folded handkerchief. One of these comes from the Litchfield Historical Society. On the white silk moire cover ornamented with painted cupids, the title is embroidered in white silk. The block letters read:

WHISPERS TO A BRIDE.

What the interior really contained remains a secret, for the little volume is well protected from the curious by a large glass case as tightly shut as the book.

Sometimes instead of the books, "pocket cases" were used, which the Moravian sisters so wonderfully embroidered in silks on silk. They were made in an envelope shape and covered with enchanting flowers. Silk-embroidered reticules of satin with drawstring tops were often stitched with chenille-made flowers, or worked with flat silks in the Moravian style. Flower embroidery of high excellence was developed at this time in silks. Undressed India silk was most commonly employed for such needlework upon breadths of thick, soft, cream-white satin.

WAISTCOATS

Extremes in the modes and manners of American life were evidenced and expressed in needlework. Exquisite sophisticated works in the cities and in cultured homes in the immediate vicinity were being wrought by ladies who read poetry and played the harpsichord, while in outlying regions designs embroidered on homespun and with the more substantial crewel wools were being stitched by sturdy women who also understood poetry and the social graces but who had to dispense with these qualities while managing the homes of men who were creating new boundaries for the future United States.

During these years, the prosperous bridegroom was as handsomely adorned as the bride. He had his satin waistcoat, silk-embroidered with miniature flowers scattered over the front and formed into a border at the edges. These, too, may have been worked in Bethlehem by Moravian women. There is a silk-embroidered waistcoat in the Moravian museum which was worn by Count Lemke, a close friend of Count Zinzendorf, organizer and protector of the Moravian refugees, while in residence at Philadelphia. One of these was designed along the same elaborate lines as the waistcoat described, with dainty flowers worked on its borders and atop the pockets. In the same style is the waistcoat in the Litchfield Museum, handsomely embroidered on its cream satin in pale rose, pink and green silks and presumably worn by Colonel Benjamin Talmadge, aid-de-camp to General Washington, who resided with his family at Litchfield, Connecticut, in 1784.

White wedding waistcoats of linen worn by 1832 bridegrooms, were gorgeously embroidered to match the gowns of their brides. At Litchfield are several examples of this beautifully designed and executed needlework. One made of white piqué embroidered in white with a pattern of grape-vines and leaves, was worn at the wedding of Joseph Moss White in 1852.

Equally magnificent, in fine tucks and elaborate white-embroidered panels, were shirt bosoms of the same period. Undoubtedly the bridegroom in this lovely finery looked as stunning as his bride.

≈≈≈≈≈≈≈≈≈≈≈≈≈≈≈≈≈≈≈≈≈≈≈≈≈≈≈≈≈≈≈≈≈≈≈≈≈≈≈

CHAPTER XI

NEEDLE LACEWORK, DARNING ON NET AND TAMBOUR

"For sweetly here upon thee grew
The lesson which that beauty gave,
The ideal of the Pure and True
In earth and sky and gliding wave.

And it may be that all which lends
The soul an upward impulse here,
With a diviner beauty blends,
And greets us in a holier sphere."
JOHN GREENLEAF WHITTIER.

≈≈≈≈≈≈≈≈≈≈≈≈≈≈≈≈≈≈≈≈≈≈≈≈≈≈≈≈≈≈≈≈≈≈≈≈≈≈≈

 ACEWORK WAS USED TO MAKE A variety of filmy edgings for costumes, and included many techniques. It was applied to borders for handkerchiefs, wedding veils, shawls, collars and other dainties worn by Miss America through the eighteenth and nineteenth centuries. One of the needlework methods used to achieve a lacy effect was called

TAMBOUR

It is said that Madame de Pompadour set the fashion for tambour work, which was introduced into France from China during the Louis XIV period. It became a great fad. So enthusiastic was the famous lady over this stitchery that she had her portrait painted while engaged upon her needlework sample.

In America tambour work was a favorite occupation of many women from 1780 up to and including the 1850's. They learned the art from the French or through the Moravian school where the technique was taught. Applied to costume accessories the work was extremely beautiful and marks a high point in creative needlework since many women evolved their own designs.

An idea of the principle of tambour operation may be gleaned from the

METHOD OF WORKING

In this type of embroidery a notched or tambour needle is used, which loops the wool or thread through to the surface of the material to be decorated. The needle then passes through the loop of wool and pierces the material again, making a stitch similar in character to a chain stitch. Tambour work has also been compared to crochet stitches.

The material to be worked must be placed in a frame and the pattern drawn on it. The needle used resembles a very fine crochet needle. The thread is held in the left hand under the work, and caught upon the upper side by the hook, forming a loop. This loop must be kept on the hook and inserted again at a short distance, when another loop is drawn up through it. This makes a chain stitch which must follow the outline of the pattern first and then gradually fill it up. It has been used in appliqué work with success, and some patterns on satin or velvet have been worked with silk mixed with gold. But chain stitch, which is nearly the same thing, can be done with a common needle with much less trouble.

A variety of stitches create lace effects when

applied to silk netting or machine-made fine cotton net. Designs of leaves and flowers upon rhythmic vines stitched in this method against a fine net background, achieve the effect of lace. Muslin and cambric have been used also but without exciting results.

This stitch technique has been adapted to many uses such as rugs done in heavy wools on coarse material, upholstery coverings for chairs and stools and also decorative panels in which wools have been replaced by silks intermixed with gold and applied on satin. Braids have also been employed in the execution of this stitch and worked in shadings elaborately designed upon merino or cashmere. The latter fashion was inspired by work done in the Levant.

Another explanation of the way in which the work was accomplished comes from Miss Margaret Whiting, pioneer creator of the Deerfield Blue and White Society, who explains tambour needlework stitching as her mother worked it while making a fine net shoulder cape of her own design. "My mother placed a strip of sheer mull under her design and after working it on the right side with many delicate stitches, cut out the spaces between the items of the pattern on the back."

Possibly the net was mounted upon a frame similar to that in the Essex Institute in Salem, which was prepared for working a piece of

LACEWORK: DARNING ON NET

This bears a close resemblance to the tambour work just explained, since the needlework on the border appears to be worked in a small chain stitch. Eyelets also were featured in both tambour and darned-net lacework. Indeed the chief difference between the two lies in the fact that in the first emphasis is on chain stitches while in the second it is on the woven patterns created by filling the net areas with various styles of needle-weaving or darning.

Strips of net footing were pinned or sewn to paper and sewn or darned in patterns to be used for insertions on dresses, bonnets, and caps. Usually these narrow widths were worked in simple patterns. A design was first pricked on the paper in outline with a pin and then filled with various stitches. One of the early needlework authorities recommends that "Those dis-

posed to try this sort of work, should select a net with no dress in it, and allow amply for the inevitable shrinking. Evans Moravian No. 70, (thread) would be suitable for heavy parts, and their Boar's Head for the darned fancy stitches."

Some lace-worked veils have employed seventeen varieties of stitches to compose the pattern fillings. These darning patterns were executed either on black net with black threads or on fine white net with very fine white cotton.

The lacework fashionable in the 1820's and 30's, was carried out in unique ways. The darnings were very ingenious with different fillings within their lacy outlines. Circles were needle-woven in as many odd styles as the embroideress could command.

Other techniques of embroidery on lace are distinguished by the various names of English Lace, Valenciennes, Brussels, Mechlin, Point Lace, Honiton, Guipure, etc. Many of these laces are, and have been, successfully imitated by American women at different times. *Harper's Bazaar* in 1855, published full instructions for making the point lace stitches. Honiton was made with needlework stitches for handkerchiefs and much ingenuity has produced interesting results.

Lessons in embroidery on lace were advertised prior to the Revolution. Mrs. Sarah Wilson in Second Street near Walnut, Philadelphia, refers to these techniques along with "sattin stitch, quince stitch, cross-stitch embroidery curtains or chairs, writing and cyphering."

Needle lacework was taught in Boston as early as 1775.

LACEWORK EXAMPLES

An original bonnet, made about 1825, shows a darned net wedding veil fastened on the front, as they were worn during this period. There is a little drawstring at the top of the veil with which to pull it across the face. This was the accepted style for the marriage ceremony, and making one of them was a delightful, hopeful occupation. Fortunately dozens of these lovely needleworked veils remain intact and in most cases are in an excellent state of preservation.

An unfinished veil of machine-made net, worked in 1825 by Lucinda Vail Moser, is in the Metropolitan Museum of Art, and shows very effectively the method by which the nee-

Wedding Veil net embroidered in tambour and darning stitches. 1825, by Maria Hustace, New York. Gift of Mrs. Samuel T. Hubbard.

Wedding Veil Borders; black silk embroidery darning and tambour stitches on black net. Period 1830, Connecticut.

Upper, left to right.
(A) Fichu; net embroidered, darning stitches, cross bars, pattern 1790-1800, New York. Gift of Mr. and Mrs. Ernest Vietor, 1938.
(B) Wedding Veil; tambour stitched on net, 1825-1830, New York. Gift of William C. Morgan.
Lower, left to right.
(C) Wedding Veil; white net embroidered lace work. 1820, New York. Gift of Mrs. Homer Foot.
(D) Wedding Veil; worn and made in tambour and darning stitches by Maria Hustace, 1825, New York. Gift of Mrs. Samuel T. Hubbard.

Group of Wedding Veils.
Upper, left to right.
(A) Wedding Veil; tambour stitched on net, lace work. 1840. Gift of Mrs. J. F. Tams.
(B) Wedding Veil; cream net. Darning lace work stitches. 1820-1830. New York. Bequest of Miss Ellen Bates.
Lower, left to right.
(C) Veil, white net embroidered. Drawstring top. 1820-1830. New York. Gift of Miss Caroline Anderson.
(D) Wedding Veil; embroidered net worn by Mrs. Daniel Talmadge in 1836, New York. Gift of Robert Swartwout Talmadge.

1. *Courtesy of:* THE ESSEX INSTITUTE.

Bonnet and Lace Work; darned net, wedding veil made and worn during the 1820 and 1830's. Massachusetts.

2. *Courtesy of:* MISS MARGARET WHITING, Deerfield, Massachusetts.

Shoulder Shawl of Net; tambour stitched and designed, in 1835 by Mother of Miss Whiting, Mary Goodrich Whiting, Troy, New York.

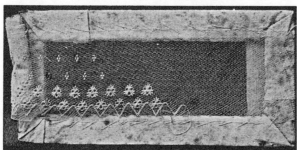

3. *Courtesy of:* THE ESSEX INSTITUTE.

Unfinished Lace Work Darning on Net; mounted on frame as worked in 1830, Massachusetts.

4. *Courtesy of:* THE METROPOLITAN MUSEUM OF ART.

Unfinished Veil, Lace Work; darning on net, 1825, by Lucinda Vail Moser.

dlework progresses. Spaces are prepared for taking the different darnings and may be seen clearly in the illustration. This is a most interesting example which came to the Museum through Mrs. Thomas L. Rushmore. Other lovely examples of lacework in both the black and white techniques may be seen in this same collection.

In the Litchfield Historical Society are a few wedding veils which have been worked in black silks on black silk net. They suggest the black Spanish lace mantillas in their effective style. The designs are very beautiful. Caroline Canfield's patterns are exhibited there in the veils she made from them about 1830. Her book was filled with excellent designs which she drew, evidently by the dozen, and later constructed in able stitchery. Some of her patterns were copied from designs which came from Paris. Others were created by students who were taught the art of tambour and net embroidery at leading finishing schools.

A wedding veil of white embroidered net with its drawstring top, made in New York between 1820 and 1830, has an extraordinarily fine design of cornucopias filled with flowers for its central repeat theme, and an elaborate star-flowered border with beautiful stitch interpretations. It is a gift of Miss Caroline Anderson to the Museum of the City of New York.

Paired with this example and made in the same decade is a fine white net wedding veil embroidered in the manner of the others. Its darning patterns fill in large sprays of single chrysanthemums. The border has the appearance of carnations worked in a row. It came to this collection through the bequest of Miss Ellen Bates.

Also to be seen in this collection is a wedding veil of embroidered net showing an unusual border of upright and drooping flowers suggestive of classicism. The sprays of flowers needle-woven above the border possess something of the same quality and their stitch fillings are charmingly rendered. The veil was worn by Mrs. Daniel Talmadge in 1836 in New York. It was given to the Museum by Robert Swartwout Talmadge.

Embroidered on white net in white is a gorgeously designed and worked veil of the 1820 period, which has a double row of large floral spray units. Considerable artistry is exhibited in the execution of the needlework. Mrs. Homer Foot contributed this lovely addition to the collection of the Museum of the City of New York.

In the same collection is a fichu worked in the same technique and style. This net embroidery was made in New York between 1790 and 1800. Its design is unique in the Museum collection in that its net center is worked in a pattern of cross bars over the entire area. The lilies and leaf motifs used for the edging are very interesting and distinctive. Mr. and Mrs. Ernest G. Vietor were the donors.

EXAMPLES OF TAMBOUR WORK

Miss Gertrude Whiting has kindly loaned a reproduction of a net shoulder shawl, tambour stitched, the pattern of which was designed and worked by her aunt, Mahala Goodrich, of Troy, New York. This and a tambour collar embroidered on net by Miss Whiting's mother in 1835 were worn with the low-necked dresses of that period. The graceful design of circles enclosing a petaled flower is bordered with an inner circle made of small eyelets and an outer one tambour stitched. The leaves and bird motif produce a lacy effect on the sheer net which is charming.

A dainty cap-crown of tambour-stitched net, embroidered about 1825 with eyelets surrounding the tambour-stitched pattern, is shown at the Memorial Hall in Deerfield, a gift of Ellen and Margaret Miller.

Tambour embroidery on net has been worked upon many lovely collars, several examples of which are in the Museum of the City of New York. One in particular, made in New York in 1820, shows exceedingly fine and intricate work in its stitched design of flowers. The border edge is like dragon flies' wings in its transparent delicacy. It comes from Mrs. Eliot Norton.

A veil in the collection, made in 1825, is embroidered on net in tambour and darning stitches. It was made by Maria Hustace, born March 13, 1803, the daughter of Benjamin Hustace who lived at 323 Greenwich Street, New York City. It is one of the best examples of the entire collection. A great variety of darning stitches form many intricate fillings in the strawberries which compose the border. To achieve the filling patterns great concentration and patience were required. The stitches were often counted out. It is amazingly well done.

A beautiful veil also included in this group is tambour-stitched upon fine white net. The lovely groupings of flowers for the border are worked with great skill. It is from New York of the period between 1825 and 1830 and was contributed by Mr. William M. Morgan.

Mrs. J. T. Tams gave a similar veil made in 1840 in New York. Using the customary fine white net with tambour-stitched flower patterns and handsome border, the needleworker has taken pains to cover the entire background with tiny dot stitches which greatly enhance the lacy effect.

At the Essex Institute is a very fine net collar in tambour work. It was worn by the daughter of John H. Andrews of Salem, Massachusetts, in 1835, over the shoulders of a billowing pink satin wedding gown. Her veil was draped from a pink satin bonnet which was ornamented with pale green sprigs supporting flowers composed of pearl drops. Pink satin ribbons fastened the bonnet under the chin with a large bow.

The invention of the sewing machine and its mechanical chain stitch destroyed much of the fascination of tambour work. Likewise the net embroidery with its dainty darning stitchery, which looked, when finished, like so many stars caught into a web of gossamer with myriads of ferns and flowers painted by Jack Frost, has given way to machine-made products. But America is still privileged to witness and enjoy precious examples of what proved to be one of the finest and loveliest expressions in the history of her needlework.

CHAPTER XII

WHITE WORK, COSTUME EMBROIDERIES
AND ACCESSORIES

"Great are the symbols of being, but that which is symboled is greater;
Vast the create and beheld, but vaster the inward creator;
Back of the sound broods the silence, back of the gift stands the giving;
Back of the hand that receives thrill the sensitive nerves of receiving."
RICHARD REALF.

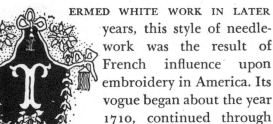 ERMED WHITE WORK IN LATER years, this style of needle-work was the result of French influence upon embroidery in America. Its vogue began about the year 1710, continued through the middle eighteenth century and flourished strongly during the early nineteenth century up to 1842. After that time its popularity declined and its character changed, due perhaps to an increase in the importation of imitation needlework and the introduction of other fabrics for dresses which supplanted white muslin to some extent.

By 1710 many colonists had had time to grow prosperous. With prosperity came more leisure for the women and a desire for dainty clothes. By this time the technique of crewel embroidery had been mastered; something new in the way of ornamentation was desired. So it was that needlewomen from France, some of them of noble birth, who with their families had sought refuge in this country from religious and political oppression, found solace and sometimes sustenance in teaching the fine art of white work which they had learned in their youth.

Linens, cambrics and muslins of various qualities imported from India and the Old World were the backgrounds used. Sheer as gossamer, the very delicacy of the fabrics gave rise to designs equally delicate in theme. Compositions were arranged and executed in the most exquisite manner.

DESIGN AND TECHNIQUE

In linen damask the warp and weft threads are run in different directions so that even in this all-white material changes in color or tone are produced. The same principle applies to white on white embroideries. Surface changes brought about by varying the stitch, accent the light vibrations, and the direction in which the threads are placed or woven against the white background of linen, gauze or muslin, serves to reveal or diminish details of the design.

Painters are well acquainted with the variety of colors or shades to be seen in white. Their practiced eyes will spot differences in tone and color reflection playing upon a pristine surface, and with the wizardry of their brushes and palette, they will work into their canvases a surprising amount of color; pastel pinks, yellows, and pale blue notes to accent high lights, shadows and half tones playing over a white fabric section.

The embroiderer substitutes threads of silks, floss, cottons, chenilles, linen, flax and wool for the oils of the painter. They may all be white threads but the difference in composition creates changes in tonal value. With needles for brushes and a chosen background of white linen for canvas, the needle artist may proceed with all the technique at command to make the all-whites tell a story or reveal a mood. The play of color occurs through the building up of one kind of thread against a contrasting surface and where the painter has to make his surface changes by employing other colors to create high light, the needle-painter obtains this through the actual fact of bas-relief. Light reflected upon it automatically paints in the rest.

The ancient needleworkers of the Orient knew well how to produce these high lights and shadows and applied their knowledge with highly artistic results. The old Persian embroidery in which white silk is needleworked with great skill upon fine white linen is most effective. The needleworkers in India have for centuries accomplished wonders with their technical flourishes. Chinese artistry is well known in their costume embroideries of white silk upon white silk damask or brocade while their use of white silk against white crêpe de Chine backgrounds is lovely beyond words.

Paintings of ladies in ancient China portray them sitting at a long frame plying their needles upon silk embroideries, while a poem is read to them by an attending maid. The mandarin's bride is occupying her time in the creation of a needleworked poem while her lord is away at war. She will surprise him upon his return with a beautiful panel dedicated to him with love woven into all the stitches. Its charm may help him to forget the ugliness of the battlefield.

Something beautiful to be given, to endure as a constant reminder of the devotion with which it was made, speaks to the heart in a language of its own. That is why a machine-made work will never be able to imitate the feeling that is produced through the personal touch. Thought combined with deep feeling bestows a special quality upon the work toward which it is directed. A gift so made is transfused with a peculiar beauty and becomes to the recipient a treasure without price.

Such a labor of love is speaking very quietly to its companions in the Historical Society's Museum in Litchfield, Connecticut. On the wall hangs the portrait of a family group. A colonial lady with filmy embroidery about her throat is seated by her husband who was an aid-de-camp to General Washington. He is wearing a silk-embroidered waistcoat, the original of which is hanging in a case below him. Their baby is wearing an exquisite white on white embroidered muslin. Beneath the portrait, in a case, is the dainty, lovely baby dress embroidered in white, with garden flowers enchained in its stitches. Beside it lies a bonnet, fresh as a breath of spring and light as a feather in its white wispy needlework of eyelets and sprigs of tiny flowers. Mother may have worn the larger white cap close by which is heavily embroidered with white laurel leaves on white muslin. Classic white patterns border and accent themselves against the sheer gray-white muslin of other bonnets. Flowers in white satin stitch adorn others of finest white linen.

Innumerable lovely things recording the history they have helped to make are gathered in this one large room. They speak of other days with an eloquence that only those who know their language can understand. But there are many who are inspired by their beauty and among their admirers are some who will carry their banner of worthy traditions forward.

HANDKERCHIEFS

The white on white embroidery that dominates the room, however, is aloof in a glass case. In fact it has the distinction of two glass coverings—one on its frame and the other on the case. That it is a priceless treasure is true. It was a labor of love expressing all through its composition idealistic admiration for two illustrious figures in American history—Washington and Lafayette.

The New Orleans lady of long ago who contributed this lasting memorial in their honor, matched their fineness of character with the finest stitchery at her command and upon a tiny square piece of muslin worked a handkerchief with exquisite lacy embroidery, all in pure white. It tells in its circular pattern the story of Lafayette's first arrival in America. His ship lies at anchor. He is being greeted in warm em-

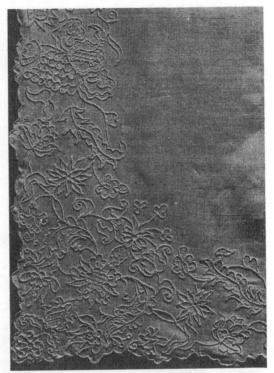

1. *Courtesy of:* MRS. ROBERT COLEMAN TAYLOR, New York.

Alberta G. Gary's (Daisy's) Portrait by Austin Street, Philadelphia; showing white eyelet embroidery on child's costume. Period 1858-1864. Baltimore.

2. *Courtesy of:* THE MUSEUM OF FINE ARTS, Boston, Massachusetts.

Kerchief; white embroidery on linen. 18th century, American.

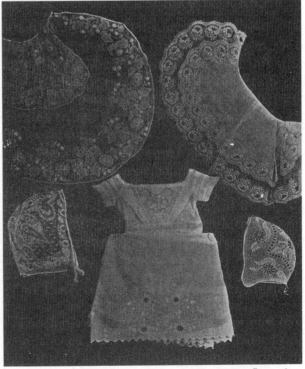

3. *Courtesy of:* THE MUSEUM OF THE CITY OF NEW YORK.

Collar Embroidered on net; tambour work. 1820, New York. (Bequest of Mrs. Eliot Norton, 1934.)
Fichu; white embroidered mull. 1795, New York. (Gift of Mrs. Albert Morrow, 1932.)
Shawl; white embroidered, Empire style with English bobbin border. 1795. (Gift of Mrs. Walter Oakley, 1932.)

4. *Courtesy of:* THE LITCHFIELD HISTORICAL SOCIETY, Connecticut.

White Embroidered Collars on Mull, Infant's Caps and Christen-Dress. 1830 Period, American.

White Embroidered Mull Handkerchief; 1824, Generals Washington and Lafayette portraits. New Orleans, Louisiana.

White Embroidered Handkerchief; 1832, by Sarah E. Pollock, Roxbury, Massachusetts.

White Embroidered Linen Bureau Cover; 1820, by Ann Scott. Baltimore, Maryland.

brace by the figure of America, symbolizing the cordial welcome given to him here. A small lunette follows in the design with two figures dancing to commemorate the fiestas, receptions, and balls given in Lafayette's honor. A large portrait of General Washington is worked next to the lunette.

In another section two ladies are earnestly exchanging confidences under a tree, apparently representing France and America in friendly conference. The costumes are delightfully executed in a variety of stitches. On the opposite corner is a large portrait of General Lafayette and his name, like that of Washington, is written out in needleworked script. Likewise "The Arrival of Lafayette at Charleston in 1777" is stitched at length.

The final episode represents General Lafayette upon the occasion of his second visit in 1824. He stands sadly beside the tomb of his great friend, General Washington. He is laying a wreath, his personal tribute, upon it, while to the right the classic figure of a lonely Muse gazes heavenward.

Spaces are filled in with graceful trees—pines, willows, poplars and other varieties of plant growth. The introduction of Chippendale's little mandarins and Chinese temples shows the influence of this great cabinetmaker, artist and designer upon embroideries of the day. The windows in the tiny houses are worked with delicate drawn-lace stitches. The mounds of grass and small hills are made in the same way, with darned lacework stitched in many different patterns. In combination with fine white satin stitches, they produce a handsome effect. The border is composed of drawn threads worked with darned patterning. This dainty lacework is exceedingly beautiful. The whole is a work of art. Its actual size is that of the average man's handkerchief.

At the time when this handkerchief was embroidered, approximately 1830, this type of needlework flourished and large ornamented squares were quite a vogue, being made primarily for women to use. All over the country ladies were sewing them for their loved friends and relatives. However none has appeared thus far worked with such elaboration or skill as that shown in the Lafayette example. Usually the four corners were ornamented with the all-white combined satin and drawn-lace stitches. In New England such a work was made in 1832 by Sarah E. Pollock of Roxbury, Massachusetts, to be given to her sister Susan. It is adequate in its large dimension and is daintily made, though capable of enduring the winter's sneezes. This linen cambric handkerchief has the name of the sister written in the center with indelible ink in the graceful fine penmanship studied so assiduously in that period. The date also is included. According to directions published about 1850 for marking handkerchiefs, this was the fashion.

METHOD OF WORKING

White work requires careful drawing so that the different designs may be identified sufficiently to follow the outline in satin or other stitches. The edges of the over and over stitch must always be kept evenly together and match each other perfectly on their outside lines; otherwise the work will have a ragged appearance. Likewise featherstitches, fagoting and French knots used to fill in their separate areas must be exactly confined within the intended design limits or the effect will be spoiled.

Earlier needleworkers used primitive methods to transfer their designs, often charred twigs. In later years inks were substituted. A system used in the early nineteenth century is explained as follows:

MARKING

One of the accomplishments which every lady should learn and try to excel in, is the ability to mark well in indelible ink. Clothes of every kind, and particularly handkerchiefs, are constantly in danger of being lost; and there is no security so great against their total loss, as an intelligible mark. An embroidered wreath with the name in ink is very handsome, and so is one all embroidered. The stitch used in embroidery is the same as for any fine muslin work. After acquiring the necessary knowledge for marking in ink, a little careful practice will enable a lady to copy any beautiful embroidery pattern in ink, even to close the shading with the pen. Embroidered handkerchiefs look very beautiful when the corner containing the name is marked in ink with a corresponding design. For instance, the embroidery may contain roses, pinks, etc., or a set pattern of block work or scrolls. If the corner containing the name is marked to correspond, it makes the handkerchief very elegant. The name can be written in the leaf or in the flower.

We have used an Indelible Ink prepared by Mr. Blair, corner of 8th & Walnut Streets, Philadelphia, for several years; and never had it wash out or fade, and it is free in the pen, never blotting the article. The directions are on each bottle, and carefully followed the result is always good. Some inks wash out directly, and some (from some injurious ingredient) cause the place to become so tender that it washes into holes, and in one instance we had a very elegant handkerchief in which the place containing the mark, came entirely out in the first washing.

It is best to practice on ordinary material before trying a fine handkerchief, as thin material is harder to mark than one which is closely woven.

WHITE WORK TECHNIQUE

In an embroidery treatise of the day, many names were given to white work technique; among them were "French embroidery," "broderie Anglais," "Mountmellick embroidery" and "white work."

FRENCH EMBROIDERY: This term was applied to all white stitchery but in particular to exceedingly fine and dainty work stitched solid in satin stitch, mostly on muslin. The designs were usually tiny florals in the character of French brocade patterns. Delicacy was emphasized in the most expert needle craftsmanship and to emulate the work of these women who had been taught in convents, was considered highly desirable by American women.

A definition of the next term has been extracted from a Philadelphia treatise on the subject written in the nineteenth century.

BRODERIE ANGLAIS: "Broderie Anglais is the simplest of all the different kinds of white embroidery, and its rapid execution makes it very desirable for ladies' under garments and children's clothes. It is simply holes of various shapes and sizes sewed over carefully and neatly. Some of the patterns are very handsome." This really applies to patterns worked entirely in eyelet embroidery as a substitute for open work hemstitchings heretofore applied to sheets, pillow cases, etc. For ornamenting petticoats, blouses, linen dresses and children's clothes it was exceedingly practical for the stitchery withstood constant wear.

MOUNTMELLICK EMBROIDERY: This term applied to white embroidery is of Irish origin. It is a heavier style and does not include the eyeleting or open drawn-work stitchery. The materials used are coarser threads applied to strong linen or "jean." Floral patterns were rendered in bold stitched effects quite in contrast to the dainty French work. It was used for bolster-end decorations, pillowcases, table coverings, sometimes costume bags and wherever heavier white designs were required.

WHITE WORK: This term applies to all needlework made in all-white on white and is usually associated with the average technique. Stitches employed in this embroidery include satin stitch, outline stitch, backstitch, stem stitch (sometimes thick stem stitch; also named crewel stitch), all forms of featherstitch (these derived from chain stitch), bullion stitch, French knots. French knots and the satin stitch were most generally used, alone and in combination.

Hand frames of all sizes were employed. Many women stitched in the hand without a frame but to keep the needlework smooth and even called for a high degree of craftsmanship.

MATERIALS

The finest and the most desirable cambrics, linens, muslins of all kinds, were used. For delicate work India mull and linen and cambric backgrounds were preferred. White embroidery threads of linen and cotton floss were imported. "For Broderie Anglais, a very fine long cloth, or the same material of which the garment is made, jaconet, linen, etc., are used." For muslin work and other "fine embroidery, such as collars, sleeves, etc., fine French muslin is used. For Swiss lace and appliqué work, a close but clear muslin should be chosen. For pocket handkerchiefs, fine linen cambric is the only suitable article, and it is much the best also for infant's caps, shirts, etc."

Some of the finer and most beautiful examples of early white work embroidery have been left to the textile collections of leading museums, including the Metropolitan Museum of Art, the Museum of the City of New York, Cooper Union, the Litchfield Historical Society, the Museum of Fine Arts in Boston and many others. These provide a wealth of inspiration in design for interested students.

The examples include:

GOWNS

These were elaborately embroidered in the most intricate and delicate stitchery. The early Empire gowns of 1800 were very lovely, made of sheer muslin embroidered in classic designs. Later costumes became more elaborate, such as the bride's morning costume described in detail in the chapter on wedding gowns.

PETTICOATS

The excellent white embroidery designs for petticoats and edgings drawn in a pattern book by Caroline Canfield of Litchfield, Connecticut, have already been mentioned. Children's petticoats also were ornamented with a tremendous amount of embroidery. Illustrating the style in the 1860's and even earlier, is a gracious portrait of Alberta G. Gary by Julian Street, a famous Philadelphia painter of that time. The little girl, nicknamed "Daisy," is wearing the sheerest of white mull dresses. Underneath an embroidered white petticoat reveals dainty eyelet embroidery and below the hem pantalette edges appear with matching eyelet borders. The needlework borders have been fastidiously rendered by the artist. It is a charming picture of a sweet little Baltimore maiden as she looked in the 1860's.

Tops of gowns often were finished, especially before 1830 and immediately after, with

FICHUS, SHAWLS AND COLLARS

Harper's New Monthly Magazine in 1855, describes the fichus illustrated in the fashion plates of that issue as made

> of tulle, plain in the body, with bouillonee bordering the entire outline, and crossed with very narrow ribbons in large lozenges.... Figure 4 is a fichu, likewise of tulle, gathered in folds, which are confined by rosettes of narrow white satin ribbon, plaits of which form the edge and traverse the front. A fall of lace completes the whole.

These costume accessories were elaborately and preciously embroidered with infinitesimal stitches. Fichus and shawls of collars of needle lace and white work were made and worn for many years, from the muslin embroidered collars of the colonial Empire period in 1795 up to

1830. A large triangular piece of India muslin, embroidered in raised satin stitches and with small clusters of flowers for border and corners worked in fine white thread, is unusually lovely. Tiny French knots add delicacy. This choice gift to the Museum of the City of New York by Mrs. Albert S. Morrow reflects the best needlework in this technique produced in 1795.

Eyeleting was frequently used for bringing airiness into an embroidery design which might otherwise be too heavy. A shawl treated in this manner is a gift by Mrs. Walter Oakley to the Museum of the City of New York. It belongs to the Empire style of 1795 and is a lacy, cobwebby piece of white mull, adorned with satin stitch, French knots and featherstitch. English bobbin lace has been sewn on the edge and makes a very charming finish.

Kerchiefs in delicate embroidery were an eighteenth century fashion. The Museum of Fine Arts in Boston owns a very dainty example with the delicate raised tracery in satin stitch worked over raised fine threads. The pattern is an outline design of leaves, grapes and flowers the centers of which have small eyelet holes added for daintiness. The background is fine linen.

Another kerchief in this collection has interesting drawn work and embroidery executed on fine India muslin. It was made in 1750 and is initialed by Rachel Leonard of Plymouth, Massachusetts. A carnation motif has been interestingly embroidered on an eighteenth century kerchief which is also in this group.

SLIPS AND SACQUES

Ruffles, edgings and scattered sprigs of flower leaves or dotted eyelets ornamented these additions to every woman's wardrobe all through the nineteenth century.

INFANTS' WEAR

Christening robes were lavishly covered with the most precious and exquisite embroidery. White interlacing vines worked in wispy featherstitching were augmented with flowers worked in satin stitches raised over an underlay of threads, or eyeleted in lacy effects through myriads of openings carefully buttonholed with stitches so small that a magnifying glass would be needed to trace their direction. A delicate christening robe remains in the Litchfield Museum which has an entire front panel etched with fragile needlework.

Baby-dress yokes came in for an equal amount of stitched decoration. Miss Madeline Evans of Williamstown, Massachusetts, owns baby dresses and caps which are exquisitely embroidered. She thinks her great-grandmother, Isabella Holloway, who married James Lee in 1800 and lived in New York, made the little wardrobe. The yoke of one of the dresses is worked in a deep "V" formed by flowers traced in white embroidery up both sides and around the neck and topping the little shoulder lapels.

Baby caps from this period remain in quantities, worked with the most graceful designs and showered with flowers or tiny leaves to adorn the bobbing head of the adored infant. These were always white on white traceries, with sheer muslin for the material.

A little girl's dress worn by a New Yorker about 1780, is a gift of Miss Carolyn Ferriday to the Museum of the City of New York. It is hand-embroidered on fine white linen edged with Mechlin lace. It was worn by Jane Barr Stuart who was born in 1775.

HOUSEHOLD LINEN

Utilitarian needlework included pillowcases which were enhanced with handsome needlework particularly in white. Every technique was employed upon them.

Bureau-cover ends also received adornment. An example belonging to Mrs. Carroll R. Williams, formerly of Baltimore, Maryland, was made in 1820 by her great-great-aunt, Ann Scott, of the same city. Her initials have been marked upon it and the design repeated around the ends has been worked in white eyelet embroidery combined with French-knot fillings, satin stitch and fine buttonholing. The fringe also is hand-made, an evidence of still another technique understood by Victorian needlewomen.

This craze for all-white needlework spread throughout the country and lasted for almost a century. Rich and poor, the matron in the city and the farmer's wife, all carried their bit of embroidery wherever they gathered. It was the chief occupation outside of household duties. Patterns were exchanged among friends. Not only were women's accessories needleworked, but passionate attention was lavished upon the gentlemen, whose embroidered shirt fronts were impressive indeed. Ruffles, too, were handsomely edged and decorated with French knots and satin stitch, and made delicate with drawn work touches.

Enterprising manufacturers were evidently to blame for the sudden stoppage of this graceful embroidery. Looms at home and abroad were turning themselves inside out, around and about, to imitate this style of needlework and finally succeeded so well that the disconcerted ladies found it difficult to tell whether Cousin Eliza was wearing a gown of her own workmanship as she stated, or whether she had bought it through Uncle Ezra Courtney when he went to Switzerland last year and returned with so many mysterious packages.

When the twentieth century opened its infant eyes it could hardly see any home-made baby caps or dainty trimmings in the process of completion. The christening robe was foreign born and in all probability made in France. European women were busy plying their needles for those in America who still preferred the hand-made embroideries. And it was thrilling, anyway, to import your embroidery from abroad; even more distingué to pack the many steamer rugs well wrapped with leather straps and travel to Paris or London yourself, to bring back the cherished fineries.

But few women could afford such luxuries as travel in this period, and contented themselves with manufactured imitations. Hamburg was used for petticoats and edgings, and was effective in its semblance to hand embroidery. Out in Ohio or other distant states they might eyelet and embroider, but the women in the big cities hadn't any time or interest for what to them seemed tedious work. After a couple of centuries of capable and healthy needlework expression among almost all the feminine members of the family, the great alibi arose in the late Victorian period "that my eyes are too weak for embroidery." Lack of exercise would weaken any muscles—eyes included. Or it may be that Papa would buy Mamma that marvelous allover cut-worked hand-made French-embroidered gown at a few hundred dollars, if she really couldn't do a stitch herself any longer. Besides, the Ladies' Culture Club kept her so busy preparing that paper on Venetian Art to be read at the Wednesday meeting, that she just couldn't find time to sew.

Then and there needlework lost its pure white innocence and became cultured, too. The Venetian Art began to do things to stitchery and we find the huge cross-stitch pictures of European hamlets and other landscapes completely absorbing the energies of any needleworkers who survived.

CHAPTER XIII

MORAVIAN WORK: MEMORIAL SAMPLERS
AND SILK ON SATIN EMBROIDERIES

"My heart is awed within me when I think
Of the great miracle that still goes on,
In silence, round me—the perpetual work
Of thy creation, finished, yet renewed forever
Written on thy works I read
The lesson of thy own eternity."

WILLIAM CULLEN BRYANT.

COMPLETE ABSORPTION IN STITCHING damsels on memorials followed the early sampler era. The mood of the worker turned from moralizing to mourning, from melancholy to gloom, and at last gave itself up to abject sorrow. It is claimed that the fad for making these memorial pictures sprang from the teachings of the Moravian sect.

These people had migrated to this country from Moravia, which is a part of present-day Czechoslovakia. They settled first in Georgia, where they practiced silk cultivation. Finding Georgia too close to Spanish marauders and becoming unpopular with their neighbors because they refused to bear arms, they moved north to Pennsylvania and settled at what is now Bethlehem in 1740.

Nine years later the congregation founded two schools, one for boys which was the nucleus of Lehigh University, the other for girls. The girls' school was presided over by the religious Sisters of Bethlehem, who developed the art of fine needlework, particularly in silk, which became famous all over the country. These schools soon established a reputation for culture and learning. Enrollment was sought by prominent

Americans who considered the environment appropriate for children during the formative years of their lives. As branches of the school for girls were established in other states, the art and practice of good needlework was extended.

This feature of the Moravian school established its supremacy above all others. Included in the curriculum were tambour and fine needlework, the techniques of ribbon work, crêpe work, flower embroidery and pictures upon satin. During this transitional period when the contrast between the pioneer's hardship and the abundant life enjoyed by the prosperous colonists was most marked, the gentle Sisters of Bethlehem in their quiet way cultivated among the impressionable and tender flower of American womanhood a love of the beautiful and a respect for excellence in technique. In consequence their contribution to the panorama of needlework history in America has been of considerable importance and lasting value.

An inscription on the back of a needlework panel records the tranquil atmosphere which pervaded the school. It was worked in brown silk to resemble finely penned lines and reads:

WORKED WHERE THE PEACEFUL LEHI FLOWS

A sect wandering over the world in search of a place where they could worship in peace according to the dictates of conscience had found a home at last.

MEMORIAL SAMPLERS

That the art of embroidering. the memorial samplers was taught in schools other than those established by the Moravians, is indicated by examples found in various states. It may be that the pattern came from Bethlehem, for many of the teachers or "preceptresses" who taught young ladies this new art of dainty silk stitchery had attended the school there.

Evidence of the use of a repeat process occurs in two memorials reproduced facing page eighty-two. One is in a private collection in New Jersey; the other, almost identical in design and theme, is in the textile collection of the Metropolitan Museum of Art. Both were embroidered, apparently, in New York State, and possibly at the same school. George Washington's demise was memorialized in stitchery, no doubt, as a preparatory work in anticipation of the time when the young lady might wish to make a more personal memorial.

A comparison of the samplers is interesting, for although the principal composition is the same, the embroiderer, in each case, has varied the design to suit her own taste. In the sampler by Ellen Bange Bevier, the architectural details of the tomb have been changed. The oval is a different shape, and the inscription, "Sacred to the Memory of the Illustrious George Washington," though identical in its wording, is stitched in a different script. The urn has assumed a different top and base; also the fluting decorating the bottom of the tomb. Ellen Bevier has stitched more luxuriant leaves on her mounds and the costumes on her mourning ladies have been varied in the neckline treatment and in the draping of the black veil. In the Metropolitan Museum memorial the curls of the hair are more abundant, falling below the arm in beautiful spirals. The background is worked a little more elaborately with the grass presented in little furrowed rows, whereas the Bevier panel is "laid" in flat stitches and shaded in the opposite direction from that of the other example. It is interesting to compare the willow trees and firs in respect to mass and decorative interpretation. The Metropolitan Museum picture is far richer and more graceful in design and shows greater attention to detail. This may be due to the fact that the designer had a little wider area in which to work; that she has consciously used this space for her effect is shown by the introduction of a little plant between the figure at the left and the tree trunk, a touch which is omitted in the Bevier sampler.

Both pictures have equal charm. They were worked in the classic manner popular during this period as a result of the Napoleonic influence and the Greek revival prevalent during the late eighteenth and early nineteenth century not only in needlework, but in architecture, interior decoration and costume design.

THO LOST TO SIGHT YET DEAR TO MEMORY

The letters of many such inscriptions have been stitched with the hair of the departed one, this "thread" giving a fine line and making the sampler deeply sentimental. This particular inscription is embroidered upon a silk-stitched gravestone erected in a landscape of carefully laid silk stitches which create the effect of light and shade falling upon a lawn of well-kept grass. Chenille oak leaves decorate the tree shading the sorrowful mother, and the traditional weeping willow droops over the tearful father, dressed in a finely stitched black silk costume of the period. A little silken bird hovers sympathetically above the tomb, silhouetted against a delicate blue sky tinted in water color. The church architecture is naïvely recorded in flat and outline stitches, and the house, of lesser importance, is worked simply. A most effective use of shading and stitch direction is shown in the handling of the draperies and folds in the mother's gown.

The work was made by Ellen Wychoff. The dedication reads:

SACRED
To the Memory of
Altia Wychoff,
Who Departed this Life, Dec. 12th, 1807,
Aged 18. By E. Wychoff, 1810.

It has been donated by the granddaughter of Ellen Wychoff, Miss Anne Doughty, to the Museum of the City of New York, the city in which it was embroidered.

The mourning sampler inherited by Mrs. Henry J. Miller of New Jersey from a Moravian ancestor living in the vicinity of Philadelphia is of particular interest since it originated at the re-markable Moravian school. The design possesses all the essential characteristics found in memori-als worked in other states. The tomb is in the same style; the inscription is similarly located; the initials are embroidered on the same Greek urn and the usual garland of roses is present. The pose and costume of the figures, including the heavy veil of the matron, are typical. In the land-scape treatment the same willows worked in the same stitches occur, and the inevitable pairs of firs and poplar trees, also. The church may be seen in the background with the "pool of tears" consistently placed.

In this picture, sacred to the memory of Daniel Goodman who died at the age of 18 years in the year 1803, a novelty is introduced into the design. A little painted angel bearing a painted scroll inscribed with some legend is making her entrance from heaven through bil-lows of painted clouds. The little boys who are shown mourning the affectionate brother were cousins of Jane Niles whose sampler was de-scribed earlier in this book.

From the Connecticut Historical Society in Hartford, comes a mourning sampler worked by Elizabeth K. Bennet approximately in 1809, judging by the date embroidered on the tombs. The left one bears an inscription to the mem-ory of Mr. John Bennet who died in 1777 and Susannah, his wife, who followed him in 1779. Mrs. Martha Emmons, who died in 1808, is commemorated on a large Grecian urn and mourned by a lady in a striped gown who is seated beside it. At the right, a little lady is almost overcome beside the tomb of Mrs. Titus King, who died in what appears to be the year 1791.

The setting of this little scene is admirably executed in the most benevolent silk weeping willows, caressingly drooping over each un-happy lady. Tender little trees abound in the background and numbers of small chenille-embroidered plants cheer the foreground be-tween the mounds of elaborately shaded silk grasses. The pebbly paths about the tombs are effectively represented by myriads of tiny silk French knots. From every angle the picture is a most impressive work in silk embroidery. The only apparent break from the traditional pattern occurs in the omission of the little lake which was probably symbolical of the vale of tears.

Belonging to the same school of needlework memorials is the sampler embroidered in silks by an unknown worker and to be found in the collection of the Essex Institute in Salem, Mas-sachusetts. The legend on the work dates the sampler. It reads:

SACRED
TO THE MEMORY OF
MAJR.
ANTHONY MORSE
OBIT MARCH 22D 1803
AE'49.

The tombstone upon which the inscription is embroidered has been elaborated by the intro-duction of a painted angel, life size, who points heavenward. In this particular example the let-tering on the tomb appears to have been painted in with a fine brush. The figure of a young woman kneels beside the urn, making a graceful line and tying in the weeping willow tree with the foreground masses. The draperies of her gown flow in rhythmic stitches and enfold the form completely. The portrait, hair and arms are painted on the heavy satin. The willow trees are most poetically designed, not only in the patterning of the individual leaves and branches, but also in the solidly stitched back-ground masses which bring the leaves into dec-orative silhouette. The interplay of light and shade effects is handsomely balanced in the fore-ground as in the rest of the picture. The origi-nal is unframed and it is interesting to observe that the edges of the square satin panel were sewn to strips which had eyeleted holes about an inch apart, through which cords were passed to bind and stretch the panel upon a frame for embroidering.

While this sampler is similar in theme to the other memorials, it shows much originality and selectivity in its composition. The stitchery also shows a high degree of technical excellence.

SILK BIBLICAL PICTURES

In each period of needlework history one finds religious expression. Delightfully quaint is the silk embroidery reproduced opposite page 83, showing the costumes of the 1800's. It is de-scribed as follows by Miss Jane Kerr who in-herited it:

1. *Courtesy of:* MRS. HENRY J. MILLER, New Jersey.

Moravian Mourning Sampler; silk embroidered on satin painted sky and angel. Worked by ancestor of Mrs. Miller. Daniel Goodman died age of 18 years in 1803, dating period of picture.

2. *Courtesy of:* THE METROPOLITAN MUSEUM OF ART, New York.

Silk embroidered memorial sampler to "The Illustrious George Washington," about 1800. Worker unknown.

3. *Courtesy of:* THE CONNECTICUT HISTORICAL SOCIETY, Hartford, Connecticut.

Mourning Picture, Embroidered with silk and chenille, painted portraits; memorial to three persons, worked 1807 by Elizabeth K. Bennet, Connecticut.

4. *Courtesy of:* THE MUSEUM OF THE CITY OF NEW YORK.

Silk and chenille embroidered Memorial Sampler; painted portraits appliquéd, tinted sky worked by E. Wychoff in 1810, New York.

5. *Courtesy of:* MISS HELEN BRAINARD SMITH, New Jersey.

George Washington Memorial Sampler worked in silks on satin, tinted sky, painted portraits. Approximately 1806, by Ellen Bange Bevier, Ulster County, New York.

1. *Courtesy of:* MISS JANE KERR, Oregon.

"Moses in the Bulrushes"; silk, sequins, chenille embroidered picture on satin, one, set of five biblical pictures saved, others destroyed in great Chicago Fire. Worked by Lucretia Colton, 1800, Massachusetts.

2. *Courtesy of:* CONCORD ANTIQUARIAN SOCIETY, Massachusetts.

Embroidered picture illustrating Sterne's "Sentimental Journey" worked in silks on satin, painted portrait, arms and hair, by Lydia Hosmer, 1812, Concord, Massachusetts.

3. *Courtesy of:* MRS. E. S. HARKNESS, Connecticut.

Silk embroidery on satin. Water color painted sky and portraits. Design of the Early American School, or "American Primitives" influence. Worked by Harriet Denison in 1800, Connecticut.

4. *Courtesy of:* MRS. J. W. WEINLAND, New York.

Silk embroidered picture. Edward the 4th, King of England and Elizabeth Gray imploring the restoration of her husband's estate. 1829, by Anne Conrad; Philadelphia, Pennsylvania.

This needlework picture, "Moses in the Bulrushes," is one of five biblical pictures, the only one saved from the great Chicago fire. It was embroidered by my great-great-grandmother, Lucretia Colton, of Long Meadow, Massachusetts, the year in which it was done, unknown. She was born December 29, 1788, so I imagine it was done in about 1800 or thereabouts. The embroidery is soft shades of greens, yellow and browns, silks on white satin. The eagle at the top is in gold thread, raised, and the figures and sky are hand painted in. It was left by my great-great-grandmother, Lucretia Colton, to her daughter, Lucretia Colton King, who in turn left it to her granddaughter, my mother.

Along with thoughts of Biblical scenes, Lucretia Colton demonstrates her patriotic fervor and love of country with the inclusion of the national emblem in her picture. The eagle embroidered in gold thread carries in his beak a garland of flowers done in the same manner as in Laura Sherril's embroidery, "Meditation," described hereafter. This use of gold embroidery shows the influence of court costumes worn in England and France during this period, and similarly ornamented. One finds some resemblance also to the Stuart embroideries in the naïve arrangement of the figures and the ornamental backgrounds which have however been simplified to their basic essentials. There is, in all these works, a delightful freshness of interpretation and in their spirit the same directness found in early American paintings, the so-called primitives.

In the same class, but different in design conception, is another religious subject in silk needlework from the collection of the Metropolitan Museum of Art. Worked in silk embroidery on satin and entitled "Christ and the Woman of Samaria," it was stitched by Caroline Ridgeway in 1812, and about the same period as the "Moses" picture. It was made, however, not in Massachusetts but in Philadelphia, and may very likely have emanated from the Moravian school.

SENTIMENTAL AND CLASSICAL PICTURES

Simultaneously with the gloomy subjects used for the silk mourning samplers, appeared silk embroidered pictures in happier mood showing maidens in their gardens reading poems, romantic or otherwise. The frontispiece is an excellent example of the new attitude. It is owned by the Berkshire Museum and is reproduced from their collection of Americana. Titled "Meditation" and embroidered by Laura Sherril, it presents a gentle lady dressed like her sisters of the mourning pictures. Like them she is worked in silk upon satin, but she has become a patriotic expression and instead of being in a reverie beside a tomb beneath the wings of a dove, she has ventured out upon the hillside, and sits in meditation beneath the broad protective wings of the American eagle.

In contrast to the usual representation of the eagle with head up as it appears, for example, on the ornamental brasses adorning the mirror panels of the Adam, Chippendale, and Sheraton periods, the eagle embroidered on this picture and similar examples, is pictured with the head posed downward, holding in the beak the garland designs which compose the border decorations of most of these pictures. It may have been that the design was drawn or inspired by the same artists who made the engraved designs used by the cabinetmakers of the day, for in their advertisements, found in the journals of the period, the same styles may be noted.

In another mood, and from the collection of Mrs. E. S. Harkness, Connecticut, comes the work of Harriet Denison, an embroidered picture on satin, made in 1800. It is delightfully naïve, reflecting the tender sentiment of the young lady. The drawing seems to have been inspired by the immediate locality in which Harriet lived. The salt box house is typical of the architecture of New England homes. The red-roofed Georgian house, the brown-shingled old house and the three-story house of the more modern type are all characteristic of the locale of the Connecticut Valley and seaport communities during this period.

In American needlework pictures, irrespective of period, swans on a pond are apt to be included. Even in a contemporary panel from Oregon, the same motif appears. They are as universal as the sheep and the eagle. The swans in Harriet's picture are of an early period, amusingly stitched upon a silk pond of iridescent pale blue and green, bordered with an original style of fence. The hedges, the grass and the trees are worked in with much spirit and in delightful planes of variegated color. Blues, greens, pale cream golds, yellow greens are used, and large acorns in the tree to the right of the picture are amusingly interpreted from nature.

Particularly interesting are the costumes of the period, exactly rendered. Peppermint pink-and-white striped trousers on the young man are topped with a cream waistcoat striped with silver bands. A French-gray jacket, a very broad brimmed black hat, silver edged, and black flowing tie complete this ensemble, including, of course, the handsomely buckled black shoes. The young lady wears an Empire gown of beige-colored silk. The skirt reveals an underskirt of rose red. Long panniers top this skirt, tied in front with gold cords. A little white vestee edged with black velvet ribbons covers the bosom. The hairdress of curls is painted in very realistically. She is unhappily weeping into a generously large handkerchief. The slippers are powder blue with silver trimmings.

In painting the bands of blue sky above, the young artist has used the color adroitly, matching the blue of the silks in the foreground. The effect at first glance is that of a completely embroidered panel. That the houses are out of proportion with the figures, animals, trees, is not offending, since the picture is so well composed, being both decorative in color balance and sensitive in stitch feeling. One senses a lyric interpretation of the scene, similar to the early tapestry designs of hunting episodes created in Europe in the twelfth century primarily for wall pictures. In the same way the artists of that period took their models directly from nature without preconceived ideas of draughtsmanship. In the simplicity of this rendering one finds the sort of direct charm and joy which the worker felt in the conception.

The classic revival reflects current literary interests, much as did the earlier samplers. The needleworker also was influenced by the painters of the day and copied the style of their pictures, indirectly or intentionally, as the case might be, even supplementing the embroidery with water-color painting. Infinite variety of subject marks this period of silk on satin embroidered pictures. The general expression was less set in pattern and needleworkers freely drew their inspiration from numerous sources. Dominant among the influences were the effective classical

paintings of the popular Angelica Kauffman, whose works were exhibited all over Europe during the late eighteenth century and were first beginning to be known in America about 1800. Admiration spread throughout the country for her murals and restrained classic lunettes which depicted subjects from ancient history. Her decorative drawings illustrating Greek and Roman mythology were adapted for embroidery and her painted illustrations for Sterne's "Sentimental Journey" were particularly popular.

In the Concord Antiquarian Society in Massachusetts may be found Lydia Hosmer's classical scene, worked by her in 1812 while attending a young ladies' finishing school. It is called "Maria." The picture is painted on white silk, the embroidery done in long and short stitch with French knots. It depicts an episode in Sterne's "Sentimental Journey," the design being adapted from an illustration in the book. Tristram Shandy's melancholy acquaintance is here shown sitting at the foot of a large tree, her elbow in her lap, and her head upon her hand, exactly as described by Mr. Yorick, who may be discovered at the coach window in the background. The coloring of this embroidery picture is difficult to describe, but very lovely. It is beautifully worked in untwisted, possibly India, silk. The dress is a cream color, shaded with tan. The young woman's face, hair and arms are painted in natural colors. The shrubbery is done in tiny French knots in blue green, olive green, off-white and tan. The sky is painted in subdued sunset colorings.

From the Essex Institute in Salem comes another excellent example in "Cornelia and the Gracchi," worked in silk and chenille stitchery on satin. This, too, may have been adapted in design from the painter's work, since a canvas exhibited prior to the stitching of this picture was titled "Mother of the Gracchi." There was an early exhibit of Angelica Kauffman's work at the Pennsylvania Academy in Philadelphia where her exquisite drawings of classic figures may have inspired many needlework pictures of graceful ladies playing upon harps, surrounded by embroidered festoons of delicately shaded silk flowers, the latter showing the influence of the Moravian school. The borders were arranged either in classic squares or in shield compositions. Used for fire-screen panels, these chaste and delicate needlework pieces made admirable decorations when mounted on Sheraton stands and placed in Adam drawing rooms.

Elizabeth Tryon has left us a delicately stitched embroidery in this style. She was the grandmother of Mr. Eugene Phelps Edwards of Stonington, and her work, a silk on satin pole-screen panel showing a lady playing a harp in the best Angelica Kauffman manner, was embroidered by her in Connecticut. The date assigned to it is 1830, although the design seems to belong to the period around 1810. Today it graces the home of Mrs. Frederic C. Paffard. It is as handsome and as stately as it was a hundred years ago, and the silk as well as the little hand-painted miniature portrait retain their original beautiful color.

Of the same school in both design and technique is another graceful figure beside a harp. Embroidered with fine silks and gold thread upon satin with touches of silver thread on the harp strings, and using water colors on the portrait and the sky, this panel is a very fine example of the period. It is at present in the Litchfield Museum collection in Connecticut. "Malvina" is the title, and it was worked by Mary Bacon, October 15, 1808, in Woodbury, Connecticut. There is a possibility that both this picture and the pole-screen panel were worked while the girls were at school and that school was, in all probability, Miss Pierce's School at Litchfield, Connecticut. Mary Bacon's "Malvina" came from the Taylor and Masters families of New Milford, Connecticut, and almost all the girls of the leading families in that vicinity attended this exceptional pioneer school for successive generations. The great similarity in style suggests that both pieces were worked under the guidance of the same preceptress.

Combining classicism with the romantic style and related to the preceding pictures in the floral composition, the use of water colors for portraits and sky and silks for the embroidery, are three oval pictures of high merit. Two come from the needlework collection of Mrs. Harrold Gillingham in Philadelphia and are exceedingly handsome in every respect. The first is a silk-embroidered picture which has been drawn and worked on satin. The title, "Paul and Virginia," explains the story of the tender couple under the finely worked blue and green leaves of the silk tree. In the distance, faintly sketched in

water color, a sail boat may be seen upon which one would assume Paul is about to embark. The needlework has been executed with great refinement and skill, the silks being laid with an artistic sense of direction and form, and with technical smoothness. They are all simple over and over or laid stitches, but give great rhythm in line and mass through the careful interplay of color and high-light values. The design is also excellent, being well balanced and selective. The treatment of the foreground bears a strong resemblance to the color and stitch sequences found in the early crewel embroideries of the eighteenth century. It was worked about 1800 by a great-grandmother of Mrs. Gillingham.

Also designed in oval form but quite different in composition, is another exquisite silk on satin embroidery with water-color portraiture. The center oval has been very finely stitched in with a highly decorative arrangement. The foreground showing shade trees and an abundance of fruit trees in the landscape includes the figure of a little girl who is touching pears and grapes which have been made in design as large as she is. Around this oval the entire background has been filled in with a gorgeously worked silk flower spray, about six inches in width. The delicate workmanship on the flowers would seem to indicate acquaintance with the Moravian school of embroidery, for this was their specialty. Having been embroidered in the vicinity of Philadelphia about 1800, it is quite likely that the inspiration came from the teachers at Bethlehem.

Belonging to the same group in technique and design is the very fine picture, "Cupid and Psyche," made by Lydia Welles of Boston, Massachusetts, about the year 1800 before her marriage to John T. Hall. It shows splendid craftsmanship and artistry in the handling of the silk stitches forming the folds of drapery in the gown upon the reclining figure. The shadow-forms in the folds of the dress, the high lights and the drawing in stitchery of the various lines and masses are rendered with fine ability. Excellent also is the arrangement of the general composition of trees and foliage and the distant mansion with its garden walls, elements which are combined with the figures in a pleasing rhythm. The leaves on the trees and bushes pleasantly interrupt the straight flat satin stitches of the remainder of the picture through the use of French knots worked with silks of various shades. The picture is a delicious harmony in color on the soft pastel range in mellow golds, pale blues, and creams, with faint rose touches. Cupid's little wings are embroidered, while the rest of the figure is delicately painted in flesh tints. The painted house in the background presents a rather stern front to all this romance, as if to suggest a firm anchorage, substantially holding to earth these mortals in their flights of fancy.

It is interesting here to note family interest in needlework repeated through several generations. Lydia Welles, creator of the Cupid and Psyche picture, was the great-grandmother of Mrs. Kenneth Budd, an ardent contemporary needleworker in both silk and needlepoint embroidery, who frequently exhibits beautiful examples worked in both techniques. Mrs. Budd's daughter, Mrs. J. Oliver O'Donnell, also has created a number of lovely needlepoint panels to her own and the family's credit. The art of embroidery seems to have been handed down in a number of other American families, the particular technique used by the ancestor being reflected in the contemporary work of the descendant. Although the newer needlework design may be related entirely to the contemporary scene the fundamentals remain, denoting aptitudes inherited from the immediate background.

SHEPHERDS AND SHEPHERDESSES

Romance governed the needle's flight of fancy into the realms where eighteenth century shepherdesses kept trysts with shepherd lovers. The drowsy little white sheep made of French knots in silk or wool, paid no attention to these tender meetings and unromantically minded their grass or gazed at the delightful silk-embroidered landscape or looked tactfully at the old homestead of classic architecture surrounded by an immaculate white silk fence in severe contrast to the gayer mood of the lovers under the tree in the foreground.

Flocks of these contented sheep were embroidered in various settings ranging from backgrounds suggesting foreign shores with castles in the distance, to those which show a quaint American village. The costumes of the lovers likewise varied with the fashion prevalent at the time of execution. In four of the pictures selected as representing this school of imagery, there is to be found an amusing diversity in arrangement and idea. The subject no doubt reflects the popular vogue for shepherdess pictures which was particularly evident in England and France during the eighteenth century. The fad, due perhaps to the slow traveling by packet-ships in that time, did not reach America until some years later making its first appearance here in the early nineteenth century.

The large number of these silk panels which were worked simultaneously in adjacent sections of the country suggests that the design and technique was taught in private schools. Most picture examples, however, seem to be based on direct observation rather than reproduced exactly from a model or formula as in the similar memorial samplers. It is this absence of sophistication and self-consciousness which gives many of the little pictures their chief charm.

Much has been made of the effects created by the light which, falling upon the silks at a calculated angle, dramatically changes the shades. Unfortunately this quality is lost in photographic reproduction, but in the originals the play of color is most effective and important in supplementing or accenting the idea and the composition. In the laying of the silks, stitch direction is carefully studied and the tempo of the scene heightened or lowered according to the emphasis placed on the sheen or high lights reflected from the angle in which threads are placed or massed. An amusing example of this sheen, effectively emphasized in the foreground stitching of the grass, may be noted in a picture called

"THE SHEPHERDESS OF THE ALPS"

Worked in silks on satin, the radiation of the silks follows a circular direction in laid and backstitches which are very lively in effect. The "Alps" have been rendered in dot stitches over the hilly surfaces. The vineyards have been made delightfully suggestive of a bright sunny climate through the use of heavy dots *en masse* to indicate shadows under each tree. Emily Trowbridge, who worked the panel in Connecticut about 1800, was fond of using this dot treatment to give her embroidery substance and light contrast; she uses the same method to give back-

1. *Courtesy of:* THE WADSWORTH ATHENEUM, Hartford, Connecticut. Gift of Mrs. Susan T. Darling.

The Shepherd Boy, mate to the shepherdess picture; silk embroidery on satin, worked about 1790, by Sally Wilson Belcher, Connecticut.

2. *Courtesy af:* THE WADSWORTH ATHENEUM, Hartford, Connecticut.

The Shepherdess; silk embroidery on white satin. Worked about 1790 by Mrs. Sara T. Kinney's mother's mother, Sally Wilson Belcher, Connecticut.

3. *Courtesy of:* MUSEUM OF THE CITY OF NEW YORK.

Shepherd and Shepherdesses; silk needle work picture, 1800, by an ancestor of Mrs. James W. Halehurst, New York.

4. *Courtesy of:* MEMORIAL HALL, Deerfield, Massachusetts.

"The Shepherdess of the Alps," silk on satin embroidery, about 1800, by Emily Trowbridge, Connecticut, mother of Bishop John Williams, Connecticut.

1. *Courtesy of:* MRS. HARROLD GILLINGHAM, Penn.

Silk on satin embroidery, water color portrait and sky, about 1800, Pennsylvania.

2. *Courtesy of:* MRS. KENNETH BUDD, New York. the great granddaughter of Lydia Welles.

"Cupid and Psyche"; silk on satin picture with painted portraits. About 1800 by Lydia Welles, who married John T. Hall of Boston, Mass.

3. *Courtesy of:* MRS. FREDERIC C. PAFFARD, Connecticut.

Silk on satin embroidered pole screen panel by Elizabeth Tryon, 1830, Conn.

4. *Courtesy of:* LITCHFIELD HISTORICAL SOCIETY, Connecticut.

Embroidered picture, "Malvina"; silk and gold thread on satin, worked by Mary Bacon, October 15, 1808. Woodbury, Connecticut.

5. *Courtesy of:* MRS. HARROLD GILLINGHAM, Pennsylvania.

"Paul and Virginia"; silk embroidered picture on satin with water color portraits. About 1800 by great grandmother of Mrs. Harrold Gillingham, Pennsylvania.

ground fullness to the leaves in the very capable tree.

The figures are dressed characteristically in the best American mode of the day. The young shepherd "of the Alps" is romantically debonair, with the present of a wreath of flowers for which he has climbed the highest mountain, in one hand, and the small round black hat of the early nineteenth century in the other. The high stock about his neck is far removed from the rustic Alpine shepherd, but he is charming with his carefully arranged curls. The fair shepherdess is likewise in the mode and decoratively awaits her admirer in a white silk gown, stitched in perfect detail even to the gathers of the high waist over her bosom and the little scallops embroidered around the neck. The gown is the style which was worn at weddings of that day and has a train. The increasing shortness of the bodice in costumes of this period disturbed many persons. A contemporary journal ridiculed the trend in a couplet:

Shepherds, I have lost my waist.
Have you seen my body?

The curls of the shepherdess are as admirable as those of her swain, and the slight gay tilt to the bonnet shows a spirited departure from the heavy veils worn by the mourning maidens.

Morality is touched upon in the exclusion of the black sheep from the pasture; his eager look into the fold where all the fair white sheep remain, bespeaks his loneliness and dismay most effectively. Emily Trowbridge was the mother of Bishop John Williams of Connecticut, who made a gift of the engaging little embroidery to the Memorial Hall in Deerfield, Massachusetts.

A beautiful pair of silk-embroidered pictures made between 1790 and 1800 by Sally Wilson Belcher, were given to the collection of the Wadsworth Atheneum in Hartford, Connecticut, by Mrs. Susan T. Darling, in the name of Mrs. Sara T. Kinney, Sally's granddaughter. One picture shows a little shepherdess in the costume of the period. The embroidery is worked on white satin. A garland of silk flowers in shield formation is tied at the top center with a ribbon bow, from which is suspended an oval medallion containing the embroidered landscape. The girl or shepherdess in the foreground is carrying a basket of wheat on her left arm and holding a bundle of it in her right hand. The embroidery is beautifully and expertly done. The sky has been entirely stitched in fine technique which is also evident in the handling of the cloud effects. The costume, ground and trees, are embroidered equally well, with the feeling of a painting. French knots for curls are attractively used. Basket stitch on the basket, diagonal stitch, satin stitch and laid work are all combined with masterly relation to the subject. The flower work is lovely and delicate as an etching.

The mate to this picture, the little shepherd boy, is exceedingly well done. The little lunette has been worked with great feeling, both for design and for tone. Even the little dog expresses tired sleepiness as he crouches at his master's feet. Again costume details are accurately rendered, the stripes on the knickers being clearly indicated. The jacket and vest are well stitched and have almost the effect of a painting. Her trees show inventiveness in the play of light and shade on the trunks, and in the variety of stitches used for leaves. The flower embroidery is really handsome, each species being delicately and accurately rendered in excellent needlework.

These examples are exceptionally fine and are representative of the best effort made in their day.

It is interesting to observe the fashions arriving in America from foreign sources, as depicted in the silk pictures. The Museum of the City of New York has an oval embroidery worked in 1800 by an ancestor of Mrs. James W. Hazelhurst who presented it to the Museum. The two shepherdesses are wearing dresses in the Empire style with small panniers adapted from the French, costumes which were fashionable in New York City at the time the picture was embroidered. The scene, however, is laid in the country and the ladies are shearing sheep, which certainly no lady ever did in the costume pictured. Styles arriving by way of India are indicated in the turban which one shepherdess is wearing. It seems to be of velvet and is decorated with a "banditti" plume. The other maiden is wearing a style of headdress also popular between the years of 1800 and 1810 and called a "gypsy hat." Both have the handsome curls to be noted in portraits of the period. These curls do not necessarily represent nature's kind abundance in this respect. In fact in most cases ladies wore closely curled wigs, which were exceedingly fashionable as we may gather from a letter which Eliza Southgate, visiting in Boston during this period, wrote to her mother in Maine.

> I must either cut my hair or have one. I cannot dress my hair at all stylish. Mrs. Coffin bought Eleanore's and says that she will write to Mrs. Summer to get me one just like it; how much time it would save—in one year we could save it in pins and paper, besides the trouble. At the Assembly I was quite ashamed of my head, for nobody has long hair. If you will consent to my having one do send me over a five dollar bill by the post immediately after you receive this; for I am in hopes to have it for the next Assembly.

"ENGRAVINGS," ARCHITECTURE AND LANDSCAPE

In quite an original and distinctly different style are the three "engraved" embroideries made by Elizabeth Anne Barker, the great-great-grandmother of Mrs. Raymond Lefferts of New York. They are painted and stitched in shades of silk chosen to simulate a steel engraving and ranging from sepia black to pale taupe and light gray against the ivory colored satin. The young designer has produced delightful tonal values in her work. Obviously copied from old engravings, the hatched lines are imitated in the same direction as the originals. Where the lines become too fine to be imitated by thread, thin brush-strokes of water color have been laid on to continue the stitched effect. Without close examination one does not immediately detect the substitution. This combination, technically, has been used in ancient Chinese embroideries and the idea may have come from such pieces imported to America.

That Elizabeth Anne Barker had a style of her own is shown in the flocks of birds stitched in each of her engravings, and the use of broad, sweeping, couched lines of silk to suggest masses of grass in the foreground or stone in the bridges. These are excellent illustrations of effects which may be obtained by the use of stitch direction. In the tree and leaf arrangements there is strong resemblance to the technique found in Japanese prints and described in their laws for brush painting of such subjects. The architecture is naïvely rendered, but effectively conveys the period and general feeling of the building with its attendant landscaping. The stitches are varied and represent the traditional English forms, long and short, laid stitches, couching, brick stitch, outline and satin stitches. The fly or Y stitch is used for the trees with their leaves of Oriental shape. The tones and shadings in the originals are exceedingly soft and well related. They are little gems.

Following these monotone embroideries came the introduction of chenille silk-work, applied to foregrounds or mass stitchery and replacing the long sleek threads of silk. The pictures developed a trend away from the sentimental and probed the mysteries of architectural reproduction with landscape effects. The young ladies either had patterns to follow, or they were taught this new style of needlework by "instructresses." The two examples opposite page 91 suggest some common source since the design in each of the scenes, which portray Mount Vernon, shows a landscape effect in which the trees, shrubbery and boats are almost identical in arrangement. The only real variation occurs in the use of materials and stitchery. One picture, worked by Abigail Parker Noyes in the year 1812, in Hartford, Connecticut, at Miss Patten's Boarding School, shows the entire ground worked in silk chenille threads. Her large tree is carried out in flat silks, one clump of leaves being chenille. Some of the bushes are chenille and the smaller trees to the left are stitched in flat silks. The other picture, worked by Caroline Stebbins in 1804 while a student at Deerfield Academy in Old Deerfield, Massachusetts, where the picture may be seen today in the quaint Memorial Hall which was the original old school building, shows an opposite treatment in several details. The foreground is worked in flat silks. The trees and bushes are developed in chenille, the distant trees, only, matching those of Abigail Noyes' work in the use of little silk French knots to indicate the leaves.

In both pictures the Mount Vernon Mansion is rendered in virtually the same way, in drawing particularly, but the values in coloring are reversed. In each we also find the same style of hand-painted boats, river and hills. The pictures typify the variation to be found in almost all works copied or adapted from one original theme. Inevitably the personal touch or idea of the worker changes in some degree the idea or design of the originator.

An elaborate bit of architecture combined with a romantic scene in the foreground is displayed in the embroidery by Euphemia Acheson of New York, an aunt of Miss Anna Culbert of Stonington, Connecticut, to whom the panel now belongs. Worked in 1853, with silks and chenille threads on satin, the landscape repeats some of the favorite motifs found in other pictures in this period. The little boats are almost the same as those in the Mount Vernon pictures. The tree technique is similar and the stitching of the church is related, although finer in craftsmanship. Euphemia waxes eloquent in her introduction of a colonial officer who is strolling under the trees with his lady love. She provides further interest by adding a hunter with his dogs. Sheep in clipped chenille upon the distant river bank, little swans and birds, are reminiscent of the earlier school of shepherdess designs.

The entire picture has been executed with skill, artistry and inventiveness. The usual stitches have been employed with one exception. The leaves on the large tree in the foreground have been worked in silk with a loose *S* or loop stitch, giving a breezy look to the composition. The careful use of colors and a variety of unusual greens provide charm and vitality and contrast luminously with the antique satin background. It makes a lovely wall decoration for the living room where it remains in company with other delightful examples of needlework made by the antecedents of the owner.

SILK FLOWER PICTURES

An eighteenth century vogue in European needlework included the stitching of many dainty panels of flowers gracefully arranged in Watteau-esque clusters and bowknotted with ribbons embroidered in pastel silk. Inevitably this passion reached America in the course of time, and our 1800's found shepherdess bouquets worked in the same technique as the Moravian flowers but grouped in a handful rather than distributed in a garland festoon around the border as taught by the Bethlehem school.

Two early and very lovely silk on satin flower pictures of this type were made by Mrs. Jeremiah Mason of Massachusetts, between the years of 1775 and 1828. Their pastel coloring is as delicate and charming as the draughting and stitchery. The usual American flowers drawn, no doubt, directly from the owner's garden, are represented in the tulip, carnation, morning glory, rose, sweet pea, the modest violet and the honeysuckle, shaded with particular delicacy.

Of the same period is a group of posies arranged and stitched in the same manner, which comes from the American Collection of the Essex Institute in Salem, Massachusetts. It was embroidered by Miss Maria Cheever, daughter of Captain James W. Cheever. Worked in her girlhood, about 1795, the composition is almost identical in character with that of the Mason needlework although the flowers are different. It is beautifully worked in the most delicate coloring.

Equally lovely is an oval silk-embroidered flower picture made about 1830 which comes from the family of Mrs. Frank Burroughs of Chicago, Illinois, and Stonington, Connecticut. Like many other early American embroideries which come from the West or Middle West, it was inspired by or made in the East, and is a memento of the migration from the old colonial homesteads to the then wild West. Descendants from this pioneer American stock are responsible for the revival throughout the Middle and Far West of an interest in needlework as strong as that displayed by needleworkers of like descent in the Eastern States.

From Elizabeth Anne Barker, designer of the engraved embroideries, comes another work of different quality and in the fashion of the preceding pictures. She has clustered her bouquet into a basket, a very original conception for her time, combining woven chenille stitches with the silk. She has taken another liberty in piling up a finely shaded silk mound much in the manner of the memorial sampler technique, thereby placing this picture pretty close to 1800. It is lovely in color, dainty and quaint in effect and nicely stitched.

Leaving the garden we go to sea with the embroideries of beloved sailing vessels also worked in this period.

SHIPS AND NARRATIVE PICTURES

Silken sails stitched on satin seas with waves smooth as the material of which they are made, grace the pictures made by two persons who loved these embroidered ships dearly and wished to perpetuate them in some artistic form. Here they are, still bearing their sails and masts proudly aloft, as good as new. One is "The Abby Bacon." She was formerly the "Barque Pocahontas" which was built in Salem in the 1850's. She was embroidered in the silk picture by her great admirer, Sailor Merrill of Salem, Massachusetts, while she lay at the Wall Street wharf. There is a painted picture of her today in the Lee Mansion at Marblehead. This interesting ship picture now rides at anchor in the harbor of the Essex Institute in Salem and her American flag still flies in the sky as patriotically as she did 83 years ago. A proud sailor's masterpiece!

The other ship picture is in the Metropolitan Museum of Art and was embroidered in America between the eighteenth and nineteenth centuries. The picture portrays the town of Londonderry, England, which has been painted on the satin background in water colors. The ship, pointed homeward toward America, has been embroidered in silks in tans, browns and white, with an outlining in black. The waves are worked in the same tones, while the sky indicates good weather ahead in its clear blues which are hand-painted.

Narrative pictures became popular a little later carrying an impetus into the mid-nineteenth century. Large areas of canvas were elaborately covered with cross-stitched pictures of every conceivable romantic subject.

"Cornelia and the Gracchi," previously noted as a subject popularized by the painter, Angelica Kauffman, combines with its silk embroidery the additional technique of velvet work. This material has been inlaid on sections of the satin and indicates a later period of execution. It was worked by Mrs. Lydia Very of Salem, Massachusetts, at the age of sixteen, while attending Mrs. Peabody's School. It is now in the Essex Institute collection. The draperies have been worked with care and understanding, the figures ably drawn. The composition is fairly well arranged, and was probably copied from an engraving or painting. The portraits are very well painted, almost professional in their rendering. It is possible that a more experienced hand assisted in this part of the work. It has been said that little miniatures were painted and sold

separately by traveling artists for this purpose with different poses of heads and arms dictated by the taste of the embroiderer.

Highly romantic, dramatic and most effective in costuming and composition is the embroidered silk picture "Done by Ann Conrad, in the year of our Lord, 1829," and portraying "Edward the 4th King of England and Elizabeth Gray Imploring the Restoration of her Husband's Estate." Court subjects became the fashion about this period and included pictures of presentations, and other episodes pertaining to the throne. The history of foreign countries became attractive to women who had spent long years concentrating upon the homeland. It was restful to allow one's mind and thoughts to attend these functions which means would not actually permit.

Most of the embroidery in this picture has been worked in satin stitch, and long and short stitch, the silks varying between brown, tans and golds. Pastel shades of blue and red in the billowy redingote costume of Elizabeth Grey afford a contrast. This gown is particularly interesting in its reflection of the day's fashions. The embroidered roses edging the redingote are characteristic. The dogs have been done exceedingly well and the touches of spangles or gold-metal dots show a new note in needlework introduced in the middle nineteenth century. With very able hand-painted portraits to complete the capable stitchery, this picture is a creditable example of a Philadelphia girl's ability in her chosen field.

A unique and rare example of silk needlework in a Connecticut collection of antiques is an early diploma of a famous school conducted for the education of the daughters of prosperous Americans. It was established in Litchfield, Connecticut, by Miss Sarah Pierce, who opened the school "for the instruction of females" in the year 1792. It has a brilliant historical background, being the first school in the country for the higher education of young women. Students came from nearly every state in the Union, from sections of Canada, the West Indies and other distant countries. They traveled by stage coach or horseback, riding on a pillion behind their fathers. Such difficult traveling required courage, endurance and a great desire for cultural development.

The diploma was, to all appearances, cut out

1. *Courtesy of:* THE METROPOLITAN MUSEUM OF ART, New York.

2. *Courtesy of:* THE ESSEX INSTITUTE, Salem, Massachusetts.

3. *Courtesy of:* THE ESSEX INSTITUTE, Salem, Massachusetts.

5. *Courtesy of:* MRS. FRANK BURROUGHS MULFORD, Chicago, Illinois.

4. *Courtesy of:* MRS. RAYMOND LEFFERTS, New York.

6. *Courtesy of:* MRS. GORDON K. BELL, New York.

1. Silk embroidered ship picture on satin with water color painting. 18th and early 19th century, America. 2. Silk embroidered ship picture made by Sailor Merrill. About 1855. Salem, Massachusetts. 3. Silk on satin flower embroidery by Mary Cheever, worked when she was a girl. About 1795. Massachusetts. 4. Silk embroidered flower picture by Elizabeth Anne Barker, great-great-grandmother of Mrs. Raymond Lefferts, about 1800, New York. 5. Silk embroidered flower picture on satin; about 1830. Illinois. 6. Pair of silk on satin embroidered flower pictures by an ancestor of Mrs. Gordon K. Bell, Mrs. Jeremiah Mason; 1775—1828. Massachusetts.

1. *Courtesy of:* THE ESTATE OF THE LATE MRS. HENRY P. MOSELEY, California.

Mt. Vernon embroidered picture worked in chenille, silks; and painted sky, by Abigail Parker Noyes (Mrs. Henry Perkins), at Miss Patten's Boarding School in Hartford, Connecticut, 1812.

2. *Courtesy of:* MEMORIAL HALL, Deerfield, Massachusetts.

Mount Vernon embroidered silk on satin picture by Caroline Stebbins, 1804, while student at Deerfield Academy, Massachusetts. Donor, George Sheldon.

3. *Courtesy of:* MISS ANNA CULBERT, Conn.

Silk embroidered picture on satin worked in 1853 by Euphemia J. Acheson of New York.

4. *Courtesy of:* MRS. RAYMOND LEFFERTS, New York.

The "Monument of General Daisey" Silk embroidery on satin. After an engraving in steel tones, touches of water color for fine lines. About 1800 by Elizabeth Anne Barker, New York.

5. *Courtesy of:* MRS. RAYMOND LEFFERTS, New York.

Embroidery in steel engraving style with silks on satin, water colors, supplement stitches. Worked about 1800 by Elizabeth Anne Barker, New York.

and sewed under a piece of satin, then embellished further with borders of delicate flower embroidery in pale silks. A final border-frame around the square was formed of black lacework stitchery about an inch wide. Under the small circle in the center, where the engraved figure of the young lady studying a globe has been applied, is worked in chenille embroidery the phrase, "Merit Wins the Prize." This original conception made about 1800 in Litchfield, Connecticut, was the needlework of Charlotte Sheldon, a daughter of Dr. Daniel Sheldon, a physician who was prominent in the affairs of the state.

THE "MORUS MULTICAULIS" MANIA

It is still a question whether the materials employed by the many needleworkers of this age were obtained from abroad or if many silks might not have been a product of the great effort made by Americans in both North and South during the seventeenth century and on through the eighteenth, to grow, spin, and reel silk. Individuals in North Carolina, Georgia and Virginia attempted to perfect this industry and did achieve some success in its cultivation. Purrysburg in South Carolina was the scene of considerable activity among the Swiss immigrants to this community. Some years after the failure of the Purrysburg effort Charleston saw the establishment of a silk reeling industry. This venture was made possible by a grant from the legislature.

Heretofore raw silks had been sent to England and reeled, the colonists concentrating primarily upon its cultivation. In the eighteenth century many individuals were raising silk and women showed much ability in this field. The daughter of a colonial governor of South Carolina, Mrs. Eliza Pinckey, was so adept at silk raising that she took some to England in 1755 and, according to Mrs. Frances Little, "from it made three dresses" one of which "was presented to the Princess Dowager of Wales, a second to Lord Chesterfield, and the third, it is said, to her daughter, Mrs. Horry of Charleston." A silk-net wedding veil made and worn by Martha Harness of Moorefield, Virginia, on June 17, 1817, was also a domestic product. The silkworms were grown on the plantation and the little bride reeled the silk, spun the fine thread and netted it into the delicately meshed veil which, tubular in form, entirely enveloped her figure.

Various accounts of the American silk industry refer to the accomplishments of other women who spun their own silk. Silk thread for sewing was made in the state of Massachusetts about 1800. Mulberry trees were raised by that time in numerous states, due to the activity of Dr. Stiles, President of Yale College, who sent mulberry seeds all over the country. To arouse further interest, he appeared at a commencement in the year 1788 wearing a black silk gown sewn and woven from Connecticut silk. Cultivation of the trees was attempted in Connecticut, Maine, Vermont, Massachusetts, Rhode Island, New Jersey, Delaware and Pennsylvania. In the last state the Moravians were busy with silk cultivation, encouraged by their former experiences in South Carolina and Georgia. In Lancaster County the Quakers were represented by the accomplishments of Susannah Wright, who had achieved the honor in 1770 of having her silk made into a court gown for England's Queen.

Benjamin Franklin promoted the industry in the late eighteenth century by raising funds for reeling silk in Philadelphia mills.

Bounties were established in different communities to aid in the raising of good silk. National enthusiasm grew by leaps and bounds. In Savannah, Georgia, a revival of earlier efforts persisted, and in Kentucky sewing silk was manufactured. By 1830 the manufacture of fringes, silk trimmings and the like for use in needlework had been added to the making of sewing silk. The year 1831 contributed braids, ribbons and silk plushes, as well as broad loom fabrics. These novelties were made possible through the Mansfield Company in Connecticut, the looms of Joseph Pepka in Manayunk, Pennsylvania, William H. Forstman in Pennsylvania, the Monotogul Mill in Boston, Massachusetts, and many others.

Further progress was achieved through the enterprise of Samuel Ryle, termed the "Father of the Silk Industry." It was he who took over the management of the Paterson silk center and made it prosperous. This center was founded by Christopher Colt, Jr., who had turned from interests in Hartford, Connecticut, to the weaving of silk in New Jersey. Here in 1839 were introduced Paterson's first broad-silk looms, which were a product of the talent and ingenuity of Samuel Ryle.

In the same decade, around 1834, the four Cheneys, Rush, Ward, Frank and Ralph, became interested in the culture of silk and later, in the year 1838, started the Mt. Nebo Silk Mills in South Manchester, Connecticut, giving birth to the first phase of what became in later years the great silk industry of the Cheney Brothers. Here in this first factory silk was reeled and other processes started. Furthering these interests and broadening their enterprise, the Cheneys purchased lands in Georgia, Florida and New Jersey for the purpose of raising silk, and upon them planted their own mulberry trees. Finally they became so engrossed in silk culture that they closed the mill, abandoned the weaving, and moved to Burlington, New Jersey, to take charge of their silk plantations and the large cocooneries.

By 1840 the peak of general interest was reached. Chinese mulberry trees were imported into the country in quantities and grew rapidly. From New England to Florida, the silk raising mania spread. It became the chief topic of conversation and the leading speculation for numbers of prominent citizens. Then suddenly the bubble burst. The panic of 1837, the gradual introduction into the American product of "a little mixture of foreign silk," the persistent difficulties in cultivating the mulberry tree, all may have contributed to the collapse of silk culture.

That we have such a large representation of silk pictures in this period is possibly due to the patriotic impulse of every young lady and matron to use the materials made in their native land. The same patriotic motive may account in part for the fact that the national emblem, the eagle, is represented as holding in his beak a wreath of silk flowers; the country would foster the flowering of the industry through the support and thoughtful effort of its women.

CHAPTER XIV

EMBROIDERED MAPS AND NEEDLEWORK RUGS

"Eternal Truth! beyond our hopes and fears,
Sweep the vast orbits of thy myriad spheres!
From age to age, while History carves sublime
On her waste rock the flaming curves of time,
How the wild swayings of our planet show
That worlds unseen surround the world we know."

OLIVER WENDELL HOLMES.

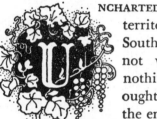

NCHARTED SEAS AND UNMARKED territories meet the eye, the South and the North are not what they now are; nothing seems what it ought to be according to the embroidered map of the United States made by Eliza Jones in 1810.

This was the period when silks on satin were popular for needlework and Miss Jones used her threads very well, adding a lyrical garland of chenille and silk flowers around what appears to be, at first sight, the thirteen original states. Ohio and Indiana are represented, however; Kentucky, Tennessee, and East and West Florida occupy all the land along the Mississippi. Louisiana is among those missing, East Florida taking her place in this record. Eliza Jones must have learned her geography pretty well, for all the states and their principal cities are lettered in stitchery. Even if there was comparatively little territory to cover, it was probably a pretty big world for her to embroider. Mrs. Francis D. Brinton owns the original and it is presumably a Quaker work from Pennsylvania.

Maps in embroidery which began to appear about the end of the eighteenth century, are impressive primarily because they record boundary lines and names of towns which have been changed or completely lost. Comparatively few examples made in this country have come to light. Those known seem to have been worked principally in the nineteenth century.

A map of North America stitched on satin with silks bears the title, worked on a scroll, "North America, Sarah Willis, New Bedford, 1803." Embroidered roses and morning glories are entwined about it. The map, very accurately copied in engraved stitch, is a reminder of how widely the United States has expanded since 1800. The tract of Louisiana extends almost the entire length toward the northwest. "New Albion" occupies California's place and Washington, Oregon and other far western states do not exist. The area called "Western Territory" extends above the Ohio River to the Mississippi and the Great Lakes. Illinois is mentioned only as a river. There is no mention of the state of Michigan. Canada extends above the St. Lawrence River only, its boundary line stopping short of the Great Lakes. In this small section is lettered the title, "Lower Canada." "New Britain occupies all land either side of Hudson Bay." "New South Wales" is at the lower western end, to the left of the Bay, and "North Wales" is the name applied to northwestern land on the opposite side. These sections have no

boundary lines and apparently are divided only
by the small rivers which have been very carefully stitched. All the western part of America,
including California, makes one big sweep of
territory without a break until it meets the
dividing line of Louisiana, which extends as far
north as Lake Winnipeg in the section now
known as Canada. This very fine example of
map embroidery is owned by Mrs. Patten of
New Jersey.

A rare map of the world was made in New
England in 1802 by A. Mather, said to have
been descended from Cotton Mather of early
New England history. It is embroidered with
very fine black silk thread on white silk in the
"engraving manner." The two hemispheres of
the New and Old World are beautifully worked
and. the geographical boundary lines of North
America are exceedingly interesting, as are the
names of the countries. As in the North American map there are no states beyond the Mississippi River; all the section is named "Louisiana." California is called "New Navarra."
Southern California and the Central American
States are incorporated under one name, "New
Spain." There are very delightful decorations
added in the four corners; little lunettes in
stitching, after the manner of engravings, depict
Asia, Africa, America and Europe. These are
charming in design detail. The panel measures
fifteen-and-a-half inches by twenty-eight-and-a-
half inches.

From the famous collection of samplers
owned by Mrs. Henry E. Coe, of New York,
comes the embroidered map sampler by Elizabeth Ann Goldin. It varies considerably from
the two already described in that geographical
and historical facts have been added to the map
in the sampler manner. The information recorded is as follows:

LAKE ERIE IS THE CELEBRATED SCENE OF
   PERRY'S VICTORY
OVER A BRITISH FLEET, SEPTEMBER 10, 1813.

LAKE CHAMPLAIN IS CELEBRATED FOR THE
   VICTORY GAINED BY
MACDONOUGH OVER A BRITISH FLEET OF FAR
   SUPERIOR FORCE, SEPTEMBER 11, 1814.

LONG ISLAND IS THE MOST IMPORTANT ISLAND
   BELONGING
TO THE STATE OF NEW YORK, 140 MILES IN
   LENGTH AND FROM 10 TO 15 BROAD, CON-

TAINS THREE COUNTIES AND NUMEROUS
FLOURISHING TOWNS, POPULATION 7000.

POPULATION OF THE STATE OF NEW YORK IN
   1820 WAS 1,372,812.
ALBANY IS THE CAPITAL.

Here follows Ann's signature and the date,
May, 1829. All the counties of New York State
are lettered including "West-Chester" and two
on Long Island, "Queens" and "Soffolk."

A very interesting and unusual map of
"North and South America" as embroidered by
Frances Wade in Savannah, Georgia, in 1798,
shows an absence of countries in both conti-
nents. Only Mexico is printed in the Central
American section. Venezuela is called "Cuyan."
To the south of that country it is merely "Ama-
zons Country." The Guianas are also among
the missing and in their place extending below
along the Pacific Ocean a small area of land is
marked "Peru." Brazil occupies her usual place,
but she is smaller. Below her is Paraguay. Chile
is marked on the South Atlantic Coast with her
boundary lines extending all the way from the
lower end of South America to Peru on the
west coast, interrupted only by "Patagonia" and
a section named "Incultan."

North America also lacks certain familiar di-
visions. In the west, territory belongs only to
Louisiana and New Mexico. The United States
area is tiny, as outlined in Elizabeth Jones' map.
The only land marked Canada lies around the
western part of the Hudson Bay which has been
called "M Bay." Miss Fanny Bleecker Seaman
is the owner of this fascinating embroidery.

METHOD OF WORKING

A frame is usually necessary in making silk
and satin embroideries, so maps worked on
these materials would require the same mounting. This method permits a smooth, even appearance while working. Puckering and rough
surface on the thread would destroy the unity
of the needlework composition. Nothing must
interrupt the smooth, glassy lines which should
look as undisturbed as the surface of an un-
troubled sea.

Silk embroidery technique is a special study
and requires particular attention in the use of
stitch direction. Most stitches used on maps are
Kensington, cross-stitch, satin stitch, stem stitch

Map of North America; silk embroidery on satin, 1803,
by Sarah Willis, New Bedford.

Embroidered Sampler Map of New York State; worked
in cross stitch, stem stitch and outline stitch by Elizabeth
Ann Goldin, May 21, 1829.

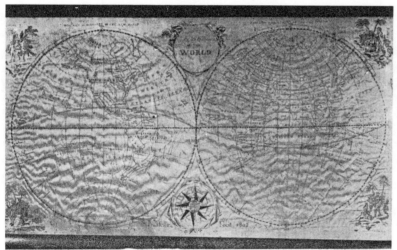

A "Map of the World"; embroidery in silk on satin, 1802. By A. Mather.
New England.

"A Map of the United States"; silk embroidered on satin, dated May 10, 1810. By Eliza
Jones, Pennsylvania.

Hand Embroidered Carpet Tambour. Stitched 1835 by Zeruah
Higley Guersney, Vermont.

2. *Courtesy of:* THE METROPOLITAN MUSEUM OF ART,
New York.

Turkey Work Rug: used as a bedcover, dated
and signed M. B., 1809. American.

3. *Courtesy of:* THE MEMORIAL HALL, Deerfield, Massachusetts.

Needlework Rug; Indian House built in 1698 at Deerfield, Massachusetts. 1845 by Arabella Stebbins, Sheldon Wells, Massachusetts.

4. *Courtesy of:* THE METROPOLITAN MUSEUM OF ART, New York.

Embroidered Carpet; cross stitched on canvas, 1812 by
Ann and Sophie Moore and Harriet Hicks, Champlain,
New York.

and outline stitch. Materials are linen embroidered with wools or silk thread, and satin embroidered with silk. The Mather Map shows the use on its white satin background of an exceedingly fine black silk thread nearly as delicate as the sewing silks used today for everyday use. It carries the look of an old engraving or etching, which was the intention.

NEEDLEWORK RUGS

The famous "Caswell Carpet" is probably one of the most delightful and extraordinary examples of early embroidered rugs made in America. It was tambour stitched in 1835 by Zeruah Higley Guernsey, who later became Mrs. Caswell White. The design is naïve in some respects, and there exists a quality reminiscent of old Persian paintings of flowers and birds, or early patterns on textiles from India. It is not entirely unsophisticated. Eighteen squares, each worked separately, have been joined to make a carpet which measures twelve feet wide by thirteen-and-one-half feet long.

METHOD OF WORKING

The technique used in the embroidery is the same as the method of working the tambour stitches on net described in Chapter XII, the only difference being in the use of coarser materials. The chain stitch effect is the same. Each of Zeruah's squares was worked on a tambour or other large frame, placed on two tables or chair tops.

MATERIALS

This example was made upon a coarse homespun foundation and the wools came from Zeruah's own sheep. Every step, shearing, carding, spinning and dyeing the woolen threads, was performed with her own hands. A large wooden needle was made for the stitchery by her father, it is said, who made spinning wheels and other kindred equipment professionally.

DESIGN

The general colorings are deep brown, sage green blending to a lighter shade of the same tone toward yellow, rose pinks, and pale brick reds toning into deeper cherry red. Blues in the royal range, deep brown gold, yellow gold, beige, cream, and pale, off-white also appear. The black background has faded to a brownish black, some squares have changed to a green black and others are of a deep wood tone, a shade often seen in the early East Indian textile prints. Every square is treated in different patterning. The designs have been well composed individually and each odd flowering plant has its own definite character and coloring. The leaves are all unlike and, rhythmically placed in their square areas, produce a highly decorative effect. Some squares remind one of the old botany prints of the era which may have been the inspiration for them. A pair of doves, resting in the flowering branches of one square, is poetic in its consideration of line. Father and Mother, in another square, might easily have changed places with Persian characters similarly rendered in their miniature painting. A pair of peacocks stitched under a flowering bush resemble early Indian painting in execution and design.

It is claimed that two young Indians of the Patawatomi tribe who were studying in the Castleton Medical College, resided for a while with the Guernsey family. The young men were considered guests of the town and so interested were the townsfolk in helping them through college that they took turns in boarding them. While Zeruah worked on her squares, the Indians, it is said, took a hand at designing two squares which are marked with their initials.

Two other squares bear a resemblance in design to early Victorian themes in the use of glass urns filled with fruit upon a table. One is in the section placed nearest the hearth and was removable in the winter in order that sparks from the fireplace might not ruin the precious needlework.

Pussies on their mats of blue and white occupy two squares. Two Manx cats in their tawny colorings are stitched on other squares against striped backgrounds. Around the corner is a pair of pet puppies. Shells have been introduced amusingly; also the crowing cock. Beneath the signature and date section is a flowering heart.

This is a work expressing in every embroidered inch a love of home and all nature about it. Although over a hundred years old, it still retains effectively its soft, warm colorings and charm. The late Mr. Homer Eaton Keyes was its appreciative possessor.

An appliqué rug from the home of Mrs. N. Stanton Gates in Mystic, Connecticut, is a very early example of this type of needlework. It is a small dresser rug for the bedroom and was made about 1840, when the application of cloth on cloth became attractive to American women. It was a thrifty mode, for the little colored patches with which the flowers were made were cut from old materials. These were usually pretty good fabrics, often hand-woven and worth needleworking into interesting colorful patterns for rugs. This example has the brightly colored materials appliquéd to a dark woolen cloth foundation with buttonhole stitches. In four corners may be seen the raised clipped-wool motifs which have been worked in the same manner as the Deerfield rug made by Arabella Stebbins Sheldon Wells, about 1845.

This rug presents a picture of the old Sheldon homestead with its overhanging first story, built in 1698 and called Indian House in Deerfield. The rug, presented to the Memorial Hall in Deerfield by the brother, George Sheldon, has an odd technique. It was made of narrow strips of cloth stitched to the foundation with the top edge turned outward, giving it a deep pile. A large, thick homemade wool fringe borders the rug picture.

From the same collection is a rug designed and made by "Little Mary" Hawks. A red broadcloth coat, which belonged to William Bloddard Williams, has been used for the background of the fine wool-embroidered flowers, executed in the soft colorings of morning glories and roses. The leaves are in the sage greens and go very well with the red, which is not unlike Chinese red. Carrie Gale Chapin of Cleveland, Ohio, presented this historic example to Deerfield's Memorial Hall.

A few examples of Turkey-work rugs, used as bed coverings and later as rugs and vice versa, remain. The nineteenth century example from the Metropolitan Museum of Art measures approximately twelve by fifteen feet. It is signed and dated M. B. 1809, and was used as a bedcover. It has been worked with wools using about eight to ten strands when stitched through and puffed, then clipped on the surface to give a rich pile. The background is black wool. The large flower motifs measure approximately eighteen by twenty-four inches. Each is worked in the following colors: deep rose, henna, tan, peach and cream leaves; yellow, green, pale and deep apple-green centers; the border outside on the left is taupe with black on the opposite side; the vase is worked in cream with sage green outlining both it and the flowers; the sage-green leaves are outlined in blue green, cream and yellow. This is a handsome work of a type exceedingly rare.

From York Village, Maine, comes a unique and equally precious Turkey-work bedcover. Its original border is gone and the remaining square measures five by five-and-a-half feet. It is designed upon much the same principles as the preceding example only the florals have been carried out on a smaller and more compact scale and not clipped. It is now used as a rug in the York Museum, but Miss Elizabeth Perkins states: "No one must walk on it."

Another embroidered carpet worked in tambour stitch in 1844 is similar to the Caswell Carpet in that squares have been worked separately and used later for a carpet. The design in these units is less simple in construction and line, the general composition reflecting the nineteenth century trend toward more realistic elaboration and fulsomeness. The immediate environment in Canton, New York, where it was made, is reflected in the bouquets of flowers, the cattle and the game birds. In the typical romantic trend of the age, Mrs. Miner has introduced far-away European ideas in some of her designs. For example a hunter in Moyen Age costume, derived, no doubt, from a tapestry, is driving a frothing bull in front of his white steed. The motif of shepherd with his shepherdess has been borrowed from the silk-on-satin embroidery designs prevalent a little earlier. Other inconsistencies occur but the whole is delightfully arranged and only a professional critic might note the unrelated themes. The general impression is that of rich colorings and great charm. It is a rare specimen in technique. Mrs. Fanney E. Wead is the owner.

A very engaging Pennsylvania Dutch carpet embroidered about 1825 is in the collection of Mrs. J. Insley Blair. It is about five feet by two and is worked in cross-stitch with a design very like those used by this group on their embroidered towels. What may be conventionalized peacocks or geometric drawings of pompous pigeons border the edges from which many conventional trees and potted plants are rising toward the center.

A cross-stitch carpet worked on canvas of great size, eighteen by fifteen feet, is the nineteenth century example belonging to the Metropolitan Museum of Art. The design carries the Greek fret motif popular in the decoration of the day. Innumerable shells are stitched on either side in scattered spacing. The entire center simulates interlacing brocade ribbons of French origin which were made and used in this period. The burlap strips after being cross-stitched were sewn together and after that the separate border was added.

This rug was made by Ann and Sophie Moore and Harriet Hicks, begun in 1808 and completed in 1812. Ann and Sophie were the daughters of Judge Pliney Moore and the rug was made for the drawing-room floor of his house in Champlain, New York, where it remained from 1812 to 1825. A stair carpet was made to match the rug; also a fireside rug measuring six feet by two, which shows a hound in pursuit of a deer. Both rugs have a Greek fret border like the drawing-room rug.

Needlework rugs had been made in Europe prior to the eighteenth century. In America they were made in that century and up to the middle of the nineteenth century, the high period being in the early 1840's. After this manufactured rugs became more numerous and the urge to stitch for beauty's sake was all that remained. Hooked rugs were quicker and easier to accomplish, and they became popular. With ease of execution the art of needlework declined into a handicraft which produced myriads of spotty scatter rugs, hooked from remnants of the family leftovers or made as a hobby when time hung too heavily. The earliest examples showed the finest qualities artistically. Later works being mostly copies of the earlier examples were less inspired and consequently had less character.

METHOD OF WORKING

The technique of making these rugs varies from the early Turkey-work described in Chapter VII, to the tambour-stitched carpets using heavy doubled "threads" in large wooden needles employed as in the lacework technique and treated in detail in Chapter XIII. A tambour frame was used for the rugs, or any other frame of convenient size. The method, of course, includes first the use of the Oriental chain stitch and then the cross-stitch, followed in turn by hooking, a technique not usually referred to as embroidery.

Drawings of the design, which was usually original, were most often applied to materials such as homespun linen, canvas or a coarse burlap, as in the method used for quilting, with charcoal as the main draughting medium. The system of paper-pricking transfer was sometimes adopted as in the lacework method, only on a larger scale, the patterns being worked onto the canvas in sections.

Threads were whatever came to hand, depending upon the accessibility of towns or cities. Almost everything has been used, from cloth strips of all types to yarns and flax, and applied with ingenuity in stitchery and design.

CHAPTER XV

EMBROIDERED COATS OF ARMS, BANNERS, FLAGS; FLAG PRESERVATION

"When Freedom from her mountain height
Unfurled her standard to the air,
She tore the azure robe of night,
And set the stars of glory there.
She mingled with its gorgeous dyes
The milky baldric of the skies,
And stripéd its celestial white
With-streakings of the morning light;
Then from his mansion in the sun
She called her eagle bearer down
And gave into his mighty hand
The symbol of her chosen land."

JOSEPH RODMAN DRAKE.

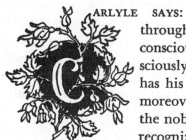

ARLYLE SAYS: "IT IS IN AND through symbols that man consciously or unconsciously lives, moves and has his being. Those ages, moreover, are accounted the noblest which can best recognize symbolical worth and prize it at the highest." Down through the long ages there is a pennant streaming against the blue, a flag flying, calling for sacrifice and high endeavor, topping all effort, a symbol of man's ideals. It illuminates the way in which man would travel along the highway of time. Through it, he would match the pattern of his existence nearer to the ideal woven with spirit into the standard for which he would give his life, his all.

Into these emblems have gone the thought and purpose of countless women who have stitched each part and portion, worked the mottoes and legends, helped in their designs so that the symbols would reflect a truly inspiring meaning. Needlework has played an important part in this symbology; it has expressed abstract motifs with decorative feeling and warm color. As in other countries, America's story has been told symbolically in her many colorful flags and banners.

AMERICAN FLAGS AND BANNERS

The earliest record of a flag symbolizing the union of colonies in the New World was the flag of New England. Made in 1686, it was received from England's King during the administration of Sir Edmond Andros. The emblems were the Cross of St. George and the King's Colors at the time, borne on a white field. The center of the Cross was emblazoned with a yellow or gilt crown over the cipher of the sovereign. The Union Jack was ordered for the merchant service of American ships in 1701 and replaced the former New England emblem.

A later New England symbol was the pre-Revolutionary Pine Tree Flag, needleworked with a design of a green tree upon a white ground. It represented, according to the legend it bore underneath the tree, "An Appeal to Heaven," a phrase quoted from the closing sentence of a document sent by the provincial congress of Massachusetts to Great Britain, appealing for justice to the colonies. The flag was used by the Navy in 1775 and the next year was adopted by the Massachusetts council as its symbol for the sea service, signifying freedom. An early New Hampshire flag made its protest at the same time, with the embroidered inscription:

LIBERTY PROPERTY AND NO STAMPS.

A pre-Revolutionary flag from New York has a beaver embroidered in its center and a small tree. The design symbolizes the fur trade.

Most of the flags of the Revolutionary period were made of homespun and used the thirteen stars and thirteen stripes in the design, but it was not until 1777 that the standardized flag appeared throughout the colonies. The first American flag is said to have been made by Mrs. John Ross, popularly known as Betsy Ross. The house where the first Stars and Stripes were sewn together is in Philadelphia, at 239 Arch Street. Records state that in June, 1776, a committee of Congress composed of Colonel Ross and Robert Morris, with General Washington, called upon Mrs. Ross, who was an upholsterer, and engaged her to make the flag. It is said that General Washington was familiar with Mrs. Ross' skill with the needle for "she embroidered his shirt ruffles for him" prior to his receiving command of the army. Mrs. Ross made a rough sketch of the flag, based upon their suggestions, which was revised by General Washington. When the gentlemen asked if she could execute the final design, she replied: "I don't know whether I can, but I'll try," immediately "suggesting that the design was wrong, the stars being six-cornered, not five-cornered or pointed." This was attended to and the Star-Spangled Banner finally created. It was put in general use soon after the Declaration of Independence. Beginning in 1794 a star was sewn into the flag for each new state added to the Union.

Other flags followed in quick succession. The famous embroidered banner used by Count Pulaski of the continental army, who later became a general, was made by the Moravian Sisters as a tribute and presented to him in 1778. He had been wounded in the Battle of Brandywine. The Moravian Sisters at Bethlehem nursed him back to health and when he organized a corps of cavalry, they prepared a beautiful banner of crimson silk with designs embroidered by them and sent it to him with their blessing. This event has been commemorated by Longfellow. The banner was received by General Pulaski with grateful appreciation and he carried it through his battles until he fell at Savannah in 1779. The banner was rescued by his first lieu-

tenant. The lieutenant, however, was badly wounded and delivered the flag to Captain Bentalon who, upon his retirement, carried it to his home in Baltimore, Maryland. It was used in the procession which welcomed Lafayette in 1824 and then it was ceremoniously retired to Peale's Museum. It now rests in a glass case under the care and watchful protection of the Maryland Historical Society. Although a tired banner, its spirited words are still strong and visible: "Unitas Virtus Forcier" ("Union makes valor stronger"). On the other side in the center is embroidered the all-seeing eye, and the words: "Non Alius Regit" ("No Other Governs").

A flag said to have been presented to Andrew Jackson by the ladies of New Orleans, January 8, 1815, shows a soaring eagle with a long pennant in his bill. The lettering upon it can hardly be seen now. About this scroll a garland of roses has been embroidered in silks; to the upper left is a scattered group of stars whose number must be significant. These are apparently silk-embroidered also. In the Civil War this flag was used by the Louisiana Regiment. It was captured at the Battle of Black River Bridge on May 17, 1863. The State of Illinois later returned it to New Orleans where it remains in the Museum collection of the Daughters of 1812.

A COAST ARTILLERY FLAG

In the Museum of the City of New York is hung an embroidered silk banner which in 1840 belonged to the 6th Company, National Cadets Artillery of New York. The royal-blue silk background serves to emphasize the silk and chenille embroidery of the symbols. The upper part of the cannon is worked in gold silks, the rest of the cannon in heavier brownish-gold chenilles. The guardsmen's jackets are embroidered in chenille above very white trousers. Their portraits are painted. The flags which they carry match the jackets. The eagle is shaded and stitched in various browns, golds, and tan chenille threads while the New York seal has a plain silk background against which the small brown leaves have been embroidered in chenille. Against the stacked rifles at the right is hanging a knapsack initialed, presumably by the embroiderer, C. G.

This banner is characteristic of the period in which it was embroidered. The whiskers, mustaches and sideburns of the gallant guardsmen, as well as the design of the uniforms, reflect the mode. It is a proud and triumphant symbol of the 1840 Cadets. It was inherited from his father by Mr. De Lancey Kountze who has loaned the banner to the Museum for exhibition.

THE STATE OF LOUISIANA PELICAN FLAG

The Pelican flag, silk-embroidered on silk and now in the Louisiana State Museum, was made during the Civil War period. The emblem was adopted in December, 1860, upon the occasion of a general demonstration in New Orleans over the secession of South Carolina. "One hundred guns were fired, and the Pelican flag unfurled. The Southern Marseillaise was sung as the flag was raised amid reiterated and prolonged cheers for South Carolina and Louisiana." Its adoption as a state flag was later opposed, however, by a committee of the convention which "did not approve of the pelican as a symbol for the State of Louisiana," and reported the pelican as a bird, "in form unsightly, in habits filthy, in nature cowardly." Also they learned to their amazement from Audubon "that the story of the Pelican feeding its young with its own blood is gammon." The convention proceeded to adopt a flag of thirteen stripes, four blue, six white and three red; in the center was a pale yellow five-pointed star. General Beauregard wrote a letter to a friend in 1872 saying the significance of the devices was not apparent and that it was far inferior in beauty to the old national ensign.

The Pelican flag is a beautifully needleworked example of fine stitch direction especially in the laying of the silk-embroidered feathers. Possibly the thirteen spaces in the nest represent the thirteen colonies.

THE G. A. R. PHIL H. SHERIDAN POST 34 FLAG

This embroidered silk flag was made following the Civil War by a group of ladies in Salem, Massachusetts, who presented it to the G. A. R. Phil H. Sheridan Post 34. It is now in the collection of the Essex Institute. On one side of the heavy, ivory silk taffeta is embroidered the emblem of Post 34. On the other side the present seal of the State of Massachusetts forms the central design. The arms are worked in sapphire silks. An Indian figure dressed in shirt and moccasins has been worked in shades of tan, golds and brown. In his right hand is a bow and in his left an arrow, its point toward the base. On the left side of the Indian's head is a large star representing one of the United States of America. Underneath the crest a motto is embroidered on a ribbon scroll which reads:

ENSE PETIT PLACIDAM SUB LIBERTATE QUIETAM

This ancient motto is often quoted. It is the second of two Latin lines written several centuries ago in Copenhagen. The first line is "Manus haec inimica tyrannis." Several translations of both lines were made by John Quincy Adams. The version quoted at a lecture is as follows:

This hand, the rule of tyrants to oppose,
Seeks with the sword fair freedom's soft repose.

FLAG PRESERVATION NEEDLEWORK

One of the most romantic achievements recorded in the story of American needlework is the salvaging and preservation of the nation's tattered flags and banners. This distinctive work was originated by Mrs. Amelia Fowler, a Boston woman, an artist and an expert needlewoman, whose appreciation and love of American history had often been expressed in embroidered pictures and tapestries.

Before Amelia Fowler thought of preserving the great emblematic standards and flags of the nation she used to practice the art of embroidery outside the traditional dictates of the day's fashions. Very radically to some person's minds, no doubt, she turned from Berlin woolwork to creative effort and chose to make portraits of the Indians. The instinct for preservation was busy in her nature in many ways. Not only did she record impressions of the physiognomy of a vanishing race, but in doing so, she used all the antique silks collected and saved since her girlhood from skeins belonging to her grandmother in 1818.

METHOD OF PRESERVATION, STITCHERY

The method for the preservation of flags employed by Mrs. Fowler was devised by her at the request of the late Rear Admiral William Cary Cole, who was desirous of saving the historic flags of the Naval Academy. These flags included the ensign flown by the "Constitution"; the "Don't Give Up the Ship" flag which commemorates the command of Commodore Perry at the battle of Lake Erie; battle flags from the Revolutionary War, and others from before and after the Civil War. She experimented with many methods before she would attempt to work on one of the Naval Academy flags, and it was not until she had made a study of the famous tapestries exhibited at Bayeux that she received the inspiration which led to the adoption of the process which she has used with such success.

Mrs. Fowler decided that linen must be used as a foundation for the preservation of the flags. The question then arose of how to secure the tattered pieces of silk and bunting to such a background. All adhesive materials were found to make flags stiff and unreal; they lacked the qualities of permanence and flexibility which she wished to attain in her work. Finally she hit upon the plan of fastening the flag to the linen back with a peculiar stitch much like a wide, square, open buttonhole stitch. These stitches cover the entire surface of the flag with a hardly visible network of meshes made of thread dyed to conform to the colors of the flag no matter how faded or stained they may be. Where there are gaps or missing parts of the original, the needleworked threads are dyed to match the adjacent parts of the emblem, and complete the original design.

HISTORICAL FLAGS

When the restoration of one of the flags had been completed, Admiral Cole took the flag and the remains of Perry's famous battle flag before Congress, exhibiting the two side by side. When the members saw the restored flag in contrast to the dilapidated condition of the other, they were deeply affected and impressed by the beautiful work and speedily granted the necessary appropriation for the restoration by Mrs. Fowler of all the others in the collection at the Naval Academy.

One of the most treasured exhibits in the National Museum today is the original Star-Spangled Banner, the flag that Francis Scott Key saw flying above Fort McHenry from his position as a prisoner aboard a British ship in Baltimore Harbor, September 13 and 14, 1814, and which inspired him to write the words of our national anthem. Mrs. Fowler restored this flag at the Smithsonian Institution in 1914; singularly enough, this year marked the beginning of the World War. Over a million six-sided stitches were used and worked by many women helpers to secure the flag to its linen background, thus insuring its permanency for generations to come.

During her lifetime Mrs. Fowler also restored the battle flags of the State of Missouri which include emblems carried by Missourians during the Civil, Spanish, Mexican Border and World Wars. These preserved flags hang today in the halls of the State Capitol. One of her most cherished labors was the work upon the colors of the battleship "Maine," recovered after they had been within the sunken ship for ten years.

THE NEXT GENERATION

Working with Mrs. Fowler at the time of her death fifteen years ago, was her daughter, Katherine Fowler, wife of Thomas B. Richey, then Production Officer at the New York Navy Yard, Brooklyn. Mrs. Richey inherited the secret formula for the restoration of flags and had the additional advantage of many years of personal instruction in the art by her mother. Her studio consists of five rooms located at House D at the Brooklyn Navy Yard. Here is carried on the combination of art, heraldry and history expressed in needlecraft. Over two thousand flags, rich in lore and historical significance, have been preserved by Mrs. Richey since the death of her mother. The method, considered the best in the world, is now being imparted to Mrs. Richey's daughter and namesake, Katherine, in order that she may carry on the work.

Each flag that has come to Mrs. Richey for the prolongation of its existence, reincarnates the courage and valor of heroic men and deeds. Among them are the defiant banner of Texas which emboldened the spirits of the followers of Sam Houston at San Jacinto. When she received this flag it was so far gone that many of its pieces were not longer than one's thumb. When it was reconstructed there was found a beautifully painted figure of Liberty, a scroll and a sword, and over the sword the motto "Liberty or Death."

Other flags which live again through the artistry of her needle are the three hundred and seventy-five banners in the Boston State House. Because it would have required an act of the legislature to allow them to leave the state, Mrs. Richey had to do this work at the State House. On the other hand the flags of the State of New Jersey were shipped to her at San Francisco where Captain Richey was stationed at the time.

Banners of the Emperor and Dowager Empress of China taken by Americans during the Boxer Rebellion have been restored by Mrs. Richey; also a Korean banner sent by Admiral John Rogers to the mother of Lieutenant Hugh W. McKee, killed when the United States forces took the Korean fort in 1871; the flag used by the Twelfth Regulars when they went up San Juan Hill, and the flag used by the New York First Regular Volunteers in the Mexican War, 1846; the personal flag of General Pershing with four stars, which saw service through the World War; and a pre-Revolutionary flag of silk, embroidered with a beaver symbolizing the fur trade in early New York. One of the oldest of the flags she has worked upon is the Norfolk Borough flag, dated 1736, and owned by the Bennington Historical Society, Vermont, which the owners valued so highly that Mrs. Richey had to transport it personally to and from her studio.

Here is needlework of such skill and cleverness that it is unique in its own right; sought by governments and historical and patriotic societies, as well as individuals, it is a distinct contribution to the field of American embroidery.

HERALDIC EMBROIDERY HATCHMENTS, AND COATS OF ARMS

Other emblems equally idealistic and as frequently rendered in needlework are family coats of arms. Under the feudal and monarchistic systems of Europe, heraldic shields and crests were symbolical of family achievement and position.

Identification in this manner was equivalent to being placed in the Social Register or the "Who's Who" of the Middle Ages.

Hatchments (a corruption of the word achievements) were funeral devices bearing the coat of arms of the deceased. Since they indicated one's standing in the social scale it was considered of vital importance to display them at the funeral service.

> No trophee, sword nor hatchment o'er his bones,
> No noble rite, nor formal ostentation.

Thus Laertes in *Hamlet* laments the "obscure funeral" of his father.

In America many colonists retained their last mark of identification with Old World tradition in their family coat of arms. In New England there were evidently enough aristocratic inheritors of these emblems to warrant the advertisement of instructions for embroidering them. Or possibly the art appealed to those who not being entitled to such emblems still thought them a pleasant type of decoration which would give atmosphere to the new home. Since this style of needlework was in vogue in England in the eighteenth century, it is perfectly natural to find the fashion followed in Massachusetts. The *Boston Gazette* of May 16, 1757, contained the following announcement:

> To be taught by Jean Day at Mrs. Cutler's up William's Court, opposite Brazen-Head in Cornhill, viz. Dresden, Embroidery with Gold and Shell Work, Coats-of-Arms, Tent Stitch, and a Variety of other Work, all in the neatest, and newest Fashion. N.D., The above Mrs. Cutler takes in Young Ladies to Board.

A few years later, on May 1, 1769, the *Boston Chronicle* carried the advertisement of Amy and Elizabeth Cummings who

> Hereby inform the public that they have This Day opened their school for instructing young ladies in embroidery, Coats-of-Arms, Dresden, Catgut, all sorts of Colored Work, at their house on Cornhill, opposite Old Brick Meeting, where they have to see, a great variety of Goods suitable for the season. Also blue China and yellow ware.

Thirty-nine examples of registered coats of arms belonging to American families have been embroidered in this country. Most of them are from New England. There are doubtless others

1. *Courtesy of:* THE LOUISIANA STATE MUSEUM.

Embroidered Apron, Masonic Order, Scottish Rite. 1850-1860. New Orleans, Louisiana.

2. *Courtesy of:* THE LOUISIANA STATE MUSEUM.

Embroidered Apron with Pelican; Masonic Order. 1850-1860. New Orleans, Louisiana.

3. *Courtesy of:* THE ESSEX INSTITUTE, Salem, Massachusetts.

Embroidered Coat of Arms of the Curwen and Russell Family. Eighteenth century American. Massachusetts.

4. *Courtesy of:* THE LOUISIANA STATE MUSEUM.

Embroidered Priest's Vestment; from an old St. Martinsville Church. Early nineteenth century American.

5. *Courtesy of:* THE ESSEX INSTITUTE.

Embroidered Coat of Arms of the Fisk family by Lydia Phippen, wife Major General John Fisk, 1780, Massachusetts.

1. *Courtesy of:* THE DAUGHTERS OF 1812, Louisiana State Museum.

Andrew Jackson's Flag; silk embroidered. 1814. New Orleans, Louisiana.

2. *Photograph by courtesy of:* MRS. THOMAS B. RICHEY.

Pre-Revolutionary Flag of New York State; embroidered preservation by Katherine Fowler Richey.

3. *Courtesy of:* THE ESSEX INSTITUTE, Salem, Massachusetts.

Silk Embroidered Flag. G.A.R. Phil Sheridan Post 34, Massachusetts State Arms. Nineteenth century. By a group of ladies in Salem, Massachusetts.

4. *Courtesy of:* THE METROPOLITAN MUSEUM OF ART, New York.

Embroidered Hatchment of Arms; of the Isiah Thomas Family of Boston. 1749-1831.

5. *Courtesy of:* MRS. KATHERINE FOWLER RITCHEY.

Portrait of an Indian and His Horse; embroidered in antique silks by Mrs. Amelia Fowler, mother of Mrs. Richey, Massachusetts.

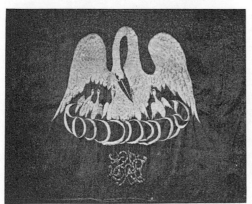

6. *Courtesy of:* THE LOUISIANA STATE MUSEUM.

The Pelican Flag of the State of Louisiana; embroidered in silk, 1860. New Orleans, Louisiana.

7. *Courtesy of:* MR. DE LANCEY KOUNTZE and THE MUSEUM OF THE CITY OF NEW YORK.

Embroidered Banner of the 6th Company National Cadets, National Guard Coast Artillery. 1840. New York.

in other sections of the country which have not yet found a place in the collections.

EXAMPLES OF EMBROIDERED HATCHMENTS

A hatchment bearing the arms of the family of Isaiah Thomas of Boston, of the 1749-1831 period, has been embroidered upon black satin with colored silk. The arms are worked in black and white. The helmet and the crest are blue and the mantling is in blue, red, white and tan worked mainly in chevron patterning, with silk twist in satin stitch. The hatchment is framed in an eighteenth century pearwood frame with gilded moldings and is in the collection of the Metropolitan Museum of Art.

The Curwen and Russell coats of arms in the Essex Institute at Salem are embroidered on cream satin with silk. This is an eighteenth century example of American needlework. The entire panel has been worked in plain satin stitches with the exception of the demi-unicorn at the top which is made with outline and backstitches in the engraving technique. A little water-color brushwork seems to have been used in its shadings.

The hatchments were square, but in most cases the coats of arms were placed cornerwise upon them so that when framed and hung upon the wall the top corner of the hatchment pointed toward the ceiling. Sometimes, however, the coat of arms has been embroidered in the square rather than the characteristic diamond position. Illustrating the square style is the embroidered coat of arms of Robert Hale Ives, made by Rebecca Ives Gilman in 1770 and owned by Mrs. Robert Hale Bancroft of Boston. Particular interest attaches to the shield, upon which the heads of three Moors are amusingly embroidered in silk.

METHOD OF WORKING

Coats of arms embroidered in America in the eighteenth century were usually placed on a frame of some sort. The patterns were drawn first upon paper and blocked off in squares, then transferred free hand to the satin, canvas (catgut) or other material. Sometimes the design was lightly sketched on with water color.

The ribbon or scroll band was frequently worked in cross or tent stitch (needlepoint) and the motto embroidered on it in black silk. In the best work, however, the entire design was executed in one stitch style. The earlier examples were worked exclusively in satin stitch. The embroidery was related in style to the early church or ecclesiastical needlework of European origin. Gold and silver threads were employed and applied to the background material of silk, velvet, satin, linen or canvas with couching stitches. Used also were long and short stitches, Kensington and split stitch.

EMBROIDERED RELIGIOUS SYMBOLS

Embroidered vestments, robes, aprons and accouterments used for religious and other ceremonies are represented in various collections and are of great beauty and interest. Not many of them were made in America, however; much has been imported from Europe.

Masonic emblems embroidered on the aprons used in their ceremonies in New Orleans between 1850 and 1860 are at present in the Louisiana State Museum. They show the elaborate Old World embroidery technique characteristic of that period. One was worn by Charles Tennent; another by the father of Charles Gayere; a third by A. Fanchier. Each has been embroidered with gold threads combining appliquéd materials with silks and small gold spangles or sequins. In one central design may be discovered the old Louisiana symbol of the pelican. Above is the cross with the word, "INRI" embroidered at its top. The canopy covering the group is appliquéd and embroidered. The background is satin.

Abstract symbols of the Masonic Order appear on the second apron. They are worked in silk threads, spangles and gold bullion. Apparently a pearl has been encased in the device above the square and compass. Within the triangle may be seen three Hebraic letters signifying God. At the very top is a five-pointed star encasing the initial G.

The third apron is embroidered very elaborately with silks on satin, using an eighteenth century design of the Master Masons Lodge. The apron is covered with abstract religious symbols significant to the Order: the initial G, four triangles, a six-pointed star on either side of the floral design. In the center an altar is approached by seven steps set in a mosaic pavement. Above the altar is a pair of compasses opened at 45°. In the center of the altar is a skull and crossbones on a black ground; above are the scales of Justice. The altar is supported by eight columns. On the left and right side are columns surrounded by flowers and beside each is a sprig of acacia. At the base of each column are Masonic emblems, including the trowel, the square, and the plumb. Over the top of one pillar is a blazing sun and over the other a moon and stars; at the top is embroidered the number 121. All of these motifs are needleworked in gold threads and fine silks with the application of a few sequins.

In the Louisiana Museum also is a priest's vestment from an old St. Martinsville Church, embroidered in the nineteenth century. Its rather simple lettering is surrounded by a design of religious symbols. In the center a cross has been beautifully worked, apparently in silks upon a heavy brocade. The needlework decoration which forms the outline of the cross has been chosen with great taste. It is finely and chastely embroidered.

Thus with hearts full of zeal American women, often with simple means, have managed to inspire the spirit by making manifest through emblems, the religious, patriotic or family ideals which they were intended to represent.

The Finding of Moses

Courtesy of: MRS. EUGENE LEVERING, JR., Baltimore, Maryland.

THE FINDING OF MOSES

A large needlepoint mural worked in small tent stitch or petit point, measuring fifty-nine by fifty-one inches. It was awarded first prize, a gold spoon, as a work of Fine Art in Embroidery by the Maryland Institute of Arts, Baltimore, when exhibited by Mrs. James A. Gary in Baltimore, after its completion in 1865.

PART IV

THE VICTORIAN ERA

CHAPTER XVI

NEEDLEPOINT PICTURES AND UPHOLSTERY

"Back of the canvas that throbs the painter is hinted and hidden;
Into the statue that breathes the soul of the sculptor is bidden;
Under the joy that is felt lie the infinite issues of feeling;
Crowning the glory revealed is the glory that crowns the revealing."

RICHARD REALF.

ENT STITCHERY, KNOWN AS TAPESTRY or needlepoint today, was used profusely throughout the nineteenth century. The country abounds in embroideries worked in needlepoint and the even more arduous cross-stitch which differs from needlepoint in that the stitches make a complete cross as against the half-cross used in needlepoint, necessitating a double coverage of the area. Our Victorian sisters intended that their work should possess solidity and permanence. The complete thoroughness with which they worked, the intensity with which they escaped into their dreams through the medium of their stitchery produced treasures that will endure for many years to come.

Although their art had to be applied, in most cases, to such trifling adornments as Algerian smoking caps for men or braided and embroidered Turkish effects for their feet, this was no detriment to these romantic ladies who lost themselves in fervor whatever the subject. Every spare moment in days and evenings extending over a period of years was devoted to the reproduction of historical episodes and scenes from the Bible. Here were sources of pure and vir-

tuous release. When all the household duties and other demands had been attended to, when the nineteen children had found their several beds, then the lady of the house forgot the fatigues and cares of the day by stitching romantic episodes while mind and heart traveled abroad into a world she was too poor or too busy to visit in person.

The making of needlepoint pictures was most extensively practiced in the middle of the nineteenth century, but it was by no means confined to this period.

NEEDLEPOINT PORTRAITS

From the eighteenth century until about 1830 needlepoint was used in embroidering portraits. Maintaining the popularity noted in the mourning samplers, George Washington ranked first as a needlework subject. Some of his portraits are very large, like that in the Louisiana State Museum which was made in the late eighteenth or early nineteenth century. No doubt the design was taken from a professional pattern since another example in raised woolwork, exhibited in the Jumel Mansion in New York City, is identical. The resemblance could not be accidental since the portrait is very elaborate and difficult to execute, not only because of its size but also because of the number of shades needed to reproduce the costume, draperies, furniture and so forth.

In the collection of the Concord Historical Society at Concord, New Hampshire, is another large portrait of General Washington, and a very good one, showing the head and shoulders. The patriotic border is original and effective in design. The whole is ably worked, the stitches on the portrait, the leaves in the border and the shields all being carefully studied and expertly rendered.

The portrait of Benjamin Franklin in the same collection shows the statesman in his library among books, maps and atlases, while outside through the window may be noted the lightning flashes which led him to the extraordinary discovery of electricity.

Henry Clay was another great personage sufficiently admired by the gentler sex to be immortalized in needlework. His portrait in the Louisiana State Museum suggests his interest in agriculture through the plow and the farm animals which appear in the background. Upon this scene, however, he turns his back with a gesture indicating his concern with world affairs, the latter symbolized by the flag draped across a globe.

ROMANTIC AND HISTORICAL SCENES

The popularity of needlepoint portraits began to decline toward the 1840's. Landscapes and Biblical scenes replaced them. Like the silk on satin pictures of the earlier period, these needlepoint pictures were often copies of paintings by contemporary artists. Whatever was fashionable in the art exhibitions was immediately reproduced in embroidery. The Hudson River School which turned from European scenes to glorify the American landscape; the tremendous canvases of Church and Bierstadt and Moran; historical scenes, particularly the well-known painting of Washington crossing the Delaware by Emanuel Leutz; the Italian villas of Frank Duveneck—all inspired the Victorian needleworkers.

Size meant nothing. When paintings were large, embroideries also were on a grand scale. When paintings became small again, so did the needlepoint pictures. These ladies were not to be outdone. Discouraged by the prevalent no-

tion that painting was a masculine pursuit, they covered their canvases with hustling needles nearly as swiftly as the men with their brushes, for this was the day when brush-strokes were carefully laid in to express every little detail of the scene depicted.

This needlepoint "painting" continued to be popular for more than three decades. In the late 70's Berlin work and scattered techniques finally dissipated the energies of the needlework artists.

"THE SICILIAN MAID"

This cross-stitch picture, made over one hundred years ago by a relative of Mrs. Frank T. Clark of Cheshire, Connecticut, was copied from a painting of the romantic school. The panel has been finely worked with intricate shading and tonal values softly blended and quaintly colored. Delicate rose and pink are cooled with Egyptian turquoise and colonial blues. The draperies on the costume are admirably rendered in deep to pale blue on the skirt, oyster whites and blue on the apron, highlighted with silk floss in stripes. The shawl in rose and browns is tenderly rendered and the portrait beautifully toned in flesh tints. High lights on the face are again accented by the use of silk floss in a little lighter key than the wool of the same shade. The water jar in rose and gold ochre is a rich note. It is silhouetted against a sky stitched and blended in the most delicate pastel shades from the palest blue tint at the top, through cream-white and oyster-pink tones into the palest orchid tint of the violet shades on the distant hills. All of the off-white scale is included. This color treatment gives much atmosphere and harmonizes well with the brownish pink walls of the ancient city. The costumes of the small boys are splendidly toned in soft gray green and reddish browns, offset with touches of antique turquoise blue. Altogether it is a "painting" in cross-stitch typical of the nineteenth century and most able in its technical expression and feeling. It measures twenty-seven by thirty-one inches.

"THE SCOTTISH CHIEFTAIN"

This picture was worked by the same needlewoman. The setting is the interior of a castle in Europe, also adapted from a painting of the

Large needlepoint portrait of Benjamin Franklin, American, about the late eighteenth century.

An early needlepoint portrait of General George Washington. Made about 1780, worker and locality unknown.

1. *Courtesy of:* THE CONCORD HISTORICAL SOCIETY, New Hampshire.

Portrait Head of George Washington; in needlepoint and cross stitch. Early nineteenth century, New Hampshire.

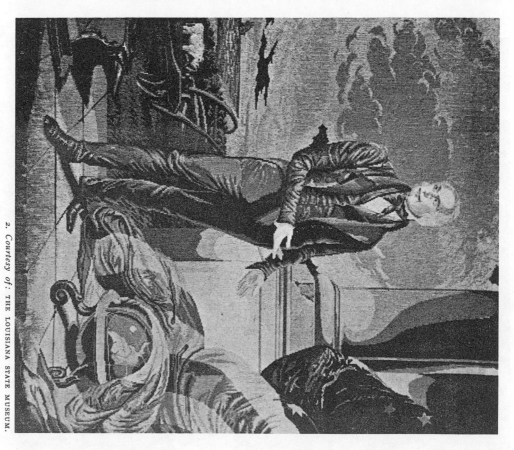

2. *Courtesy of:* THE LOUISIANA STATE MUSEUM.

Portrait of Henry Clay; needlepoint and cross stitch. Early nineteenth century, Louisiana.

day, and with the same careful attention to tone and shadings. The stitched rendering of the walls in tones of gray and beige browns is amazingly well done, as are the portraits, quite full in character and expression. The design is contained in a panel twenty by twenty-six inches. Chenille has been introduced in addition to silk floss and wool to give the needed quality to the hair and beard. The fur on the tunic border and the fluff of feathers on the beret or tam-o'-shanter have also been worked in cross-stitched chenille in varying shades. On the cape of the central figure at least five shades of white have been used, with cream-white silk as the highest light. In contrast to the crimson reds in the costume and the various cool grays in the walls the effect is quite handsome.

"MARY, QUEEN OF SCOTS"

This needlepoint "painting" has been worked upon a grand scale, measuring approximately six by five feet. It was made by Mary Rothmann, born in 1850 in New York City, who started to work on this wall piece at the age of eighteen. Her instructor was an artist whose name is unknown to the granddaughter who now owns the tapestry. Because of the young needleworker's talent, the artist requested her to reproduce in needlepoint this picture which he had painted in oils. The Queen is depicted on her way to the block. She is mounted on a charger and accompanied by her lady-in-waiting and page under the watchful eye of her guard. On one side are her countrymen of Scotland, and on the other are the English. The needlepoint was done on plain canvas without any tracing, so that it was necessary to count the stitches. Mixed wools, silks, chenille and beads were used.

Mary Rothmann worked on this tapestry in her spare time for eleven years, completing it in 1879. When it was finished the artist was so elated that he destroyed his original painting stating that she had produced a masterpiece which could never be duplicated.

Between the period of 1868 and 1870, while working on "Mary, Queen of Scots," she completed another needlepoint tapestry known as the "Arabian Scout," also done in wool, silk, chenille and beads. Her granddaughter, Miss Beatrice Zeigler, states that a special room in

the house was devoted entirely to this tapestry, and that a great range of colored wools had been gathered in it by her grandmother to have at hand when embroidering, exactly as a painter collects his colors on a palette.

The colorings are well preserved for their age. Those in the purple robe of the Scottish Queen have softened a trifle and some of the blues in the page boy's costume have lightened. The horse's hoofs are outlined in beads which have also been used for armorial touches on the soldiers' uniforms. It is an extraordinary accomplishment.

BIBLICAL SCENES

Two needleworked pictures have come to light depicting "Moses having His Hands Upheld by Aaron and Hur during the Battle of the Israelites and the Amalekites."

The Wadsworth Atheneum in Hartford, Connecticut has a handsome version of this event in a panel worked on canvas with colored wools in cross-stitch by Mrs. Anne Strong of Portland, Connecticut, in 1859. It is approximately forty-five inches high by thirty-nine inches wide and was given to the collection by her son, Ellsworth B. Strong.

The same design has been worked by others in similar technique, but each has introduced certain changes, as always happens in the copying of a pattern. Eliza R. Fish of Mystic, Connecticut, made her interpretation of Moses holding up his hands for victory in battle in 1860, when she was eighty-seven years old. It is finely and ably worked in small cross-stitches with great contrasts in the shading. It has the strong feeling of an old tapestry. The faces have been worked in petit-point stitches and the horses in chenille silks. High lights are worked in with floss. Mrs. Charles Noyes of Mystic is the proud owner of this fine example of Biblical needlework made by her great-grandmother.

A Biblical picture in the author's collection is more violent in theme. It shows Abraham about to slay his son upon the sacrificial altar, a subject which was popular in the period. The dagger is about to descend, but from the needleworked heavens an angel in handsome white robes is emerging in the nick of time with the message that the patriarch has proved his faith to Jehovah's satisfaction. It is vividly and dramatically embroidered in the finest detail. Not a quiver of emotion is omitted.

"THE FINDING OF MOSES"

An amazingly fine Biblical picture is the large cross-stitched tapestry called "The Finding of Moses," embroidered in 1865 by Mrs. James A. Gary of Baltimore. This large "mural" was worked from a small picture in color sent her from the Sisters of Mount Saint Vincent, a convent in what is now Central Park, New York. Mrs. Gary had been educated there as a girl when her great-aunt, Mary Jerome, was Mother Superior. It was here, also, that she learned to embroider. The picture was sent to Mrs. Gary with a recommendation that she copy it in the large needlework panel to keep herself from brooding over the loss of her small daughter who had just died. The sympathetic Sisters wisely proffered the advice that Mrs. Gary work at least an inch a day, which was more than followed, for the embroidery, worked entirely in delicate petit point, was finished within the year. It is a fine memorial to sweet "Daisy" Gary, whose portrait is included earlier in the book.

The colors are soft and show a large range of shadings. The high lights have been emphasized with white silk, as was the custom in all needlework during the period. The design of the picture is consistently Victorian in the drawing of the popular calla lilies, which grow out of the water where Egyptian lotus buds ought to be, and the bassinet of baby Moses is not at all related in period or style to the baskets which were to be found upon the Nile during Biblical times. Artistic license permits these inconsistencies, fortunately, and the panel has its own personal charm. The fashions of the 1860's have been sincerely rendered.

There are additional qualities imparted by the color harmonies and the intense feeling which accompanied the execution, as shown in the tender care with which every inch of the needlework was executed. When the picture was exhibited at the Maryland Institute of Art in Baltimore, it was hailed as a work of art and awarded the first prize, a large gold spoon with the initial "G" engraved on the handle, and "Prize for Moses" on the bowl. The mural is now in the Baltimore home of Mrs. Eugene Levering, Jr., one of Mrs. Gary's daughters. The other daughters, Mrs. Francis E. Pegram and Mrs. Harold Randolph, also of Baltimore, and Mrs. Robert Coleman Taylor of New York are today all ardent needlework enthusiasts, inheriting this talent from their gifted mother.

Another picture worked in fine needlepoint is a personification of Mercy. The womanly figure is gowned in flowing robes of finely stitched yarns, ranging in color from pale coral pinks into deeper corals and wine reds for shadows in the folds of the skirt. She wears over her shoulders a cape stitched in shades of royal to powder blue. Seated upon a grassy mound, she is offering a cup to an infant who leans over her lap to drink the water, taken apparently from the nearby spring. The landscape background is handsomely rendered with jade green and blues in the foliage. Morning-glories of pale pink and crimson are silhouetted against a deep blue sky which fades to pale peach near the mountainous horizon. Pale peach clouds are worked into the heavens in a tapestry effect. Further Victorian atmosphere is provided by a large urn reposing on a pedestal. It is of the 1860 period, New York, and belongs to the author.

SENTIMENTAL PICTURES

Needlepoint pictures showing young maidens and youths stitched in rural settings are also in the mood of the earlier silk on satin pictures. Usually little animals or flowers and plants complete the scene. Mrs. N. Stanton Gates owns such a panel which is used as an ornamental wall decoration in the famous old Denison House in Mystic, Connecticut, which she now occupies. It is worked in petit point in very soft colorings. Two little sisters are stitched in a decorative landscape. The elder is seated upon a bank of grass with a lap full of pansies and roses; the smaller is bending over to fasten a rose upon the older sister's gown. This belongs decidedly to the sentimental school and was made about 1840 by Esther Burrows of Connecticut, who learned to embroider in a French convent where she had been sent to "finish" her education.

Illustrative of this same phase is a needlepoint picture of two "infant" sisters who are gazing adoringly at their pet bunnies and a setter dog

1. *Courtesy of:* MRS. N. STANTON GATES, Mystic, Connecticut.

Wall picture in needlepoint, about 1838, by Miss Esther Barrows, Connecticut.

2. *Courtesy of:* MRS. C. J. VAN ANTWERP.

Needlepoint wall picture, about 1835, Lee, Massachusetts.

3. *Courtesy of:* MRS. EDITH WILLIAMS, Stonington, Connecticut.

Needlepoint and cross stitch fire screen panel, "The Squirrel." About 1850, Connecticut.

4. *Courtesy of:* MRS. KENNETH BUDD, New York.

Small wall picture, "Birds in Nest," worked with silk in petit point on fine scrim, about 1840, New York.

1. *Courtesy of:* MISS BEATRICE ZEIGLER, Huntington, Long Island.

Needlepoint tapestry picture, Mary, Queen of Scots. 6 ft. x 5 ft., 1879, by Mary Rothman, Long Island.

2. *Courtesy of:* MRS. FRANK T. CLARK, Connecticut.

Needlepoint tapestry picture, "The Sicilian Maid," about 1840, Connecticut.

3. *Courtesy of:* MRS. CHARLES NOYES, Mystic, Connecticut.

Biblical needlepoint picture of "Aaron and Hur holding up the hands of Moses in Battle of Israelites and Amalekites." 1860, Eliza R. Fish, Connecticut.

4. OWNED BY THE AUTHOR.

Needlepoint wall picture "Mercy," about 1840, New York.

stretched out contentedly under the stool which is holding the multiplied family of rabbits. There is a landscape background realistically rendered. This delightful example is in the home of Mrs. C. J. Van Antwerp of Lee, Massachusetts, who says it was made in that vicinity about 1835.

SMALL WALL PICTURES

Now and then a needleworker, turning from these grandiose landscapes, has discovered Mother Nature's friendly little animals and pictured them in a small detailed panel. A small panel used for a fire screen, worked about 1850 in fine cross-stitch, adorns the fireplace in an old Stonington, Connecticut, homestead owned by Mrs. Edith K. Williams. The panel, it is said, originally came from the old Denison House and may also have been made by Esther Burrows. The picture represents a bright, alert squirrel who is in the process of stealthily extracting a large grape from a bowl of fruit. He is caught in the act by an innocent butterfly of large proportions at whom he peeks very guiltily out of the corner of his eye. The picture is rendered exceedingly well in delicate wools, ably shaded, upon fine scrim of cream color. This scrim background has been left uncovered.

The squirrel is carried out in tones of red and browns and is beautifully shaded. His whiskers have been worked in long black silk stitches. The grapes are a pale green shade, the leaves carefully and realistically stitched in deeper greens and blues. The butterfly tops the coloring of the picture with its shades of red, navy blue and ivory white. Altogether the tones harmonize with graceful delicacy and present a spirited and charming work.

A petit-point wall picture stitched about 1840 in New York is in the collection of Mrs. Kenneth Budd of that city. A bouquet of poppies has been worked upon exceedingly fine cream-colored scrim with tiny tent stitches. Some poppies are worked in violet tones shaded to mulberry; others in light rose shaded to deep wine, and still others in deep brick orange shaded to deep henna and wine colorings; the leaves are in sage and pale greens. The sprays of wheat, so popular in the designs of the 80's, are worthy of note. This little flower panel is worked with plain threads or dulled floss and high lighted with silks, as are other nineteenth century embroideries of the period.

It was fashionable at this time to back the uncovered scrim with a self-colored material. In this instance antique cream satin was used. The reason for doing this was to provide a sheen of high light from the gleam of the satin seen through the scrim. When framed under glass the effect was that of a solidly covered background with an interesting quality. Many embroideries, Berlin, needlepoint or crewel, were worked on finer scrim in this fashion with an "unfinished" background effect. This does not apply to work upon coarser canvas which, when the background has been left uncovered, looks less pleasant. The method was evidently a matter of taste rather than the general rule or an evidence of fatigue, since there are a tremendous number of works on exceedingly large areas of canvas which have been most painstakingly covered, not always artistically yet, in some instances, with beautiful effect. Patience was the order of the day.

"Little Birds in a Nest" is a companion wall picture to "Poppies." It is worked in the same technique with fine silk on scrim. About twelve shades have been used on the wings, feathers, eyes and bills. Ranging from pearl-gray silks through taupe and into prune, wood brown and slate blue, the colorings are exquisitely blended. The birds' mouths are worked in yellow, red and orange, which serve to brighten the entire design, balancing the bright yellow green used in the leaves. Deeper greens of boxwood color give weight to the reddish brown branch upon which the little round nest, toned in tan and olive-brown shades, is resting.

Like other petit-point pictures, this needlepoint silk embroidery is backed with satin, the tone of the scrim giving a charmingly rich filled-in effect. Framed in brown marbelized narrow paper, it makes a graceful little wall decoration in the New York home of its owner, Mrs. Kenneth Budd.

NEEDLEWORK UPHOLSTERY

Needlepoint and cross-stitch were used with increasing frequency on chair seats, footstool tops, and benches during the entire nineteenth century.

A handsome example of early needlepoint

very finely stitched upon cloth upholsters the top of an Empire piano stool. The piano and stool were both made in New York about 1825, copied from Napoleonic pieces by Robert and William Murns, cabinet makers at 172 Chambers Street, New York. The needlepoint design is composed of lilies and roses delicately colored. This group, an inspiring example of design and craftsmanship characteristic of the period, has been given to the Museum of the City of New York by Mrs. Dess Murphy, Mrs. Robert McAllister Lloyd and Mrs. Paul Townsend Jones in memory of their parents, Mr. and Mrs. Robert Lenox Belknap.

An amusing combination of poppies and scrolls surrounded by a conventionalized border was used in the needlepoint which decorates the top of a Victorian stool made by Mrs. Daniel L. de Freest of New York, mother of Mrs. Francis H. McKnight of California who has inherited this delightful work. It is a typical example from the early part of the century when Berlin patterns were beginning to be introduced into America for such purposes.

Chair seats in needlepoint to be used upon the high-backed chairs began to be popular in the middle nineteenth century. An early Victorian example made about 1845 is in the Museum of the City of New York. The chair, a gift of Mrs. Henry de Bevoise Schenck, is made of rosewood. The back splat is carved with scrolls. The posts and legs have spiral turnings, fashionable during this period, which were not carved with cutting tools but were burned in or incised with a hot iron. The seat is upholstered in a needlepoint covering with a large morning-glory and leaf pattern. The background is worked in deep royal-blue silk floss; the leaves, flowers and borders are wools in shades of browns, reds, coral rose, with grays and gray greens for the leaf coloring. It was

worked in 1854 by the mother of the donor, Mrs. Richard Van Wyck (Catherine Berger Johnson), who was born in 1829 and lived at Tenth Avenue and Hewes Street, New York, in the house built in 1812 by her great-grandfather, Brigadier General Jeremiah Johnson.

Another chair of the same general style and period came from the old Goelet mansion at Nineteenth Street and Broadway, New York. The needlepoint, an allover pattern of conventionalized roses and ribbons, was worked by Miss Goelet (Mrs. Thomas G. Gerry) of New York, the grandmother of Mrs. William Warner Hoppin. Mrs. Hoppin has adapted and worked this pattern in needlepoint for another Queen Anne chair covering which she uses in her living room in New York today, thus matching the heirloom chair which stands outside in the entrance hall.

A chair from Charleston, Massachusetts, belonging to the Fosdick family, has been inherited by Mrs. Albert L. Mason, a descendant. The original needlepoint, which was damaged has been painstakingly revived by Mrs. Mason, also an enthusiastic needlepoint devotee. The design is striking in its diagonal patterning intricately worked with warm Oriental colorings. This heirloom graces the foyer in Mrs. Mason's home in Stonington, Connecticut.

Mrs. Harrold Gillingham of Germantown, Philadelphia, owns several very handsome chair seats worked in the fine needlepoint in the allover geometric or mosaic "spot" patterns chosen for coverings in that day. They were often small squares or diamonds or triangles repeated at inch or half-inch intervals. Other pieces in her collection are delightfully representative of this needlepoint phase, their warm Oriental color notes being mixed with the sober tones suitable to their application upon staid walnut, mahogany and rosewood furniture.

1. *Courtesy of:* MRS. ALBERT L. MASON, Stonington, Connecticut.

Needlepoint Chair seat revised from nineteenth century by Mrs. Albert L. Mason. Original chair from Fosdick family, Charleston, Massachusetts.

2. *Courtesy of:* THE MUSEUM OF THE CITY OF NEW YORK.

Needlepoint Seat and Chair from family residence, General Jeremiah Johnson, 10th Ave., Hewes St., New York. 1845 by Mrs. Richard Van Wyck (Catherine Berger Johnson) mother of Mrs. Henry de Bevoise Schenck.

3. *Courtesy of:* MRS. WILLIAM WARNER HOPPIN, New York.

Needlepoint Chair seat (one of set) on chair from the Goelet Mansion, 19th St. and Broadway, New York, by Miss Goelet. Mrs. Thomas G. Gerry, mother of Mrs. William Warner Hoppin.

5. *Courtesy of:* MRS. FRANCIS H. MCKNIGHT, California.

Needlepoint Stool Top. Early nineteenth century by Mrs. Daniel L. de Freest, New York. Mother of Mrs. Francis H. McKnight, California.

4. *Courtesy of:* THE MUSEUM OF THE CITY OF NEW YORK.

Needlepoint Empire Piano Stool Top. Early nineteenth century, New York.

Frank Leslie's Lady's Magazine and Gazette of
Fashion for September, 1868

Original Pattern Louis XV jacket from Frank Leslie's Lady's magazine and Gazette of Fashion for September, 1868, showing braiding patterns.

CHAPTER XVII

GODEY'S, LESLIE'S, AND PETERSON'S NEEDLEWORK PATTERNS

"While rosy cheeks thy bloom confess
And virtue thy bosom warms
Let virtue and let knowledge dress
Thy mind with brighter charms,

"Daily on some fine page to look
Lay useless sports aside
And let the needle and the book
Thy fleeting hours divide."

FROM ROSAMUND PACKARD'S SAMPLER, 1820.

CHOOLS FOR YOUNG LADIES OFFER-ing "education in a genteel manner" and featuring embroidery before all other branches of learning, remained for a long period the chief means for the dissemination of knowledge concerning patterns and technique. Pattern books appeared from time to time, but very early ones are scarce.

There is a legend that Adam, Chippendale and Sheraton brought pattern books to America from which many needlework designs were adapted, and judging from some of the motifs remaining on embroideries of the period it would appear to be true. A particular example reflecting Chippendale's influence, is the Lafayette-Washington handkerchief in white embroidery made in New Orleans and previously described.

In 1821 needlework lessons and rules were published in book form and young girls were instructed how to prepare their materials and sew them in both plain and decorative stitchery. Following in the footsteps of these pioneers, other publishers issued more and better books and pamphlets of instruction. During the last half of the century patterns for embroidery to embellish the costume or for household knick-knacks were issued profusely by the recently established magazines for women and particularly by *Godey's Ladies' Magazine, Frank Leslie's Ladies' Gazette, Peterson's Magazine* and, somewhat later, *Harper's Bazaar*.

EARLY PATTERN BOOKS

A series of small pattern books now in the First Editions Collection of Americana belonging to Mrs. Robert Coleman Taylor was published in 1843 by J. S. Redfield, who offered "popular books wholesale and retail" for sale at Clinton Hall, corner of Nassau and Beekman Streets, New York City. The titles give an idea of the subjects covered.

No. 1. BABY LINEN: containing plain and ample instructions for the preparation of an infant's wardrobe; with engraved patterns. "Indispensable to the young wife."—*World of Fashion*.

No. 2. PLAIN NEEDLEWORK: containing clear and ample instruction whereby to attain proficiency in every department of the most useful employment with engravings. "It should be read by every housekeeper, and is highly useful to the single lady."—*Ladies' Court Circular*.

No. 3. FANCY NEEDLEWORK AND EMBROIDERY: containing plain and ample directions whereby to become a perfect mistress of those delightful arts; with engravings. "The directions are plain and concise, and we can honestly recommend the volume to every reader."—*La Belle Assemblée.*

No 4. KNITTING, NETTING AND CROCHET: containing plain directions by which to become proficient in those branches of useful and ornamental employment; with engravings. "A more useful work can hardly be desired."—*Court Gazette.*

No. 5. EMBROIDERY ON MUSLIN AND LACE-WORK, AND TATTING: containing plain directions for the working of leaves, flowers, and other ornamental devices; fully illustrated by engravings. "It should find its way into every female school."—*Gazette of Education.*

No. 6. MILLINERY AND DRESSMAKING: containing plain instructions for making the most useful articles of dress and attire; with engraved patterns. "In this age of economy, we are glad to welcome this practical book."—*La Belle Assemblée.*

From this last review, it appears that it was smart to be thrifty in that age, as it is now.

BONNET MAKING INSTRUCTIONS

In "Directions for Bonnet Making" the author of *Millinery and Dressmaking* aforementioned, states:

That there is a charm in a neat and well made bonnet, is a fact that no one will be disposed to deny, because all feel it; and it appears almost like an instinct of our nature to desire that the head-dresses of those forms of loveliness which move around us, and whose sweet smiles constitute the sunshine of our lives, should be worthy of the fair faces they are intended to adorn. Fashion is ever changing, so that to lay down invariable rules for any portions, and especially those which may be considered the ornamental ones, of female attire, is altogether impossible; still, the general principles are invariable, and the alterations demanded by a fickle goddess who presides over the ladies' wardrobe exhibits her power, not so much in the alterations of general costume as in an ever-varying attention to details; so that of most articles of dress it may be said, "Ever varying, still the same."

A footnote is added:

The latest fashions can always be seen, however, at Mrs. Deuels, 297 Broadway, a

lady of taste and judgment, who stands at the head of her profession.

Here we may introduce "Belinda," discovered in Stonington, Connecticut. She is a little hand-painted model who may have looked out from a milliner's window on the Broadway of long ago. After years of residence in an old "wall-paper decorated hat box," she was revived and restored to her former dignity by her present owner, Mrs. E. P. York. Belinda is a little battered as to face but still proudly carries upon her head a dainty hand-made cap of needle-work netted lace, and attempts to demonstrate the charm derived from "wearing with smiles" a "neat and well-made bonnet." (See page 149.)

From another publication come directions for making a dress cap which read as follows:

This is made of net, and is formed of two pieces, exclusively of the border and trimmings. The pattern must be cut in paper both for the head pieces and the crown. The head piece is when opened twelve and a half nails long, and two wide.

Many bonnets made according to these patterns have found permanent homes in museums throughout the country. They are an important record of artistic needlework attainment.

PAPER PATTERNS

A pattern typical of the early tissue paper pattern is shown opposite page 113. The original was inserted in *Frank Leslie's Gazette of Fashion* in 1868. It is a pattern for a paletot, a snug fitting jacket which in this case was to be made of velvet and trimmed with chinchilla or other fur. A braiding design to be worked on the sleeves and skirt of the jacket is included.

Dressmaking was much more complicated then than it is now. Each pattern section had to be traced off the original tissue and cut out separately before the complete pattern could be applied to the material. The tissue patterns of today may seem complicated, but trying to pick out the various sections which were printed one over the other on one sheet of paper, as shown in the illustration, must have been a tussle.

Transferring the embroidery design also often meant tracing the one motif again and again. This was done either with chalk, a pencil or stitching. For such embroidery much chenille was used, also silk in satin stitches; or the design might be braided in color contrasting with the material.

Paletots also were fashionable for children and were equally elaborate, with wool braiding on merino or with white embroidery on muslin for summer.

FASHION NOTES

Costumes in those days were elegant in the quality of the materials used as well as the lavishness of their embroidered decoration. Dresses were meant to be worn for a long time and the workmanship was elaborate because the costume would be lasting. That many of them are still in excellent condition is testimony to their solid worth.

Even then, however, advocates of dress reform were making themselves heard, and protests were by no means confined to Amelia Bloomer and other radical representatives of the gentler sex. During 1869 campaigns were carried on by contributors to *Peterson's* and other magazines against the foolish fashions. In an "Editorial Chit-Chat" which appeared in *Peterson's* about 1871, the following note appeared, written by a bachelor:

The health of American women is suffering seriously. There is no hope that they can accomplish much till a radical reform is effected.

To this a lady replied:

Women have dressed for thousands of years, substantially as they dress now, that is with flowing skirt to give grace to the figure; with a corset of some kind to keep the weight of the skirt off the loins; with a girdle or belt around the waist and with bodices high or low, according to the occasion, and they will dress so to the end of time, because it is in the fitness of things that they should. The fashion of the particular garments varies with all climes and all ages and every generation; we respectively suggest that old bachelors whether in pantaloons or petticoats, know nothing of the subject."

With this retort the case for reform seems to have rested. It was not until after the advent of the bicycle that skirts began to leave the ground and rise above the ankles. And it was some years after that before the dust ruffle was permanently retired. Further concessions to health and comfort were made during the World War when many women went into nursing or took over positions in industry hitherto occupied only by men. In the dizzy days of the post-war period, skirts rose to the knee. Today, in spite of a downward trend, they are still from twelve to fifteen inches above the ground.

The life of women has swung into new channels. Sports, business and the many activities in which women now engage outside the home require a costume on which elaborate needlework would be entirely out of place. But while we do not regret the change because of the freedom of movement allowed us, we can still admire the elegance and the flowing lines which the lady of 1871 so confidently predicted would last "to the end of time" and which actually are reappearing in the evening dresses of today.

TYPICAL EMBROIDERY PATTERNS

A running commentary on the type of needlework which preoccupied ladies during the latter half of the nineteenth century to the neglect of the more creative efforts characteristic of earlier periods is supplied by a list of patterns taken at random from women's magazines which undoubtedly encouraged this frittering away of time and talent.

1842—SLIPPER PATTERNS: in needlepoint, calla lily design.

1843—A BOY'S NECKTIE: "A RICH BORDER IN GUIPURE": for an infant's robe. AN EMBROIDERED SHIRT FRONT.

1850—"CASE FOR PRAYER BOOK OR BIBLE": for tambour or embroidery.

1853—"RETICULE": to be worked on rich, deep blue velvet with network gold braid laid flat; the fleur-de-lis must be worked in white silk, the rose in red silk, the five dots in the center in gold beads. "GOLD FISH GLOBE MAT": to be worked in three shades of emerald green Berlin wool, one scarlet drag stag's cotton and to be bound with white skirt cord. (*Frank Leslie's Gazette*.)

1855—ANTIMACASSAR: in scarlet and white appliqué. "WELCOME CUSHION": to be embroidered or appliquéd. "THE NATIONAL CUSHION." BRAID WORK DESIGN FOR "TOILET CUSHION." "RUBY VELVET TOILET CUSHION BEADWORK

PATTERN." PIN CUSHION COVER: for white silk floss on satin. (*Godey's Magazine*.)

1856—"THE CHECKER COLLAR": white embroidery in checkered squares, lacework edging. (*Godey's Magazine*.)

1860—"TRAVELING SATCHELS." "CARRIAGE RUGS": Point Russe embroidered on crochet—Victoria stitch. "RUG STRAP HOLDERS IN NEEDLEPOINT." "BEADING PATTERN FOR A CHRISTMAS OR NEW YEAR'S PURSE": Chinese red, gold, white, maroon, turquoise and blue composed the color scheme. (*Peterson's Magazine*.)

1861—"A FRENCH CARRIAGE BAG FOR SILK OR FLOSS EMBROIDERY." (*Frank Leslie's Gazette*.)

1862—PIN CUSHION IN APPLIQUÉ. "ETRUSCAN HAND SCREEN": designed in Pompeian red background with black and gold figures, for needlepoint or cross-stitch. (*Peterson's Magazine*, July.)

1864—EMBROIDERY, BRAIDING AND RIBBON SHIRRINGS: the paper pattern reproduced from *Leslie's Magazine* illustrates the styles for "edgings," to be embroidered usually in white on cambric, swiss, muslin, flannel, or fine linen. These borders were designed to decorate the flounces of petticoats, sacques, jackets, sleeves and for pantalette edgings. There are many examples in collections all over the country. "BREAKFAST HANDKERCHIEFS." "NEEDLEPOINT PATTERN FOR CHAIR, OTTOMAN, SOFA, PILLOW, CAMP STOOL, ETC.": geometric designs in blue, red, brown, tan, white and black. (*Peterson's Magazine*, December.)

1866—"QUILTED BED POCKET": with a place to contain a watch; to be quilted in blue with added ribbon work. "APPLIQUÉ AND EMBROIDERY FOR WHAT-NOT:." (*Peterson's Magazine*, February.) MUSIC PORTFOLIOS AND OTHER ACCESSORIES: these were made of navy-blue cloth and embroidered with flower scrolls in colored silks in satin stitch and chain stitch. Handles and mountings were applied in blue or natural colored leather. These were appropriate containers of such sheet music as "The Bower Schottische," arranged for the piano and dedicated to a Professor John Bower; "Il Bacio Waltz"; or a Scottish ballad to be faithfully practiced and rendered by a young lady accompanied on the piano by her "gentleman music teacher."

1867—NEEDLEPOINT OF CROSS-STITCH PATTERN FOR "THE RAILWAY TRAVELING BAG": cherry red, gold, grass green, sky blue and maroon with white were the colors suggested for this capacious bag. (*Peterson's Magazine*, February.) A NEEDLEPOINT SLIPPER: combining silk floss or wools in an allover design, Fleur-de-lis motif. (*Peterson's Magazine*, April.)

1868—A LAMBREQUIN: it may be worked either in wool and silk or entirely in beads. The outer edge to be finished with silk cord or a string of beads. (*Harper's Bazaar*, May.) TIDIES. ANTIMACASSARS: of embroidered pieces of linen. (*Harper's Bazaar*, October.) "A LARGE PAPER PATTERN FOR A LOUIS XV JACKET": the description claims the jacket is "Extremely pretty made in black silk of the same material as the skirt. For the chilly mornings of September it will be found useful to wear over muslin dresses and for this purpose should be made of cashmere or de laine and ornamented with braid." The edging is to be hand-embroidered in buttonhole stitch. (*Leslie's Gazette of Fashion*, September.)

1870—"THE POMPADOUR BOW SLIPPER": in Berlin wool and beads. Red, green, black and white are the colors. (*Peterson's Magazine*, November.)

1871—"MAT IN ASTRAKAN WORK," PATTERNS FOR "SEGAR CASE": oval in shape. (*Peterson's Magazine*, February.) MAT IN ASTRAKAN WORK, JUDY'S ANTIMACASSAR, CARRIAGE CUSHIONS IN HONEYCOMB NEEDLEWORK, TIDY FOR EASY CHAIR, NETTED TIDY: design contributed by a lady of Boston, Massachusetts, to be netted and darned with coarse knitting cotton. (*Peterson's Magazine*, May.)

1872—"TURKISH WORK" BAGS: parallel stitch combined with cross-stitch in turkey red, blue and black. Penelope canvas—Berlin eight-thread wool, Turkey red twill. "PATCH WORK": pieces of silk, beads worked or wools on canvas in light and dark shaded geometric square designs.

1873—"DESIGN FOR FIRE SCREEN AND BORDER." (*Peterson's Magazine*, February.)

1874—"EMBROIDERED WASTE PAPER BASKET": the frame to be made of black varnished bamboo bars ornamented with gold buttons. The embroidery to be worked with "green sadler's silk and gold thread in satin and half-polka stitch embroidery." The basket is to be lined with pleated green silk, and finished on the upper edge with a box-pleated ruche of the same. On the corners of the basket bamboo rings are to be set, on which to fasten tassels and fourfold green silk cords tied in a knot. This typifies the period of combined techniques when embroidery began to go into the doldrums. Over-elaboration was the general rule in this as in all other decoration. Through all the stuffiness, however, fine, clean-cut and tasteful works were executed.

1886—SCARFS, TABLE AND BUREAU COVERS: Mrs. Jane Weaver designed for *Peterson's Magazine* Kate Greenaway figures in outline embroidery which were extensively used to decorate ends of scarfs and table and bureau covers. They are done in red and blue French working cottons or on wash crewels.

1887—"DESIGN FOR A CHAIR SEAT": one of several designs made by the South Kensington School of Art Needlework introduced by *Harper's Bazaar*. It is a working pattern of floral forms in simple, clear spacing with a refreshing quality which is in contrast to the fussy designs directly preceding them. A two-fold screen pattern was adapted by the school from an old English design and is an excellent arrangement in spite of the fact that the directions recommend "dark blue velveteen with the design to be appliquéd with cut out gold brocade and bordered with their gold. The flowers are then worked in terra cotta shades of silk from dark red to pale pink. The centers of the roses to be filled with French knots, etc." (*Harper's Bazaar*, May.)

Such patterns as these listed were exchanged between members of the church sewing circles who during this period were industriously embroidering. Beginning in the 40's and continuing through the 90's bedspreads and quilts, "throws" and couch covers were produced from scraps of silk, satin and cotton preserved for the purpose. In the late 60's embroidery stitches in great numbers were mastered by the members of these "sororities" and used to outline the bits of silk, velvet and satin made into crazy quilts.

A little later came the fashion for embroidering pillow shams. Such cheerful sentiments as "Good Morning" and "Good Night" were issued in pattern form in *Peterson's Magazine* and were copied in Kensington stitch with red thread upon white linen. Sometimes a long piece of tape was stretched across the head-board of the

bed to keep smooth the smiling, chubby face of the "Dolly Dimple" who was represented as uttering these salutations.

At the same time "splashers" for the wall space back of the wash-stands were designed to be embroidered in outline stitch with cat-tails at the side springing from the rippling water lines. At the base pond lilies and their leaves provided further decorative touches. Bees gathering honey from clover blooms were embroidered to remind the tardy that they should be hustling down to breakfast. Flower motifs, bluebirds, every conception imaginable absorbed the stray drops which splashed from the roomy washbowls.

As may be gathered from the pattern notes, colors were limited to the primary scale. The wholesale manufacture of shaded wools had not yet been achieved; color reproduction in the magazines also was limited. Hence the use of red, yellow, green, pink, blue and black was general.

NAMES FOR MARKING

Embroidered table linens were not in evidence prior to 1890 except for the tray-cloths, and these were few. But names for marking were widely popular and full patterns of printed names were included in the magazines to be worked in English script or block letter outlines. They were embroidered on almost everything in solid satin stitch or outline stitch. Many were carried out in fine white work on handkerchiefs and other accessories. Some of the names are familiar in songs and stories of the period, such as:

EMILY: English block letters.

URSULE: Victorian lettering with flower inserts.

GEORGIE: in script.

MADELEINE: in script with French knots in middle of letter.

AGNES: in feather stitch outlining of script.

CHARLOTTE: in flowers and outline script.

ISABELLE: in satin stitch script.

AMELIA: in block letters and scroll borders.

LIZZIE: in floral script.

LOUISE: in Gothic lettering.

NELLY: in fine "eyelet" script.

Letters for marking alphabets upon linens, departing from the earlier cross-stitch of sampler days, were published in *Godey's, Leslie's* and *Peterson's Magazines* worked in the following techniques: Guipure d'art (on net), interlaced letters in satin stitch, eyeleting, cross-stitch (occasionally), braid-work, white needlework.

A SCHOOL FOR ART NEEDLEWORK

The persistence of an ambition to achieve something beyond utility and fussy decoration and to scale Parnassus by way of needlecraft is evidenced even in this period of mediocrity by an advertisement which appeared in *Designs in Outline for Art Needlework,* edited by Lucretia Peabody Hale and published in 1879. The advertisement was inserted by the School for Art Needlework which had been established at the Museum of Fine Arts in Boston. Thus we learn that in spite of the production of much that was in questionable taste, embroidery was still recognized as a potential cultural expression in the same category with the other fine arts of painting, drawing and sculpture. At this time a school was actually functioning in an American art museum to encourage an acquaintance with the technique of needlework in its highest artistic form.

The price of tuition was five dollars for six lessons; eight dollars for twelve. Private lessons were two dollars an hour. On Mondays and Thursdays there were free lessons. Other classes met on Tuesdays and Fridays. There was a session on Wednesday for those taking only one lesson a week. "Materials and designs," so the advertisement reads, "will be furnished at a moderate price."

On the board of Managers were Mrs. G. W. Hammond, Mrs. W. B. Rogers, Mrs. W. G. Weld, Mrs. J. W. Wheelwright, Miss L. P. Hale, Mrs. C. G. Loring. The members of the Committee on Designs were Mrs. W. G. Weld, Mrs. J. P. Marquand, Miss W. R. Ware, Miss Susan Hale, Miss Annie Dixwell, Miss F. W. Cushing, Mrs. J. W. Wheelwright, Mr. Frank Hill Smith, Mr. B. C. Porter, Mr. Arthur Little, Mr. John H. Sturgis.

Whatever may be said of the "fancy work" of this period, the ambitious program of this school in the Boston Museum of Fine Arts must not be overlooked. And although in general public taste left much to be desired, certainly industry was not lacking. In the Victorian era may be found stitched examples expressing idealism, patriotism and sincerity, as well as superficiality.

CHAPTER XVIII

FASHIONABLE BERLIN WOOL-WORK

"No endeavor is in vain;
Its reward is in the doing,
And the rapture of pursuing
Is the prize of vanquished gain."
HENRY WADSWORTH LONGFELLOW.

 ERLIN WORK IS A TERM WHICH was generally applied to all types of needlework on canvas made during the Victorian era. The craze for such work developed about 1856 and spread throughout America, becoming the most popular needlework fashion for the next thirty years. The name was derived from the fact that the best patterns used for it came from Berlin and were commonly known as Berlin patterns. The work is characterized by the use of very brilliant worsteds, also of German make and marketed especially for working these patterns in needlepoint or cross-stitch upon a soft canvas, also supplied from abroad.

The patterns were blocked into designs on squared paper and hand painted to match the wools. They gave impetus to quantities of floral panels which were copied from them for chair seats, pillows or stools. Pet dogs were designed in every posture, begging a crumb from the little Victorian mistress, as illustrated, or sitting patiently awaiting the master's recognition. Leo, the Lion, was a very smart subject for footstools and floor mats. Herds of deer stalked through American parlors. Most popular of all

were the parrots perched upon wreaths, sprays or bouquets of roses, these in turn being entwined with festoons made of lilies or ivy leaves. Some patterns used flocks of woolly birds, but instead of stitching them entirely in cross-stitch or needlepoint, the ladies of the 1880's and 90's combined techniques and worked the patterns in various styles of stitching.

One design, a beautiful example from this period from the embroidery collection of Mrs. Harrold Gillingham in Philadelphia, has the Polly and flowers entirely worked in silks with satin stitches upon black cloth. The colorings are softer than most Berlin patterns and the work is replete with artistry.

Other examples of Berlin work include wall pictures, screens, banners and, particularly, lamp mats. Worked to use upon a table top is an amusing and quaint piece made about 1850, which is in the home of Miss Esther D. Waterman in Southport, Connecticut. This lamp mat is described by her as being a round piece of Victorian needlework made by Eliza Rathbone Dodge, wife of Henry Lucius Fox, who lived in the northern part of New York State. She was the grandmother of Miss Aline Kate Fox of Southport. The needlework begins with an outer circle cross-stitched in fine wools of an Egyptian turquoise blue which blends to a deeper blue. The center is an eight-pointed design having a border cross-stitched with pansies in an intense purple, and pink rosebuds. The background is worked in two shades of beige and red brown, high lighted with yellow floss meeting the inside points of the squares which in turn are outlined with rows of deeper red brown and one row of black wool. Within this border, the background is worked in a yellow-brown ochre. Little corner motifs are embroidered in ivory silk floss, giving a lift of light to an otherwise monotonous color scheme. Toward the center the turquoise blue band joins another circle of flowers which is made of pansies and roses, repeated as in the outer points of the squares. The center of the background is filled finally with a third shade of lightest turquoise, a blue which is a shade higher than the outer border of the mat, upon which is stitched a bunch of little white lilies worked in ivory white, gray green, and white, and picked out a bit here and there with cross-stitched ivory floss.

Looking at this mat framed under the glass of the table top, with the glow of lamp light falling on the embroidery, one would seem to catch a glimpse of an old-fashioned garden, enclosed by yew and evergreen trees with their ground-sweeping branches, and hedges of boxwood and privet, and, in the center, a sunlighted spot of brilliantly colored flowers. The table bearing it would immediately have caught the eye in the old days, since it would be placed with exactness in the center of a room furnished with heavy walnut pieces. These extreme contrasts in color distinguished the interiors of most homes during the Victorian age.

DESIGNS AND STITCHES

Pattern designs for Berlin work were so numerous and so easily obtained that it is almost superfluous to say much about them. Although quantities were imported, a great many also were invented at home. Of course there was a great variety of tastes to suit; and, as in painting, what will please one eye, will be offensive to another. As a general rule, however, "set" patterns or exact allover repeated motifs were more pleasing than any others. Next were those handsome bouquets which have been so much used for ottomans, chairbacks, and so forth. A group of exquisite fuchsias, beautifully grouped,

is a handsome novelty. At least forty shades of color have been used, worked in tent stitch on fine canvas with the black background which was consistently used for almost all needlepoint throughout the Victorian period.

Leslie's Ladies' Gazette, Godey's Ladies' Magazine, Peterson's Magazine, and the others, provided patterns in Berlin work which might be copied from their publications. Many were engraved in full colors. Two particularly soft, lovely patterns in the author's collection are chair seat designs from *Godey's,* about 1860. One is a pheasant, with surrounding florals reminiscent of old English chintz, tinted in soft cerulean blues, pale peach tones and delicate greens. Another grape and vine pattern is equally interesting and quaint. These plates were of fairly large proportions, folded in quarters and placed in the volumes as special features during the Christmas season.

Mrs. Stephen M. Harrisson owns several original Berlin patterns which were published during the 60's and found by her in an old trunk belonging to the family. They are all fresh in color and clearly countable. They measure approximately eight by ten inches.

The fair young maiden with her pet dog Tray was a design much in demand during this period and madly cross-stitched for wall pictures, stool tops and pillows. A favorite touch was the addition of a bead to simulate the animal's eye. Polly's eye was usually a large topaz bead. Likewise Leo, the Lion, looked far more fierce when he stared out at you from his cross-stitched landscape, watching your every move with a bright eye of yellow glass. Patterns of crosses entwined with ivy leaves, roses or lilies were applied in various ways on touching mementos, cross-stitched, perhaps, upon a bookmark to send to the minister at Eastertide as a token from a devoted parishioner.

Mrs. William Alfred Robbins of Brooklyn owns a hand-painted Berlin pattern made in 1860 which was used for needlepoint and cross-stitch by her mother, Mrs. Thomas H. Robbins. She also has inherited a strip of crocheted wool from the original large afghan on which the design copied from the Berlin pattern was worked with cross-stitched wools. Her mother changed the original color scheme in the Greek key design from red browns to violet, deep mauve and gold shades and used coral tones in the flower group instead of the heavy magenta shades painted in the pattern design.

Apparently copied from a Berlin pattern also, is a small black satin "toilet cushion" of the 1850 period, which has been cross-stitched with flowers in gaily colored worsted. It was made for a relative of Mrs. Alban Richey of Brooklyn who now owns it. A scroll border has been stitched around the edge in a characteristic pattern and the four corners edged with black satin ribbon bows, a finishing touch fashionable at the time.

The same type of design has been applied to backgrounds of black horsehair, to be used for antimacassars or for chair seat coverings either on the "hair pin" backed chairs or the carved rosewood Victorian side chairs.

Donated to the Witte Memorial Museum in San Antonio, Texas, by Mrs. Adolph Wagner is an interesting needlepoint panel which was inspired by a Berlin pattern. It was made by Miss Christina Wagner, a member of a German family which settled in Texas in the 1840's. The design, worked in 1872, is in an oval shape on fine scrim. The wreath of flowers is fashioned with a cluster in the center, and the needlework has been mounted on the inside of the cover of a leather portfolio of the period. Possibly it was intended to remind the user that tender thought had gone into the creation of the gift.

With engines to take the place of stage coaches, traveling became a more usual event in people's lives. All manner of accessories were needleworked for the traveler. Most attractive, so the Victorian ladies thought, were the "railway bags" which were not unlike the carpet bags in shape, except that they were made of canvas and needlepointed or cross-stitched from the never-failing Berlin patterns. The designs ran mostly to stripes. Now and then a scroll or flower would interrupt the tradition, but on the whole they adhered to the strictly conventional.

Preceding these novelties were the shawl straps. Mrs. Emily Barnes Callen has one worked in 1873 by her mother, Julia Huntington Barnes, of East Cleveland, Ohio. The design used on the straps was a conventional scroll pattern with a few flowers worked in needlepoint. The initials were worked across the top panel of the canvas strap-holder.

This was another period when men's accessories were being gaily decorated with embroidered ornament, from needlepoint suspender bands to elaborately embroidered "segar" cases worked in beads (see Chapter XXIV), or silk-work. Slippers and smoking or lounging caps, paper weights, tie racks, match holders and innumerable gadgets were gaily flowered with countless stitched blossoms. These were tokens of love, indicated by doves and other touching symbols expressive of sentimental devotion.

MATERIALS USED

In the years between 1838 and 1890 materials for embroidery were consistently the same. In the 60's many books and articles were published which give the requirements for needle-work of the day. Wools, silks, chenille and beads were generally used in Berlin work, the foundation being canvas or sometimes perforated cardboard. A detailed description of the styles of canvas and other materials best adapted to different types of Berlin work is given by Florence Hartley in her *Lady's Handbook*, published in Philadelphia in 1859. The quotations which follow are from that book.

BERLIN OR CANVAS WORK

The materials for canvas are, silk, cotton, thread, and woolen; these are styled coarse or fine, according as they contain a greater or less number of threads within a given space; the threads of the coarser kind being stouter. Canvas is also distinguished by a number, corresponding to its size, such as twenty, and twelve, canvas; these distinctions are, however, arbitrary, and vary according to manufactures of each country.

The finest canvas, of either material, is distinguished under the general appellation of "Mosaic."

SILK CANVAS

Silk canvas, more commonly called Berlin canvas, is generally used as a substitute for grounding; it is well adapted for flower, vignette, gem, and all kinds of set patterns and also for articles of furniture, but is not so strong as the grounded work for the latter purpose; but for many articles, such as screens, etc., it may be used with great saving of time and labor. It can be had of almost any desired color; but white, black, and claret are most generally used. Working on this canvas requires greater neatness in finishing off the stitches at the back, than work intended to be grounded; the wools and silks must not be carried across from one part to another beneath, but cut off as closely as possible, otherwise, when mounted, they would show through the meshes of the canvas.

Berlin canvas is expensive, and therefore, imitated by an inferior manufacture, and it requires care to select; the best being clear and free from knots, and firm and even in its texture. It also varies in width, from an inch to a yard and a half, but there is not so great a variety in this respect as in other descriptions of canvas; four sizes in general are manufactured, which are numbered about 21, 29, 34, and 40 threads to the inch.

COTTON CANVAS

Cotton canvas is made of all qualities, sizes and widths. There are English, French, and German canvas. The French is superior, not only on account of firmness, but also from the great regularity and clearness of its threads, and the squareness of the meshes—an object of great importance, as many patterns would be distorted and ruined by being lengthened one way and diminished another.

German cotton canvas, although of an inferior description, is as well adapted for many purposes, as the French, and costs much less, and it is generally made with every tenth thread yellow, which many persons consider a great assistance in counting stitches; it can be procured in all sizes and widths, and both stiffened and limp; but in texture, it is not so strong as either the English or French canvas. It should not be used with light or white grounds, as the yellow thread will show; nor where much tension is necessary to be used....

WOOLLEN CANVAS

Woollen canvas is of German manufacture, and used when grounding is not to be done; but is not so rich in appearance as grounded work. The usual colors and widths can be procured.

BOLTING

Bolting is a very fine woollen canvas, manufactured principally in England but is not much used. It was formerly much in demand for children's samplers and generally very narrow....

WOOL AND SILK USED IN CANVAS WORK

German wool or zephyr merino is adapted for working all kinds of Berlin patterns, and is of various sizes. When very fine, it is called Split Zephyr. It is commonly knotted in small skeins, making it very convenient, and the varieties of shades and colors are almost innumerable. It can be used doubled or trebled on very coarse canvas. It requires skill and attention in selecting. When the quality is good, it is soft and curly in its texture, and round in its form, and comparatively free from the smell of the dye. When using this wool, it is better not to wind it, as it deprives it of its elasticity. In selecting the wools for working, great care and taste are required to blend the colors harmoniously, avoiding gaudiness, and yet making contrasts. Some patterns are very pretty in design, and yet the coloring is very bad. Of course, the arrangement when altered from the printed patterns must be left to the taste of the worker.

ENGLISH WOOL FOR CANVAS WORK

This is sometimes used with German wool in the same piece of work. In large articles particularly some of the shades are quite equal to the German. Victorian authorities claimed the following English colors were equal to the German, namely scarlet, some shades of blue, green, gold, browns, clarets, and neutral tints. For grounding backgrounds, English wool is preferable to the German. It is stronger and less apt to soil.

WORSTED FOR NEEDLEWORK

This was formerly much used for embroidery but not at the present time. Its advantages are that it takes a fine dye and has a brilliant glossy appearance in large articles, such as carpets and rugs. It is much cheaper than wool. Hamburg wool, or German worsted, is a common kind of wool usually containing four threads, but can be had as thick as twelve threads. It is very good in color, and very suitable for coarse canvas. There is an English imitation of this wool which is not desirable.

The "Orne Balls" are used for embroidery on canvas as well as for crochet. It is used in what is called fluted embroidery.

SILKS USED FOR CANVAS WORK AND OTHER NEEDLEWORK

Mitorse, or half-twisted silk, is much used for all kinds of embroidery, and is less likely to become rough in wearing than the floss silk. It can be introduced with good effect in some parts of wool embroidery, for small articles.

The Dacca silk should always be used for copying Berlin patterns in silk, or for very fine canvas. The varieties of colors are almost equal to those of German wool. It may be used mixed in with wools or fine canvas, and will bear dividing. It is usually done up in knotted skeins.

Floss silk is a thicker description of silk used for tapestry work or for gem patterns, when silk is required to brighten up the effect of the wool. It can be employed for grounding in canvas work with beautiful effect. It can be procured of various sizes.

Filorelle is not a pure silk but is glossy and beautiful, and can be used to advantage in the coarse kinds of Berlin work. It requires care in the selection, some being very brilliant, others having a look like cotton.

Gold and silver thread, called "Passing," is a smooth thread of uniform size. It is the finest material of this kind manufactured. It is used in the same way as silk, being mixed with it or with wool (for ecclesiastical work).

Gold cord is much used mixed with wool in some kinds of canvas work, and sometimes with beautiful effect, when used as a grounding of course, only for very small articles of luxury.

METHODS OF WORKING

Directions for embroidering on canvas offered to readers in the 60's present some new ideas in methods of work. Others are quite familiar, being used in needlepoint today.

One of the best effects of Berlin work can be produced by the Irish or Railroad stitch, as it is called from its rapid execution. It is difficult to describe, but simple to work. A beautiful effect is produced by using four or five shades of fawn color, and stripes crossed over the crimson at regular intervals; the stripes formed by the fawn colors running diagonally, and the four shades of crimson the same.

The squares formed by the pattern meeting are filled in with black wool. It has the appearance of being raised from the canvas. A set of furniture in this pattern is very handsome.

We do not admire the figure and landscape patterns for canvas work, though some are handsome; but the sky is seldom good, or the faces.

Autumn leaves, in their beautiful natural colors, form the most elegant designs for canvas work, and persons of good taste can arrange them for themselves, either repeating them in rows all over the cushion, or in groups on a grounding of black or green.

Armorial bearings, Heraldic devices, &c., can be more readily copied from checked patterns (or designs outlined on square paper and worked by counting off their spaces with matching squares of the canvas mesh).

All fine canvas work is improved by a judicious mixture of silk; and "Gem" and "Set" patterns look best in all silk.

What are called tapestry designs have no shading, and a few bright colors are used. They look better in silk than in wool. Whatever color is used it must be surrounded by a line of black. It may also be done with half wool and half silk.

In the period of 1864-1868, Turkish stitchery was introduced probably through the Berlin patterns. Its name may be accounted for by the popularity in Germany of Daood Pasha, a literary man and a Christian just added to the Turkish Cabinet. He is said to have been the second literary gentleman and second Christian ever called to the highest council of the Ottoman Empire. He was attached to the Ottoman Legation in Berlin, where he published two volumes called the "Histoire de la Legislation des Anciens Germans," dedicated to Jacob Grimm and considered a remarkable work. Our Ottomans also may owe something to this statesman's influence.

Designs in Turkish stitch appeared on needlework coverings which were sent to this country from Berlin. They were copied and used in the parlors of the "cultured ladies." Other items which they decorated with embroidery reflecting the Turkish craze were smoking fezzes to be worn at home by the tired business men; likewise Turkish slippers in the Oriental motifs.

The Victoria stitch was created in honor of England's Queen, and point Russe was obviously inspired by Russia. The Czar stitch and the Princess Frederic William stitch were other names adopted in this period. But in spite of their new names, these were the same traditional stitches, centuries old.

In order that one may have a conception of the demand for Berlin patterns from the 1860's to the 1890's, some material has been garnered from contemporary authorities who were active in offering advice and encouragement in this field.

An idea of the items to be adorned may be gathered from Mrs. Pullman's *On making up of Fancy Work*. It contains suggestions for presents "suitable for ladies to make," and adds that "a few hints for the proper fitting up and completing of the most prominent article will, I am persuaded, not be unwelcome."

Among these articles were:

"NOTE CASES, PORTFOLIOS AND SIMILAR

THINGS": to be made of cardboard, leather, canvas (Berlin work) or silk beaded.

"SHAVING BOOKS": braided cloth, cardboard or velvet, embroidered.

"CARRIAGE BAGS": Berlin work on canvas.

"SHAWL STRAPS": Berlin or other needlepoint on canvas and leather.

"TOBACCO BAGS": canvas and silk embroidery.

"HAND BAGS OR EUGÉNIE BAGS": combinations of a straw base, silk top and canvas embroidery application.

"MATS": Berlin-worked, beaded, braided on canvas or cross-stitched on cardboard foundation.

"HAND SCREENS": silk or wool cross-stitched on satin, beaded or Berlin-worked and finished with quilled ribbon-work, or bound with silk fringe with long handles which were ribbon wrapped and fastened at the end of the handle with a sweet bow.

"WHAT NOTS; BERLIN-WORKED OR BRAIDED": "Very commodious little articles, which are meant to be suspended between windows, or in any other convenient place. The front is the only part that is worked; and it is done in canvas (embroidery) or crochet, or simple braiding on cloth. A stout cardboard frame is made, on which the work is sewn. It is lined with fluted silk, and the back covered with silk or cloth. Being suspended to the wall, this part is not seen." The description ends with the direction to add quilled ribbon-work for further embellishment, finished off with numbers of tassels.

"OTTOMAN": usually in Berlin work.

"SULTANAS," OR "HANDKERCHIEF CASES": braided or embroidered.

"D'OYLEYS: OR DOYLEYS": braided, embroidered on linen, beaded or "jeweled."

"ANTIMACASSARS": usually netted or knitted.

"BRACES" (suspenders): generally cross-stitched on fine canvas in black or white.

"CIGAR CASES": embroidered, braided, beaded and crocheted.

"FOOT MUFFS": embroidered or crocheted.

"LAMBREQUINS OR MANTEL DRAPERY": Berlin-worked. These were long strips of canvas, scalloped and shaped to suggest a draped piece cut like window valances, and worked in elaborately cross-stitched or tent-stitched patterns in fairly vivid colorings. Very smart and fashionable also over large marble mantelpieces!

Patterns for embroidered galluses or suspenders for gentlemen were frequently shown in *Godey's* and all other ladies' magazines, along with ideas for paper weights and ink stands for the office, to be handsomely needleworked. Many men brought up in this atmosphere developed a positive distaste which to this day makes it difficult for them to tolerate even the mention of art needlework, or "fancy work" which it really was. Possibly they remember fearful and wonderful presents embroidered by various feminine members of the family and which they received at Christmas time—Aunt Delia's napkin ring made of cardboard, cross-stitched with the motto "Don't Forget Me" in baby blue flowers and edged with tiny sewn shells; or that key-ring basket Mrs. Washburn-Hicks sent for his room at college, all embroidered with poppies and edged with shirred red ribbon trimmings (he would never forget that); and the high-topped black velvet boot embroidered all over with silver beads and lettered on the top, "Love from Niagara Falls." (It was meant to fasten on the wall to hold a whisk-broom. He never did learn who sent it to him, and to avoid hurting someone's feelings had to hang it up next to the dresser, along with the shaving book with its embroidered cover lettered in cross-stitch, "I Am Always Near When You Need Me.")

After the 60's followed the period when the backs of gold and jeweled watches were painstakingly filled with locks of hair made into roses or clasped hands, lilies or other decorative creations symbolizing the same everlasting devotion expressed on the embroidered watch-holders. These watches have ceased ticking away the minutes of the 80's and have been silent a long time, but in their carefully stitched cases they are still bright reminders of this sentimental era.

3. *Courtesy of:* MRS. THOMAS H. ROBBINS.

4. *Courtesy of:* MRS. WILLIAM ALFRED ROBBINS, Brooklyn, New York.

Afghan Strip crocheted and cross stitched from Original Berlin Pattern. About 1860.

Original "Berlin Pattern" for Cross stitch and Needle-point strip. About 1860.

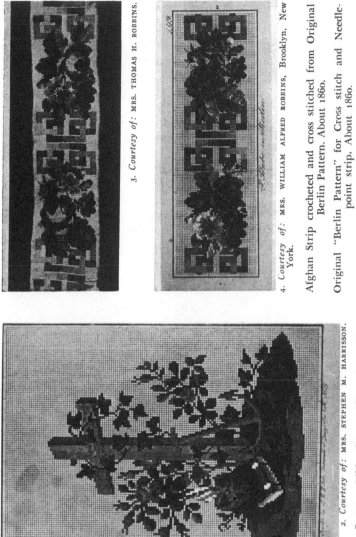

2. *Courtesy of:* MRS. STEPHEN M. HARRISSON. New York.

Berlin Pattern, Bible, Cross and Anchor. 1860.

1. *Courtesy of:* MRS. STEPHEN M. HARRISSON.

Original Berlin Pattern "Girl with her Dog, 'Tray,'" 1850.

7. *Courtesy of:* MRS. ADOLPH WAGNER, Texas.

Needlepoint panel made for the inside of a leather portfolio, in 1872, by Miss Christina Wagner, Texas.

6. *Courtesy of:* MISS ESTHER WATERMAN, Connecticut.

Lamp Table Mat. Needle-point or "Berlin Canvas Embroidery." 1850 Connecticut.

5. *Courtesy of:* MRS. ALBAN RICHEY, Brooklyn, New York.

Pincushion—Needlepoint in wools worked on black satin, 1850, Brooklyn, New York.

1. *Courtesy of:* MISS ISABEL ELY LORD, Brooklyn, New York.

Canvas lace cross stitch panel of silk and wool on fine canvas; made by Mrs. Rose in Pennsylvania. Cir. 1850.

2. *Courtesy of:* MISS ESTHER WATERMAN, Connecticut.

Raised clipped embroidery in wool and petit point in wool and silk floss on scrim, uncompleted panel. Cir. 1850, Connecticut.

3. *Courtesy of:* THE WASHINGTON HEADQUARTERS ASSOCIATION, Jumel Mansion, New York.

Portrait of George Washington in clipped or cut wool work. American, about the early nineteenth century.

4. *Courtesy of* MISS ANNA M. CULBERT, Stonington, Connecticut.

Raised wool work Parrot with needlepoint background, pole screen panel, about 1845. New York.

CHAPTER XIX

CANVAS LACEWORK AND RAISED WOOL-WORK

"All truths wait in all things,
The insignificant is as big to me as any,
(What is more or less than a touch?)
WALT WHITMAN.

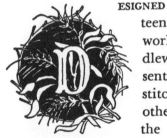

ESIGNED IN THE MIDDLE NINE-teenth century, canvas lace-work was a popular nee-dlework fashion. It repre-sents a unique type of stitchery included among other pattern novelties in the *Ladies' Hand Book of Fancy Ornamental Work,* published in Phil-adelphia in 1859. Its technique is explained in the following quotation:

This is an imitation of black lace, done on canvas, and for which patterns of square crochet will answer. The close stitches are done in four thread Berlin wool. The open squares in fine black silk. All done in cross stitch. It is very pretty for some purposes. Bags worked in colors with a black edge, ottoman covers, sofa pillows, &c. A lamp mat in our possession is made in this way of an oval shape, with cards—the eight of diamonds—white ground, scarlet spots; the six of clubs—white ground, black spots; this is surrounded by a narrow line of light brown, and then again by a border about an inch wide, of three shades of red. The whole finished by an imitation lace border about an inch and a half wide. It is sewed on to cardboard and lined with thick silk. It is very pretty.

At an earlier date, Miss Lambert describes the same technique in the *Hand Book of*

Needlework, published by Wiley and Putnam, at 161 Broadway, New York City, in 1842.

IMITATION OF LACE

Numerous patterns in imitation of lace have been lately introduced, and where judgment is used in the application of them, they cer-tainly have some merit;—the best are prin-cipally adapted for small articles; but lace and canvas work being somewhat at variance with each other, it is doubtful whether they have much claim to good taste. The ground is worked in various stitches of fine silk, the pat-tern on it being in cross stitch of thicker silk or wool.

An example of canvas lacework, a lamp mat, is shown opposite this page. It was worked in black silk and wool on fine canvas by Mrs. Rose in Pennsylvania about 1850, according to the present owner, Miss Isabel Ely Lord. The lace border, worked in black silk, encloses ribbon scrolls cross-stitched in fine wool in shades of red, from wine through cherry tones into the high light of coral rose. About five shades are used. The ribbons are effectively outlined with a single cross-stitch edging of golden yellow. This shades into the cream of the fine canvas, which looks like linen scrim and softens the otherwise obvious reds. There is a note of violet in two of the corners which are decorated with a little pair of morning-glories enclosed in yellow and deep green shaded leaves. In the opposite corners is a pair of little roses, worked in pale pinks shading into the deeper reds of the ribbons. These little flower bouquets bring harmony to the entire panel and keep it from being too raw in color. The stitchery is finely worked and lends quality to the design which was fashionable in this period. Few examples of this technique have come to light in this country.

RAISED OR CLIPPED WOOL-WORK

Inherited by Miss Esther D. Waterman is an example of needlework showing combinations of raised or, as it is sometimes called, clipped wool-work. It is reproduced opposite page 125. Such examples were filled in with cross-stitch or needlepoint backgrounds and were a favorite diversion in the middle nineteenth century. Miss Waterman says of the work: "The piece of needlework of cut wool was made by my grandmother, Esther Dimon Wakeman, the wife of Warren D. Gookin who lived in Southport, Connecticut."

The design is centered upon finest cream-colored scrim. It shows a cross-stitched basket shaded in three tones of cinnamon brown, high lighted slightly with ivory silk floss stitches. Four very large, lush roses which have been stitched in raised wool embroidery are in the basket. The wool stitches on the surface are clipped closely after looping, making the woolly flowers stand out in relief about a quarter of an inch above the rest of the cross-stitch. Two are coral pink roses, one shading into a flesh-toned light pink center, the other into ivory white. The inner-heart petals are shaded in pinkish beige and the outer petals are of ivory, shading into gray greens for outline. Another rose is worked in deepest crimson colorings, high lighted in tone with coral and shaded into its deepest outline color with two wine reds. Surrounding these are delicate rosebuds, a few small flowers of baby blue and a cluster of five-petaled posies, worked in regular fine cross-stitch from a center of "spots" of rose and pale crimson, into deep brown gold which blends toward the outer edge of the petals into pink brown through to light pinkish beige. Some edges are outlined, or "picked up" as painters

say, with a high lemon-yellow or light, shining, gold silk floss.

The only floss stitches in this design are the few touches on two of the little blue flowers and a few beige-colored flowers. The rest of the needlework is stitched in plain yarns. These little lifts in tone help the entire work immeasurably by taking away any possibility of monotony in the effect of the finished piece. It is comparable to the dash of spice with which an experienced cook adds zest to a dish. The leaves vary from blue-green branches through to yellow green, with brownish or faded-leaf shades of yellow brown, touched with gold, giving additional tonal variations. A group of flowers arranged as carefully and tastefully as this indicates a needleworker gifted with fine artistic perceptions. The embroidery is delightful in every way.

It was the intention, judging from a few inches of cross-stitch started, to set the group off with a background filled with black, in the usual Victorian style. We, today, are inclined to reverse this effect, selecting for our backgrounds any of the lightest tones we may find that are practical for our use.

A raised and clipped-wool portrait of George Washington was made from the same pattern that was used in the needlepoint portraits of Washington in the Louisiana State Museum in New Orleans. It is in the Jumel Mansion in New York City, once used as Washington's Headquarters. The exact date and name of the worker are unknown but the pattern appears to have been circulated in the late eighteenth and early nineteenth century.

This is an ambitious work in wools, approximately thirty-six by twenty-eight inches in size. The colors are elaborately shaded in a manner decidedly suggestive of painting. Deep, rich tones are used in the costume of the President, the draperies and the interior details. To stitch in the details of the chair ornament so that it came out with such accuracy after the wool was clipped, required careful arrangement and close figuring. Likewise the portrait and the achievement of the satiny high lights on the silk stockings and velvet of the breeches bespeaks skill. Even the lace jabot and sleeve frills have been rendered with amazing effect. The original is used as an ornamental decoration in the room where it hangs and where the Father of our

Collection of: MRS. HARROLD GILLINGHAM, Philadelphia, Pennsylvania.

Cushion Top. Silk embroidered parrot worked on black broadcloth in gay colors. About 1860, Philadelphia, Pennsylvania.

Courtesy of: MRS. BENJAMIN TILTON, New York.

Cushion Top. Needlepoint background, bead leaves and raised wool-work parrot. 1860's New York.

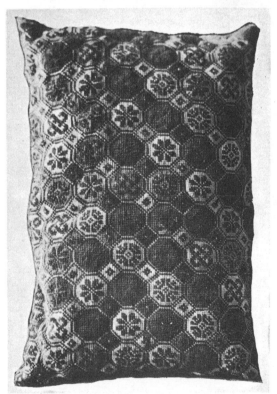

Collection of: MRS. HARROLD GILLINGHAM, Philadelphia, Pennsylvania.

Cushion Top. Fine Cross Stitch in all over small conventional design. About 1870, Pennsylvania.

Courtesy of: MRS. EMILY BARNES CALLEN, New York.

Cushion Top. Worked in Queen Stitch and Cross Stitch about 1868, Ohio.

1. *Courtesy of:* MRS. WILLIAM W. HOPPIN, New York.

2. OWNED BY THE AUTHOR.

3. OWNED BY THE AUTHOR.

1. "God Bless Our Union"; portrait of George Washington, flags, patriotic emblems wool embroidered on perforated cardboard in satin, outline and cross stitch. Dated 1776-1876, Long Island.

2. "Maud Muller"; perforated cardboard, embroidered wools, satin stitch and tent stitch. About 1877, Pennsylvania.

3. "The Virgin Mother and Holy Child"; painted paper portraits applied. Silk, chenille, and bead embroidery on perforated cardboard. About 1860, Pennsylvania.

4. Group of Bookmarks; embroidered on perforated cardboard with ribbons. Made between 1825 and 1875. Collected by Miss F. S. N. Allen and Miss M. C. Whiting.

5. Early American Embroidery; silks, on heavy paper. Deposited at a "Sanitary Fair" Civil War benefit in Baltimore, Maryland, as "antique" by Eleanor Boyd, its owner. Cir. 1830.

6. Sampler; wool cross stitch on perforated cardboard by Master Nathaniel Palmer Stanton, 1861, Stonington, Connecticut.

4. *Courtesy of:* THE MEMORIAL HALL, Deerfield, Massachusetts.

5. *Courtesy of:* MRS. CARROLL R. WILLIAMS, a great-great niece, New York.

6. *Courtesy of:* THE LIGHTHOUSE MUSEUM, Stonington, Connecticut.

Country spent many sleepless nights planning for the nation's security, no doubt.

Cockatoos, parrots and parrakeets were exceedingly popular and were embroidered on countless fire screens, panels and cushion tops. Like most other birds worked in the same period, they are silhouetted against a cross-stitched or needlepoint background. The leaves, flowers or scroll borders were either made in the same technique or worked, like the parrot, on the reverse side of the scrim or canvas. When completed, the wool on the right side was clipped to give a raised, fluffed surface simulating bird feathers.

The technique has been described in detail in an old pattern book of 1858 as follows:

RAISED BERLIN-WORK

In this, one or more prominent objects in a design, are raised; the remainder being done in cross stitch. Birds, animals, and flowers, look handsome when so worked. Do all the plain parts first. Then thread needles with the various shades you want, and obtain fine flat netting meshes. Begin from the left-hand corner, lowest part, with the proper shade, the wool being "doubled." Bring the needle up "between" the two upright threads of the first cross-stitch. Take a tapestry-stitch to the left, bringing the needle out in the same hole. Put the wool round the mesh, and take one to the right, the needle coming out again the same x. Thread round the mesh, and take a tapestry-stitch from the hole of the last down to the right, the wool to the right of it. Thread round. One to the right x. A figure V is thus constantly formed on the wrong side. When done, wash at the back with gum; cut the loops, and shear them into shape from the pattern, giving proper thickness and form to each part. Sometimes this is done across one thread only.

A cockatoo worked in raised wool, with wings and feathers clipped, sits as proudly today on a pillow top in the home of Mrs. Benjamin Tilton as he once did years ago in the mansion of the Stevens family in Hoboken, New Jersey, from whom Mrs. Tilton inherited the piece. The background, needlepointed in antique green-brown wools, sets off the parrot to advantage and blends with the embroidered and bead-worked leaves. The roses have been clipped also. The pillow has been bound with fluffy antique brown wool fringe to match the cut wool-work.

Another cockatoo, made in the same raised work with the sheared wool surface, decorates a handsome needlework panel in the Brooklyn Museum of Art. It was worked in the middle nineteenth century.

Embroidered for a pole screen panel is a parrot of raised wool-work made in wools of gray greens, with blue for the top of the head, and red for the tail and a spot on the wings. Touches of beadwork and silk floss are introduced in the scrolled border which is worked in cross-stitch with gold, blues, rose and brown wools against a fine cream scrim canvas, uncovered. It is a beautiful piece and came to Miss Anna M. Culbert of Stonington, Connecticut, from a member of her family who made it in New York in 1845.

The popularity of bird patterns may have sprung from the fine hand-colored plates which were being published during this time in England and from the delightful Audubon plates in America.

CHAPTER XX

EMBROIDERY ON PAPER: BOOKMARKS AND MOTTOES

"Maud Muller looked and sighed: 'Ah me!
That I the Judge's bride might be! ...'

"The Judge looked back as he climbed the hill,
And saw Maud Muller standing still....

" 'Would she were mine, and I today,
Like her, a harvester of hay; ...' "

JOHN GREENLEAF WHITTIER.

APER EMBROIDERY WAS ANOTHER form of fashionable pick-up work for the occupation of leisure hours during the nineteenth century. All ages, and evidently both sexes, enjoyed practicing this art with which they made the needlework greeting cards and Valentines of that day. Beginning from small mottoes, accompanied by crosses, anchors and lambs and mounted on old brocade ribbons for bookmarks, the impulse grew until large "God Bless Our Home" mottoes were lavishing color in bright green and red yarns to give vibration to their earnest message. Mother would hang this bit of handicraft above the door with deep sentiment. If it was not securely fastened, the first slam would cause it to make an emphatic impression by dropping on someone's head. These mottoes seemed to have an unhappy faculty of falling down at wrong moments. Nevertheless, a number have survived and in future days will doubtless be much sought after as antiques dating from a queer period!

The background upon which these messages were embroidered was "Bristol board," as described in the 1860's, known today as perforated cardboard.

METHOD OF WORKING

According to a description from a publication of 1842, the paper used was

a card with minute holes at regular distances throughout it. It is of various degrees of fineness, and can be bought in whole sheets or parts of sheets. It is used for many ornamental articles, and it is easy to work on, and when nicely done, is nearly equal to fine canvas work. It is very nice for children to employ themselves on. Beautiful bookmarkers, portfolios, needle-books, etc., can be made with it. The pieces for bookmarkers, side of baskets, etc., can be obtained with borders.

Be careful in working that the needles are not too large, or the holes will be broken through. The small patterns must be worked in silk, the larger can be done in wool, or silk and wool. Sometimes the flowers are worked in chenille, and the leaves in silk.

Mottoes and designs can also be worked in gold, silver, steel or colored beads.

The printed Berlin patterns are also guides for cardboard work.

PAPER EMBROIDERY—1830-1900

An example of paper embroidery is presented in the sampler shown opposite page 127. It is in the collection of the Stonington Historical Society and was made on perforated cardboard by Nathaniel Palmer Stanton in 1861. According to the lad's statement, it was worked at a school conducted there by Miss Sheffield and was intended as a present for his mother. The cross-stitches on this sample of lettering have been carried out in bright shades of gold, rust, green, blue and rose reds. That Nathaniel knew his technique pretty thoroughly is evidenced by the variety of stitches in which the lettering has been worked.

Patriotism and portraiture may be found in cardboard embroidery also. An example made on Long Island to commemorate the one hundredth anniversary of the signing of the Declaration of Independence and bearing the dates 1776-1876, is a needleworked portrait of George Washington. To reproduce details in the face the needleworker used a pencil; a little color was pressed into service to produce the shadows under eyes, eyebrows and cheek bones. Surrounding the portrait is a border formed by the motto "God Bless Our Union," and flags and other emblems. Mrs. William W. Hoppin, a well-known needlewoman, has placed this naïve little picture in the dining room of her country house, where it is much enjoyed. It is typical of the wave of nationalism which swept over the country after the Civil War.

Made in Pennsylvania about 1877 on perforated cardboard with sheer wool threads is a picture of Maud Muller, the rustic beauty who

> . . . on a summer day
> Raked the meadows sweet with hay.

She is returning from the fields in a dress stitched in red and blue wool, her rake in one hand, a bunch of flowers in the other. The gaily colored wool foreground delights ultramoderns because of the diagonal shafts of light in bright green and yellow penetrating the deeper green bands beside them. Maud is finely worked, and she wears an expression which is quite amusing to visitors who chance to spy her in the author's studio. She is thinking of the Judge, probably.

In contrast to this child of nature is a Virgin Mother and Holy Child, worked solidly in beautifully shaded fine chenille silk threads. A few small gold and silvery-nickel beads add a Victorian touch to the crowns and halos. The portraits are hand-painted miniatures on paper, appliquéd. The entire figure of the Christ Child is painted. It is a tender version of this type

of work and came in its original frame to the author's collection from an old Philadelphia family. It was made about 1860.

From Baltimore comes a unique Early American paper embroidery which was worked in silks, in satin stitches, on heavy plain paper, not perforated. It was donated to a "Sanitary Fair" in Baltimore given during the Civil War to raise funds for the soldiers. Antiques and other objects were brought to these fairs and sold in the same way that Thrift Shops raise money for charities today. This embroidery was listed at the fair by Eleanor Boyd as an "antique." Her great-great niece, Mrs. Carroll R. Williams, states that it was made about 1830. Design arrangement and shadings are freshly original, direct and highly effective from the viewpoint of a painter.

"Love in Absence," a wee bookmark dating from 1834 and made in New York, and "Home Sweet Home," a motto of a later period made in Vermont and worked on a large scale with elaborate shadings in cross-stitch and satin stitched wools, belong to the author. Each is characteristic of their time. Patterns for these subjects were published in early magazines such as *Godey's*, *Leslie's* and *Peterson's*. *Harper's Bazaar* developed a large needleworking audience in the 80's and 90's through its elaborate instructions and reproductions including numbers of the increasingly popular

MOTTOES AND BOOKMARKS

Mottoes for the wall varied in color and design according to the several contributing factors of originality in execution, the all-important angle of taste and the materials to be found or procured.

A bookmark stitched on perforated paper by Nelly Custis when she was an old lady now reposes in the museum at Mount Vernon. According to the inscription on the bookmark, which does not show clearly in the reproduction, it was made "for Miss Jackson of Philadelphia, from one who has loved and respected her during sixty years." It is initialed and dated

E. P. L. AGED 72. JULY 1851

E. P. L. is Eleanor Parke Lewis née Nelly Custis. The design consists of a cross and other symbols of eternity, and the Bible. The embroidery is mounted upon an early brocaded ribbon.

In the collection of the Litchfield Historical Society is an amusing bookmark which has cross-stitched upon its narrow paper strip the "Oaken Chair brought over by Gov' Carver in the May-flower, 1620." It is mounted on a silk and em-bossed ribbon. The needleworker is unknown, but it belongs to the early Victorian period.

A court-plaster case made in 1830, with per-forated cardboard covers, was cross-stitched with a motto. It is lined with rose silk and was used in a sewing basket, ready for the occasion when scissors misbehaved or pins and needles pricked the wrong way. It is in the Museum of the City of New York.

The Memorial Hall in Old Deerfield, Massa-chusetts, has a case filled with all manner of mottoes and bookmarks, embroidered on card-board and applied to brocaded ribbons, worked between 1825 and 1875. They were collected by Miss F. S. N. Allen and Miss M. C. Whiting, the originators of the Deerfield Blue and White Industry in that community. The messages, sen-timental and pictorial, are worked in cross-stitch. The following are typical:

"Katy's Love," "Sincerity," "I'll Keep the Place," "Love Your Sisters," "Forget Me Not," "Love," "Amour," "A Token of Love," "Look to Jesus," "Sweet Home," "Hope of the Soul," "Holy Bible," "Le Dieu."

Later cardboard embroidery was concerned with a strange assortment of subjects which were applied to an equally strange collection of ob-jects. The following list gives a good idea of paper embroidery at its peak:

PICTURES: Swiss hamlets made by the dozen, rustic pictures and "The Old Church," with emphasis on the graveyard.

WATCH HOLDERS: "to hang on the wall and put the watch in." (1900.)

KEY BASKETS: early keys to houses often being of great size and made in hand-wrought iron a basket was necessary to hold a number of them.

THERMOMETER STANDS cross-stitched, handy for the ladies when they had the "vapors."

GLASS GOBLET HOLDERS: a precious idea in which the cardboard was cut an inch deep and sufficiently long to run around a glass goblet, "preferably the red Bohemian or garnet-col-ored glass." A design like the Greek key or some other Grecian motif was worked upon it with chenille, silk zephyr and beads.

CATCH-ALL BASKETS: beautiful elegancies "for waste matches, etc." These tasteful little affairs were intended to be suspended from a glass lamp or chandelier or other convenient place "for receiving the spent matches which would otherwise be cast upon the floor and perhaps do mischief."

BASKETS FOR COUNTERS: embroidered paper receptacles were also made by ladies "to use when playing cards," or "to throw clippings into when engaged in sewing." Brown cardboard was fancied for this purpose, and embroidered in point Russe.

ALBUM COVERS: to contain the family por-traits of Father, one hand tucked into his coat in the Napoleonic manner, the other resting upon the back of a high chair in which Mother is stiffly seated. Clutching her skirt is little Swinburne, who was named after the great poet; he is wearing a large bow tie emerging from under a white starched collar and his hair is immaculately parted and plastered down. The velvet suit is snugly fitted over his spindly lit-tle legs, one of which is neatly crossed at right angles over the other. He looks into the camera and defies the birdie to make him smile.

This hand-embroidered book usually con-tained also a few pressed flowers gathered on bicycle rides into the country and placed on an inserted page cross-stitched with the motto "Remember Me."

After this phase was exhausted the fashion died a perfectly natural death, about 1910.

CHAPTER XXI

BRAIDING, VELVET-WORK AND CHENILLE STITCHERY

"It is enough of heaven, its sweet success,
To find our own. Nor yet we crave the dower
Of grander action and sublimer power;
We are content that life's long loneliness
Finds in love's welcoming its rich redress,
And hopes, deep hidden, burst in perfect flower."

FRANCES LAUGHTON MACE.

ZOUAVE SOLDIERS WERE HAVING A great influence upon costumes worn in America between the years of 1870 and 1879. During the Civil War volunteer regiments had adopted the name and the uniform of the dashing Algerian regiments of the French infantry and some years later romantic wives reproduced the characteristic jacket for their sons, thus recalling the days when Father was in the army and love was young. Little boys all over the North blossomed out in these braided Zouave jackets.

They were not the first boys to be decked out in braided costumes, however. The application of braid had long been popular. In 1830 Peter Cooper had an unknown artist paint the portrait of his little son Edward who later, in 1879, became Mayor of New York City. The portrait is now in the Museum of the City of New York. Fortunately for posterity Edward wore at the sitting his blue jacket braided in black silk tape. The design is typical of the early use of braid when it was applied sparingly. The effect is handsome even upon such a very young man. His pantaloons are white, full at the top and narrowed about the ankles. His lace collar was, no doubt, handmade. He is holding

the whip which he carried when he drove his pet goat harnessed to a gaily painted carriage, a miniature copy of his papa's equipage.

In 1860 appeared the Scotch suits for boys with a braided pattern similar to that on Edward Cooper's jacket. Instructions for making such a suit "for a little boy four to five years old" was published in *Peterson's Magazine* in that year.

It may be either of plain or colored poplin, plaid serge or white pique. If the latter, trim with black braid. The skirt is cut bias, and very full, and plaited in deep plaits, put on a band at the waist, with shoulder straps; but we suggest an under body as better.

The jacket is cut like a lady's basque in the back, with side bodies, and straight in the front, and somewhat loose. The lower part of the jacket is cut in five deep points, which are trimmed with two or three rows of worsted braid, and three buttons upon each point. The braid continues up the front and around the neck, where it is finished with a cambric ruffle. This is a very pretty style for a little boy.

A little girl's dress and cape made of blue merino and handsomely braided in intricate designs with white wool tape was made in 1870. The original was given by Miss Sally Crane to the Museum of the City of New York. The tape stands up on one edge in an interesting way which is particularly effective in the tightly scrolled sections where deep shadows intensify the design. Whoever made this charmingly designed dress no doubt followed the directions for raised braiding published in magazines of the day. The method is described as follows:

BRAIDING

This is among the simplest of all kinds of fancy work, but it requires great care and taste to make it look even and smooth. The pattern used must be a continuous one, as it cannot be pieced to look neatly. The material may be silk, worsted, cotton, or gold braid, of any width or color. For children's dresses, which are not to be washed, raised braiding is much used. This is worked by sewing it only on one edge, so that it stands up. It is very handsome, but troublesome to do.

Cotton braiding is much liked for children's dresses which are to be washed, and even for common collars and undersleeves. The braid should be chosen thick.

Baby clothes also were adorned with braid. A pair of baby shoes made in 1859 of white cashmere were decorated with scarlet silk braid.

Costumes for women were braided throughout the 60's and on up through the 1890's. Among the fashion notes for street suits in 1868 *Harper's Bazaar* published the following:

For plainer suits, cloth and serge are the most acceptable material. Sailor's blue, Humboldt purple, and Olive green are fashionably worn. The trimming is silk or a wide black worsted braid. These costumes are suitable for shopping and morning walks, and should be made plainly, without any effort at display. The bonnet and gloves should be of the same shade.

Even bathing suits were braided. A pattern published in *Peterson's Magazine* in July, 1870 is thus described:

Bathing-Suit of Maize-Colored Woolen trimmed with a red worsted braid put on in a Greek pattern. The trousers are made full below the knee. The tunic is a little shorter and the low basque is belted in at the waist. The bathing cap is silk-lined cloth trimmed with red worsted braid.

Our Victorian lady was then properly garbed to face the great ocean and all censorious eyes.

Costume braiding included such details as "Ornamental Cloak Fastenings," "Rosettes of Cord and Jet," "Braided Trimmings for Under-Skirts" and "Chest Protectors." These last were little undervests worn beneath a cloak made of the same material and ornamented with the same braided design. There were also special designs for sleeves, collars, waist-bands, sacques, pockets and cuffs of velveteen suits for eight-year-old boys, tunics for girls' dresses, the toes and side pieces of slippers in velvet, silk or cloth.

In the earlier years when the use of braid was still fairly discreet it was used for ornamenting dainty

LADIES' CAPS AND OTHER ACCESSORIES

Between the years of 1845 and 1850 ladies' caps were often braided. Mrs. Albert Morrow has given a cap of that period to the Museum of the City of New York. It is made of white net, embroidered with blue braid and bound with blue and white silk brocaded ribbon which ties in a small bowknot at the base of the neck. In shape it is a larger version of the baby bonnet. It must have looked quite fetching on the fair New Yorker whose curls it adorned.

A choice accessory was the "French Feather Fan." Full directions for making it were published in Philadelphia in 1859.

The fan is now essential for full dress in most public places and as it is also an article of great elegance, we're happy to introduce a new one which has just arrived from Paris.

In this new-fashioned fan a little fancy work does all that is required, if we except the purchase of the handle, which we only class as coming into the list of the very few indispensable materials. The center of the French Feather Fan is made of white watered silk, braided in gold thread, according to our design. It consists of two pieces of cardboard cut to the form with as much neatness and regularity as possible. The front may be tacked down with small stitches round the edge, the gold thread being couched in silk, as it does not appear to the eye. This can be sewn round the edge, so that the tacking threads, which have been put in as for patch-work, may in the same way be taken out. A row of small gold beads over this sewing makes an excellent finish and hides all the stitches. This being done, a row of small Marabeau feathers are to be laid all round the back of the fan, their stalks being fastened down to the lining. This requires to be done with regularity, so that their outer margin should possess a perfect sweep. After this, the front of the fan, which has already been prepared, must be laid on, which, fitting the back exactly, all the stems of the feathers are completely hid and secured.

The handle, of course, must be purchased, and ought properly to be flat.

We have said white for this fan, but it is equally elegant in pink or plain blue, in which cases the Marabeau feathers must be tipped with either of the colors which may be preferred.

This is the new French Feather Fan; but as many ladies in the country, and some from abroad, are in possession of many kinds of very beautiful feathers, we suggest to them such an appropriation as being both elegant and useful. If not sufficiently bushy, two or three rows may be sewn around.

The application of braid became so popular and was such fun to do, since it could be accomplished much more swiftly than other embroidered decorations, that in time everything that could possibly stand it was ornamented with elaborate patterns. The women's magazines offered countless designs for a great variety of objects including fire screen banners, chair cushions, baskets, cloth envelopes for stationery and other purposes and sermon cases for the minister.

Wall pictures using braid were made in 1840. Two from the author's collection are illustrative of the various techniques employed. The design includes the shepherd and shepherdess, popular in the satin embroideries of the same period. But these braided figures have had their portraits and the entire costume painted with water colors upon velvet which has been cut out and appliquéd to the fine cream scrim. The trees and foreground have been amusingly stitched with brownish silk chenilles and to adorn the oval panels in a scroll arrangement, braiding was used. The pictures are quite small and demonstrate the growing tendency toward experimentation with various techniques, an impulse that finally ran entirely out of bounds and resulted in the production of strange conglomerations.

Some idea of the technique employed in braiding may be derived from extracts taken from published accounts during the 1860's.

MATERIALS AND METHODS

Fancy Braiding is applied to almost any article for which canvas work is used, such as sofa-pillows, slippers, watch-cases, boxes, &c. One, which has been much used, is, to draw the pattern accurately on tissue paper, the color of the groundwork of the article, and then baste it on carefully, and run the pattern with cotton the same color. Then tear off all the tissue paper and sew the braid over the run lines. Others baste on the drawn pattern, and sew the braid on without running it, removing the tissue paper when the pattern is done. Another way, is to use Pounced Patterns. This is done by marking the pattern, first drawn on fine thin paper, with a coarse needle at equal distances. Then lay the pattern on the material to be worked, and with the finger rub pumice-stone, very finely ground, and mixed with a very little powdered charcoal if the material is light, over the perforated lines. When the pattern is removed, it will be found nicely marked on the material. For muslin or cambric work, the pattern can be again traced with a camel's hair brush and indigo.

In putting on silk braid, it is best to use threads of silk drawn out from the braid, and an extra yard or two should be provided for this purpose. Wide braid must be sewed down on both edges; narrow, run through the middle; raised braid is sewed only on one side, but the other side is held up, instead of laying flat on the cloth. There was a very pretty braid in use some years ago, called Coronation Braid, which was formed into leaves and then adjusted into various forms. It seems to be wholly out of use. Colored worsted braids are very brilliant plaid checks, &c., for children's aprons, sacks, and dresses. It is also used on merino and cashmere. Little boys' sacks are very handsome braided all over the front in some pattern designed expressly for the garment, and braided in the same color as the dress. It also dyes well, taking a shade lighter than the material. Silk braid, however, is much more elegant, but it is also more expensive. Of course, there are a great many different braids in use, in silk, worsted, and cotton. The best worsted is Russian.

Silk braids included plain Russian braid, star braid, Eugénie braid, Sardinian braid, Albert braid or cord. Cotton braids were French white cotton, Russia cotton, waved braid, Eugénie tape, linen braids, worsted braids, mohair braids.

Another writer of this period explains that

Linen braid is not desirable for braiding, it is so thin. It is only suitable for imitation lace.

Gold and silver braid is much used for ornamental articles and for slippers. The French is best in quality. It can be had of any width.

In English books on needlework, the term "Soutache," which properly means Braid, is applied to all kinds of fancy braids of every kind and color.

The waved cotton braid is very pretty on children's dresses and easily put on. It looks well on plain French chintz. Little boys' summer overcoats of jean or gingham, with a large cape, look very pretty braided in white braid.

In braiding, great care must be taken to make the "points" neatly, and a stitch should be put across to keep them in place, under the braid, and "curves" should be carefully adjusted. If the braid used is of two colors, one side different from the other, the points must be made without turning. Broad braids must, of course, be "mitred" at the corners.

In using worsted braid, hold it rather loosely, for it will shrink in washing. Use wool of the same color for putting it on.

There is a kind of braiding done with beads. It is troublesome to do, and requires care to prevent the beads from looking confused. It can be done on the same lines as are marked for any kind of braiding. The beads, of course, are strung on silk. Leave the needle at the end of the silk, after you have secured your silk by a knot, on the wrong side of your cloth, and passed it through to the right side at the beginning of the pattern. On this, string your beads, which must be fastened down at regular intervals, by a stitch taken across the silk, between the beads; say, between every two or three.

When this bead braiding is done with gold beads, an edge of gold braid adds very much to the effect. In the velvet bag mentioned under bead work, the strings of beads are alternate gold and steel, about eight rows in all. Of course, they must be of the best quality.

In using cotton braiding on muslin or lace, there must be an edge worked in button-hole stitch, or if hemmed a very narrow edging sewed on.

It must have been with considerable relief that devotees of braiding in 1890 read the following item in *Harper's Bazaar:*

An ingenious and useful novelty just introduced is a new cloth plate attached to the Wheeler and Wilson sewing machine, which will produce a lockstitch, a double loop stitch, and an ornamental stitch for braiding and embroidery. The threads of different colors may be introduced into the braiding pattern if desired, and it can be easily adjusted to materials of every thickness, from the sheerest muslin to heavy cloth or velvet. The work when finished resembles star-braiding. The price is $10.

VELVET AND CHENILLE-WORK

Velvet-work was an exception in needlework rather than the general rule. The term applies to the application of silk braiding or chenille to velvet.

Typical of this style of Victorian ornamentation is a chatelaine pocket, the design of which, so it was announced, was copied from an original model exhibited at the Vienna Exposition. It was of black velvet, chosen to match the black velvet dress of the wearer. It was embroidered in the bright silks so popular at this time, and was fastened to the belt. It contained handkerchief, keys and a note-book. A lead pencil attached to a fine cord hung at the side.

Various accessories were made in much the same fashion; slippers, and occasionally a Turkish smoking fez for Father, which might be handsomely worked with braid in the Zouave fashion. Long panels of velvet to drape the mantelpiece were rather elegant braided with gold tape and then filled in with silk-embroidered flowers. This fashion appeared in the very late 80's and continued well into the 90's.

A nice gift to make for a gentleman was an embroidered cigar case. A handsome bit of velvet-work for this purpose was suggested in *Frank Leslie's Ladies' Gazette* in 1855. The materials recommended were rich, dark green or blue velvet, one quarter of an ounce of dead gold bullion, and the same quantity of bright gold.

The greater part of the design is worked in dead gold. The brilliant kind is introduced judiciously into those places where the light falls as also into the upper parts of the leaves on the reverse side. The heart of the rose is formed by little knots of bullion.

Velvet, satin or kid when put in a frame to be embroidered, should be lined with fine but stout linen, which makes the work much firmer and the article more durable. Shaded silks, instead of gold bullion, look well for this style of embroidery. Ombre violet on green velvet, scarlet or amber on blue, and almost any color on black, look well. Ladies' card cases may be worked in the same manner.

Scroll initials were designed to occupy the center of the cigar case with a border around the edge of roses and leaves.

A particular bit of "fancy work" engaging the ladies' attention for the afternoon's or evening's diversion were the velvet balls used for trim-

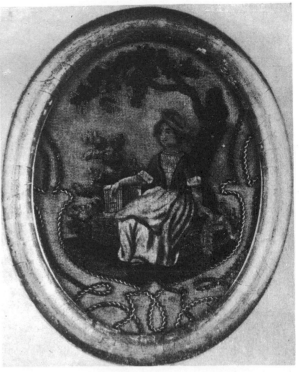

The Shepherd picture in chenille embroidery on scrim; painted velvet, appliqué and braid work.

The Shepherdess; painted velvet figure chenille embroidered picture on scrim with braid appliqué. 1840, New York.

Portrait showing braiding on jacket, Edward Cooper 1824-1905; Mayor of New York, 1879-1881; Son of Peter Cooper, 1791-1883. Artist Unknown.

Child's dress, Blue Merino braided in white wool tape, Cape with dress, 1870, New York.

Smoking or Lounging Cap.

I. OWNED BY THE AUTHOR.

Appliqué pattern, Gentleman's Smoking or Lounging Cap, December, 1867, Peterson's Magazine.

2. *Courtesy of:* THE METROPOLITAN MUSEUM OF ART, New York.

Quilt, Early Nineteenth Century, American, with entire design composed of appliquéd and embroidered patches of colored calicos and cottons, in fine stitchery, Made by Ann Walgrave Warner, American, 1758-1826.

3. *Courtesy of:* LOUISIANA STATE MUSEUM.

Opera Cape, appliquéd and silk embroidery with chenille and beads on Cashmere; Cream and White, 1889, by Madame E. Hureau, New Orleans.

4. *Courtesy of:* LOUISIANA STATE MUSEUM.

Appliqué Patchwork, embroidered testimonial quilt, gift to General Zachary Taylor, 1848, by the Ladies Needlework Society of Dansville, Virginia.

mings on the aforementioned "mantelpiece banners" or for "trimming rigolettes, etc."

The pretty balls with which so many articles of dress are tasselled are made by tying a number of strands of wool at regular distances, and cutting through the wools between every two ties. You may wind over the hands of another person, or on a winding machine; but not on anything that will give way, as it is necessary to use some force in making your knots secure and compressing the wool as much as possible. About forty-eight strands will make a full, handsome ball, tied at every half-inch or a little more distant.

For making tassels, at least double the number, cut at nearly an inch apart. You may vary the pattern (if two colors are employed) by the mode of winding. By using two colors together, winding both at one movement, a variegated ball is made. Wind eight white, four colored, alternately, and spots will appear.... If cut at all unevenly, they must be shaved afterwards.

These ideas were suggested in 1858 and evidently took firm hold. They were used on fancy work well up into the 90's at which time there was a gradual cessation of interest in this style of ornamental needlework.

CHENILLE-WORK

Threads of chenille were generally introduced into all the Victorian needlework. Its pliability and quick covering qualities made it universally liked for filling in foregrounds, leaves of trees, and so forth. Its use also provided variety in tonal effects when large areas of one material might seem monotonous. An expert from a magazine states:

With the exception of the precious metals, chenille is the most costly material used in embroidery. It is mostly used on fine silk canvas, for flowers, arabesque patterns, birds, etc. It is used with beautiful effect on table covers, sofa pillows, being worked in Irish-stitch. Chenille is made of both silk and wool, the former being much the handsomer. If it is good, it presents the appearance of a roll of the best velvet, the surface being smooth and even. If not good, it separates. There are many sizes. The finest is used for embroidery on cloth and velvet. Chenille Wire is much used for flowers, leaves, etc. It is also of various sizes. Chenille, especially scarlet or black, is extensively used for ladies' head dresses, and is very beautiful. Some in the form of a net enclosing the back hair, with a rich fringe and tassels, are elegant. Some are plain; some mixed with gold, silver, coral, or jet ornaments.

The nineteenth century embroidery palette was provided with all sorts of materials with which to achieve masterpieces in needlework. So much variety became the ruin of the finer work since women finally gorged their canvases with bits of everything at hand, departing by leaps and bounds from the simple good taste expressed so beautifully by their forebears in the preceding century.

CHAPTER XXII

APPLIQUÉ, ARASENE EMBROIDERY AND RIBBON-WORK

"But the great Master said, 'I see
No best in kind, but in degree;
I gave a various gift to Each,
To charm, to strengthen, and to teach.'"
HENRY WADSWORTH LONGFELLOW.

IMILAR IN TECHNIQUE TO THE AN-cient needle art practiced by Spanish embroiderers of the twelfth century and later adopted by various tribes of American Indians is the ap-pliqué work of the nine-teenth century. The style, however, was considerably changed by our Victorian ladies.

Patterns and designs were totally foreign to the original European work, with the possible exception of the appliqués derived from Levan-tine sources, such as the Turkish smoking fezzes. These were very popular. *Peterson's Magazine* in December, 1867, published a pattern to be made up in scarlet cloth with royal-blue ap-pliquéd leaves bound with gold braid. Another pattern for a smoking cap published in this magazine for October, 1870, borrowed its design from Persia. The conventionalized cypress tree in red cloth embroidered in jade green and turquoise-blue silk or braid was to be applied to the cap or fez, material and color for which was optional, possibly for the gentleman to choose for himself.

Not all designs for lounging and smoking caps came from the East, however. In 1864 *Peterson's Magazine* presented a "Design for Smoking Cap . . . Scotch Shape." This cap was to be of black velvet on which blue grape leaves bound with white embroidery were to be ap-pliquéd.

Great effort was expended upon this style of needlework from the 1840's to the 1890's. Costumes and accessories were appliquéd as well as decorations for the home. Such items as bags and portfolios, caps, pincushions, what-nots, sachets, table covers, borders and otto-mans are typical.

A New York publication of 1842 suggests that for larger pieces of work a "set (allover) pat-tern may be used with good effect, where em-broidery can be introduced into some of the compartments, giving it a very rich and Persian-like appearance." It adds further:

Appliqué, combined with embroidery was much in vogue a few years since, particularly for handscreens, where the flowers and leaves were formed of velvet and the stalks embroid-ered with gold bullion. Some of these "fleurs de fantaisie" were made flat, others were raised by numerous small velvet leaves, carefully laid one partly over the other and tacked down with a fine silk; these leaves (lames de velours) required to be accurately cut with a steel punch.

About 1855 *Godey's Ladies' Magazine* offered its feminine readers novel designs as follows: pattern for "Antimacassar in scarlet and white appliqué," pattern for "Welcome Cushion" to be embroidered or appliquéd, pattern for "The National Cushion." This last was a version of the Stars and Stripes with red, white and blue notes indicating national independence and patriotism.

A cashmere opera cape embroidered with silks, chenille and bead work may be seen in the Louisiana State Museum. It was made in New Orleans in 1889 by Madame E. Hureau who was an American of French descent. The wrap is ingenious and artistic. The various materials used in the needlework have been combined with excellent consideration of line and composition. The colors also are well balanced in weight of tone and form a fine decorative unity.

Many wraps were decorated with needlework of various kinds during the last half of the nineteenth century. In the 50's, 60's and 70's tight-fitting jackets were made along the lines of the paletot, edged with braiding, embroidery and sometimes touches of appliqué. In the late 70's "Mantles" made their appearance, finally becoming cloaks in the early 90's when bell sleeves were added.

Mantles in 1871, illustrated in *Harper's Bazaar* of that year, were heavily embroidered with braid in combination with appliqué and ribbon-work and silk satin stitches. Black velvet mantles were edged with four-inch flounces of black lace. These ruffles rested very prettily over the large bustles of the polonaise.

The little round hats were laden with ostrich feathers; a lace and beribboned jabot hung from the back over the long corkscrew curls which rested on the shoulders. The ribbons were wide enough to carry sprays of flowers upon them, embroidered with smaller ribbons or arasene.

Appliqué in home decoration was used on borders for table covers in all sorts of designs incorporating Persian motifs. Hangings and window curtains were so embroidered. Those made of net were appliquéd around the edges with muslin leaves or lace pattern effects and then buttonholed, eyelet stitched and satin stitched. Such draperies required an enormous expenditure of time and effort.

PATCHWORK AND APPLIQUÉ

An exceedingly rare and handsome work in appliqué embroidery and patchwork has been ac-quired recently by the Metropolitan Museum of Art. It is a large quilt made by Ann Walgrave Warner between the years of 1758 and 1826. Words are inadequate to describe the amazing technical perfection and artistry with which infinitesimal bits of calico, chintz and cotton are sewn and applied to the cloth background. Taste and feeling is shown in selecting for each motif the patch of printed cotton most nearly matching the natural color and in harmony with the object portrayed. The calico used for the butterflies' wings appears designed to order. The tiny details of the bird cage held by the elegant gentleman, the little bird perched upon his hand, the lady's gown, bodice, bonnet and hair, the details of the children's costumes, the large bowl of variegated flowers, as well as every detail in the landscape bespeak the greatest care, patience and observation.

The large birds perched among the flowers are rich in pattern and color. Flowers, trees and leaves are simply beautiful. The animals, dogs, deer and sheep, and the costume of the watchful shepherd are first appliquéd and then embroidered about their edges with a wealth of different stitches. All the motifs, indeed, are finely embroidered along the edges and amplified to add quality when needed, as in the little faces.

Not content with this display of talent in the central panel, Ann Walgrave Warner added a magnificent border of scrolls composed of vines, leaves and flowers which is in itself a work of high artistry and fine craftsmanship. Buttonhole stitch, satin stitch and other stitches used in early crewel embroideries have been introduced, and through the discretion with which they have been placed a subtle quality has been achieved which gives to the quilt the dignity and atmosphere of a tapestry wall hanging. It is a splendid, delightful and inspiring example of nineteenth century needlework.

A labor of love is the quilt given to General Zachary Taylor by the Ladies' Needleworking Society of Danville, Virginia, in 1848. They presented it "as a slight testimony to their admiration for one not less distinguished for his clemency and forbearance than for his valor and patriotism."

This appliquéd quilt was made of small patches of various materials used at the time—calico, percale, merino, cotton—and arranged in blocks to compose the entire area. Some quilting has been used around the central part of the cover and to hold down the blocks. Sides and tops of the blocks have been embroidered in silks with rosebuds, morning-glories, violets and other small flower designs. The center contains a silk-embroidered laurel wreath within which the testimonial of the Virginia ladies is finely written in script with indelible ink and may be read today by visitors to the Louisiana State Museum in New Orleans where the quilt is displayed as a testimonial to their fine needlework ability.

It may be interesting to note in passing that the patchwork appliqué quilts were a style of work particularly disliked by Mrs. Pullman, the needlework authority in New York in 1858. In *The Ladies' Manual of Fancy Work* she strongly recommended the use of silk, velvet or satin for the purpose of appliqué work, adding:

> Of the patchwork with calico, I have nothing to say. Valueless indeed must be the time of that person who can find no better use for it than to make ugly counterpanes and quilts of pieces of cotton. Emphatically is the proverb true of cotton patchwork, "Le jeu ne vaut pas la chandelle!" It is not worth either the candle or gas light.

However, in spite of Mrs. Pullman's decree, both of these quilts appliquéd in the despised cotton, have found a place in a museum while the rich silks, satins and velvets have taken second place in the estimation of the next century!

METHOD

Some idea of the processes used in application may be gleaned from the following observations on the technique as expressed in the Victorian age.

> Appliqué, or application, is the laying of one kind of material over another. Pieces of different forms and colors are placed one over another, and secured at the edges by braids, cords, or embroidery; if neatly done and arranged with taste and ingenuity, it is exceedingly attractive. It has been applied very successfully to ladies' cloaks, in the 1840's to the 1850's.
>
> Appliqué may be used on any material, such as cloth, velvet, silk, leather, or muslin and lace. In forming the pattern, it should be carefully drawn on the material intended for the appliqué, and a corresponding one on that in-
> tended for the ground, which may consist of the same or other material. Velvet can be beautifully arranged upon cloth, or satin upon velvet, or silk upon satin, muslin on lace, or lace upon muslin. If velvet, satin or silk is used, it is necessary to paste a thin paper over the back, before the appliqué is cut, to render it firm and prevent its unraveling. The pieces, when cut, are to be carefully tacked down on the material, and edges secured whether by cord, braid, or satin stitch embroidery, varying the colors according to taste. Where flowers are chosen, the color of the flowers or leaves is preferable.
>
> What were called Turkish designs were peculiarly suited for this kind of work. Vine leaves were also considered very handsome, the tendrils being formed by cord, chenille, and so forth.
>
> For bags of various kinds merino and cashmere were used, making the appliqué of velvet and silk. This was also considered suitable for slippers, sofa pillows, and so forth. Edgings with gold cord, braid or chenille gave a finishing touch. Slippers of kid with velvet appliqué or velvet slippers with kid appliqué were thought very handsome and desirable.

CLOTH-WORK

This is the name of a popular technique used in the 70's and 80's and described as follows:

> This is so similar to Appliqué that a separate direction may seem unnecessary. The only distinction is in the fact that in Patent Appliqué the pattern is stamped ready for finishing with braid, cord, etc., and that the term Appliqué is applied to muslin and lace. Clothwork, of course, would be confined entirely to that material. The pattern given would do for either, but cloth of two kinds would be as rich and effective.
>
> The pattern given is applicable either for an Ottoman cushion, bag, or toilet-cover. If for an Ottoman cushion, the groundwork should be of fine cloth, of any color. First decide upon size of pattern, then the color for the leaves cut out in the size you want; then mark with white French chalk upon the cloth the direction in which you want the stem to run; with thin, liquid glue, slightly moisten the back of the leaves, and place them in a natural position near the stem; they must not be again removed. Place over them a sheet of paper and book for a weight. When the leaves are laid in their proper places, commence working the stem, and edge the leaves with chain-

stitch, and let the stitches pass through both velvet and cloth. The veining of the leaves should be rather lighter than the leaves, and worked in close satin-stitch. The cushion should be filled with fine wool, and trimmed with a twisted cord, with massive tassels.

Machines for cutting and stamping were developed during this needlework craze. The following notice is from a periodical of the day:

As appliqué requires stamping tools and machinery for any extensive piece of work, it can only be used by private persons, on a comparatively small scale; but when neatly done, for bags, slippers, ottomans, etc., it richly repays the trouble taken.

ARASENE-WORK

Webster's dictionary gives two spellings for the name of the thread used in this needlework technique: "arrasene" or "arasene." It is there described as "a kind of mixed thread of wool and silk used in raised embroidery." This explanation is not very illuminating but very little was written about this style of work in the time of its popularity.

Family legends suggest that it was a form of embroidery akin to ribbon-work and inspired by the French needlework popular in America in the late nineteenth century and early twentieth. The work was seldom used for anything but floral sprays. Narrow ribbon threads were often employed in a manner resembling chenille-work, small backstitches or running stitches placed close together making a solid filling for the flower forms.

Peterson's Magazine in December, 1882, offered a pattern for "Arrasen Embroidery" in full colors as a present to its subscribers. The design shows two panels of glove-box size. Upon one is a design of orchids and upon the other, wide roses in a spray. These are to be worked in mauve pinks, violets and orchid-purple threads against the deep blue green of the velvet background. Leaves are to be made in rusty-green and yellow green-gold colors. Gold threads, in Oriental stitch, and a row of braid make a finish on the outer edges of the box.

The period when this needlework flourished was a lush one. *Harper's Bazaar* about 1884, acknowledging its indebtedness for its New York fashion note to James McCreery, Lord and Taylor, Stern Brothers and E. J. Derning stated that

Dark red, blue or changeable satin parasols will be used for driving in the Park; some of these have arasene embroidery in a single cluster, while others have a border of stripes and some are formed entirely of six or seven wide stripes of different shades.

Pongee parasols were also used, both plain and with embroidery, "for coaching."

These were the "Elegant Eighties" when ladies were lavish with embroidery and laces, silks, satins, and taffetas.

An evening dress of the period is described as made of silk mousseline taffeta in Nattier blue and designed along Princess lines with a tight-fitting shirred bodice. The skirt flared out to an exceedingly full swirl and train, the hem defined by a series of deep tucks extending to the knee line. The puffed sleeves were embroidered with arasene ribbons in floral sprays and parts of the bodice also were decorated in the same way.

When real lace was inserted to soften a high-collared neckline the ribbon embroidery extended its dainty leaves and flowers upon it, thus tying foundation materials and trimmings into a shimmering unity of design. The colors of these arasene ribbons were usually the antique pastels. The embroidery resembled in appearance the costume embroideries of the eighteenth century in France. Pale rose, dusty rose, sage green, gray green, faded purple, and pale pink violet were universally applied to dress fabrics.

Included also in costume embroideries of the day was

RIBBON-WORK

This ornamental needlework was applied to collars and cuffs of children's dresses as well as to the costumes of their elders. Indeed almost everything included in the fancy work items of the nineteenth century was likewise beribboned. Styles referred to most frequently were China ribbon-work and quilling.

"China ribbon" was used in 1842, primarily for flowers and leaves. Silk thread was run along one edge of this ribbon, pulled in to the desired shape, and then applied upon satin foundations either for pictures or for costume ornamentation.

A term used frequently in the late eighteenth and nineteenth centuries was "quilled work" or "quilling." It was usually applied to a type of ribbon trimming. In 1858, Mrs. Pullman describes the method.

TO QUILL RIBBONS FOR TRIMMINGS

This is so much used that many readers will probably be glad of a hint. Allow nearly three times as much ribbon as the length required; have a piece of very narrow ribbon tape to run it on; take a stitch or two to fasten the tape and center of the width of the ribbon; make a small plait towards the right, and another close to it, but not folding over it, to the left; run them down lightly, through the tape; and this double plait being made, leave about half the length of ribbon plain, before making another. This looks much handsomer than a fuller quilling. A gold or fancy cord should afterwards be run along the center to hide the stitches.

The French often put on this trimming by slightly gumming the tape and pressing it down in its place. I may add, they also fasten down raw edges of silk or satin in this way very neatly. It answers extremely well.

Such ribbon quilling did "extremely well" for hand screens also. These were as numerous for protection from the sun, heat from the fireplace, or to shield the face in embarrassing moments, as were the little satin parasols. An example of such a screen is in the Litchfield Museum. It is made of cream satin mounted on cardboard of an oblong shape. The center on each side has been cross-stitched with brilliant wool roses and buds, obviously taken from a Berlin pattern. The handle is ribbon-wrapped with a bow at the end. A heavy silk and wool fringe has been worked around the outer edge as a finish. Ribbons were much used to finish baskets, boxes and other items.

Philadelphia Quaker samplers of the early nineteenth century had borders made of shelled and quilled satin ribbons sewn along the outside edges, a fashion which presumably originated sometime during the eighteenth century in Europe.

Mention that the technique was taught in the schools in Boston occurs in journals of the 1770's. The Moravian School also was famous for its instruction in crêpe ribbon work, along with the other embroidery techniques.

Caps in these early days were beribboned and braided upon net. Baby caps also were sometimes ornamented with this work. But in the 80's and 90's the most extensive use of ribbon-work was on ball gowns and elaborate evening costumes. Rows and rows of ribbon embroidery was festooned on collars, bodices and low-draped sleeves, polonaises and hems. The flowers selected for representation and application in this period were heartsease, fuchsias, convolvulus and moss-roses. This particular fashion ceased in the needlework world during the early twentieth century.

It is sometimes difficult to accommodate one's mind to accept the extremes in taste reflected in nineteenth century needlework and to realize that so many women were occupying their needles merely in the business of gadget-making. Innumerable and indescribable what-nots were appliquéd in pale blue moiré silk and claret velvet, beribboned and braided with gold-threaded embroidery for a finish! Butterfly watch-hooks of white glazed calico embroidered with pink and green Berlin wool-work and bound with maize crocheted edges, with an added bead or two to make the effect irresistible, were suspended upon the wall with quilled ribbon fastenings.

At the same moment other women were conceiving and executing the appliquéd patched and embroidered quilts with their studied design, excellent taste, selectivity and good technical judgment. The means for needlework were universally the same, but to what ends were they applied!

BEADWORK WITH WOOL COMBINATIONS

"Nothing useless is, or low;
Each thing in its place is best;
And what seems but idle show
Strengthens and supports the rest."
HENRY WADSWORTH LONGFELLOW.

 O THE POOR INDIAN! HOW amazed would he have been to see the myriads of colored bits of crystal and the opalescent, shimmering steel and nickel beads provided for the Victorian ladies' needlework. Beads in hundreds of shades were imported from Berlin for their use and enjoyment, a wealth of material that would have filled the hearts of aboriginal women with the utmost joy.

With the Indians, beadwork was an ancient art passed from tribe to tribe and generation to generation. Patterns and color combinations became symbolic as well as decorative. The Victorians had the same fundamental desire to ornament their possessions, but the art with them was a new one. And instead of creating something directly from the elements or expressing something from the heart as did the Indians, the patterns already used in Berlin work were copied in beads.

Nothing could better illustrate the popular trend in fashions for beadwork during the middle nineteenth century than a quotation from *Frank Leslie's Gazette* published in 1855 in which a bright idea for a "novelty" in beadwork is set forth in all its glory.

INFANTS' CAP IN BEAD EMBROIDERY

The exquisite bead-work of Germany has long been a subject of almost as much wonder as admiration among the English women; since the examination of the beautiful display of that work in the Crystal Palace, it has been an object of ambition with us to attempt to produce something equally rich and elegant. The difficulties in the way of such an achievement were such as would hardly be believed by those who have not tried similar experiments. The great difficulty was the obtaining of a sufficient variety of beads. To produce the effect of a well-executed painting (which all good bead-work should do) the shades of the beads should be sufficiently numerous to blend together in the most perfect manner. In vain, we ransacked the city warehouses for the needed varieties. True, we saw hundreds of casks of these tiny beads, and laughed to ourselves at the idea of there being any difficulty in the matter; but when we came to examine them, we found that our utmost research would not enable us to obtain a quarter of the necessary colors. We did, at last, what perhaps it would have been wise to have done at first—applied to the fountainhead, and sent an order to the manufacturer at Berlin for a quantity of every seed bead that was made. The result astonished us. Between three and four hundred colors made their appearance; and it soon became perfectly clear, that if we did not succeed in bead-painting, it would not be for want of materials.

The next consideration was, on what article to employ our skill; and considering crochet as one of the most universally popular kinds of work, and feeling, moreover, that though screens and cushions, and knick-knacks of all sorts, might go out of fashion, that babies never would and that consequently any article for the wear of those small specimens of humanity could not fail to be generally popular, we have selected a Baby's Cap as the first example of bead embroidery.

Besides the materials we have enumerated, two ordinary Berlin patterns will be required. One should be a wreath, not more than twenty-eight to thirty-six squares wide, the other a small bouquet, thirty squares wide, and twenty-four deep. A few squares more or less do not signify. Choose such a design as will afford a variety of shades and colors. For this reason, roses are always suitable; because, even if not painted in the patten, you can make one in crimsons, another in scarlets, a third in yellows, while all possible variety of greens can be introduced in the leaves. White flowers only are inadmissible on a ground of cotton; but in bead-embroidering, in general, we must not forget that there are shades of white, as well as of any other color.

"Bead-painting" was well established when, nine years later, *Peterson's Magazine* published patterns for beadwork pictures (chiefly the popular Swiss chalets and hamlets), chess table tops in blue and white squares with a black flower in the white square, slipper holders, whisk broom holders, pincushions, D'Oyley designs and bridal purses in crochet embroidered with nickel beads.

For dressing room or bedroom adornment *Peterson's* offered in 1867

A Toilet Cushion to be made of emerald green velvet in a Greek key design to be worked in crystal beads, also fringed with bead loops.

Popular and fashionable designs from *Godey's Lady's Book* also included

A Ruby Velvet (toilet) cushion bead work pattern to be embroidered with beads, bugles and a deep looped beaded fringe.

At the same time a pattern for a tri-cornered jewel case and pincushion appeared, to be made up in velvet and embroidered with beads in an elaborate floral spray. A fringe of beaded loops adorned the sides of these triangular boxes. Card baskets in various sizes and shapes were ornamented with beads. An egg basket was a particularly elaborate contribution to the breakfast table; the chenille "basket" embroidered in imitation of woven straw rose from a heavily beaded base to contain Father's three-minute eggs.

For costume decoration beaded borders were popular. In 1868 *Harper's Bazaar* published the following instructions:

This border forms an exceedingly tasteful turning for borders and waists. It is made of black silk braid and lace, on which jet beads and bugles are sewn. The bottom is furnished with jet grelots between the leaves of the edge, the latter of which are veined with bugles.

This type of costume ornamentation included a "braiding" technique in beads which is described in detail in Chapter XXI.

Novelties in costume accessories included leaves beaded on net for the coiffure; bracelets either sewn with steel beads on black velvet bands or in white and shell colors, imitating the large cameos worn at the time; brooches and ear-rings made in the same manner and mounted upon pendants in imitation of the ruby, garnet and emerald ear-rings worn by the wealthy. Another novelty offered in 1868 was

"A Bead Mosaic Case for a pocket comb, to be made with a blue foundation worked in diamonds of steel, crystal, white and opaque beads."

Peterson's Magazine in November, 1870, presented

The Pompadour Bow Slipper in Berlin Work and Beads designed for the use of red, black and white beads in an all-over dot repeat, with a large green, black and white bead-work bow placed on the toe of the slipper.

Lamp stands and mats galore were ornamented with beads in almost every conceivable pattern. A pattern from *Frank Leslie's Gazette* shows a "Mat for an Urn, to be worked in beaded roses."

Some of these round mats were designed with considerable taste. One in the collection of Mrs. E. P. York of Connecticut has real charm in its background of Egyptian turquoise with the Persian tree motif worked in light corn-yellow gold.

Another lamp mat is an unusual example of steel-bead and wool technique. It is in the col-

Gay Nineties, Velvet beaded shoe; Whisk broom holder, about 1870, New York.

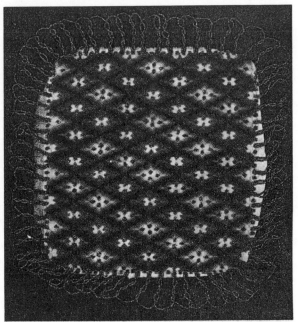

Lamp mat beaded and wool needlework on canvas. Hungarian stitches. 1850, Brooklyn, New York.

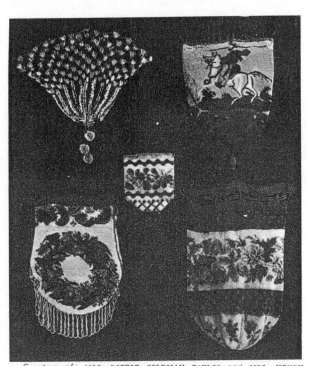

3. Detail of Beadwork and Satin Embroidery on satin skirt, worn by Mrs. Henry Pratt Janes of Baltimore, Maryland, nineteenth century, American. 4. Group of nineteenth century beadwork bags. Cantaloup seeds and nickel beads by Mrs. A. B. Collingbourne, Elgin, Illinois. Arabian Horseman, Design beadwork, 1860, New York. Honeysuckle design beadwork by Mrs. William Sinclair, New York. Persian Flower Wreath design beadwork by Mrs. Enoch Pratt, Baltimore, Maryland. Roses and Set Pattern beadwork, 1860, Maryland.

Peterson's Magazine: July, 1867.

TOILET CUSHION,
Embroidered with Crystal Beads on Emerald Green Velvet.

Toilet Cushion of emerald green velvet with Greek key design
to be embroidered with crystal beads.

RUBY VELVET TOILET CUSHION.

Ruby red velvet cushion (toilet) to be embroidered with
beads. Designs on sides for additional silkwork, if desired

TRI-CORNERED JEWEL CASE AND PINCUSHION,
IN BEADS ON VELVET.

Tri-cornered jewel case and pin
cushion to be embroidered with
beads on velvet.

LAMP STAND.

BEAD PATTERN CIGAR-CASE.

Lampstand design (in circle) for bead
embroidery, with a bead pattern for a
cigar case below.

ENGRAVED DESIGNS FOR BEADWORK FROM PETERSON'S
AND GODEY'S MAGAZINES OF 1867.

(From AUTHOR'S COLLECTION.)

lection of Mrs. Stephen M. Harrisson and came to her from her family in Brooklyn. The design is worked in what is known technically as the Hungarian or Bargello stitch. The background is on a fine mesh single-thread canvas upon which a small diamond pattern has been worked in an interesting form of "counting." The diamonds contain five color gradations, shading from the darkest color next to the black outline into the white center. The colors in which the diamonds worked are gun-metal gray, next to a diamond in cerulean blue, alternating in a row across the square. The row above begins with a diamond in red orange shading through yellow into the white center. The next diamond is in shades of green into gold and following it is a diamond in deep cherry red shading into coral pink. The sequence is repeated across the row. The design is further enhanced by the addition of little steel beads which are sewn into the centers of the diamonds and which also form a fringed border on the outside. The mat is lined with pink silk.

From 1850 on, beadwork designs were continuously published for cigar cases. A particularly fine example of this period showing beadwork at its best is in the Museum of the City of New York, the gift of Mrs. Laurent Oppenheim. It shows a small beaded landscape and a castle resting on a scroll surrounded by roses. The background is cream color. The border and case enclosing the beadwork decoration is of gold tooled leather, a very handsome setting for cigars.

This style of beadwork belongs to that class of work which rose above the chaotic, fussy designs represented by the beaded candlestands and hour-glass lambrequins which flourished in this era. An attempt was made by many women in America to achieve some of the qualities inherent in the lovely sablé beadwork famous in France during the period of Louis XIV. This work, a lost art, was revived by Madame de Maintenon at her school of needlework in St. Cyr outside of Paris. It was called sablé because the tiny beads used were as fine as grains of sand. They were made into exquisite landscapes, flower panels, and so forth, sewn with slender curved needles and strands of hair. Mrs. De Witt Clinton Cohen, a collector of these sablé examples, feels that most American beadwork has

been derived primarily from Viennese and German sources but it is possible that this delicate French work also was an inspiration. Certainly finer workmanship did appear and while far removed from the French work and coarser in its beadings, this American work reflects a greater refinement in design than was to be derived from the Berlin patterns alone.

Some of these artistic beadwork bags made in the last half of the nineteenth century are to be found in collections today. They are in an excellent state of preservation. Made with great skill by immediate ancestors, they have been accorded reverent care. From the collection of Mrs. Robert Coleman Taylor is an ingenious bag made by A. B. Collingbourne of Elgin, Ohio, when she was fifteen years of age. It is composed of dried cantaloupe seeds which have been sewn together in a bag design with nickel beads at the intersections. The work shows great skill.

A very handsome bag introduces the beaded technique applied to pictorial effects. The figure of an Arabian scout is seated upon an elaborately beaded horse stitched in browns. The landscape is in opalescent beads of powder blue which have a pinkish cast in their high lights. The top part of the Arabian costume is deep turquoise; the pantaloons are carried out in two shades of Oriental pink; the boots are red-orange beads and the turban in red and green beads matches the saddle. The foreground is composed with a variety of greens. The base is nicely weighted in color with light and dark green oak leaves which are silhouetted against a background of maroon beads. It is most effectively and delicately made.

Another bag of fine beadwork in Mrs. Taylor's collection, which was made in the same period, presents a banded effect typical of the designs used on many other purses of that day. The strip is composed of roses, trumpet flowers, asters, chrysanthemums and the Virginia creeper. Other bands of brown beads above and below have a set repeat-pattern of dots. The color scheme is a lovely blending of oranges, yellow reds on the wine tone, rose and whites. Browns and a cream background supply the border tones and among the sprays of roses below are a few touches of blue to offset the many warm colors. This bag is charming and reflects the period at its best.

Equally delicate and original is the tiny purse in beadwork designed and worked in a honey-suckle pattern which belonged to the mother of Mrs. Robert Coleman Taylor, Mrs. William Sinclair, of Hudson-on-the-Hudson. The tiny beads used in the flowers are of pink and gold. Emerald and dark green beads make the leaves, and the lattice border design uses green and gold. The background is an oyster white worked with opalescent beads. The little purse was lined, according to the 1870 fashions, with a checked taffeta material which matched the owner's skirt, which, by the way, measured twelve yards around. The original is without any top but a similar purse, which belonged to the author's great-grandmother, has a round gold-clasped top resembling the round tops of powder cases used today. Such tops were engraved rather elaborately and were either initialed or had the first name written in full across the center.

Mrs. Henry Pratt Janes was given a bead-work bag by Mrs. Enoch Pratt of Baltimore, Maryland, designed and made in the 1860's with a panel called "A Persian Wreath" executed on one side. The colorings are charmingly soft and delicate in tones of pink and wine. The deep fringe is made of intense rose-colored beads, creating a very dainty effect.

The Essex Institute in Salem has an interesting collection of bead purses and bags, some with landscape patterns. One interesting design features a row of little white ducks along the border, instead of the usual flowers seen on most examples. The Litchfield Historical Society also possesses some fine examples of this art.

Among representative examples of nineteenth century beadwork on a larger scale is the front panel of a reception dress of bronze brown satin. The elegance of this gown lies not only in the material, which is heavy enough to stand alone, but in the embroidery which sweeps from hem to bodice. Beautifully balanced sprays of American flowers form the central motif, including spotted tiger lilies, Virginia creeper and blossoms of the bleeding heart whose bell-shaped tongues serve to unite the panel with the graceful scrolls at the sides.

The embroidery is composed of bronze beads and silks ranging from cream to deep gold browns, done in satin stitch technique. The gown was worn by Mrs. Henry Pratt Janes of Baltimore, and is now owned by Mrs. John K. Sloan.

The technique most frequently used for bead embroidery is described in the *Ladies' Hand Book* by Miss Florence Hartley published in 1859.

METHOD OF WORKING

This work is done in tent-stitch, on canvas, of silk or imitation silk. The beads must be very carefully adapted to the canvas, that each one may just cover the space allotted to it.

A great number of articles are now ornamented entirely in bead-work, such as small tables, sofa-cushions, mats, baskets, slippers, screens, etc. The largest sized beads, No. 1, are used for tables; No. 2, for cushions, mats, etc.; and No. 3, for hand-screens, watch-cases, slippers.

The stitch used is always tent-stitch (needle-point).

The designs for bead-work are generally taken from the Berlin patterns. The material used for attaching the beads to the canvas, is a waxed sewing-silk, or a fine twisted cotton thread. The last is mostly used by the Germans, who greatly excel in all kinds of bead-work, and who apply it to nearly all kinds of ornamental articles. They use beads of all kinds, mingling them with patterns worked in silk or worsted.

A great difference exists in the quality of beads, particularly in the gilt and steel ones.

Where colored glass beads are used, it is better to arrange them in separate bags, with the color written on the outside of the bag.

By the twentieth century this art had vanished almost as quickly as it came, leaving us but a few gay and tenderly beaded nosegays as a memory of the mauve and lavendar decade.

CHAPTER XXIV

SEWING ACCESSORIES

"No man is born into the world whose work
Is not born with him. There is always work,
And tools to work withal, for those who will."
JAMES RUSSELL LOWELL.

URIOUS AND QUAINT ITEMS IN the way of sewing aids and accessories have been handed down by mothers to daughters for centuries. Each generation has successively treasured these vital implements which have made fine needlework possible, and it is only fitting and proper that these humble aids should receive a passing word in recognition of the great assistance they have given.

EMBROIDERY FRAMES AND WORKTABLES

In large colonial homes the living room usually contained an embroidery frame. This was often finely made. The frame shown opposite page 150 is from a room in the Mount Vernon mansion used by Nelly Custis. It is a handsome example of furniture craftsmanship, with its delicately turned legs and baskets for containing wools. Upon this stand today remains a framed piece of canvas with the needlepoint design uncompleted just as she left it years ago.

When friends gathered in the living room for an evening's visit, the hostess would work at her frame while lending an ear to merry chatter or serious discussions of national importance. It was not uncommon for a guest to take a turn at the frame, adding a few rows of needlepoint or cross-stitch for her hostess. Such an exchange was not surprising and was as usual as sitting in for a hand of bridge today. In Europe it was not uncommon in the eighteenth century for the visiting beau also to take a stitch or two at the needlework frame. Many men of that day could embroider or execute needlepoint as handsomely as their ladies, as many men are doing today.

Embroidery stands were not as numerous as worktables. Martha Washington was a most enthusiastic needleworker, and many mahogany saddlebag worktables have been named for her. These reproductions reached the height of their popularity in the 1900's; since then they have been on the wane and one scarcely ever hears of them.

A worktable fashionable in the 1800's was of Sheraton design, circular topped and having little bronzed feet. Three drawers were arranged underneath to hold beads used for the making of bags. The table top opened in the center to allow space for the needlework, while at the back a little raised shelf provided room for a candle or the little sewing bird whose bill would open and patiently hold the round embroidery hoop, or the end of a long seam, while the young mistress of the house performed her needlework chore. Both were too busy for song!

From *Godey's Magazine* in 1833, a fashion plate for correct morning costumes shows a lady wearing the customary embroidered sewing apron, and beside her to contain her materials is a dainty little basket sewing-stand. The cup on the leg of the stand is for yarns or threads and is quite like those designed for the Nelly Custis embroidery frame.

That the Hepplewhite Sheraton period contributed lovely tables for this purpose is evidenced by collectors' reports of such items. Possibly Chippendale gave inspiration for one or two. The Empire and classic revival period brought in several styles with central columned legs, brass trimmings and brass lions' feet upon the branched base. Black lacquer stands came by way of the Orient for a fortunate few to enjoy. The beautiful top would open to disclose beneath a nest of little squares like jewel boxes, all decorated with lacquer, each compartment having its own ivory-knobbed cover. All manner of sewing tricks could be tucked away in such a cabinet and just a look at all the little Chinese figures posing under enchanting golden trees and flowers was enough to start a wagonload of ideas whizzing past the mind's eye. One had to sew them down quickly while such enchantment lasted.

SEWING BASKETS

In the museum at Mount Vernon is a memento of Martha Washington's interest in stitchery, her hand-woven workbasket. Substantial yet graceful in make, one pictures Mrs. Washington carrying it about filled with yarns of gold and browns with which to complete the twelve chair seats designed in a shell pattern which she was making as a gift for her grandchildren.

Made in about 1790, a little later period than Martha Washington's sewing basket, is a handmade version used in Mystic, Connecticut, by Nancy Noyes Denison, the grandmother of Mrs. N. Stanton Gates. This eighteenth century basket has a deep center which is left free for the needlework while around the upper inside edge are woven little nest-shaped cups which

were intended to hold the spools, scissors, and anything else needed for embroidery or sewing.

A vital part of the equipment for needlework, these baskets often were made at home by the housekeeper herself. From Georgia to New Hampshire basketry was another handicraft practiced by colonial women. They used the materials at hand, from the long pine needles in the South to the rushes in Rhode Island. Hickory, willow, ash and oak splits were used in many types of baskets employed for various household purposes.

Another style of basketry and a most important asset to good grooming were the indispensable cap baskets, also hand-woven in various shapes and styles. These were made to carry within their silk-lined folds the exquisitely embroidered fragile caps, so fashionable in the late eighteenth century and worn well into the nineteenth.

When Milady removed her bonnet these little caps were donned for wear in the house. Often three or four were carried in a basket. They were delicate bits of needlework made of muslin, lacework on net or braiding on the same material, neatly laundered and starched, ready to adorn the coiffure of curls after a long journey by coach to the prescribed destination.

Nancy Noyes Denison of Mystic, Connecticut, also owned one of these carriers which, no doubt, held a precious cap of her own handiwork.

In the Memorial Museum in Deerfield, Massachusetts, may be found such a basket large enough to hold three or four caps. Since the owner, Anne Grant of Virginia, was a famously beautiful Southern belle, it was highly important that she have many changes in caps to enhance her charms during frequent visits about the country for balls, assemblies and other social events.

A pattern for an embroidered cap bag appeared in *Harper's Bazaar* as late as 1869 and the method of making it is described as follows:

> This bag consists of two parts of fine straw braid covered on the outside with fine brown cashmere, which is embroidered in the manner shown by the illustration with Point Russe of brown silk twist. The two parts are joined along the middle of the bottom so that they can be wholly opened out. A button and loop in the middle of the top of the bag serve for fastening. The outer edges are bordered with

heavy brown silk cord. The bag may be made of pasteboard, and covered with cashmere on both sides. Striped drilling embroidered with "Point Russe" of different colored silk is also very suitable for such a bag.

Before baskets were made but continuing along in their company came the fashion of wearing

SEWING APRONS

Until comparatively recent years, aprons were a necessary accompaniment of sewing and needlework. In the early days of America housewives wore what are termed "pockets," some of which were described in Chapter V. They were in reality what their name implies, only they were aprons in shape and had a deep pocket slit down the middle front which held within its spacious cavern everything needed for sewing or embroidery. Tied with tape around the waist, these early aprons were handy in the extreme since they held everything in the lap and if a traveling hawker of wares arrived at the door with his array of tempting household utilities, Madame Housekeeper could jump up and investigate the novelties without having yarns, needles and other paraphernalia scattered in all directions. So also could she tend the roast over the fire, turn the spit or take a hand with the baby in the cradle near by.

These pockets were thrifty items, too, since they were usually made from the odds and ends about the house. Leftovers of homespun linen were patched together to compose the area needed and then beautified with crewel embroidery in flowery patterns. Such adornment not only served to make the apron attractive but had the added feature of covering the seaming of the bits of linen. The pocket back was usually made of cotton or a material of less consequence than the treasured homespun.

A crewel-embroidered pocket-apron made by Mrs. Eunice Lyman, wife of Captain Seth Lyman of Northfield, Massachusetts, and dated 1770, is on exhibition in the Memorial Hall at Deerfield.

A similar apron, crewel-embroidered on white cotton, was made by Lydia Lambert. She married a soldier in the French and Indian Wars, which would date this needlework as belonging to the middle eighteenth century. Lydia Lambert belonged to the Salem community and her apron remains there today in the Essex Institute as a silent testimonial to her housewifely occupation.

The thrifty spirit of earlier America is reflected in another apron made obviously from left-over scraps. These odd bits of cloth are arranged in a pattern so that they balance each other in a semblance of symmetry. The border of the apron has been carefully bound with a rolled edge of the same patched materials. In the "pocket" were odds and ends of yarns to make useful little gifts for relatives and friends. One of them, a quaint potholder, remained with the pocket. It was cross-stitched in alternate squares in blue-green and cherry-red yarns. It bears the inscription:

EXCEPT THE KETTLE BOILING B.
FILLING THE POT SPOILS THE T.

Both apron and holder were made by a Quaker of Monroe, New York, known as "Grandmother Heaton." Her descendants date her work in 1823, but its style and material might have belonged to an earlier period.

Silk-embroidered taffeta aprons became fashionable in the 1800's. A lovely example in the Litchfield Historical Society collection was made in 1830 in Connecticut. It is of pearl-gray taffeta "that stands alone." It is embroidered with clusters of white silk flowers and small green silk leaves around its borders. Small pockets to hold the scissors, threads and so forth, are edged with the same needleworked pattern.

About the same size is the *Godey* apron worn in the 1833 fashion plate of morning costumes previously referred to. The material in this apron is violet taffeta edged with black lace and embroidered in black and gray braiding. The dress is white; the lady's collar in corn yellow is braided in black with gray tassels on the ends of the tie. The needlework in her hand is evidently a strip of white embroidery.

Sewing aprons passed out of general use in the late nineteenth century and with them departed a graceful as well as a very useful addition to feminine apparel. Possibly they will return to favor in the near future.

PINS, NEEDLES, NEEDLECASES

It is claimed that the earliest needles were made of thorns and that Eve's first covering was put together with such means. From that time on through history needles have been of various materials, of bones, pieces of wood, shell and iron. The steel needles made in tremendous quantities in later times have been a great boon to women.

The history of these modest little implements follows a long winding maze down the corridors of time. In colonial America sewing materials and accessories were expensive, evidently due to costs of importation. Needles were precious and there is a story from Virginia telling how the one and only needle, borrowed for use by the visitor, had to be "sharpened up" for the occasion. Eliza Southgate of Maine stated in 1800 that she could save five dollars for the purchase of a curly wig by the careful use of "pins and paper."

The old term "pin money" must have originated around this time from the saving of money for their purchase. English and French ladies used quantities of pins to fasten their clothes and, in a degree, American society women did likewise.

Needles and pins, needles and pins,
When a man marries his trouble begins.

The old adage may have reflected the sentiment of this period. In a fashion journal of 1802 the comment was made that, "fashionables now-adays make almost as little use of a pin as of a needle." This may have been an attempt to encourage economy in the use of pins, or it might be interpreted as a satirical comment on the growing ennui in this class.

Early pins were made of wire with a top added to make a head. The first all-in-one pins, combining the head and stem together in a single process, were invented in America in 1824 by an American, Lemuel Wellman Wright, but it was not until many years later that pins were manufactured in such quantities that they might disappear by the dozen without anyone minding.

"HOUSEWIFES" AND NEEDLE HOLDERS

Needlecases have served all races for many ages. Oriental princesses kept spoons in their cases as well as needles. Margaret of Austria possessed a case which included besides needles, scissors, a stiletto, little tweezers, and other implements.

Needlework "caskets" in sixteenth century France belonging to the King of Navarre were embellished with precious stones. These too were made to hold other valuable items along with the sewing aids. In the seventeenth century the small boxes were made in a more delicate manner and in the next period boxes were developed of great beauty and charm. Mother-of-pearl, enamels, precious woods, ivories, gold and silver, all the odd and rich materials, composed the needlecases of the well-to-do in the eighteenth century.

It was not until well into the nineteenth century that the term "Housewif" or "House-wife" was applied to cases which held sewing appointments. A pattern for such a sewing case is reproduced from *Godey's Magazine* of 1860. It is called a "Housewife for a Gentleman." The pattern is for a roll case and the design could be copied by any ambitious lady as a gift for her favorite admirer. The American Indians had such rolled cases made of skins with pockets to contain needles, threads, and thimbles.

Another gay pattern shows a doll to be made for a sewing "Work Table Companion." All the implements are attached to her dress which is red with blue bands and suggests those worn by young ladies who nursed the wounded soldiers during the Civil War, sometimes called "Daughters of the Regiment." This also was published in *Godey's* in 1860.

The few cases used by our colonial antecedents have been designed in many ways. In the famous needlework and embroidery collection of Mrs. De Witt Clinton Cohen in New York, is a pincushion, needle and thimble case which was used by Martha Washington while at Mount Vernon. It has been made from scraps of silk gowns in the spirit of economy exercised by all colonial women during those days. The case is designed to fold up like an envelope and contains a series of small pockets for holding the needlework accessories.

A case in the Museum of the City of New York contains a fascinating group of sewing aids used by early New York women. In the groups opposite pages 148 and 150 are shown:

THIMBLE IN A FITTED CASE, 1800: gift of Miss Jennie Moore.

TAPE MEASURE, 1830: in an acorn-shaped

1. *Courtesy of:* THE MEMORIAL
HALL, Deerfield, Massachusetts.

2. *Courtesy of:* THE MUSEUM OF THE CITY OF NEW YORK.

3. *Courtesy of:* THE ESSEX INSTI-
TUTE, Salem Massachusetts.

4. AUTHOR'S COLLECTION.

5. *Courtesy of:* MRS. N. H.
WANNER, New Jersey.

6. *Courtesy of:* MRS. N. H. WANNER, New
Jersey.

7. *Courtesy of* THE LITCHFIELD HISTORICAL
SOCIETY.

1. Crewel embroidered linen pocket apron made by Mrs. **Eunice**, wife of Captain Seth Lyman of Northfield, 1770, Dea. Phinias Field, Charlemont, Massachusetts. 2. Group of sewing aides, American. Nineteenth century. 3. Pocket apron crewel embroidered on white cotton, made by Lydia Lambert. married first to Richard Palfrey and then second to Samuel Woodkind, called late in life, "Daddy Watkins," soldier in the French and Indian Wars. Embroidered early 18th century, Massachusetts. 4. Sewing costume, apron, stand and accessories. Godey's engraving, 1833. 5. Quaker, pot holder, work apron of patch work calicos made and worn by Grandmother Heaton, while stitching the holders. Around 1823. 6. Quaker potholder cross stitch, by "Grandmother Heaton." 7. Silk embroidered apron in white and greens on pale gray taffeta. About 1830, Connecticut.

Cap basket, hand woven.
About 1790. Belonging to
Nancy Noyes Denison, grand-
mother of Mrs. N. Stanton
Gates, Mystic, Conn.

Bonnet; hand embroidered
in white on mull. Belonging
to Isabella Holloway Lee,
great-grandmother of Miss
Madeline Evans. About 1800,
New York.

"Belinda" milliner's hand painted model for
caps. Handmade needle thread lace bonnet, tied
with cotton ribbons. About 1840, Connecticut.

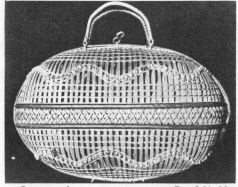

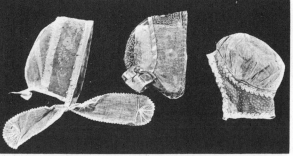

Cap basket, hand woven, belonging to Anne
Grant, famous Southern belle. About 18th cen-
tury, Virginia. Doner Mrs. S. N. Mercer,
Richmond, Va.

Group of ladies' caps, white embroidered. 1800-1845.
Organdy, braiding on net and mull. New York.

winder. This belonged to Selina Vose Morris. Gift of William M. Morgan.

PIN AND NEEDLE CASE, early nineteenth century: Beaded blue and white pediment with roses, greens, and a canary-yellow bead edge. It is of matchbox size. Gift of Mrs. Harold E. Lippincott.

OVAL PIN CASE, nineteenth century: Flowers worked in petit point on scrim in soft coloring; about three inches wide. Gift of Mrs. Walter Livingston Oakley.

PIN HOLDER, 1860: a miniature shoe made of silk. It is a gift of Mrs. Elizabeth H. Spalding.

PINCUSHION, 1850: another miniature shoe made in white. It has been decorated on the toe with a poppy design. It was given by Miss Emma Fellowes and Miss Genevieve Taylor.

COURT-PLASTER CASE, 1830: it is made of perforated cardboard and is stitched with the following motto to comfort those who have clipped or pricked their fingers:

OH MAY YOU NEVER FEEL
A WOUND TOO DEEP
FOR ME TO HEAL.

PINCUSHION, 1806: made with silk embroidered flowers by Sarah Jones and is a gift of Miss Florence Choate.

IVORY SPOOLS and a FLAX AND TATTING BOBBIN, 1784: of fine workmanship, and among the earliest accessories there. They belonged to Mrs. Philip Rhinelander, an ancestor of the donor, Mrs. John Frelinghuysen Talmadge.

NEEDLE CASE, early nineteenth century, about 1860: it is beaded, decorated with silver bugles on white and corn-colored velvet.

SEWING CASE, 1832: made by Mrs. Ephraim Peabody, another delightful variation of these containers. Silk-embroidered white flowers with delicate green leaves are worked on a pale pink silk background.

NEEDLE CASE, 1860: is another delightful exhibit made from pieces of cloth cut and bound in the bell shape of a poppy, the needles and pins to fit inside the petals. There are other amusing items to see, equally ingenious and delightful.

From the collection of Mrs. Robert Coleman Taylor is an ivory sewing box containing sewing implements of steel. "Lady's Companion" is lettered on the cover. This was made in the Civil War period, about 1860. The cover shows a spread eagle painted in natural colors with a ribbon scroll in its beak bearing the inscription "The Union Forever."

Treasured sewing silks newly arrived by packet from Europe or coming by the clippers from China and India, or made at home on the plantations were carefully kept by being wound on cut-out "stars" of cardboard or on beautiful mother-of-pearl or exquisite ivory silk winders of Oriental make. Three of these are shown in the group illustrated and were used in 1800.

Some silk winders were carved from ivory tusks of the narwhal by sailors cruising the Arctic seas on whaling ships and waiting for a catch. These when finished would be dyed red or indigo blue for a happy finishing touch.

SPOOL HOLDERS

Among the other New York sewing tools in the Museum of the City of New York is a spool holders made of ivory-colored bone, finely carved. These holders were universally used during the eighteenth and nineteenth centuries. Many designs have been contrived to contain one or many spools.

Miss Gertrude Whiting, the writer, is the owner of an Early American spool holder made of inlaid mahogany. It holds about a dozen spools on its long pins which are placed in rotation around the top of a box containing other sewing implements. A round pincushion tops the box, completing a quaint and practical aid.

In her book *Tools and Toys of Stitchery*, Miss Whiting describes "the handsomest spool rack I have happened upon" as belonging to Mrs. Burrage of Maine.

It is some ten or twelve inches tall, of silver with wrought platforms to uphold the layers of spools, and bird finials perched at the tips of the silver rods, to screw down and hold them in place.

EMERY BAGS AND WAX BALLS

While the most familiar design is the well-known red strawberry or tomato which reposes in today's sewing box, emery bags have known other days when they were dressed in amusing character. A pattern for a novel covering appeared in *Harper's Bazaar* in 1868. It was to be made in the shape of a fish and measured two inches in length.

Another indispensable article for the work-basket, used in the olden days more than now, was the wax ball. Enterprising *Harper's* in the year 1869 introduced a pattern for one of these.

SEWING WAX SIMULATING A STRAPPED SHAWL

This wax is used for waxing the thread, and when put up in this fantastic shape forms a pretty ornament for the worktable. The strap which goes around it is made of gold or colored silk braid, which is worked over with long button-hole stitches of black or colored sewing silk; gold, steel, or crystal beads being strung on with each stitch. First work one side of the braid, then work another row of stitches so as to bring the beads also on the other side.

SCISSORS

The history of scissors would take volumes. They made their appearance several centuries before the time of Christ, and have been used constantly the world over since that time. Throughout their long evolutionary process they have retained their fundamental close-cutting blade but have assumed many shapes, principally in the designs applied to the handles. These have represented human figures with swords held aloft for the two scissors' points, entwined hearts, or the legs and body of storks, their bills making the points. Most generally the handles have been shaped in flower forms or abstract curves. They have been developed in various materials such as enamel, mother-of-pearl, gold, silver or ivory to enhance their beauty. The blades remained true steel.

Those most widely used in America have been inherited from many countries. The average design has been rather simple. In recent years the little stork or bird scissors derived originally from the Persian design have been the most popular for dainty work. Otherwise modern scissors have left their sentimental shapes behind them and in the spirit of modern efficiency are simplified to the bare essentials required for cutting and snipping, without fuss or feathers to disguise their functionalism.

THIMBLES

Ancient, too, are these finger shields or needle pushers and some of the daintiest creations in design have graced them. The Alaskan women had them in crude skin bands and later in ivory or bone. Rare examples survive, early Egyptian thimbles, the bronze Roman type, the silver bands from China, the Russian brass thimbles, the French ivory examples, the lovely porcelain thimbles, the Crown Derby, old pink Battersea, Old English pewter, mother-of-pearl, antique French, and the lovely old-gold thimbles worn by our grandmothers in the United States. For ages they have lived fully and served well in their protective capacity, that of preserving faithfully the busy fingers which have given so much pleasure to others through the medium of fine needlework.

THE SEWING MACHINE AND AFTER

An estimate of the number of stitches required to make a shirt was published in *Harper's Bazaar* for August, 1869. It goes far toward explaining why sewing machines were eagerly adopted.

The following curious calculation of the number of stitches in a shirt, which somebody has had the patience to make, we mean the calculation not the shirt, by any means, may induce some gentleman to present his wife with a good sewing machine. Stitching the collar, four rows, 3,000; sewing the ends, 500; buttonholes and sewing on buttons, 150; sewing the collar and gathering the neck, 1204; stitching wristbands, 1228; sewing the ends, 68; buttonholes, 48; hemming the slits, 264; gathering the sleeves, 840; setting on wristbands, 1468; stitching on shoulder straps, three rows each, 1880; hemming the bosom, 393; sewing the sleeves, 2335; setting in sleeves and gussets, 3050; tapping the sleeves, 1526; sewing the seams, 848, setting side gussets in, 424; hemming the bottom, 1104. Total number of stitches, 20,530.

It is to be hoped that some busy housewife did become the proud owner of a sewing machine as the result of this calculation. Good sewing machines were available in 1869, but they were expensive. Since Elias Howe's epoch-making patent of 1846, improvements had been added by other inventors. When their patents ran out in 1878, the price of sewing machines dropped fifty per cent. After that there were few seamstresses who took as many as 20,000 stitches by hand in an entire year.

Patterns likewise made great advances in convenience and readability over the *Godey* period.

1. *Courtesy of:* MOUNT VERNON LADIES' ASSOCIATION OF THE UNION, Mount Vernon, Virginia.

2. *Courtesy of:* THE MOUNT VERNON LADIES' ASS'N OF THE UNION, Mount Vernon, Virginia.

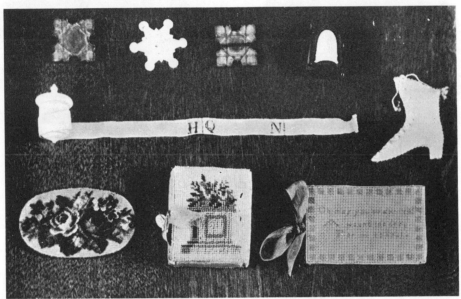

3. *Courtesy of:* THE MUSEUM OF THE CITY OF NEW YORK.

4. *Courtesy of:* MRS. N. STANTON GATES, Mystic, Connecticut.

5. *Courtesy of:* MRS. N. STANTON GATES, Mystic, Connecticut.

6. *Courtesy of:* MRS. ROBERT COLEMAN TAYLOR, New York.

1. Sewing basket of Martha Washington. About 1789, Virginia.   2. Embroidery stand and frame, Mount Vernon, Virginia. Nelly Curtis room with partially worked panel on the frame. About 1840.   3. Group of sewing and needlework aids. 18th and 19th century American, New York.   4. Sewing bird, hand wrought iron. Eighteenth century American. Used by Grandmother of Mrs. Gates, Connecticut.   5. Handmade sewing basket used and probably woven by the Grandmother of Mrs. N. Stanton Gates. About 1790. Connecticut.   6. "The Lady's Companion" needlework case. About 1860. Maryland.

WORK-TABLE COMPANION.

"Work Table Companion" or Sewing Doll. Period of 1860. (Front & Back View)

Housekeepers' Chatelaine with sewing materials fastened to embroidered ribbons.

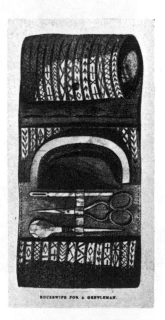

"Housewife" for a gentleman, sewing case of 1860.

ENGRAVED DESIGNS FOR SEWING AIDES, FROM GODEY'S AND PETERSON'S MAGAZINES, PERIOD OF 1860.

The mass production of pins, needles and other sewing accouterments made these articles so numerous that small respect is now paid to such necessities. Machines also have made possible a profusion of fabrics. Embroidery silks and yarns in hundreds of delectable fast colors are easily obtainable. Baskets to contain our needlework requirements do not have to be woven by hand.

In the midst of this feast we have often been famished for the exquisite taste and craftsmanship displayed by our great-grandmothers. Today, however, the creative spirit in needlework is once more manifesting itself and is making use of twentieth century sewing aids to produce a greater magnificence in expression than has ever before been seen.

CHAPTER XXV

DEERFIELD BLUE AND WHITE WORK REVIVAL; CANDLEWICKING AND NETTING

*"They cannot wholly pass away,
How far soe'er above;
Nor we, the lingerers, wholly stay
Apart from those we love;
For spirits in eternity,
As shadows in the sun,
Reach backward into Time, as we,
Like lifted clouds, reach on."*

JOHN BANISTER TABB.

EERFIELD, MASSACHUSETTS, IN 1896 saw the arrival of two painters fresh from their study of art in New York City. They were Margaret C. Whiting and Ellen Miller who had decided to revive the art of early colonial blue and white crewel embroidery, dear to the first women of New England.

They came to this quaint old Massachusetts town not only to stage this revival but to be themselves revived in the spirit of early New England, evidenced all about them in the beautiful craftsmanship to be found in the ancient homesteads resting peacefully along the wide street with its stately old elm trees. Some of these houses treasured relics reaching back to America of the seventeenth century.

Originally called Pocumtuck, the land which became Deerfield was sighted in 1638 by Major Mason, Mr. William Wadsworth and Deacon Stebbins who had traveled "up the Connecticut Valley, one hundred miles," to buy corn from the Indians. It is said they "were the first Europeans to enter Deerfield Valley." They were followed about 1670 by early settlers. Some of those who planted stakes were "the Worshipful John Pynchon with his neighbors, Serg Fuller,

Isaac Bullard, Rob't Ware, Nathaniel Fisher, Joh. Bacom."

Here the early farmers supplanted the Pocumtuck Indian tribes, tilled the soil, planted crops, raised sheep and built their homes of pine, placing within them great hearthstones taken from the Connecticut River. They lived and worked peacefully until the Indians made life miserable for them.

While the women spun, wove and sewed the needed garments, and embroidered hangings with their homemade crewel wools, the children were learning their A, B, C's, and sampler making. Here it was that Dame Hannah Beaman conducted her Dame School outside the stockade in the period of King Philip's War, during the course of which the settlement was destroyed. A few years later it was resettled only to be destroyed a second time in 1704 in a war in which many settlers were killed, their wives and children taken captive or slain on the way to Canada.

Among the many early homesteads which survived to become Deerfield's glory are "The Old Indian House," "West Lots," Christopher Stebbins' house, 1715, which later became the studio and home of Augustus Vincent Tack; the Childs-Russell Williams house, which became the residence of Elizabeth Williams

1. Courtesy of: THE DEERFIELD SCROLL, Deerfield, Massachusetts.

Symbolic Landscape Embroidery of the Blue and White Society, 1899, Deerfield, Massachusetts.

2. Courtesy of: MISS MARGARET C. WHITING, Deerfield, Massachusetts.

Detail sketch from old Blue and White Embroidered bedspread of Miss Rose Clark of Buffalo, New York, by Miss Margaret C. Whiting.

3. Courtesy of: MISS MARGARET C. WHITING, Deerfield, Massachusetts.

Large detail drawing. Copy of Early American Bedcurtain Embroidered in Blue and White for revival in Blue and White Society, by Margaret C. Whiting.

4. Courtesy of: MISS MARGARET C. WHITING, Deerfield, Massachusetts.

Blue and White Embroidery made by the Society, 1899, Deerfield, Massachusetts.

1. *Courtesy of:* MRS. GERTRUDE COCHRANE SMITH, Deerfield, Massachusetts.

Contemporary Cover, an adaptation designed from an old bedspread, made in knotted candlewicking on linen of Spanish weaving. About 1900.

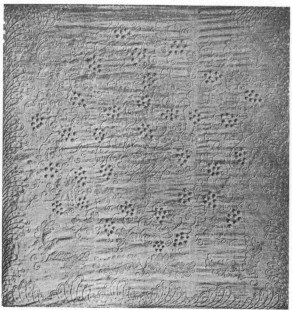

2. *Courtesy of:* MRS. GERTRUDE COCHRANE SMITH, Deerfield, Massachusetts.

Antique bedspread, candlewicked grape design on hand woven linen, about 1800, Connecticut.

3. *Courtesy of:* MRS. GERTRUDE COCHRANE SMITH, Deerfield, Massachusetts.

Early American Tester Bed from Huntington House, North Hadley, Mass., with netted and candlewicked covering.

4. *Courtesy of:* MRS. GERTRUDE COCHRANE SMITH, Deerfield, Massachusetts.

Netting Patterns, old and new ones, revived from early American Colonial examples.

Champney and the studio of J. Wells Champney; the Joseph Stebbins house built in 1768; the John Sheldon house, 1708; the house Parson Williams built in 1709; the "Block House"; "The Old Manse" built for Joseph Barnard in 1768, with its hip-roof wing which had been the Samuel Carter house of 1694. This house contained the "silver tankard made to order by Paul Revere for Joseph Barnard and also the English piano, the only one in town." The Allen Homestead became the wing of Lawyer Sam Barnard's great house in which three sisters, Sally, Nancy and Rachel, wove their linens and sewed their wedding gowns in 1791. One of the most ancient houses on the "Old Street," formerly known as the Albany Road, was the Godfrey Nims Homestead. It became at the end of the nineteenth century the home of the Blue and White Society, newly organized by Margaret C. Whiting and Ellen Miller. This was where all of their embroideries were made.

The two revivalists found a sympathetic understanding of their objective and full co-operation was extended to them by their neighbors. At that time, too, other artists joined the community inspired by George Fuller's landscape paintings of Deerfield. Sculptors and poets made their homes there along with men and women associated with Deerfield Academy which was fostering and continuing the finest values of the pioneer spirit through its able director, Mr. Frank L. Boyden.

Thus a beautiful unity of interests existed in the town which enabled Miss Whiting and Miss Miller to proceed with the establishment of a group of Deerfield women to embroider together for the creation of the blue and white needlework. They gathered day after day, delighting in this work, the result of their mutual effort and pride.

In working out her program, Miss Whiting went to the immediate environment for the atmosphere which she desired to revive in her work. In every old homestead were to be found bits of old needlework, scraps of lace made in later and more peaceful years, secrets in old note-books, early dye formulas. All provided a wealth of ideas full of interest to these two women who, fired with zeal, proposed to take the helm and steer American needlework out of the doldrums of bad taste and poor design, back into its former glory by building an interest in

the fundamentals of good design as expressed in the simpler examples of earlier American blue and white embroidery. Interest was stimulated by this fresh effort. The Society's needlework became known far and wide and women flocked to Deerfield from great distances to buy the embroideries designed by Margaret Whiting and worked by Deerfield women under her direction.

Miss Whiting's effort was probably the first group activity in the nineteenth century to give a practical demonstration of art and industry in combination. Upon each embroidery made in Deerfield was the society insignia, an initial D placed in the center of a spinning wheel. By this symbol of industry their work was recognized. It was sought for its excellent craftsmanship and the high standards in needlework which it maintained.

A small example in Memorial Hall in Deerfield illustrates the technique in stitches which are similar to those used in the early crewel embroideries. Flax has been substituted for the wool thread, and Russian linen for the homespun of New England.

The World War interrupted this great activity. Materials could not be obtained to continue the work and the women of the community were being called to other duties. Thus ended a stimulating chapter in American needlework.

DESIGN

The designs used for the Deerfield blue and white work were derived from early colonial bedcovers, which were embroidered about 1750 in New England. While the early blue and white embroidery designs were cruder perhaps than the English Jacobean work of the same period, they possessed great charm and distinctive quality. Miss Whiting contributes one of her drawings which she copied directly from an early blue and white crewel-embroidered spread of this period. Permission was given by the owner of the original, Miss Rose Clarke of Buffalo, New York. She has since died, and the bedcover has disappeared. The design fortunately has been perpetuated through use on the creations of the Blue and White Society.

Blue and white crewel embroidery of the late 1700's and the 1800's, while handsome was, according to Miss Whiting, "too sophisticated in design and workmanship to be typical" of the sort of needlework which the group wished to emulate.

MATERIALS USED

Flax thread was substituted for the earlier wools. This change was effected "on account of moths which have destroyed a good many specimens of the old crewel work." The use of linen thread is perfectly authentic, but that spun from wool was produced more easily and was also less difficult to use and, as Margaret Whiting goes on to explain, "bad workmanship could more easily be disguised."

Imported linen foundations were used in this revival work and most often Russian crash. After the World War began this material was difficult to procure which was, according to Miss Miller, the secretary of the Society, one of the main causes of the curtailment of the output.

The curtain shown in the illustration is a typical example of Miss Whiting's fine designing and the skillful workmanship of the Deerfield needlewomen. It was executed upon old Dutch linen. The design is full of grace and rhythm, a refinement over the earlier blue and white work of the colonists. Miss Whiting's training in Fine Art evidences itself in a more profound understanding of line, composition and disposition of leaves and floral units. While reflecting the personal feeling of the artist, it possesses elements related to the great decorative works of Oriental make and is also reminiscent of the embroideries of Oriental inspiration made in Europe. It embodies fundamental themes in the use of the vase and the scroll arrangement of the stems and vines, which may be seen both on East Indian ornament and on embroidery worked in the Elizabethan period in England.

Confusion in appraising a design may sometimes arise in the mind of the layman when he looks at motifs which have been seen before in different works of other periods. But it must be remembered that it is not the form itself that counts, but its arrangement, its adaptation from one rhythm to another reflecting the taste and feeling, the thought and personality of the designer. Herein lies the difference. Designing may be compared to music; the notes used are

traditional but the arrangement and the resulting harmonies are the work of the individual composer and reflect his personality and his period. Certain fundamental elements are contained in all good design. To use them well requires a deep understanding of their subtle essence and value and a holy reverence and respect in making the adaptation.

DYES

To obtain the particular shades of blue for dyeing the flax used by the Society was a delicate and touchy matter. It required infinite patience and understanding not only of color, but of the chemical factors necessary to achieve the subtle tones.

Miss Whiting was the chief aid in reviving this old art, not only because of her understanding of tonal values of color, but also because of her knowledge of dyes and their basic elements. Much study was made of old dye formulas found in manuals published in the early days and inherited from ancestors who had dyed their own crewels for needlework. Practicing the same methods and, of course, adding personal methods, Miss Whiting finally mastered this art to perfection, even making allowances for weather conditions. Atmosphere, it seems, may change the shade of blue from one tone to another and must be considered when working. It was not an easy task because the water must be cold, and the day preferably cold also. Altogether working over the large kettles of coloring liquids was a chilling experience.

The blues finally achieved are absolutely identical with the colorings of the eighteenth century pieces, and provoked deep admiration from women everywhere when embroidered into the new designs.

Indigo was the first dye mastered but since other shades and formulas used in old examples of crewel-work presented interesting problems, the Society proceeded to experiment with other colors. Miss Whiting added to her palette of thread colors shades obtained with dyes from madder, fustic and barks, supplemented with some colors which were imported. It may be of interest to compare these elements with the foundation dye ingredients used on Cape Cod for crewels, noted in the chapter on Crewel Embroidery.

That much experimenting with different native materials has been productive of varying results is true. Formulas, even though fundamentally the same, may change their scheduled colors due to various causes. The metal of the pot in which the dye is cooked may create a chemical change. The water used will sometimes effect a shade. The time of the day adds its impression. When the sun is setting is the best hour to dye with indigo, according to legend.

It is generally conceded that the director of this artistic industry, so active in pre-war days, became a first-rate authority on dyes and their temperamental changes. Examples of needlework made by the group are still holding their blues admirably, through many scrubbings and much wear and tear, for most of the embroidery was utilitarian in character. Luncheon sets, scarfs for dressers, hangings, bedspreads, and so forth, were the pieces executed in greatest number. The survival of the fugitive shades through such continued usage is excellent testimony to the thoroughness and careful industry which made the work of this Society one of Deerfield's important contributions.

CANDLEWICKING REVIVAL

Also wishing to revive the fine artistry prevalent in Early American needlework especially as expressed in early examples of candlewicking and netting, Mrs. Gertrude Cochrane Smith of Deerfield is preserving and reproducing old designs and patterns in this type of work. Many of the early pieces have fallen apart during their long sojourn in ancient attics but from the remnants Mrs. Smith manages to create new designs in the same fine traditions, and, of course, adds ideas of her own.

An example reproduced is described by her as follows:

"It is a copy of an old spread done in knotted candle-wicking on lovely cream linen for Spanish weaving. The original spread was completely covered with designs of great variety and entirely unrelated to this very lovely grape motive."

Like her friend, Miss Margaret Whiting, Mrs. Smith simplifies her designs over the older ones by eliminating superfluous decoration, and creates new compositions which show easy, rhythmic, flowing lines and a nice balancing of form. Like Miss Whiting and many others of the newer school also, she considers that complete covering of the background surfaces is unnecessary. In her spreads air or undecorated space is left around the central motif and the uncovered linen is allowed to express balance. In very early periods of decoration in the Orient and in Europe, this balancing of values by contrast is well understood.

DESIGNS AND METHODS

Patterns for candlewicking bedcovers were invented by women in different communities in olden times. They used to delight in introducing variations and creating new directions for their stitchery. Today Mrs. Smith enjoys revising old designs and planning new ones in the same manner.

Even now the application of the pattern to the cover is difficult. It is usually accomplished by sketching the design upon brown paper. The cloth is spread out upon the floor, the drawing placed over it and transfer paper placed between it and the cloth. The paper drawing is then retraced and the design is transferred to the material. This marking is washed out after the candlewicking has been completed.

Linen is the foundation material used today, replacing the hand-corded dimity and homespun of grandmother's era. The covers are placed upon large frames for the wicking. Large needles and regular wicking cotton are used for the design stitchery and knotting.

Working with twenty helpers at once Mrs. Smith has made thirty-two of these covers in a year's time.

NETTING REVIVAL

Coverings and valances for tester or four-poster beds are the prime use for netting covers made today. These also are revivals of the popular fashion of colonial America. Mrs. Carrington, a guest of Martha Washington at Mount Vernon, wrote to a friend from Virginia in 1799 saying of the First Lady:

Her netting is a source of great amusement to her and is so neatly done that all the younger part of the family are proud of having their dresses trimmed with it.

Netting was included in the needlework teaching of the early finishing schools along with samplers, quillwork, gold and silver embroidery, and the making of wax-works. It was derived in plan and technique from the earliest fishermen who made their own fish nets. Eskimo women of Alaska were adept at making intricate meshes in netting and the ivory and bone needles used for the purpose are primitive works of art, carved by the men into whale shapes and other emblematic symbols to bring luck on their fishing expeditions.

The patterns of the colonial women are mostly combinations of geometric forms with tassels introduced to create lacy effects. It was their object to achieve dainty coverings. When they no longer required the heavy crewel bed hangings to shut out the night draughts and cold as in the earlier days of settlement, and since they were not able to obtain draperies of a light, filmy quality, netting was created as a substitute. The early patterns of 1765 are distinguished by their long points. The art flourished up to 1822 and then disappeared, to be revived much later in the nineteenth century.

The early patterns revived by Mrs. Smith have replaced originals on the tester bed in the Maple Room of the Van Cortlandt Museum, New York. The Washington Room in Longfellow's Wayside Inn at South Sudbury, Massachusetts, contains a netted canopy of her make, along with forty-two other noted examples of netting made elsewhere and used in the colonial manner for the edging of coverlets, curtains, testers and valances of high post beds.

METHOD OF WORKING

Netting is an intricate process requiring a teacher and much practice and dexterity in forming the various meshes. The precise method for working is as follows:

The implements used are a netting-needle, which is a bar of steel or ivory, open at both ends, and with a small round hole in which to fasten the end of thread; a plain bar, flat or round, which is called a mesh; with cotton, silk, or other material. A stirrup is useful for holding the work. It is a strip of embroidered canvas, an inch wide and five or six long, lined with ribbon, of which about a yard and a quarter is left, forming a long loop, from one end of the canvas to the other. This is worn on the foot, the foundation of the netting being attached to the ribbon, which ought to be long enough to come within a pleasant range of sight. But, though not so neat and pretty, a fine cord passed round the foot answers all the purpose; and still better is a small cushion screwed firmly to the edge of the table.

Some of the stitches used for the various meshings are known as square netting, honey-comb netting, round netting, Grecian netting, long twist stitch, French ground netting, spotted netting, diamond netting, spotted diamond netting, Vandyked square netting, pointed edge, shell edging (in several methods). What a stitch repertoire to learn and execute with the "neatness" ascribed to Martha Washington!

Netted purses and costume decoration were made with fine silks and threads upon the same principle as late as the middle 80's, but since then netting has been confined to the coarser technique.

Interest in and appreciation of old colonial needlework arts has been directly stimulated by these leaders of the late nineteenth and early twentieth century. They continue to contribute new values to the present scene through their creative treatment of the designs found and developed by them in the earlier revival days in Deerfield.

Stump work picture embroidered with fine silks on satin employing several needles at once to execute the variety of intricate lace and weaving stitches, by Mrs. Richard Aldrich, 1900. New York.

PART V

EARLY AND PRESENT TWENTIETH CENTURY EMBROIDERIES

CHAPTER XXVI

THE TRANSITION PERIOD

"Our little lives are kept in equipoise
By opposite attractions and desires;
The struggle of the instinct that enjoys,
And the more noble instinct that aspires."
HENRY WADSWORTH LONGFELLOW.

S A SLOWLY REVOLVING STAGE-set turns upon the mechanical disk and changes the scene, so the nineteenth century slowly recedes from our view and with it the needlework arts, fads and fancies of the Victorian era. But we find as the twentieth century enters upon the stage that views of the other set are still in sight. Even in this day there are those who cling to certain designs and maintain a color consciousness which belong to the 1890's.

In the closing decades of the last century we have seen evidences that needlework was seeking a higher level. The Needlework School already described which flourished in the Boston Museum of Fine Arts in 1879 was one of the earliest of these indications. The school was inspired no doubt by the William Morris revival in England, and the output of the Royal School of Art Needlework at South Kensington where Morris, Burne-Jones and other artists created designs to be carried out by the students in embroidery and other mediums. This movement, which emphasized fine craftsmanship and good design, found followers on both sides of the Atlantic.

At the Centennial Fair held at Philadelphia in 1876 to mark the one hundredth anniversary of the nation's independence, an exhibition of Kensington embroidery attracted considerable attention. Many American women, vacationing in England, seized the occasion to attend classes at the South Kensington school and to learn a few of the stitch techniques not taught at home. They learned how to make copies of the lovely Queen Anne embroideries in the Kensington Museum and the Elizabethan needle-threadings in silk on satin. These delicate traceries of splendid design were truly inspiring. Stuart and Georgian needlework pieces also were studiously examined and copied. This schooling in London served as a reminder that needlework had been practiced in the past as an art, not only in England but at home as well. Determined to encourage higher standards in America, these women stimulated the magazines to publish, along with their usual patterns, novelties designed by the Royal School of Art Needlework. A series of designs for blotters, introduced from London, was described in *Harper's Bazaar* for December 17, 1887.

These designs were excellent in character and taste having been cleverly adapted from the ornamental letters of the old English alphabet. The scrolls upon these provided a good embroidery theme to be executed in braid or silk stitches.

Also contributing to the conception of needlework as a fine art were the essays and lectures of John Ruskin. In articles written for *The Art Journal* and through a series of letters, he recommended that needlework should be nominated for the highest place in the chambers set aside in museums for the exhibition of such Muse-taught arts as writing, sculpture, painting, architecture and pottery. He suggested further that the municipality make available to the public for their education and edification a needlework exhibit which should present all phases in the development of the art from the basic materials used, such as wools, hemp, flax, silk, and so forth, through the spinning, dyeing and weaving to the completed works. All nations and all stages of civilization were to be represented.

That Ruskin was such an ardent champion of embroidery as an art expression was due, no doubt, to the impression made upon him as a boy by the beautiful needlework executed by his mother.

There never yet has been presented an exhibition of needlework such as that urged by Ruskin. His discourses did bear fruit, however, when in 1900 a splendid exhibit of English samplers and tapestry embroideries was held at the Fine Arts Gallery in London. It covered a period of two hundred and fifty years. One or two examples from America were included. Remarkable interest was shown by the general public, which had not appreciated the history and growth of this art. They enjoyed this opportunity to see a comprehensive review of its different phases as shown in a series of works arranged in chronological order.

France too had its influence in the changing conception of what might be accomplished through the medium of needlework. In the prosperous years of the new industrial age which followed the Civil War, many American women, now able to experience the joys of travel, took their embroidery in hand and, still yearning for romance and for grand subjects, went to Paris. There discovering the beautiful tapestries in the Cluny Museum, they decided straightway to copy them in needlework "tapestries" for home decoration. For a long time thereafter "Ladies with Unicorns" met one upon the wall of every grand staircase in American mansions. Sometimes they were paired with copies of Watteau's paintings or reproductions of woven tapestries of the Louis XIV period. This fashion resulted in the idea that all needlepoint was "tapestry" rather than embroidery. In reality each art employs an entirely different technique.

Few American painters of the late nineteenth and early twentieth century made any direct impression on needlework. An exception is James McNeill Whistler whose work had great influence in popularizing the Japanese style of decoration. The great popularity of this artist, whose studio was entirely ornamented with lacquer and embroideries from the Flowery Kingdom, was responsible for the quantities of Japanese motifs which were applied to decorations for the home.

Reproductions of cranes and bulrushes, butterflies like the signature Whistler used on his paintings, fans, vases and other objects of Japanese art became extremely fashionable. The vogue for bamboo beaded portières and gold-embroidered black satin panels for wall decorations followed. The climax was reached in the screens embroidered with peacocks, chrysanthemums and scenic effects in the Japanese manner which engulfed the country during the 80's and 90's.

An excellent example of the Whistler influence is the wistaria silk-embroidered screen designed and worked by Mrs. L. W. Gary of Baltimore at the beginning of the transitional period. The themes are from Japanese prints. According to the memory of her daughter, Mrs. Robert Coleman Taylor, Mrs. Gary sketched her outline for the embroidery on the black satin with opaque white water color. The colorings used are violet in shades from red to pink violet on the flowers, offset with greens for the fine leaves. Shadows are worked in with soft grays, and tans in long and short stitches. It is a beautiful piece of work executed with the same sense of good craftsmanship as the needlepoint picture of "Moses in the Bulrushes," previously described. It is also equally large, each panel measuring sixty-two by forty-three inches.

It seems strange that artists like Winslow Homer, John Singer Sargent, John W. Alexander and the many other distinguished painters of this period had no imitators on embroidery canvases. Possibly it was because needlework was floundering about in a myriad of assorted influences from every direction while the scene was changing too fast to allow much time for reflection. Later, however, the figure painting of William Morris Hunt had some effect, and likewise the work of painters who, following his style, went back to the portrayal of figures in the nude, except for a wisp of veil here and there arranged with proper discretion.

Silk embroiderers were impressed by these pictures. Immediately there followed large silk on satin embroidered panels of sky blue with a crescent moon placed usually near the center upon which was seated a semi-nude lady with long silken hair enveloping her figure as a substitute for the filmy veil. (It was easier, probably, to embroider hair than to create the effect of a semi-transparent veil.) Invariably the lady would be gazing upward with a dreamy expression and the title might be "The Crescent Maiden" or "The Dawn Sybil." Romance was still having its day, enveloping even classic subjects in its rosy veil.

NEEDLEWORK GROUPS

Of all the influences which were contributing to a more artistic use of the needle the most potent was that emanating from William Morris, which gave rise to all sorts of arts and crafts groups both in England and America. In America it brought about the making of the California Mission furniture, the Grand Rapids morris chairs, and "art embroidery" on rough crash appliquéd with bowls of varicolored flowers to hang upon the wall in tune with natural oak dining room sets. Such needlework panels were on display in countless arts and crafts shops throughout the country.

More important, however, was the group activity stimulated by Morris and Company. In New York City the Society of Decorative Arts was organized by Louis C. Tiffany, the designer of stained glass, Samuel Coleman, textile designer and colorist and Robert W. de Forest, authority on carved and ornamental woodwork. This was very much in the spirit of the South Kensington school.

Included in this group was Candace Wheeler, who embroidered in silks and who, in the 1880's, dreamed of needlewoven tapestries of purely American creation which she hoped would be lasting works of art. Miss Wheeler was notable among those who strove in the late nineteenth century to further high standards, and many fine embroideries were accomplished mostly with silk threads manufactured by the Cheney Brothers. Large needlewoven embroidered wall hangings or "tapestries" were executed under her direction in the 80's and 90's by the Associated Artists.

Cornelius Vanderbilt was one of the patrons of this needlework art who ordered during this period a set of embroidered murals to be made in silk for his mansion at Fifty-seventh Street and Fifth Avenue. The designs belonged to the crescent moon school of design.

Another patron, Mrs. Potter Palmer, ordered large embroidered panels to place in her palatial home on the lake shore in Chicago. These were scenes from nature, such as Minnehaha listening to the waterfall.

In the same period, about 1884, Lily Langtry ordered a set of bed hangings to be embroidered by the Associated Artists for her London house. "Sunset colored" roses embroidered in silk formed the canopy design; scattered rose petals embroidered on the coverlet were as realistic as if they had fallen from the wreaths on the canopy above. The coverlet was lined with delicate pink satin to match the roses.

Two examples of Candace Wheeler's own needlework now have a permanent home in the collections of the Metropolitan Museum of Art. Each is a silk portière showing an allover repeat of embroidered silk flowers. While most portières during her day were bamboo creations, this artist used her highest abilities and artistic knowledge to apply to these fashionable draperies new forms that would maintain the best standards in design and craftsmanship. There is a suggestion of the Japanese theme in the use of the decorative lily buds, leaves and flower forms, but while the portière which uses iris in an allover repeat shows the Whistler influence, one may see the William Morris influence also in the manner of arrangement. Here the feeling leans toward the antique European brocaded patternings.

The iris were embroidered in tones of yellow, green, lavender, and gray silks in filling stitch. Applied palettes and small, bronze cut beads accent the design. The border is of old gold plush. The panel measures ninety-seven inches in length by sixty-two inches in width.

Although reflecting two schools of influence in her needlework, Candace Wheeler has remained true to herself in the understanding she shows of the fundamentals of design as expressed in the artistic flow of line and mass composition and also in her awareness of the importance of stitches which she has chosen to carry out and further emphasize the flowing qualities of the design.

The Society of Decorative Arts was only one of many needlework groups formed in the closing decades of the nineteenth century and preparing the way for the artistic triumphs of the present. The Society itself encouraged the formation of arts and crafts guilds in smaller towns. It provided small exhibits of native and foreign needlework which accomplished much in the building of an art consciousness and in stimulating a growth of good taste in the general public.

In Boston the Woman's Educational and Industrial Union was organized in 1871 by Dr. Harriet Clisby and others to increase fellowship among women and to foster better needlework. In general it was their aim to promote the best practical methods of achieving educational, industrial and social advancement. Mrs. Eva Whiting White was the president and Mary Tolman the secretary of this group.

The Needlework and Textile Guild of the Art Institute of Chicago fostered by Mrs. Potter Palmer and other women of the city worked with the same objective.

This period also witnessed the development of the Woman's Exchange Groups, the Needlework Societies, Household Art Societies, as well as the Deerfield Blue and White Industries already described.

Many factors fostered the growth of these groups. Women who had studied needlework abroad were quick to aid in the promotion of needlework groups as a means of encouraging better design. Women trained in cultural pursuits which afforded a sympathetic background for appreciating the objectives of the needlework artists took the lead in forming groups in their own communities. Whether the source of their inspiration was at home or abroad, they worked in unison like beavers to rebuild a finer appreciation of good embroidery. Badly

designed needlework was gradually discouraged; the frou-frou examples were frowned upon and taste generally was slowly improved.

Another factor in the success of this united effort was, strangely enough, the sewing machine. While the machine served to alleviate the toil of the seamstress at the same time it created new difficulties. Sewing could now be accomplished with such speed that one woman could do the work of several and countless sewing women therefore found themselves unemployed. This situation was remedied to a large extent by the new growth of the needlework societies which found among these women the talent and the industry necessary to produce the decorative pieces which were in increasing demand in the social groups which were being wakened to the desirability of needlework art as a means of enhancing the beauty of their homes.

When the century was fourteen years old, the stage was set for the catastrophe of the World War and members of all the guilds in all the towns plied their needles busily to give aid in the emergency. The popular song "Sister Susie is Sewing Shirts for Soldiers" was literally true, for thousands upon thousands of women all over the world occupied themselves with sewing and first-aid needlework.

Following the war and taking up the slack in interest, a new guild movement was started in New York. A group of embroidery and lace collectors which had been organized through the interest of Miss Gertrude Whiting united with the People's Institute to establish the Needle and Bobbin Guild. They proposed "to stimulate and maintain interest in the handmade fabrics of foreign and native make; to assist in preserving the racial character of the fabrics in so far as they are worthy in design and workmanship, and to assist in the production and marketing of the same." Miss Gertrude Whiting became the first president of the organization and Mrs. Howard Mansfield, chairman. In 1920 with a board of directors composed of prominent women and Mrs. Robert Coleman Taylor as chairman, a significant needlework and handmade textile exhibition was held in the Arden Gallery in New York. It was called "America's Making." The event was held under the auspices of the State Commissioner of Education, the Honorable Franklin K. Lane, and many public-spirited men and women who gave their ardent support to this project.

The Guild was active for many years and its chapters were spread all over the country. It was effective in providing employment for foreign-born women and, what was equally important, at the same time it encouraged these new Americans to retain their Old World embroidery techniques. Thus interest in needlework of a widely diversified character was fostered. Among the subsidiary groups were the Aquidneck Cottage Industries, Beard Quilting, Fisk Weaving, Gebert Weaving, Greene Mounting Weaving, Italian Needlework Guild, Lenox Hill Studio, Russian Group, Scuola d'Industrie Italiane, Ukrainian Needle Craft Guild.

A confusion of objectives finally broke the back of this organization and in 1936 it was disbanded. Each of the groups followed their own individual destiny, some to survive and many to expire, leaving the thirty-eighth year of the twentieth century waiting for the staging of another major needlework endeavor.

OTHER EXAMPLES OF TRANSITION NEEDLEWORK

Among the leaders and promoters of the fine art of needlework during the late Victorian era is Mrs. Emily Noyes Vanderpoel of Litchfield, Connecticut. She was active not only in producing embroidery of her own conception but in wielding her pen on the subject, and stimulated wide interest not only in embroidery but in needle and bobbin laces as well. It is she who aided the Litchfield Historical Society in acquiring so many items of historical significance in these and other arts.

In their collection may be seen a large linen bedcover embroidered in 1894 by Mary Perkins Quincy after a design created by Mrs. Vanderpoel. This work is characteristic of the transition period in that it reflects many influences. The Quincy coat of arms is used and the rose of England, the thistle of Scotland and the shamrock of Ireland are worked down the sides, tapestry fashion, to show the pedigree of Mabel Harlakeaden, second wife of the Governor of the Colony of Connecticut and one of Miss Quincy's ancestors. The center of the panel has an allover pattern in the manner of twelfth century tapestry cartoons except that dots re-

place the characteristic flower and fleur-de-lis motif.

The embroidery was finely worked in colored silks by Miss Quincy and completed later upon a large linen cover which was hand-woven in 1800 by servants of Mrs. Julius Deming, Miss Quincy's great-grandmother.

Made in 1890 and showing transitional influences in the handling of the needlepoint background are two small wall pictures sketched and worked at Easthampton, Long Island, by Almy Goelet Gerry Gallatin, mother of Mrs. William Warner Hoppin. A new note appears in the costume design of the figures. The wools in which they are worked are pale yellow greens and light salmon pinks, a choice of colors which shows that this needlework artist was thinking in original terms and breaking with the traditional in a world which was seeing red in terms of Berlin wool-work. There is a glow in them like that in a Fragonard painting of eighteenth century France. The only concession to custom occurs in the use of the scroll border designs familiar in the German patterns of the 90's, and even here Mrs. Gallatin refined the colorings to conform to her own taste.

Mrs. Richard Aldrich of New York, who is a highly talented needlewoman, learned many stitch techniques in London and became interested in the intricacies of stump work. This long-lost art she has revived to her own satisfaction and that of friends fortunate enough to see the small pole screen panel which she has made in this style of embroidery. It was executed with silks on cream satin in 1904. The coloring is delightful. The technique is the same used by the little maid in Salem back in the seventeenth century. The great skill and patience required is perhaps too much to expect of many needleworkers in this streamlined age, and yet surprising things happen in every age and a technique similar to this stump work may yet develop.

Side by side with embroideries which displayed an increasing awareness of the artistic expression possible through this medium, costume embroideries and home decorations in needlework continued to absorb the time of many women. The nature of their activities may be gathered from a glance at fashion notes taken from magazines in the years between 1900 and 1905.

COSTUME EMBROIDERIES

A vogue which continued from the nineteenth century into the early 1930's was the fashion for making Honiton lace handkerchiefs. One of these handkerchiefs made by Susan Catherine Palmer in Baltimore in 1900 is in the possession of her daughter, Mrs. Carroll R. Williams, who describes it as follows:

> It is of delicate workmanship. When I was growing up, the making of these handkerchiefs was a fashionable accomplishment with which matrons occupied their leisure hours while sitting at ease, on summer days during the period devoted to afternoon teas.

Mrs. Williams adds that she has placed this example of her mother's needlework under glass and is using it as a little tray for receiving the cards of callers.

Fancy work in these years turned to the embellishment of such articles as children's aprons of white crêpe de Chine which were embroidered with "simple borders and floral sprays." Embroidered tennis aprons were considered essential for the wardrobe of the sportswoman. They were equally smart for croquet matches. Cut work appeared on waists. "Dotty Dimple" caps and bibs of lawn were daintily made for babies.

Heavy linen collar bags were acceptable gifts to hold the stiffly starched collars which women were wearing on their shirtwaists, tightly fastened about the throat like a man's collar. The turned-over edge was finely embroidered with white dots or a tiny buttonhole stitch. Double cuffs were the last word in style. Embroidered chemisette sets made of fine handkerchief linen were particularly popular. Shirred girdles and suspenders to wear over ladies' dresses were needleworked with ribbon flowers.

Women who were beginning to make their way in the business world, lady secretaries especially, wore sleeve protectors of blue or yellow linen embroidered in white.

In 1905 the "Marguerite" lace hats appeared on the scene trimmed with liberty satin and ribbon work. They were often made at home. Shirt-waist buttons were embroidered with daisies, roses and apple blossoms. Again the suspender gown appeared, the straps gaily embroidered.

The Gibson Girl of 1906 was wearing a white embroidered eyeleted summer gown and a lingerie hat of lace and eyelet embroidery which required four yards of Valenciennes edging, four and a half yards of insertion and twenty-one Battenberg rings. White embroidered coat sets were made of linen or lawn and embroidered or eyeleted to match a hat of similar construction.

The embroidered parasol made of embroidered linen was in its prime. Sunshades were of cream white embroidered with white silk or in combinations of pale green with lavender silk or pale green silk topped with a white silk-embroidered dragon—considered lovely! A handsome parasol made for a well-known society woman was of white satin with a large purple orchid embroidered on one panel. Wistaria was another floral design which lent itself effectively to parasol decoration. A favorite method was to tint the design with water colors and then work the edges in long and short stitches. A needlework journal advised its readers that

> Parasols of pink, blue or green linen to match the gown are quite within the reach of the home needleworker. If impossible to buy just the color which you want, take any well shaped parasol, rip the covering and cut out sections from the same stuff as your gown, using the old cover as a pattern, carefully marking seams and sections, embroider the different panels, put together again and mount on the frame.

This was the decade when Hardanger cloth was being used for needlework and scrim embroideries appeared with horse-chestnut designs for centerpieces or pillow tops. They were carried out along the lines of the old Berlin work except that silk was used instead of wool for the tapestry stitch and they were worked without shading.

"Jervil" embroidery also came in at this time, the result of someone's brilliant idea that bright jewels appliquéd on linen centerpieces would give an elegant effect. These "rubies" and "emeralds" were studded into flowers outlined with black silk and Japanese gold thread which formed the border of the centerpiece.

Realistic flower "paintings" were stitched with great delight. The more natural they were, the greater the achievement. Cyclamen centerpieces were embroidered on heavy white linen, the flowers filled in with solid silk needlework.

1. *Courtesy of:* MRS. EUGENE LEVERING, JR., Maryland.

"Wistaria," embroidered screen; silks on black satin; reflecting the "Whistler" influence upon needlework. Designed and worked, 1888, by Mrs. James A. Gary, Baltimore, Maryland. Size 62 inches high and 43 inches each panel.

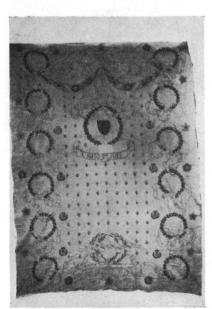

2. *Courtesy of:* THE LITCHFIELD HISTORICAL SOCIETY.

Silk embroidered bedcover, on home-spun linen designed by Emily Noyes Vanderpoel and embroidered 1898 by Miss Mary Perkins Quincy, Connecticut.

3. *Courtesy of:* MRS. WILLIAM WARNER HOPPIN, New York.

Embroidered wall picture in needle-point and "Tapestry" stitch, 1890, by Almy Goelet Gerry Gallatin, East-hampton, Long Island.

4. *Courtesy of:* THE METROPOLITAN MUSEUM OF ART.

Silk embroidered portiere, about 1900, designed by Candace Wheeler. New York.

Needlepoint sofa panels with religious symbology. Designed and worked by Mrs. Francis Leonard Kellogg, New York.

"The Good Shepherd," crewel embroidered picture for a magazine pattern. Designed and worked by Georgiana Brown Harbeson, New York. Privately owned.

"The Nativity," crewel embroidery picture worked by Lydia Mary Barwood, Brooklyn, New York, and designed by Georgiana Brown Harbeson.

"The Crucifixion," altar panel hanging, crewel embroidered on velvet. Exhibited at The 1937 Paris Exposition by invitation. Designed and worked 1930 by Georgiana Brown Harbeson.

Other popular plants and flowers immortalized in stitchery were pansies and American Beauty roses, used chiefly on pillows, California pepper berries, pine cones, Boston ferns, violets, buttercups and daisies.

There was a series of basket designs in which buttercups were combined with maple leaves. These were introduced in the so-called Hardanger embroidery which derives its name from the Norwegian village of Hardanger. This style of embroidery became a craze in 1908 because it could not be copied by machine work and was easily recognized as handmade. This was a desirable distinction.

In most European countries during the present years of the twentieth century private enterprise has made many successful attempts to revive the domestic arts and crafts which the introduction of machinery had destroyed. The art of embroidery has been sustained and schools are maintained where the best methods may be learned. Ancient traditions are preserved in technique and design along with the more modern interpretations. In this way needlework still lives and plays an active part in community life.

In America today we have only the interested individual and some remaining small groups. Schooling in the fine art of needlework in its broadest sense is sadly lacking. In the future, no doubt, some center of instruction will be developed where the newest information relating to the cultural, decorative and utilitarian branches of this art may be obtained by those who seek expression through this ancient and honorable medium.

CHAPTER XXVII

RELIGIOUS NEEDLEWORK

"Anonymous, nor needs a name
To tell the secret whence the flame,
With light and warmth and incense, came
A new creation to proclaim.
So was it when, His labor done,
God saw His work and smiled thereon;
His glory in the picture shone
But name upon the canvas, none."

JOHN BANISTER TABB.

OME OF THE MOST BEAUTIFUL embroidery ever made has been the needlework applied to the materials used for decorating places of worship and the ceremonial garments worn in them. Religion has built a significant language through the use of abstract forms. All through the centuries and up to the present time mundane materials have been glorified with tranquil needlework designs built around these symbols of religious thought and teaching. Early Christian artists gave symbolical meaning to colors, too, which are still observed in religious needlework. Embroidery technique is especially adapted to such symbolical expression and this perhaps explains the superior quality of the work done on ecclesiastical pieces. It is a sympathetic medium through which to convey the message of the Church.

The symbols used have been fraught with meaning since the earliest days of Christianity. The circle or ring represents eternity. The arrow indicates martyrdom. The palm also implies martyrdom and is associated with the saints who died for Christ. The anchor signifies hope, firmness, patience or a spiritual strong-

hold. The pomegranate when open and showing the seeds stands for immortality. The olive branch is the emblem of reconciliation and peace. The lily symbolizes purity.

Other motifs are to be interpreted according to the period in which they were created. In early Latin symbology the use of three steps in the design implied the virtues of charity, hope and faith in order of ascent. Charity, being the most necessary virtue and a foundation for the others, was the bottom step next to the earth. The second step built upon charity was hope, which led to the third and top step, faith. Traditionally these virtues are spoken of in order of descent rather than ascent. The ancient Latin sequence is to be read: Be charitable (loving), have hope and hold faith.

Canonical colors include white, red, green, violet and black. White is symbolic of purity, innocence, faith, joy, life and light. Red signifies the passion of our Lord, the suffering and martyrdom of His saints. Green is the Church color used on ordinary Sundays and ferials (week days). Its special implication is bountifulness, mirth, hope, youth and prosperity. Violet indicates passion, suffering, sorrow, humility, truth and deep love. As a rule the martyrs are represented in purple or violet gowns. Black symbolizes death, darkness, mourning and despair. Blue, the emblem of heaven, signifies piety, sincerity, godliness, divine contemplation or deep meditation. Yellow or gold represents the brightness, holiness and goodness of God; plenty, faith and fruitfulness.

Throughout the ages religious needlework has functioned as a source of comfort, being conducive to meditation and spiritual reflection. A purely wrought white silk-embroidered Easter lily glistening upon the varying tones of white brocade and adorning a simple gold cross worked in flat stitches may be just a bookmark to indicate the place where a lesson will be read from the Bible. But how eloquent this chaste, lovely bit of needlework becomes in the quiet atmosphere of the cathedral, placed where it will inspire the minister or priest as he prepares to read the message which is to refresh his people. Such simple and exquisite works have a way of bringing sustenance and solace to searching souls.

Great works of art have been left to posterity in the form of needlework made for the Church in times long past. Cathedrals have been enriched with hangings of exquisitely wrought embroideries and the altars adorned with the work of devotees who wished to dedicate their highest ability to the beautifying of their shrines. Vestments, chalices, veils, altar frontals, copes and chasubles have inspired glorious achievements in embroidery which have enhanced the services in which they have been used. It is as if the quiet nuns who worked many of these embroideries had found in the silent hours devoted to their work a means through which to approach their innermost selves, a communion with heart and soul which is expressed in the tapestries they have given to the world.

Coming down to our own day, we find many groups of women moved by the same impulse who have gathered together to stitch needlepoint and silk-embroidered coverings for prayer books or benches, altar frontals and decorative panels to ornament the sacred tables and the pulpits of chapels and cathedrals throughout the nation.

Some gifts have been made as memorials. Prayer bench covers for a small chapel in Philadelphia were very recently worked in needlepoint by its members who donated them in loving memory of an absent one. Their beautiful work has been enjoyed by many persons outside the immediate congregation. The covers were designed by Mrs. Charles Platt.

Such group effort is practiced most effectively in England today. Two years ago a needlework show was given in London to exhibit a five year task undertaken at Winchester Cathedral to refurnish the choir stalls with needlepoint cushions and kneelers. The medallions used in the design, which are, by the way, modern rather than traditional in character, present a history of the cathedral.

There are some guilds in America that make church embroideries but most ecclesiastical needlework is imported. A memorial altar frontal made for St. Michael's Cathedral in New York is a lovely example of church embroidery made by St. Hilda's Guild in that city. It is a large panel of purple brocade with three Maltese crosses. The symbols which adorn the borders are embroidered with gold threads. Interesting, beautiful and lovely sentiment has been incorporated in this work by the application of amethysts which belonged to the mother of the donor. They have been placed in the centers of the passion flowers. The stones are of an unusual color and are handsome against the gold and purple background, yet not too obtrusive in the general design.

Miss Florence Beekman, a school teacher with talent and a love of good design, created the pattern for the chalice veil which corresponds in color to the altar frontal. The needlework was executed by members of St. Michael's Church Parish in 1894. The passion flowers are exquisitely embroidered in fine silks and outlined with gold against the purple brocaded background. The design shows excellent restraint and a happy absence of over-emphasis or crowding.

Mrs. Nicholas Brown, a needlework enthusiast, presented to the chapel of St. George's School in Newport, Rhode Island, an altar cloth of fine homespun linen beautifully embroidered in white and in satin stitches, Italian cut work and laid work. The design consists of holy figures, apostles and angels in their hallowed niches. Miss Louisa Sturtevant conceived the pattern for this lovely, delicate panel which was embroidered under her direction by one of the workers in the Aquidneck Cottage Industries.

A memorial prayer book cover-binding has

been uniquely and attractively designed by Mrs. Samuel Cabot of Boston, who embroidered it in a variety of crewel stitches combined with needlepoint. Four pearls and four larger jewels have been couched upon the cross in the manner of ancient ecclesiastical embroideries. The work is contemporary in design and feeling and shows excellent taste in its composition.

Two long panels worked in the coloring and style of stained glass windows have been designed and embroidered by Mrs. Leonard Kellogg of New York City. They are done in deep rich tones of wine, red, magenta, royal blue and purples against a blue, green and black background. The little lambs, the birds, the pelican, the cross and other symbolic elements have been established in off-whites. Red orange is used in the costumes of some of the figures and forms an effective contrast to the green-blue background. The needlepoint has a mosaic quality. No studied cartoon was made, the scheme of decoration developing bit by bit as Mrs. Kellogg worked using colors from her wool basket which were to her happy in tone.

"The Good Shepherd" wall panel was designed and executed by the author for a magazine which published it after the manner of the early *Godey's*, *Leslie's* and *Peterson's Magazines* as a pattern for other women to copy. It is embroidered against a silk background, which is deep red cypress in color, with fine crewel wools in blue, greens, golds, pearl gray, whites and some navy blue. The little lambs are, of course, white. The home on the hill is bathed in sunshine tones as are the well-harvested fields toward which the weary travelers are wending their way out of the storm.

Miss Lydia Barlow of Brooklyn, New York, has embroidered a version of this design for her home and also another design of The Nativity, showing the Virgin Mary and the Holy Child, the three wise men, the angels and the ever attendant good shepherd with his little woolly lambs. Miss Barlow has embroidered the angels very effectively upon their blue linen heaven and also has carefully stitched this message, sampler fashion:

> THEN BE YE GLAD
> YE GOOD PEOPLE
> AT THIS TIME OF THE YEAR
> AND LIGHT YE UP YOUR CANDLES
> FOR HIS STAR IS SHINING CLEAR.

The panel, as you may have guessed, was designed for a Christmas gift.

An altar panel of the crucifixion was a labor of love, designed and executed by the author after the style of twelfth century Limoges enamel and inspired by the famous collection given to the Metropolitan Museum of Art by Mr. J. Pierpont Morgan. The clear turquoise and intense violet blue of the enamels were emulated in crewel wools. The cross is worked in jade green with solid backstitches. The border edge is in brown worked in a buttonhole stitch. The foreground hills are in various shades of Limoges blues and greens topped with gold. Wine shades and peach tones with touches of blue make the robes upon the sorrowful figures, while the sympathetic angels are worked in powder and navy blues and cream color. The Christ is worked in a pale shade of off-white with a slight flesh tone. An attempt has been made to convey feeling in the portraits by using wools split into small strands so that the colors might fuse more readily in tone while the observer would be unaware of the threads at first glance. The rest of the needlework has been accomplished in broad strokes of the needle on a background material of deep gray-blue velvet.

There is a great opportunity in this present age to create embroideries that will be even more abstract in quality than the examples presented. The general tendency has been to remain close to the traditional set patterns with which we are all familiar.

The evolution of new ideas in the arts as elsewhere meets with resistance. Departures from the tried and familiar formulae appear strange and are not readily welcomed. This evidently has always been so, but timid reactions have never stopped the progress of the enlightened toward their envisioned objective. When at last the new values are accepted, everyone begins to see that the new has somehow lost its strangeness and another step upward has been accomplished.

In symbolical interpretations of man's innermost thoughts and highest religious ideals, designers may be able to unite their best expression with the vision of needleworkers and, aided by the Clergy, accomplish a real renaissance in ecclesiastical art, a revival that would create a newer symbology with which to inspire oncoming generations.

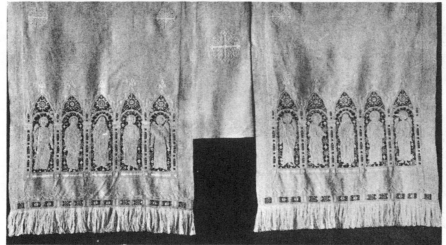

1. *Courtesy of:* ST. GEORGES SCHOOL, Newport, Rhode Island.

Embroidered white linen altar cloth from Chapel of St. Georges School made by The Aquidneck Cottage Industries, designed by Miss Louisa Sturtevant, Newport, Rhode Island.

2. *Courtesy of:* ST. MICHAEL'S CHURCH, New York.

Chalice veil, silk embroidered, designed by Miss Florence Beekman, 1894, worked by the ladies of the Parish for St. Michael's Church, New York.

3. *Courtesy of:* MRS. SAMUEL CABOT, Boston, Mass.

Crewel embroidered and jeweled memorial prayer book cover, designed and worked by Mrs. Samuel Cabot, Boston, Massachusetts.

4. *Courtesy of:* ST. MICHAEL'S CHURCH, New York.

Altar cloth, silk embroidered and jeweled, American, late nineteenth century, for St. Michael's Church, New York.

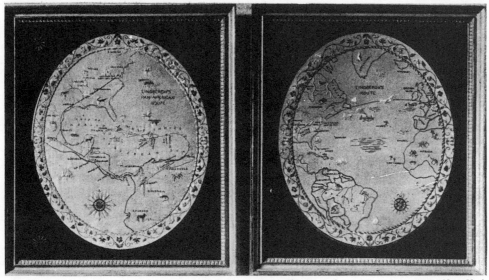

1. Courtesy of: MRS. KENNETH BUDD, New York.

Silk embroidered pictures on satin. The airplane flight of Colonel Charles E. Lindbergh to Paris across the Atlantic in 1927 and to Pan America in 1928. Designed by Aquidneck Cottage Industries and worked by Alice M. Budd, New York.

2. Courtesy of: MRS. KENNETH BUDD, New York.

Silk on silk embroidered picture of the John Jacob Astor Yacht, "Nourmahal," in Newport Harbor, 1924, by Alice M. Budd, New York.

3. Courtesy of: MISS EDITH WETMORE, Newport, Rhode Island.

Silk embroidered picture on taffeta. "Tea House and Garden" of Miss Edith Wetmore, Newport, Rhode Island. Designed and worked by Miss Louisa Sturtevant, Newport, Rhode Island.

4. Courtesy of: MRS. ROBERT COLEMAN TAYLOR, New York.

Silk on silk embroidered picture, "Flight by Airplane across North Pole by Commander Richard Evelyn Byrd, May 9, 1926. Designed and worked April, 1929 by Lillian Gary Taylor, New York.

CHAPTER XXVIII

THE RETURN TO SILK EMBROIDERIES

"Oh, there is not lost
One of earth's charms; upon her bosom yet,
After the flight of untold centuries,
The freshness of her far beginning lies
And yet shall lie . . . . ."

WILLIAM CULLEN BRYANT.

HE MODEST AND HUMBLE SILK-worms were first rendered serviceable to mankind by the Chinese, as far back as 2000 B.C. according to some authorities. Ancient embroiderers show the empresses of China surrounded by their women, engaged in the occupation of rearing silkworms and weaving the charming tissues which were finally embellished with the most delicate needlework.

From China the art of silk cultivation and embroidery passed into India and Persia. It did not reach Europe until the middle of the sixth century when, according to legend, two monks who had lived in China many years finally succeeded in conveying some of the little insects, concealed in a hollow bamboo cane, to Constantinople. There hatching was accomplished by artificial heat. It is said that Emperor Justinian used this experiment to produce a new, important and charming industry for European nations. Thebes, Athens and Corinth practiced the cultivation of silk. In the twelfth century Greece was skilled in the art. It is claimed that Roger II, King of Sicily, about the year 1130 manufactured silk at Palermo, with another establishment at Calabria which was managed by workmen taken as slaves from Athens and Corinth, cities he had conquered in his expedition to the Holy Land.

Spain acquired the knowledge of the manufacture of silk from the Sicilians and the Calabrians. The art was practiced in the southern provinces of France some time after the reign of Charles VIII, and from there it finally reached England during the beginning of the fifteenth century when the art of spinning, weaving, throwing and weaving silk was established there. According to Matthew Paris silk garments were worn at the marriage of Margaret, daughter of Henry III, when a thousand English knights appeared in "cointises" of silk. Articles of apparel were adorned with laces, ribbons and narrow silk fabrics during the reign of Henry IV. "Silk women" produced these dainties but in small quantity, for silk was still a precious rarity and apparently remained so up to 1480. It is recorded that Henry VIII wore the first pair of knitted silk stockings in England. In later years when Queen Elizabeth came to the throne, silk stockings were her particular luxury; no other women were permitted to enjoy this enviable royal privilege, and so the art did not advance very rapidly.

As time went on silk began to be more universally used and its charming qualities became available for costume and costume adornment.

The use of silks in American needlework during the 1800's and, in a smaller degree, in the late nineteenth century has been referred to, but every so often the art of silk embroidery makes an emphatic reappearance. It is doing so today in a comparatively small but very significant way. Several prominent American women have chosen to revive its ancient, graceful and knowing charms. In silken threadings they are recording events of historical import or making delicate decorations for their homes. Embroidery silk is almost unobtainable in America today and the present-day examples have been worked invariably with materials obtained from France and England.

Mrs. Robert Coleman Taylor, one of the silk devotees, learned her silk embroidery technique as a young lady in Baltimore, when, as Lillian Gary, she had ample opportunity to study the art of needlework with her mother who embroidered so beautifully.

In mentioning her earlier silk embroidery, when pansies were taken from the large garden and their every blue and violet color matched with corresponding silk shades to be worked on tea cloth borders, Mrs. Taylor states that frequent exposure and washing have not altered the wonderful staying qualities of the dyes and the silks made in the earlier years of the 1890's. Obtaining colors in silks and also in wools which would remain fast has been of great concern to all contemporary needle-women.

To work the silk on silk embroidery commemorating the epic airplane flight on which Commander Evelyn Byrd carried the Stars and Stripes across the North Pole on May 9, 1926, Mrs. Taylor used Filo wash silks, loosely woven, for the long and short stitches conveying the ice and snow. These give the sheen and effect of the snow fields in different lights, depending upon the angle of approach to the picture. Looking from the left sunlight appears to be falling on its surface, and from the right it picks up its own high light brilliantly. This dramatic quality within the silks themselves offers fascinating possibilities for the use of this medium in unusual and newly interpretive ways.

Light effects on the silk threads have been emphasized in Mrs. Taylor's composition in the way the rays of the midnight sun have been spread out from the horizon of tinted silk cloth. They are composed of lines and backstitches of rounded silk, extending behind the smooth dawn-tinted clouds of silk which have been worked in satin stitches. The airplane is effectively constructed in the heavier corded or twisted silks and is in strong contrast to the delicate sky. The walrus and the polar bear show fine stitch direction which convey their rounded structure feelingly. A double border has been made in chain stitches. Beneath the picture's inscription is stitched the date and signature of the designer and embroiderer, Lillian Gary Taylor, April, 1929.

With silks obtained from England, Mrs. Kenneth Budd, a most enthusiastic "needle painter" with silks, has embroidered many pictures in this technique. Her great-grandmother, Lydia Welles of Boston, made the lovely Cupid and Psyche silk on satin classic embroidery in the early 1800's, and this work hanging in Mrs. Budd's home today offers fresh inspiration in its fine stitch rendering. It is also lively and vital being in an excellent state of preservation.

The commemoration of the two famous airplane flights made by Colonel Charles A. Lindbergh is among the pleasurable and interesting needlework accomplishments of Mrs. Budd. This pair of pictures is worked with varicolored silks on ivory satin. The design was arranged by the Aquidneck Industries for Mrs. Budd from actual photographs taken during these events.

"The Spirit of St. Louis," the airplane used by Colonel Lindbergh on his first transoceanic hop, is shown on the first panel in an embroidered flight, its stitched lettering announcing: "Started from New York, left 2.51 A. M., May 20, 1927." The route, traced on the map in outline stitch, goes across the Atlantic Ocean to France, and the lettering shows the time of his arrival there on May 21.

Colonel Lindbergh's Pan-American flight from the North American continent, beginning at Washington, D. C., December 13, 1927, is also described in silk embroidery on satin. Mrs. Budd has stitched this information in fine lettering. The route of the Good Will flight is indicated in outline stitch. To give the feeling of old maps, each country has been outlined

THE RETURN TO SILK EMBROIDERIES

with a separate color. All the stops made in the flight are lettered. Chattanooga (Tennessee) is the first, followed by Houston (Texas); then come Tampico, Mexico City, Guatemala and Belize on the Caribbean Sea. The route then goes across to San Salvador on the Pacific, and continues on to Tegucigalpa in Honduras, on to Managua in Nicaragua, down to San Jose in Costa Rica. It proceeds on to Cartagena in Colombia; then Bogotá, in the same country, and Caracas in Venezuela; after this comes Maracay and from here the line scouts around the West Indies to St. Thomas, San Juan (Porto Rico), Santo Domingo, Port-au-Prince, and lastly, at Havana, the final day of the famous aviator's epic journey is recorded as February 28, 1928.

The map is embellished with a picture of the airplane en route, worked in satin stitches. A suggestion of the Capitol buildings at Washington is shown. Other decorative spots which enliven the color of the map are cattle in Texas, an alligator in Florida, a bird of paradise in Mexico, a mountain goat in Central America, a llama in Peru, flying fish in the Caribbean Sea, a pair of flying mallards, and an ocean liner steaming across the upper Atlantic Ocean.

A lovely floral border with delicate vine tracery is embroidered around the oval edge of both panels, framing them gracefully. Two strands of different colored chenilles have been interlaced to make the border line on this frame, giving a unique and most effective finish. The panels have been framed in the manner of earlier silk embroideries with black and gold painted glass coverings.

Silk embroideries of boats also fascinate Mrs. Budd, who has used in another example a lovely turquoise-blue silk taffeta background to convey the effect of water at Newport Harbor, with reflected sky colorings. Against this is a picture, stitched in cream-white silks, of the John Jacob Astor yacht, the "Nourmahal," gracefully riding at anchor. The lines of the yacht have been interestingly tapered through the careful use of stitch movement and direction. The American flag at its stern seems to wave gaily in a smart breeze, while the sails on the schooners and sloops are well and busily filled with ample wind. The Ida Lewis boathouse is stitched in the center of the composition where it keeps a watchful eye on the harbor traffic. Its signal station even catches a message of dashes. In the middle distance men are rowing out into the harbor in a small boat upon an errand of life-saving. Their speed is indicated by the wide lines stitched in the boat's wake.

The calm of the water near shore is ably conveyed with a few simple but telling needlestrokes which indicate a slight rolling of the water. The tree tops are composed mainly of tiny French knots and are nicely balanced in design by the flags of the "Nourmahal" crossed against the ship's steering wheel. Other stitches employed in the embroidery are satin stitch, long and short stitch, backstitch and outline stitch.

A splendid border of shells stitched in green and cream whites forms a border which encompasses the picture and, as in the Lindbergh panels, twisted chenilles of two shades make a small line around the border of shells. The embroidery is signed A. M. Budd and dated 1924.

During the present year of 1938, Mrs. Budd has completed an arresting undertaking in the embroidery in silks of the flowers of the forty-eight states. The design, by Mrs. Charles Platt of Philadelphia, won second prize in a competition held by the Amateur Needlework of Today organization at one of its annual charity benefit exhibitions in New York. Mrs. Budd decided to work this panel, intended for needlepoint, in silks. It is a major work for her in this medium. Measuring twenty-four by thirty inches, it is worked upon a background of heavy beige silk taffeta with silks matching the colorings of the flowers of the various states. Each is handsomely and ably embroidered in the varied expressions and characteristics of the floral emblems. The fine lettering which labels each blossom is carefully stitched in the smallest detail. The entire panel is a splendid decorative example of twentieth century American needlework in full flower.

Mrs. Theodore Roosevelt, Jr., tries her hand at silk embroideries also and has several pictures or rather, screen panels, to her credit. One example is a small three-fold table screen of blue silk which was worked in 1937. The central panel is a fantasy adapted in design from an illustration by Boris Artzybasheff. It depicts in fine silk stitchery two Chinese youths holding fast to a dragon horse, composed of solidly worked small silk flowers and leaves, which is silhouetted against the light blue silk sky.

The two side panels were designed by Mrs. Roosevelt with fantasies and beasties. A devil sits astride a rhinoceros blowing on a horn out of which come little devils; astride the horn sits another devil similarly blowing a smaller horn. Above is a frog carrying above his head a pond lily umbrella. All the other little figures remind one of the early illuminated manuscript paintings of *The Book of Kels,* with the funny little creatures of Celtic imagination painted among the initials and scrolls. Small branches of flowers in the spaces between the strange figures decoratively fill the background. The entire embroidery has been accomplished in fine chain stitches after the manner of ancient Chinese silk embroideries and it is beautifully done. It is initialed E. B. R., and dated 1937.

A delightful two-fold screen made by Mrs. Roosevelt has been embroidered with colored silks upon gold cloth. The design was adapted from an old illuminated manuscript found in a church in England. It bore a quaint legend which has been embroidered in large old English block letters upon the two folds of the screen, and surrounded with flower scrolls, leaves and queer little animals fantastically composed. The legend reads:

FROM GHOULES AND GHOSTIES,
LONG LEGGITIE BEASTIES AND THINGS
  THAT GO BUMP IN THE NIGHT,
GOOD LORD DELIVER US.

This example of silk embroidery has been rendered not only with delightful humor but with excellent stitch technique.

Going to the eighteenth century for her inspiration Mrs. Curtis McGraw of Princeton, New Jersey, conveys the feeling of that period in her silk-embroidered picture. The use of water-color painting on Cupid, urn, and fence is reminiscent of the early 1800 American pictures. Stitch direction has been carefully watched in the rendering of the draperies and in the treatment of the foreground where the quality of a grassy lawn has been achieved. Tiny pearls have been applied around the neck and wrist of the maiden. The panel is very small and delicately toned to harmonize with an eighteenth century room in Mrs. McGraw's home.

A silk embroidery on taffeta which also includes touches of water color has been designed and worked by Miss Louisa Sturtevant of the Aquidneck Industries in Newport, Rhode Island. Miss Sturtevant is the Aquidneck designer and a painter by profession. She uses painting angles in her needlework expression as evidenced in her rendering of Miss Edith Wetmore's "Garden in Newport" with its tea house surrounded by flowers, plants and trees. The shadings and stitched drawing of all these forms have been interpreted by Miss Sturtevant with feeling and stitch variety. To indicate masses in the overhanging trees, water color has been used between the embroidered outlines of branches and leaves and likewise on the tree trunks. This treatment suggests a compromise between the realism of the earlier schools of needlework and the simplicity in line and form stressed in more recent embroideries. A border of twisted chenilles has been laid on the edge of this silk picture, an inventive use of materials which is novel and interesting.

A "Lady Watering a Water Lily" is a fantasy on blue-green silk taffeta which was designed and worked by the author in 1926 to decorate the boudoir of Mrs. D. Belfield in Merion, Pennsylvania. The general colorings have been chosen to correspond with the chinoiserie of the eighteenth century room in which it was placed. The corals and golds were arranged to match the silks used for window draperies. The blue green of the background blended with the walls, and touches of jade greens in the room were "picked up" in the color used for the willow trees in the embroidery. Chinese lacquer red was also included to reflect other color notes used in the furnishings.

Small silver-threaded stars were scattered in the blue sky and repeated in touches on top of the water, while tiny, opalescent crystal beads were applied, spraying out from the watering pot to drop on the thriving, pale-pink Chinese lily. Deep mauve violets, claret-wine shades and deep green blue added emphasis and color depth around the corners of the embroidery to offset the higher and lighter tones of the peach and coral shades. Gaiety and spirit were most sought in this work, both in color and line, and were achieved through the play and direction of the open stitches as well as in the subject idea.

1. *Courtesy of:* MRS. THEODORE ROOSEVELT, JR., Long Island, New York.

Three-fold silk table screen embroidered with silks. Center Panel Design from Boris Artzybasheff. Two outside panels designed and worked by Mrs. Theodore Roosevelt, Jr., Long Island, New York, 1937.

2, *Courtesy of:* MRS. CURTIS MCGRAW, New Jersey.

Silk embroidered picture with painted portrait after manner of 18th century needlework by Mrs. Curtis McGraw, New Jersey. 1937.

3. *Courtesy of:* MRS. KENNETH BUDD, New York.

Silk embroidered picture, "State Flowers U.S.A.," designed by Mrs. Charles Platt of Philadelphia and worked in 1938 by Alice M. Budd, New York.

4. *Courtesy of:* MRS. D. BELFIELD, Pennsylvania.

"Watering the Water Lily," Chinese Chippendale, embroidered mural with wools, gold thread and crystal beads on silk, for boudoir of Mrs. D. Belfield, Pennsylvania. Designed and worked 1926 by Georgiana Brown Harbeson, Pennsylvania and New York.

Three crewel embroidered samplers commemorative of the World War prime events, January 1, 1916, April 8, 1917, and
July 4, 1917, by Lillian Gary Taylor, New York.

A wall memorial crewel embroidered sampler, "In Flanders Field," by Mrs. Petrina Peterson, New York.

The gradual trend in recent years toward the expression of rhythm and movement, the use of original ideas and inventive stitches seems to be increasingly evident. The silk embroideries as shown in these twentieth century examples depart entirely from traditional formulas in subject and design, in mode and in manner. The only bow to fundamentals occurs in the use of the foundation materials, real silk and satin, and the stitches employed, which have remained much the same after the flight of untold centuries.

CHAPTER XXIX

NEW USES OF THE SAMPLER

"What does eternity indicate?
We have thus far exhausted trillions of Winters and Summers,
There are trillions ahead and trillions ahead of them.
Births have brought us richness and variety, and other births will bring us
  richness and variety.
I do not call one greater and one smaller,
That which fills its period and place is equal to any."

WALT WHITMAN.

NUSUAL USE IS BEING MADE OF the sampler in this streamline age. Instead of being a practice sheet for needlework techniques as it was in the eighteenth century, it has become today a purely decorative asset applied in many ways to adornment of the home. Instead of gracing the wall primarily as a picture, hung over the mantel in the best parlor or in the bedroom as of yore, the sampler now wanders about the house inserted in a glass tray, or it graces the top of a tilt table, or it is inserted as part of a mirror panel. No longer is the sampler the main accomplishment of the young daughter, a splendid diploma to be displayed by the proud parent. Today's daughters and their mothers demonstrate their stitch abilities together on samplers. Nor are these modern samplers allowed to grow old quietly and unobtrusively in the home. They are sent out to the public exhibitions and sold to raise money for various charities. Or through their embroidered slogans they help to promote causes. These twentieth century samplers have been called

CAMPAIGN SAMPLERS

Three examples of hard-working samplers commemorate significant events of the last decade. The first one was made for the great drive of the Woman's Organization of National Prohibition Reform which, headed by Mrs. Charles Sabin Davis of New York, enlisted the co-operation of prominent women in other communities all over the country. The New York State committee adopted this sampler which was designed and made by the author to convey the spirit of the drive and to record the campaign. Hundreds of these designs were printed on brown, blue and cream linen; they were packaged with their dozen shades of wool, and sold to promote the cause through the various state committees. The linen squares bear a verse printed on the top center. One of them, which was embroidered in the fine crewel wools of reds, whites and blues, by Mrs. Mary Williams Dick, a campaigner from Connecticut, shows this verse which reads:

> BRING BACK THE OLD
> RING IN THE NEW
> TURN OUT FALSE LAWS
> RING IN THE NEW.

On either side liberty bells are being rung with ropes made of tiny chain stitches, by a man and a woman representing Mr. and Mrs. "Johnny Q. Public." They stand beneath the embroidered spread eagle and the initials of the organization, W. O. N. P. R.

Needlepoint sampler commemorating the N.R.A. Adapted from poster and worked, 1933, by Mrs. de Lancey Kountze, New York.

Sampler used by Mrs. August Belmont's "Adopt A Family" committee to help raise funds. Designed and worked by Georgiana Brown Harbeson, 1933.

Rhode Island Tercentenary, 1636-1936, crewel embroidered sampler designed by Aquidneck Cottage Industries, Rhode Island, and worked by Mrs. Nicholas E. Brown, Newport, Rhode Island.

"Oberlin College" crewel embroidered. Anniversary sampler, 1833-1933, designed and worked by Georgiana Brown Harbeson, New York.

"The Fisherman's Prayer," crewel embroidered sampler designed for a yacht by Georgiana Brown Harbeson and worked by Bettie Holmes, Long Island, New York, 1936.

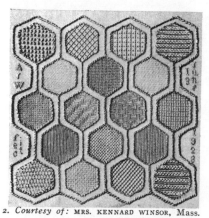

Sampler of stitches, pulled, outline, darned and drawn work, worked on scrim with sewing silk, 1928, by Adelaide Winsor, Massachusetts.

Hopi Indian sampler, 1934, made by Clarabelle Irving at the United States Indian School in Albuquerque, New Mexico.

"Repeal Sampler." Crewel embroidery on linen for the W.O.N.P.R., designed by the author and worked by Mary Williams Dick, Connecticut, 1932.

Enterprise in the farms and outlying districts is represented by the flowers growing around the house, which was embroidered next to the woman who rules over the home. On the opposite side enterprise in the cities was represented by stitched skyscrapers next to the man who presides over these towers of steel and business activities. The couple stand united and determined on the platform principle "Repeal the Eighteenth Amendment," which was the slogan of the drive and was embroidered at the base of the sampler.

The example of this sampler shown in the illustration was dated by Mary Low Williams in 1932. The stitches employed to make it were satin stitch, backstitch, outline stitch, chain stitch, Roumanian stitch and buttonhole stitch.

The second campaign sampler was used in the "Adopt a Family" drive presided over by Mrs. August Belmont, whose committee endeavored to stem the tide of depression during the year 1933. This sampler carried a verse which the author adapted from an early sampler. It reads:

WHEN WEALTH TO VIRTUE'S HANDS IS GIVEN
IT BLESSES LIKE THE DEWS OF HEAVEN
LIKE HEAVEN IT HEARS THE ORPHAN'S CRIES
AND WIPES THE TEARS FROM WIDOWS' EYES.

The verse is enclosed in a wreath of forget-me-nots which is held by two pale pink and blue angels. Bluebirds carry a ribbon inscribed "Spirit of '33," implying that the full basket, abundance, brought happiness to the little boy and girl in the needy family. The pet squirrel and the Scottie dog are begging for a share. Beneath the flowering hearts on either side of the sampler is the embroidered legend, "Welfare Relief, Work Against Want."

Packages of samplers bearing this design were sold to help raise funds and were embroidered by philanthropic women.

The third sampler was dedicated to the N. R. A. presided over by General Hugh A. Johnson, and advertised the New Deal policies. This sampler was primarily a copy of the poster which proclaimed one who possessed it to be an

N. R. A.
MEMBER
U. S.

Beneath came the spread eagle with a wheel or gear of industrial symbolism substituted for the arrows usually carried in its right claw, and in its other claw lightning flashes instead of laurel leaves. Underneath came the slogan:

WE DO OUR PART.

This poster was worked in needlepoint by Mrs. De Lancey Kountze of New York and dated by her A.D. 1933.

All three campaigns and their embroidered samplers have now become a part of American history.

COMMEMORATIVE SAMPLERS

The earliest in this group of contemporary samplers which record significant events is the group of three World War memorial samplers designed and worked by Mrs. Robert Coleman Taylor. They are embroidered on linen with Utopia floss in tiny cross-stitches, darning and satin stitches. The first was begun in 1914 and finished in 1916. The top inscription states in stitching:

THIS IS MY COMMANDMENT
THAT YE LOVE ONE ANOTHER
AS I HAVE LOVED YOU.

A pair of seven-branched candlesticks balance either side of this lettering. Beneath them is a line, and then in three columns come the names of the nations and the events of the war, as follows: in the left column, Austria, Hungary, Germany, Turkey, Bulgaria; in the right, Servia, Russia, France, Belgium, England, Japan, Italy; in the center, Belgium martyred, Poland starving, Armenia massacred, Servia devastated, Lusitania.

The date 1914 tops the margin on one side and 1915 on the other. Placed in niches down the side borders, cannon or long-range guns are centered upon all the nations. They are worked in cross-stitch. Underneath the columns is a strip of ground showing trenches and breastworks on either side manned with small embroidered soldiers sighting the enemy over the top. The German flag is on one fortification and on the other is the flag of France. Then comes the large word stitched beneath the entire picture

HUMANITY

Beneath, a temple of peace is embroidered to the left and two crossed American flags are draped to the right. Under all is the name and date, Lillian Gary Taylor, January 1, 1916.

The second panel or sampler is dated at the top center of the border 1916, which is the year in which it was begun. Underneath is stitched:

GREATER LOVE HATH NO MAN THAN THIS, THAT A MAN LAY DOWN HIS LIFE FOR HIS FRIENDS.

A pair of seven-branched candlesticks with lighted tapers are placed on a line extending across the sampler. Below this are listed the following nations, stitched in three rows with the outstanding events and battles of the year between them. In the left column, Austria, Hungary, Germany, Turkey, Bulgaria; in the right, Servia, Russia, France, Belgium, England, Japan, Italy, Roumania; in the center, Louvain, Rheims, Belgians deported, Roumania invaded, Russian revolution.

Beneath these is a scene picturing the sinking of the "Lusitania." The submarine torpedo boat is also shown. Under this is another scene with three Red Cross ambulances hurrying across the sampler, while above are three airplanes of 1917 make. This panel is signed and dated in that year. The design theme of the border is the small Red Cross symbol of first aid.

A border of laurel leaves surrounds the third and last of the World War samplers. Suspended from the top border are seven flags with the American flag in ·the center. On either side of the flags is stitched the date, April 6, 1917, when the sampler was begun. Beneath are the well-known lines:

HE HAS SOUNDED FORTH THE TRUMPET THAT
    SHALL NEVER CALL RETREAT,
HE IS SIFTING OUT THE HEARTS OF MEN BEFORE
    HIS JUDGMENT SEAT.

Then follows an embroidered underline of massed allied colors. Beginning to the left and following across the sampler is written:

PARIS, "LAFAYETTE NOUS VOILA," JULY 14, 1917.

A row of marines with an American flag cross the left side of the panel, meeting General Pershing who stands midway and who is approached from the other side by a row of soldiers representing the army of the United States.

Names of abdicating rulers and the battles of the year follow in three columns. The columns are separated by two staffs encircled with entwined leaves and topped with circular wreaths bearing the date January 1, 1919, when the sampler was completed. Its record is as follows: in the left column, Tsar of Russia abdicates March 1, 1917, Kaiser of Germany, November 9, 1918, Emperor of Austria, November 12, 1918; in the right, King of Bavaria abdicates November 8, 1918, King of Württemberg, November 8, 1918, King of Saxony, November 11, 1918; in the center the battles of the year are listed, Liege, Marne, Ypres, Verdun, Gallipoli, Piave, Bagdad, Château-Thierry, Argonne Forest.

This sampler completes the series of World War memorials which provide interesting records for present and future generations. The entire series has been executed with great needlework skill, particularly in the decorative and inventive expression to be seen in the lettering. Symbolism has been introduced with thought, feeling and selectivity.

Another World War memorial sampler has been embroidered by Petrina Peterson. It is dated 1922, New York. Two poems surrounded with a laurel leaf border comprise the design. On the left side of the panel these verses are stitched beneath British flags:

IN FLANDERS FIELDS

IN FLANDERS FIELDS THE POPPIES BLOW
BETWEEN THE CROSSES, ROW ON ROW,
THAT MARK OUR PLACE; AND IN THE SKY
THE LARKS, STILL BRAVELY SINGING FLY
SCARCE HEARD AMID THE GUNS BELOW.

WE ARE THE DEAD, SHORT DAYS AGO
WE LIVED, FELT DAWN, SAW SUNSET GLOW
LOVED AND WERE LOVED, AND NOW WE LIE,
    IN FLANDERS FIELDS.

TAKE UP YOUR QUARREL WITH THE FOE:
TO YOU FROM FAILING HANDS WE THROW
TH' TORCH; BE YOURS TO HOLD IT HIGH
IF YE BREAK FAITH WITH US WHO DIE
WE SHALL NOT SLEEP, THOUGH POPPIES GROW
    IN FLANDERS FIELDS.
                          JOHN MCCRAE.

On the right this poem is stitched under crossed American flags:

AMERICA'S ANSWER

REST YE IN PEACE, YE FLANDERS DEAD!
THE FIGHT THAT YE SO BRAVELY LED
WE'VE TAKEN UP! AND WE WILL KEEP
TRUE FAITH WITH YOU WHO LIE ASLEEP
WITH EACH A CROSS TO MARK HIS BED,

AND POPPIES BLOWING OVERHEAD
WHERE ONCE HIS OWN LIFE BLOOD RAN RED!
SO LET YOUR REST BE SWEET AND DEEP
    IN FLANDERS FIELDS.

FEAR NOT THAT YE HAVE DIED FOR NAUGHT;
THE TORCH YE THREW TO US WE CAUGHT!
TEN MILLION HANDS WILL HOLD IT HIGH
AND FREEDOM'S LIGHT SHALL NEVER DIE!
WE'VE LEARNED THE LESSON THAT YE TAUGHT
    IN FLANDERS FIELDS.

                        R. W. LILLARD.

Rows of poppies rise from the lower border. They are red beneath the poem "In Flanders Field" and beneath "America's Answer," they are red, white and blue. The sampler is signed "Tena Peterson." It was inspired by the samplers of Mrs. Taylor, whose work Miss Peterson has long admired and to whom she presented this sampler on her silver wedding anniversary.

Commemorative of the Rhode Island Tercentenary, 1636-1936, is the crewel-embroidered sampler designed by Louisa Sturtevant of the Aquidneck Cottage Industries and worked by Mrs. Nicholas E. Brown of Newport, Rhode Island. The design names in needlework the original settlers of Rhode Island, John Clarke, Roger Williams, Bishop Berkeley, Governor Coddington, Anne Hutchinson, and Oliver Hagard Perry. The seal of Newport, the Rhode Island crest and the state flower center the panel. On one side of these motifs an Indian is standing; on the other side is a colonial gentleman. A spinning wheel and a Viking ship complete the top decoration beneath which is stitched the legend on either side of the sampler,

TO PROCLAIM A   SOUL FREEDOM
TRUE AND   TO ALL THE
ABSOLUTE   PEOPLE OF THE
                    LAND.

Between the British and American flags is stitched "R. I. Tercentenary 1636-1936." Below is a reproduction of the Colony House embroidered in darning stitches, outline and satin stitches and set within a laurel wreath. Beside it to the left are United States marines and a battleship; to the right, sailors and a clipper ship. A handsome turkey centers the lower part of the sampler; to the left, encircled by a wreath, is the old market and opposite in another wreath is a stitched rendering of the Redwood Library. A colonial soldier is flanked by two old cannon and on either side of these are worked the names of John Smibert and John Goddard.

The sampler is bordered with a simple outline stitched in wool, and is initialed N. E. B. on one side and signed L. C. Sturtevant on the other, the embroiderer and the name of the designer.

The one-hundredth anniversary of Oberlin College was commemorated in a sampler designed by the author. Incidents in the history of the college are included, from pioneer days when it was organized in a log cabin made with trees hewn from the Ohio forests and became the first college in America to give degrees to women, up through its late nineteenth century days and into the present. The future is suggested by buildings stitched upon a cloud. These new halls of learning were taken from the plans of the architect. The embroidered scene is enclosed within the college seal which bears the legend:

OBERLIN COLLEGE . . . LEARNING AND LABOR

It is dedicated to "Education" which has been accomplished through the practice of "Industry," "Economy" and "Self-Denial."

This sampler was one of a series of needleworked lunettes illustrating a series of articles by Miss Catharine Oglesby published in 1934 in *The Ladies' Home Journal*. The articles dealt with the various accomplishments of American women in raising money in their communities to further civic needs and were entitled "It's Up To The Women." The illustrative panels were embroidered upon silk backgrounds with fine crewel yarns. The Oberlin College panel was a dawn-peach tone, silk-embroidered in various shades of gray pearl to deep blue and brown gray and emphasized with ivory white and black notes. Other samplers symbolized Patriotism, Culture, Suffrage, and Thrift. Each design recorded some organized effort among women. The first woman's club in America, which was organized in Concord, New Hampshire, in 1804 and named "The New Hampshire Female Cent Society," was shown on the sampler dedicated to Culture. The signing of the Woman's Suffrage Amendment, June 4, 1919, was depicted on the Suffrage sampler.

This is the first occasion on which samplers or embroideries have been definitely designed for use as magazine illustrations. They were embroidered in 1933 and 1934 and are all based on American themes.

PRACTICE SAMPLERS

Two samplers which are purely practice examples of needlework have entirely different objectives. The first is a handsome sample of eighteen stitches worked on very fine scrim by Mrs. Kennard Winsor of Massachusetts. Sewing silk was used to make the pulled and outline stitches, darned stitches worked in a variety of patterns and drawn work stitches. It is a stitch reference sampler in much the same manner as early samplers except that the design layout for the embroidery is more modern. The technical display is an interpretation of the darned lacework stitching on net made during the 1830's. It is very stimulating to see a gradual revival of interest in this style of fine needlework. The sampler is initialed A. J. W. and is dated 1928.

The other practice sampler was made by an American Indian, Clarabelle Irving, who comes from the Hopi Village of Sichumnovi on the First Mesa Reservation and who learned to embroider at the United States Indian School in Albuquerque, New Mexico. Her sampler is now in the collection of Miss Gertrude Oppenheimer. It was made in 1934 in much the same spirit as our grandmother's work, since it is a sample of technique and the designs were to be used later for a more practical purpose. In this case the Indian maiden planned to embroider a belt sash for her father and has created a very gay symbolic pattern for a bright addition to his costume, to be embroidered perhaps after her working hours on a ranch.

The background material is a discarded flour sack; sometimes sugar sacks are stitched in the same way, with brilliant wools in Indian red, green, blue, black and yellow. The stitches are flat and simple giving the effect of weaving when finished. The geometric symbols used in the embroidery have been interpreted by a student of Indian symbology. The top left motif signifies the five steps in the life of a Navajo: Childhood, Youth, Manhood, Middle Age, Old Age. The three squares cornerwise in the upper center are significant, the upper square with its white top and two triangles symbolizing a triple rain cloud, the four perpendicular lines indicating showers. The square to the lower left beseeches a heavy rainfall, the uppermost desire in the Indian mind in that section of the country. The other squares have not been analyzed. It is said they are simply experiments in conventionalized design. The small round spot on the right with T's coming out of its center, signifies the four corners of the earth. Beneath are the spread wings of a large bird, and to the left, in the upright square within a square motif, is a third smaller square which symbolizes the Omnipotent Eye (Navajo). To the left are six lines again emphasizing the desired rain.

The stitches employed in this sampler are long stitch, satin stitch and cross-stitch.

HOBBY SAMPLERS

A sampler showing not only a love of catching fish but a love of stitching them was made by Mrs. Christian R. Holmes for her yacht. The verse, a favorite with Mrs. Holmes, is embroidered on the linen sampler in fine satin stitch with crewel wool.

THE FISHERMAN'S PRAYER

LORD GRANT I MAY CATCH A FISH
SO LARGE THAT EVEN I
IN TELLING OF IT AFTERWARD
MAY HAVE NO NEED TO LIE

The lady on the bank is about to catch a large whale, crewel-embroidered in satin stitch; a small fish looks out of her basket, mouth wide open with astonishment at this catch! A turtle is busy blowing bubbles and a large fish on the other side of the picture is similarly engaged. An angelfish dots the "I" of the verse with more and truer-blown bubbles, while below the verse two dolphins leap playfully above the waves. The embroidery is signed "Bettie Holmes, Her Sampler," and is dated 1936. It was designed by the author.

Samplers depicting hobby interests have been

Needlepoint sampler, "Coronation-Jubilee" 1910-1935, "George and Mary," worked 1937 by Elizabeth Eshleman Castles, New Jersey.

Needlepoint sampler of "Recognition of U.S.S.R.,1933," by Mrs. Theodore Roosevelt, Jr., Oyster Bay, Long Island, New York.

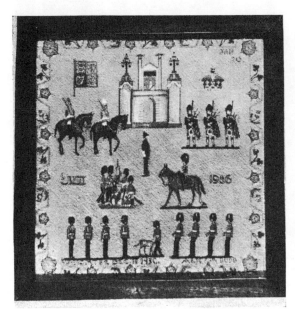

Needlepoint sampler; "The Trooping of the Colors, Edward, the VIII, 1936" by Alice M. Budd, New York.

Needlepoint sampler describing Theodore Roosevelt, Jr.'s hunting expedition. Designed and worked, 1934, by Mrs. Theodore Roosevelt, Jr., Long Island, New York.

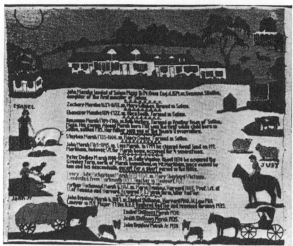

Needlepoint and french knot stitched, Family Sampler with Genealogical Record, 1938, by Mrs. John Bigelow Marsh, New York.

Needlepoint sampler portrait, by Ann F. Hobdy, of her old Kentucky homestead and worked by her.

Needlepoint sampler of the Halcott Pride Greens, designed by Margaret Green and worked by Virginia Green, 1937, North Carolina and New York.

Needlepoint and cross stitch sampler by Mrs. Margaret L. Hall, Connecticut, 1934.

decidedly on the increase and another rising trend combines this interest with others in the embroidering of

CONVERSATION PIECES

This is a name applied to samplers portraying family interests, combining background and history, hobbies, travels, occupations and any number of little or large ideas related to the important institution of the home. Many of these have been made recently in both crewel embroidery and needlepoint techniques. Examples in the latter class have been selected for description because of their diversified character.

"The Old Kentucky Homestead" was designed and worked by Ann F. Hobdy around her own home in the South. It is very Stephen Fosterish in its composition and character and gaily reminiscent of Old Black Joe with his belongings wrapped in a bandana kerchief, his tail coat left over from his service as butler, his large, soft hat handed down from the "Massa." He is seen approaching "Mandy" who is holding the little "chillun," and is intending no doubt to ask for a little support in his old age or for comforting words over his "miseries."

In the landscape patch below a happy black boy with the never failing smile is about to bite into a large crescent of watermelon. A proud strutting cock is dangerously near but he will, no doubt, fly at the slightest move to the cornfield which Miss Hobdy has indicated by four healthy cornstalks. Huge butterflies chaperon the darky figures, and the old homestead centered safely between towering old trees is beamed upon by a very large and decorative sun emerging from clouds much in the manner of twelfth century paintings.

The sampler is related in design to decorative modern Russian pictures of the Chauve Souris character, or the Remisoff and Soudekine painting interpretations of the heavenly bodies. Corner clouds match this style of design. Birds and flowers complete the decorative and jolly rendering which has been worked in needlepoint on fine canvas.

Also designed by Ann Hobdy is a needlepoint sampler which combines the qualities of contemporary landscape design with those of the early family register style. These blend amus-

ingly in the work of Mrs. John Bigelow Marsh. Life down on the farm, and the family's love of it, is depicted. The particular duties relegated to each member of the family are shown along with their special interests. Isabel, John, Jr., and Judy with their two pet collies are needle-worked into the side border. A hay wagon is included and a horse and buggy in the foreground. Above this scene and snuggling below a hill is the old homestead, embroidered in fine needlepoint detail. Part of the fine canvas background has been left uncovered in the manner of early samplers worked in this technique.

The family is "registered" in the center of the sampler. The letters are very ably stitched.

* * * * *

JOHN MARSHE LANDED AT SALEM MASS 1634 FROM ENG. D. 1674, M.

SUSANNA SKELTON, DAUGHTER OF THE FIRST MINISTER OF SALEM.

* * * * *

ZACHARY MARSHE 1637-1693. M. MARY SILLSBEE. FARMED IN SALEM.

* * * * *

EBENEZER MARSHE 1674-1722. M. ALICE BOOTH. FARMED IN SALEM.

* * * * *

BENJAMIN MARSH 1704-1786. M. RUTH WATERS. FARMED IN FRONTIER TOWN OF SUTTON, MASS. HIS COUSIN ABIGAIL MARSH BORN 1718 WAS THE FIRST WHITE CHILD BORN IN SUTTON, SETTLED 1715. HER FATHER WAS ONE OF THE TOWN'S 3 PROPRIETORS.

* * * * *

STEPHEN MARSH 1735-1800. M. NANCY DODGE. FARMED IN SUTTON.

* * * * *

JOHN MARSH 1765-1845. M. LOIS MARSH. IN 1799 HE CLEARED FOREST LAND ON MT. MARKHAM, ANDOVER, VT. FOR MARSH HOME, OCCUPIED FOR 4 GENERATIONS.

* * * * *

PETER DUDLEY MARSH 1800-1879. M. SALLY WINSHIP. ABOUT 1830 HE ACQUIRED THE GREELEY FARM, NORTH OF MARSH HOMESTEAD, ON MT. MARKHAM, SINCE OWNED BY HIM AND HIS DESCENDANTS, EXCEPT FOR A SHORT PERIOD IN THE 1880's.

* * * * *

IVORY WHITE RICHARDSON MARSH 1833-1868.M.
MARY SHEPHERD WHITMAN. GRADUATED
FROM DARTMOUTH 1857. TEACHER IN NEW-
PORT, R. I.

* * * * *

ARTHUR RICHMOND MARSH B.1861.M.MARIE
BIGELOW. HARVARD 1883. PROF.LIT. OF U. OF
KANSAS AND HARVARD. ACQUIRED P. D. MARSH
FARM, LATER RED TOP.

* * * * *

JOHN BIGELOW MARSH B. 1887.M.ISABEL STET-
TINIUS. HARVARD 1908. H. LAW 1910. LAWYER
IN N. Y. MAJOR 77 DIV. Q. E. F. RESTORED RED
TOP AND RESUMED FARMING 1935.

* * * * *

ISABEL STETTINIUS MARSH 1920.

* * * * *

JUDITH STETTINIUS MARSH 1925.

* * * * *

JOHN BIGELOW MARSH JR. 1930.

* * * * *

This interesting genealogical record registers
the survival of the old homestead and the love
of farming which has persisted in the family
since the arrival of the original colonist who
began it all in 1634.

Likewise a family story but designed and
stitched in a totally different style is the needlepoint sampler of the Halcott Greens worked by
Virginia Green formerly of Saluda, North Carolina, now of Bronxville, New York. Miss Green's
sister, Margaret, designed the pattern. She says:

> It took us about a year to assemble the data,
> or rather to pick and choose what incidents to
> use and to plan the design. It took about eight
> months to do the cross stitching and needle-
> point. The background is pale blue, the drums
> are dark blue and red, the roses shaded pink
> on gold silk background. The wide outer bor-
> der is a greeny peacock blue. The figures are
> in appropriate color. I was living in Bronx-
> ville, New York, when I did it.

Miss Green has made a key to the family story
which has been pasted on the back of the sampler and covered with heavy cellophane.

> The border of roses and drums signifies
> romance and valour. The house in the upper
> left corner stands in Princeton, Massachusetts,
> and was owned by the last Ward Nicholas
> Boylston until his death some few years ago.
> The house had been in the Boylston family

since 1799. Beneath is Farnifold Green, son of
Timothy Green, who met a tragic death at
the hands of the Indians.

The upper half of the center panel shows
the palmetto tree, emblem of South Carolina,
and the Confederate and Union flags. The Ne-
groes shown are the plantation slaves of the
rice and cotton era.

The house in the upper right corner is the
Cocke home at Bruno, Virginia. From this
original Bruno our great-great-grandmother,
Eliza F. Cocke, daughter of Bowler Cocke III.,
married Walter Cole's father's great-grandfather. Below is a scene which tells the story
of the desolation of Columbia, our home town,
after Sherman's march in 1865. The whole of
Columbia was the site of our grandfather
Thomas Taylor's plantation and his homestead
was burned.

A strip extending across the sampler midway of its length shows the Greens moving
from pillar to post. In the last ten years we
have moved from South Carolina to New York
and Massachusetts and back to North Carolina.

The left panel now continues with a square
in which is portrayed Mother, our queen, who
has ruled us with a golden sceptre (or rod
of iron) wherever we have been. In the corner,
our house in Columbia, South Carolina, where
we lived thirty-four years. Beneath this square
is another in which is shown Margaret, the
eldest, chasing the winged dollars over the side-
walks of New York. Macy's red star, her pilot
for eight years, shines in the corner above her.
In the square below Bill Dargan, Margaret's
son, our pride and joy, is shown with the rising
sun behind him, his hobbies and interests
about him.

The lower half of the center panel bears
five portraits. The dashing naval officer is
Admiral Hallowell, a maternal ancestor. The
Confederate army officer at the right is mother's
father, S. C. Boylston, who was a cadet at the
Citadel. He fired the first shot on the "Star
of the West," which started a war between the
North and South. Below on the left is a couple
marked C. & N. These are Cordes Boylston,
English professor, and his wife "Nooky" Long-
horns, by adoption of and by Texas. On the
right is brother Hal (Halcott P., Jr.), bachelor, loves good clothes and good living. Civil
engineer.

On the right panel, balancing the portrait
of Mother, is a portrait of Father taking life
easily. The cobwebs have covered his law
books. His two black cats, gardening (pot variety), an occasional game of chess are his
hobbies. Beneath is a portrait of Virginia, next
in age to Margaret whose portrait in the left
panel balances Virginia's. Of Virginia it is
recorded that she is lame but undaunted. The

American Red Cross is her favorite volunteer work. In the final square is Jessie (Mrs. Gordon Grant), slim and lovely, model wife and mother, with her children and her husband.

The four corners of the sampler show emblems of Scotland, France, Wales and England, recording the Scotch, French, Welsh and English strains in the family.

Mrs. George Hall has made a conversation piece in needlepoint and cross-stitch which shows all sorts of gay little Victorian items mixed in with a few present-day notes and scattered with apparent nonchalance over the canvas. There are teapots and pussy cats on cushions, harps, crosses with flowers, rocking horses and lambs, houses and steam trains blocked in like toys and worked in cross-stitch. Anchors and birds, a mouse and roses fall side by side. A door key is fastened in stitches under the date 1934. Butterflies, two birds, a heart and the date 1894 decorate the top of the sampler. A donkey with a saddle on its back is stitched above the initials G. F. H. 1917 and what that story is meant to tell, we will have to ask Margaret L. Hall who initialed, dated and finished this sampler in Westport, Connecticut, in 1934. It is quite unlike the others, but chatty and entertaining in its own delightful, reminiscent way.

Mrs. Theodore Roosevelt, Jr., delights in relating family episodes in needlepoint and crewel stitching. A particularly interesting sampler is the interpretation of her husband's various hunting expeditions. It is bordered with the animals hunted and Mrs. Roosevelt explains:

It is my fondest expression in needlework because it was the most difficult to accomplish accurately. Each evening, Mr. Roosevelt would examine the animal I had worked upon during the day, offering constructive and anatomical criticism until we arrived at the proper effect for each animal. For instance, the Tamaraw, native to the Philippines and now extinct, was worked out from a head in Mr. Roosevelt's collection. The body had to be designed from memory.

Mrs. Roosevelt has stitched each animal thoughtfully and with spirit. The giant panda, looking like a black and white "Teddy bear," has been especially well done. A tiny bird has perched itself quite cheerily on the round back of a huge sleeping rhinoceros. Great fun has been had in depicting Mr. Theodore Roosevelt, Jr., gun in hand, skipping along the pointed mountain tops, his head wrapped in a white turban. A large bunch of red wool suggests the red beard grown from lack of shaving facilities. A large sun is smiling upon the scene and a stitched verse beneath says:

BEHOLD HE COMETH LEAPING UPON THE MOUNTAINS, SKIPPING UPON THE HILLS.

The scrim background is fine and left uncovered; all the figures are worked in petit point. The only stitch variation is to be found in the mountains, which are worked in upright Hungarian stitches and provide interesting variety in technique. The sampler is initialed and dated

T. FROM E. 1934

HISTORICAL EVENTS

Showing even more stitch contrast is another sampler from Mrs. Roosevelt's collection of petit point panels. This is entitled:

RECOGNITION OF U. S. S. R. 1933

The sampler pictures Russian peasants marketing, with houses, walls and the round domes of the kremlin towering over all. The main part of the picture is worked in petit point. The sky and one side of a market stall are worked in a Gobelin stitch. A departure in technique is made in the leaves on the trees which are worked in long flat satinlike stitches. As explained by Mrs. Roosevelt, "I became tired of working continuously with the needlepoint stitch, it seemed to be flat and lifeless, so I made up a stitch that galloped"...and the design does just that. Vitality is achieved by thus bringing out these leaves in contrast to the rest of the composition.

Many people questioned Mrs. Roosevelt's political affiliations when the sampler won a first mention in a New York exhibition. But she called their attention to the little red devil sitting in the tree ready to pounce on the unwary pedestrians. After that the discussion turned from the political angle to art and followed along the lines prescribed by the humor indicated in this touch, which is characteristic of most of Mrs. Roosevelt's needlework.

Events in England are among those which American women have been pleased to commemorate in needlepoint. Bringing back memories of the Coronation Jubilee is the sampler worked by Mrs. John W. Castles of Convent,

New Jersey. This sampler is dedicated to "George and Mary" and bears the dates 1910-1935. All the emblems of Great Britain are stitched carefully and interestingly—the crowns, the flags, the scepter, the swords and floral emblems of the royal family, thistles, roses, shamrock, acorns. The panel has been finely worked in petit point. It is initialed E. E. C. and dated 1937.

Mrs. Kenneth Budd has chosen from England "Trooping of the Colors for Edward the VIII in 1936." This panel has been worked in petit point on a beige background. The Tudor rose borders the sampler, which shows the officers of the guard standing at attention, other officers on horseback and the Scottish bagpipers playing before the castle walls. The crown and a flag balance the top part of the picture. In the top corner is stitched the date January 20 and below is the date December 11, 1936, with the signature of Alice M. Budd.

Mrs. Budd has mounted this embroidery upon a tilt table top which makes a graceful decoration in the reception room of her New York residence.

These samplers are interestingly modern in thought as well as form. They display not only accuracy in technique and theme but reflect the artistry which travels hand in hand with imagination. The subjects are diversified and these very differences are stimulating. In samplers it is most often personal reflections which are expressed. In future efforts this introspective quality may bring forth strikingly new versions of intimate thoughts, and result in fine creative needlework to add to the distinguished list of newer samplers contributed to posterity during the twentieth century.

"Madame Amelita Galli-Curci"

Personality portrait designed and embroidered upon fine linen with a variety of wools in satin, long and short, buttonhole, outline, French knot, and chain stitches, by Georgiana Brown Harbeson, New York, 1924.

CHAPTER XXX

MODERN CREWEL EMBROIDERY

"O thou sculptor, painter, poet
Take this lesson to thy heart:
That is best which lieth nearest;
Shape from that thy work of Art."
HENRY WADSWORTH LONGFELLOW.

NALYZE IMPULSES AND YOU MAY perhaps discover why women embroider today as they did long centuries ago when Queen Matilda and her ladies-in-waiting executed many yards of crewel embroidery, called the Bayeaux Tapestry, depicting the Norman Conquest of England. Many persons wonder why people take time to embroider such records of human endeavor and achievement or why they wish to spend hours noting their particular interests in stitched form. The fact is that it has always been a fundamental impulse to state the accomplishments of loved ones and friends or to record family events of particular significance. Sometimes perhaps it is the stitched way of saying confidently, "I told you so!" Ideas, objectives or emotions which are important to us we wish to perpetuate in some way. The same impulse is behind every form of expression. Every experience deeply felt in life needs to be passed along whether it be through words or music, chiseled in stone, painted with a brush or sewn with a needle. It is a way of reaching for immortality.

Needlework is difficult to do, if well done, and by that very fact offers an interesting challenge to every sensitive, thinking person who knows that nothing that is permanently worth while is easy of accomplishment.

Crewel embroidery is probably one of the oldest forms of embroidery in its fundamental stitch technique. The name is derived from the type of yarn used for its execution. The 1892 edition of Webster's dictionary describes crewel as a "worsted yarn slightly twisted, used for embroidery." The 1938 edition states that it is "a soft worsted yarn, used in fancy-work." . . . Shades of the Victorians! Even dictionaries are affected by changes in fashion.

Crewel embroidery today employs all the stitches used in the days of Queen Anne and in the early crewel embroideries made by the first American colonists. The stitches are similar to those which appear on antique silk embroideries made by the Chinese, the Persians, and other ancient races, but in the later periods wools have been substituted for linen or silk. There are about two hundred stitches in the embroidery vocabulary which, in passing from one nation to another, take on varying characteristics. Differences in temperament and personal approach, direction of application, color and design or subject translation will often alter their effect tremendously.

The famous Bayeaux Tapestry made by Queen Matilda was not executed in needlepoint, as many persons believe. It is a form of crewel embroidery, only instead of using wools in working the open decorative design upon the linen, the ladies of that time used linen threads. The stitches applied were satin stitch, darning stitch, backstitch, long and short stitch and simple filling forms, the same as those practiced in the early Jacobean crewel-work. The linen was hand-woven in a long narrow strip. The design, recording King Harold's expedition to England, was embroidered in sequence on this strip which was two hundred and thirty feet long and nineteen inches wide. It was rolled up from end to end on a frame and each event was worked in a small section. It was meant to be hung upon the castle walls like a tapestry: hence the name. It is one of the most famous examples of needlework in history and has offered much inspiration to embroiderers all over the world through its design, color and narrative treatment.

Much of the crewel embroidery design of today can be traced to early Queen Anne or Jacobean influence. Many patterns have been copied from the early traditional designs made in colonial times. Other independent designers have evolved ideas of their own along contemporary lines, not necessarily using wool, but employing the stitches that have always been associated with this style of open embroidery. In this fashion the linen background is not entirely covered with stitches, thus contributing a value in the presentation of odd and different pattern effects. Still others are attempting to create new effects in crewel embroidery by starting with a clean slate. They hope to strike out into fresh, untrod paths and to develop entirely new conceptions in both design and stitch application.

"Needlepainting," a term coined by the author to describe certain types of modern needlework, implies an approach to embroidery from a painter's point of view. Needlework is handled the same as canvases, paint and brushes would be used, and similar decorative angles are employed in composition. This style of needlework in different forms is illustrated in the following examples of work created by contemporary artists who are discovering new ways and means to express ideas in this ancient and interesting medium. The individuality of each is clearly reflected in the manner in which the embroidery has been developed.

CREWEL-EMBROIDERED PICTURES

Contemporary crewel embroidery is ably represented in the fine work of Marguerite Zorach, who has been devoting her talents to the modernization of embroidery for many years. Mrs. Zorach is a painter who also sees great possibilities in needlework as a fine art and approaches it from that angle. Her embroidery is purely decorative and interpretive.

The "Portrait of the Rockefeller Family" represents the diversified needlework ability of this artist. This large panel of linen, measuring approximately three feet by four, is entirely covered with fine stitching which fills in the various features of the landscape, the portraits of the family, their homes, hobbies, sports, activities and pets. It was a large undertaking and required about two years for its completion. Every detail of hills, trees, sea, sky, boats, costumes, animals, butterflies, flowers and all the other parts of the design, are conveyed with great variety in both stitches and color, employed to indicate the texture of costume material and other detail. Fine crewel wools have been used for this work and fairly brilliant color has been threaded into the linen with chevron darning stitches, satin stitch, chain stitch, backstitch, dot stitch and running stitch. A kaleidoscopic quality in the needlepainting is achieved through the shading and the use of strong contrasts of color in the landscape. Further emphasis is added by the use of high lights which border rich dark colors dramatically.

In the stitching of foreground forms Mrs. Zorach has employed the technique used in eighteenth century crewel embroideries but she paints with her wools in an ultramodern manner and uses an entirely different arrangement in making the stitches in order to achieve vibration in the lines and masses. The main portraits are those of Mr. and Mrs. John D. Rockefeller, Jr., whose names are embroidered into the band at the base of the picture, followed by the names of the rest of the family. The signature of the embroiderer and the date, 1932, are included. The work is an extraordinarily fine example of modern needlepainting and a splendid heirloom for the Rockefeller family to possess.

A crewel-embroidered portrait which was intended to convey the personality of Amelita Galli-Curci was designed and needlepainted by

A needlework portrait in wools on linen foundation, of the Rockefeller family, their homes, pets, hobby interests and sport activities. A contemporary crewel embroidery designed and worked by Marguerit Zorach, 1932, New York. Privately owned.

"Washington Square Arch," New York, Needlewoven and crewel embroidered picture on cloth designed and worked by Marcia C. Stebbins, New York.

Needlepainting in wools, New England Village, by Marian Stoll, Connecticut.

the author in 1924. The portrait depends primarily upon line for its interpretation. It is the author's belief that lyrical qualities may be found in a single line through the elimination of non-essentials and the retention only of those elements required to express the mood or subject to be interpreted. One finds this quality in line in the old manuscript paintings of the twelfth century, in the early portrait paintings in India and in the portraits of early Chinese painters.

The rachel-tinted background of fine linen has been left plain for the indication of flesh tones. Solidity has been introduced by the filling in of the hair, which lends structure and background for the portrait. Sections of the landscape have also been filled in. The weaving in with backstitches of Madame Galli-Curci's costume in the foreground establishes the support of her portrait and also forms a solid background against which to silhouette the members of the orchestra. Black and deep blue wools used in the men's figures are placed against the Venetian pink background of the gown to provide vibration and thus introduce the music theme. The little birds hold a laurel wreath over the singer's head in recognition of her supreme artistry. The costume was one which Madame Galli-Curci wore upon a concert tour of the United States and it was while attending one of these concerts that the idea of needlepainting her was conceived. The date of completion was worked into the music manuscript of the orchestra leader, and the embroiderer's signature around the rim of the kettledrum.

This portrait has recently been acquired by a collector of ancient English embroideries as an example of contemporary American needlework.

A New England village has been realistically reproduced with varicolored wools on linen by Mrs. Marian Stoll of Connecticut. Mrs. Stoll has exhibited many embroideries in this style of needlework, executed in imitation of the brush strokes employed by painters. Her wools take the place of oils on her canvas and the colors are stitched into the areas and masses of foliage, sky and architecture exactly as one would paint. Her technique is loose and broad, her wools a little heavier than those which have been used to embroider the preceding examples.

Mrs. Stoll describes in a few words her attitude toward her embroideries and the materials employed in making the wool-painted pictures.

The standard wool I use is 4-ply Zephyr. But whenever I can find a new and useful shade, I get it no matter what kind of yarn it is—it's usually knitting wool. I have a good deal of Zephyr dyed to order in Vienna.

What were once my theories have become practice. After long effort I had to see that I couldn't handle any brush-medium. Then, after having done a good deal of professional embroidery in Vienna and in England, I came to think it might be possible to paint in wools. So I set out to test that hypothesis. For a long time now, I've felt that a needle with wool was just as respectable and legitimate a medium for serious painting as any other, and so I have deliberately gone out after painters' objectives, such as light effects, recession, volume, aerial perspective, atmospheric quality, texture, etc.

Of course, as any painter feels, the further I go on, the more there is yet to learn; but at least it isn't the medium that limits me, for wool as a painter's medium really has infinite possibilities. Sometimes one finds prejudice against wool, owing to so much frightful rubbish whose vehicle it has been in the past; but so soon as anyone begins to use her eyes instead of her memory, it ought to become obvious that wool used in this way has possibilities far beyond certain much-admired media—for instance, it is a hundred times more flexible than tapestry work, whose legitimacy has never been questioned. And it is tied to no formal stitch; it's as free and supple as oils, aquarelle as pastel—what more could one ask? And it offers as wide a field for personality in technique as paint does.

Great emphasis is likewise laid by Mrs. Stoll upon the direction of her stitches which are usually the elemental backstitch, long and short or outline stitches. Each shade and tone of her sketch in wools is radiated in different directions with bits of color chosen from her palette of yarns to express the required atmosphere. These stitches completely cover the linen background. Her needlework possesses strong vibratory powers in the blending and shading of the masses quite in the modern trend and along lines which have been achieved by other painters in their canvases. Mrs. Stoll has executed many dramatic and remarkable landscapes in this medium which have been acquired by collectors. This particular embroidered picture is in the possession of Mr. E. K. Waterhouse of London, England.

Marcia C. Stebbins of New York is likewise a painter who has recently turned to wools as a serious medium of artistic expression. She enjoys the value which the background fabric lends to needlework design and much of the material upon which she embroiders her figures and scenes remains uncovered, establishing a backdrop of atmosphere in the mood of the subject.

"Washington Square Arch" is an embroidered picture of this New York square which chooses the arch as its central theme. The old red brick Georgian houses lend a warm-toned relief for its creamy-white architecture, and intense colors are again repeated like chords of music in the costumes of the children playing in the foreground and in the figures decorating the park benches. The rough material, in a tan beige color, provides an effective background tone for the various shades which accent the picture.

Miss Stebbins employs the simplest stitches to convey the forms. They alternate between darning stitch, running stitch, chain stitch, outline stitch, backstitch; occasionally buttonhole stitches are introduced. Her main interest in her needlepainting, like that of her contemporaries, is the establishment of spirit, movement, idea and atmosphere to be directly registered without that interruption which is caused by becoming aware of stitch pyrotechnics in advance of the subject matter. Miss Stebbins has created numbers of interesting pictures in her own particular style which have found an appreciative audience. This panel has been recently acquired by Miss Gertrude Oppenheimer of New York for her collection of American embroideries.

CREWEL-EMBROIDERY MURALS

Elizabeth M. Roth works on the same general principles as the preceding artists in creating her crewel-embroidered murals. In the view of New York's buildings sketched from Central Park she embroiders over all her linen ground-material and paints in with her wool colorings in fairly solid coverage much as Mrs. Stoll has done. While the stitches are much the same in all the pictures, the manner or style in which each person has worked them shows a vast difference. Each expresses her own individuality. This is equally true in the divergences to be noted in

the color selections. Generally the moderns enjoy what is termed pure color; too many pastel or "faded" tones imply a lack of vitality. In the earliest and finest needlework examples both here and abroad, it is interesting to note that the colors used were brilliant. The ravages of time alone are responsible for the washed-out tones in the majority of antique needlework examples.

Mrs. Roth has expressed admirably the contrasts in light and shade in the sun-lighted buildings and also in the reflections on the lake; the latter are ably suggested through the proper placing of stitches and colors to indicate the mirrored effects. It is a difficult feat to suggest water with wools, but she has managed this splendidly. The mural is one of many which Mrs. Roth has designed for *The Woman's Home Companion* to be reproduced by readers having needlepainting ambitions. It was embroidered in New York in 1934.

Mary Ellen Crisp also "paints" murals with needles and wools on linen, often on quite a large scale. Perhaps she is inspired in this by the great murals painted by her husband, Arthur Crisp. The example chosen for description was embroidered on linen seven feet high by ten feet long. It is reminiscent in theme of scenery in the Far West and presents an interesting arrangement of rolling hills, mountains, lakes, cactus, flowers and vines. Much of the linen has been covered but not the entire surface. Compromise has been established in a combination of both methods; some of the linen has been allowed to remain as a definite part of the design and color of the picture. This is shown in the top clouds which are weighted around the edges with wool outlines leaving the centers bare while the rest of the sky and the horizon have been sewn in solidly with wools. Small horizontal stitches have been used to suggest the upright trees growing on the distant mountains. Rows of running stitches round out the outlines of the flowing hillsides in the middle distance, while short wavy stitches indicate the river in the foreground. The forms of the cactus plants have been followed by wool-stitched lines in the same manner. In the immediate foreground, horizontal darning-in stitches "cut" or interrupt the long flowing lines of the hills and water and prevent monotony, at the same time calling attention to the mountains by

Crewel embroidered mural, New York from Central Park, 1934, by Elizabeth
M. Roth, Connecticut.

Embroidered mural 7′ x 10′ by Mary Ellen Crisp, New York.

1. *Courtesy of:* CROWELL PUBLISHING CO., New York.

Crewel embroidered sampler on velvet, "Spirit of New England" by Georgiana Brown Harbeson, New York.

2. *Courtesy of:* MRS. MACDONALD DICK, North Carolina.

Modern crewel embroidered panel designed and worked 1932, by Mary Williams Dick, Stonington, Connecticut.

4. *Courtesy of:* MRS. STUART DAVIS, New York.

Embroidered "abstraction" mural, 4' x 6'. Designed by the painter, Stuart Davis and worked by his wife, Mrs. Stuart Davis, New York.

3. *Courtesy of:* MRS. GEORGE W. WHITE, New York.

Embroidered panel, "Minnehaha, Indian Heroine," 1936 designed by Georgiana Brown Harbeson and worked by S. Blanche MacDonald, New York.

directing the eye upward toward them. These forms repeat the same stitch direction and provide a continuation of rhythmical composition.

The use of contrasts in line direction is important in the newer embroidery, so much being suggested through such rhythms. This is in direct contrast to the nineteenth century emphasis upon realistic reproduction. Today an attempt is made to catch atmosphere in the spirit or mood of the landscape in preference to an exact copy of the scene.

Mrs. Crisp provides human interest by the introduction of the two figures on horseback. These serve not only to establish scale and suggest the vastness of the scene but also provide a bright diversion in subject matter.

These examples are worked in great contrast to the many grand landscapes made in the nineteenth century and one realizes the gradual rise of embroidery into its own dominion. Less attempt is made to reproduce paintings. Instead the painter is often turning embroiderer and working directly in this medium, striking out with needles and the palette of wools straight into a needlepainting, often working without a cartoon to follow. The author, in making the embroidered portrait of Mme. Galli-Curci, sketched directly with pencil upon the linen without any preliminary drawing, the composition having been well established in the mind. The wools were applied exactly as pigment would be used in a water-color rendering. Such a method, however, is inadvisable except for those who have had long training in the fine arts and the fundamentals of design and who are familiar enough with the various techniques of embroidery and painting to compose directly and without the necessity of changing lines once they have been placed upon the canvas. Otherwise a well planned cartoon is necessary and simpler to revise as one works.

Each one of the artists mentioned has had a "one man" exhibition of embroideries in New York art galleries within recent years, and all had training in the fine arts before attempting these needlepaintings. It is to be expected and hoped that many others will discover the charm to be found in experimenting with this medium and will contribute interesting new embroideries expressive of contemporary life and thought.

Experimenting with abstract qualities in embroidery, Mrs. Stuart Davis of New York has chosen to reproduce the ultramodern oil paintings created by Stuart Davis, her husband, who is also a mural painter. Her embroidered mural is four feet high and six feet wide and is solidly covered with plain back and outline stitches. She has been interested in the pattern and flow of the masses of color and has not wished to detract from the atmosphere of the various forms by any technical interruption either in stitch direction or style, although both are incorporated. This embroidery has strength, simplicity, and a directness or frankness of approach that is characteristic of the artist's work and of the age.

Mrs. Davis' needlework is entirely different in composition from any of the preceding works; it is unusual in conception, entertaining and interesting.

SAMPLER PICTURES IN WOOLS

Mary Low Williams Dick has turned her attention toward embroidering sampler pictures. They combine the qualities of different centuries and compose a needlework poem which belongs entirely to the twentieth. Her design of the leaping deer is repeated in the streamlined crane flying across the sky, whose movement is reflected below in the rhythmically wide-spread branches. This horizontal line direction is repeated again in the leaping white rabbit beneath the tree. Perpendicular lines stop this general direction toward the left and prevent the subjects from running out of the picture. Upright trees, a pair of upright rabbits and upward-moving decorative leaf columns embroidered on either side of the panel complete and effectively contain the composition.

This crewel-embroidered picture or sampler is exceedingly well balanced in design. Mrs. Dick shows in this work evidences of her feeling for music, rhythm and poetic abstraction. It is dated and initialed by her in March, 1932, and is in the possession of Dr. and Mrs. Charles Mallory Williams of Stonington, Connecticut.

Another sampler picture is an embroidery of Minnehaha made by Blanche S. MacDonald of New York. In this panel the Indian maiden has been stitched solidly, attention being centered principally upon her portrait and the costume detail. Atmosphere and locality suggestive of the Hiawatha legend and Indian life, have been decoratively rendered in the background of the picture. Stitch direction is used to advantage in the simple straight lines indicating the waterfall, the rounded lines of the hills, and in the round masses of foliage. These forms have been movingly conveyed through the use of buttonhole stitches radiated to indicate the natural growth of leaves and plants. Detached buttonhole stitch has been employed on the immediate foreground to add weight and form a firm base upon which Minnehaha stands. Miss MacDonald has made a good portrait of the Indian maiden. The colors are particularly well blended with fine stitchery.

The picture is freshly interpretive and thoroughly suggestive of the quiet forests and peaceful woodland atmosphere in which the early Indians moved and had their being. It was embroidered by Miss MacDonald in 1936 and dedicated "To Flora White," her sister, who was the recipient of the original.

Making use of white velvet to suggest a crisp, snowy landscape, the embroidered sampler of the young lady in an old-fashioned costume gazing up at a small bird on a tree has been entitled "The Spirit of New England." This conception was inspired by a verse of Oliver Herford's:

> I heard a bird sing
> In the dark of December
> 'Twas a magical thing
> And sweet to remember.

The idea continues with the comforting thought that it is nearer to spring than it was in November.

All the little forest animals may be discovered slinking along under the hedges in the background while under the scrolls, indicating the roots of the trees, the gray squirrel may be seen hoarding his nuts while the rabbit listens intently to the bird's song and wishes spring would hurry.

The colors on the figure are a tangerine-henna shade of wool worked in herringbone stitch. The central panel of the costume is pale mauve worked in wide buttonhole stitch. The muff is embroidery in dead white in contrast to the cream white of the velvet background. The hedges are worked in darning stitches in shades of green blues with an emphatic touch of deep royal blue to suggest crisp winter air and shadows. The hills are in mauve and pale

blue, one shade crossed over the other to create the effect of distance. The trees are worked in wine reds, brick red, brown and mauve violet. These colors are repeated in the plumes on the girl's bonnet. The trees are "painted" in shades of brown, tan and grays which range from deep slate-gray blue, up into light pearl and yellow grays. Color and texture were sought primarily. The author here employed darning wools of the kind used for mending her sons' woolen stockings with excellent results, since these tans, grays and browns are permanent in color and related to the wood tones. One or two henna leaves, left over from the fall, pick up the color of the dress and are worked in Roumanian stitch. The little animals are rendered in their own natural colorings in backstitch and satin stitch.

The panel was designed and embroidered by the author in 1927 and was reproduced in the Christmas number of *The Woman's Home Companion* in 1936 for other interested needleworkers to copy.

CREWEL EMBROIDERY DECORATIONS

Contemporary bedspreads are being crewel-embroidered just as they were in colonial days, except that the designs are different in character and usually the foundation also. Mrs. Benjamin Tilton has made a lovely spread with an allover design composed of native American wildflowers embroidered in fine wools in their natural colors. The violet, goldenrod, lady's-slipper, thistle, wild rose, clover and many others have been finely needleworked. In one corner an early bird is flying above a group of flowers and to the right a butterfly hovers over honeysuckle blossoms. The linen used for the background was homespun and quilted by Mrs. Tilton's grandmother, Anna Billings of Ledyard, Connecticut, a hundred years ago. The initials worked by her at that time show in one corner of the quilt today. Mrs. Tilton has made her stitches very tiny and has kept the colors of the various flowers on a high pastel tone giving an antique quality and unity to the whole cover which is delicate and charming. Her own initials balance those of her grandmother's.

Many crewel-embroidered curtains and hang-

Three-fold screen worked in crewel embroidery with wools upon twill in a variety of stitches in the style of Jacobean needlework of English origin. One original panel was worked by Mrs. Frederick Exton when 70 years old. The other two were completed in 1934 by the daughter-in-law, Mrs. Exton.

1. *Courtesy of:* MRS. EDWARD R. WARREN, Mass.

Crewel embroidered purse designed by Woman's Educational and Industrial Union, Boston, Massachusetts, and worked by Mrs. Edward R. Warren, Massachusetts.

2. *Courtesy of:* MRS. BREWSTER JENNINGS, New York.

Crewel embroidered silk taffeta cushion by Mrs. Brewster Jennings, Long Island, New York.

3. *Courtesy of:* MRS. HARRIS P. MOSHER, Massachusetts.

Crewel embroidery on large curtain designed by Miss Amelia Baldwin, Boston, Massachusetts. Embroidered 1927 by Mrs. Harris P. Mosher, Massachusetts.

4. *Courtesy of:* THE LENOX HILL STUDIOS, New York.

Crewel embroidered curtain, contemporary, adapted from ancient East Indian design by Katherine Lee Grable, New York, and worked by the Lenox Hill Studios, New York.

ings are included in today's needlework. Mrs. Frederick S. Mosley of Boston has embroidered a pair of curtains which were adapted in design from early eighteenth century patterns by the Woman's Educational and Industrial Union. This design is large and free, providing ample opportunity for stitch variety. Inventiveness and versatility is shown by Mrs. Mosley in filling the large spaces of the leaves and flower forms. The hills in the foreground include some mounds worked for variety's sake in a checker-board darning pattern which produces amusing contrast to the shaded round mounds upon which little goats and deer frolic. The curtains are handsomely and delightfully executed.

A large curtain which is used as a wall hanging was crewel-embroidered in 1927 by Mrs. Harold P. Mosher of Marblehead, Massachusetts. The design was made by Miss Amelia Baldwin much in the style of the "Tree of Life" pattern originating in India centuries ago. Miss Baldwin has departed from that pattern, however, in her floral forms and in the draughting of the different little animals, so that the suggestion of the ancient design tradition remains only in the central tree and its branches. The fillings of flowers, tree branches and leaves have been delightfully interpreted in the different stitches invented by Mrs. Mosher. The embroidery technique is spirited and gay. The animals and foreground have been worked with skill and feeling for the subjects. They seem to have personality.

Another pair of contemporary crewel-embroidered curtains have a series of delightful designs in the form of tree and figure groupings scattered alternately over their linen surface. Occasionally little animals replace the human figures and a bird or a single tree stands amusingly apart in the composition. The borders show fine trailing vines and flower arrangements that are delicate and decorative and also serve effectively to contain the otherwise isolated motifs within the curtain areas, thus holding the entire composition together. The pattern was adapted from an ancient East Indian design by Katherine Lee Grable, who also dyed the wools to match the original example. The embroidery and design was carried out by members of the former Lenox Hill Studios of New York under Miss Grable's very competent direction.

Crewel-embroidered curtains and hangings of heavy linen or twill are most appropriate in wood-paneled rooms or interiors containing Jacobean, Queen Anne or Early American furniture. They are also effective in decorating large club rooms, dining halls, or living rooms where miscellaneous pieces of furniture are combined. Prior to the depression many embroidery guilds were kept actively employed executing large commissions for decorating homes and executive offices with this beautiful and substantial needlework.

Chair seats are often embroidered to match hangings or are used quite independently. Mrs. John L. Hall of Boston has embroidered a chair seat on which is a very large and amusing squirrel worked with crewel wools. He is surrounded by leaves, scrolls and decorative floral forms which are interestingly executed in design and technique. The stitches have been given their proper direction. The foreground shows imagination in the use of different stitch fillings which give variety and style to the work. The design was adapted for Mrs. Hall by the Woman's Educational and Industrial Union of Boston.

A chair seat for a children's room was crewel-embroidered in an original way with an "Alice in Wonderland" design by Mrs. Mosher. Against a heavy twill background Alice is centered, worked entirely in back and split stitches. She is crouched down upon her knees watching the White Rabbit which is hurrying off to keep his engagement with the Duchess and is shown glancing at his watch. He is worked solidly in tiny French knots and his little jacket is back-stitched. In the four corners, carefully embroidered and expressive enough to delight the happy child whose room the needlework decorates, are the Duchess looking very fierce, the Red Queen, the Mad Hatter with his bread in hand, and the Mock Turtle dripping large tears into a puddle. The background material has been enriched and strengthened with a braiding effect which has scattered satin stitched leaves interwoven in the design. This arrangement suggests many vines and serves to surround the make-believe characters with an atmosphere of mystery and enchantment.

Mrs. Mosher also has embroidered the upholstery for a small chest, using floss in crewel embroidery technique. This design also is from the land of make-believe in its romantic suggestion of the Arabian Nights. The Sultan's costume is stitched with careful regard for line. His large sword is worked in with gold threads. The turban is studded with sequins and likewise the veil of the imploring wife. One tree in the composition is decorated with these small paillettes which also form Scheherazade's jewels. A decorative landscape completely covers the top of the chest and a diamond-shaped pattern covers the floor which is embroidered on the sides. Below the lock is a conventionalized design. Both ends are embroidered with pictures of favorite characters from the thousand and one tales.

This example is completely novel and differs from the other embroideries which Mrs. Mosher has made. No doubt it provided her with much amusement as an exercise in stitched fantasy and an experiment in the use of mixed materials.

Mrs. Brewster Jennings of New York City also finds crewel embroidery a relaxation from needlepoint. She shows able technique in her round taffeta oyster-white cushions, crewel-embroidered with flowers, leaves and vines. They are related in design to the early eighteenth century patterns, but Mrs. Jennings gives them a very French feeling through the use of a silk background and the combination of pastel colors shading from the Nattier blues, blush rose and palest pinks into light tones. These are very charming, graceful and finely worked embroideries and a little more luxurious in feeling than the linen-backed crewel-work.

Mrs. Edward R. Warren of Boston has embroidered a purse of heavy linen with an all-over pattern of crewel wool flowers and leaves. The stitching is quite fine and very expressively directed. The shading is simple but effectively placed in the composition to accentuate the lights and darks of the florals. The Woman's Educational and Industrial Union designed this purse with taste and originality. The embroidery fills the general shape and outline with discretion and a good sense of spacing, creating an accessory to the costume which is not too obvious and which yet retains quality and distinction.

A three-fold Jacobean screen of heavy linen-colored twill has been crewel-embroidered by Mrs. Frederick Exton of New York. She used varicolored wools in blue-green and green and gold shades with touches of soft coral and rose.

The fillings in the flower forms are very original and amusing in their use of an infinite variety of stitches.

This is an heirloom in the truest sense, since one panel was commenced by Mrs. Exton's mother-in-law and completed by her when she was seventy years old. Mrs. Exton completed the other two panels and the screen is now a handsome decoration in her large living room. It will become the property of her little grandchild.

Being particularly enthusiastic about crewel embroidery, Mrs. Exton has made several chair seat coverings in the same Jacobean style. The inspiration for the design comes directly from England. She has given much individual emphasis, however, by originating the "fillings" of the leaves and flower motifs. Here creativeness has been exercised in combining various styles of stitches to suggest the character of the flowers and in the blending of the different colored yarns.

Not being confined to any set pattern is the secret of the joy to be found in crewel embroidery. Here stitchery may be free in spirit. An idea may run through the needle's eye threading its way gaily without any element of fatigue because of the ease and the speed with which one may accomplish effects in this medium.

Large surfaces spontaneously stitched in this manner, however, depend upon good design to properly convey the values of the subject. An error in stitch or stitch direction is apt to stand out far more glaringly in this technique than in needlepoint or canvas embroidery. Perhaps because of its greater simplicity, it requires closer attention to the proper placing of lines and to values to be attained through the use of stitches or color.

In the newer mode, design tends to be expressed with spirited action. Color is vibrant, and inventiveness enters stitch patternings. Conscious effort is made by the most advanced contemporary embroiderers to eliminate all superficial lines in their compositions; to refine all masses down to the main thought to be expressed until only the vital essence of the scene remains. There must be sufficient substance to permit a rhythmical rendering of the subject.

As in the manner of musical composition, one may arrange stitch scales and play upon chords

1. *Courtesy of:* MRS. BENJAMIN TILTON, New York.

"Native Wildflowers"; crewel embroidered bedspread, 1936 by Anna Billings Tilton, New York, on linen, homespun and quilted 100 years ago by her grandmother, Anna Billings, Connecticut.

2. *Courtesy of:* MRS. FRED S. MOSELEY, Massachusetts.

Crewel embroidered curtain, designed by the Woman's Educational and Industrial Union, Boston, Massachusetts, and worked by Mrs. Fred S. Moseley, Massachusetts.

Crewel embroidered chest coverings by Mrs. Harold P. Mosher, Marblehead, Massachusetts.

Crewel embroidered child's chair seat, "Alice in Wonderland" by Mrs. Harris P. Mosher, Marblehead, Massachusetts.

Crewel embroidered chair on linen, design adapted from old wallpaper in Governor Wentworth Mansion by Frances M. Grace and worked by Mrs. J. Templeman Coolidge, Massachusetts.

Crewel embroidered chair seat by Mrs. John L. Hall, Massachusetts. Design adapted by Woman's Educational and Industrial Union, Massachusetts.

of contrasting colors to produce amusing original harmonies. Depth and tonal qualities are achieved through the nature of the wool itself, since the actual thread produces a certain bas-relief and three-dimensional value in the shadow which falls when it is placed upon the material. This makes another interesting angle for the artist to include and emphasize in needlework compositions.

Artists who carry out their needlework directly from their own original cartoons find an added zest in the personal touch achieved. A direct reflection of the artist's feelings as expressed in the original conception is brought through to the stitched panel when both are executed by the creator. The work is often more vital, however, when the interpretation is made spontaneously and without too great effort spent in the preparation of preliminary cartoons. One fundamental rule which applies to all needlework down the ages is that no evidence of weariness must appear in the embroidery at any time. Since it is such a personal expression, the slightest fatigue will show immediately in the result.

With the spirit of the age stressing clean-cut effort, a transition from solid, heavy needlework styles to abstract interpretive creations which seek to convey moods and decorative rhythms is natural and to be expected in today's crewel embroideries. The contemporary needlepainter realizes that one drop of originality in thoughtful design and imaginative stitching is worth tons of effort expended in technical perfection which lacks good design content, awareness and feeling. Toward the accomplishment of interesting ideas conceived with nicety of balance and expression, energy is being expended by many needleworkers whose budding ideas are unfolding in their modern embroideries like blossoming flowers turning toward the dawn of the new age.

CHAPTER XXXI

CONTEMPORARY NEEDLEPOINT EMBROIDERY: SCREENS AND COVERS

"All the soul in rapt suspension
All the quivering, palpitating
Chords of life in utmost tension,
With the fervor of invention,
With the rapture of creating!"
HENRY WADSWORTH LONGFELLOW.

 EEDLEPOINT DEPENDS NOT SO much on the quality and refinement of line as it does upon mass effects. Differing entirely from crewel embroidery, its closely woven stitches give it a heavier and bulkier effect. Its close resemblance to tapestry when used on hangings or covers imitating that style of design, accounts for its being so called, although it is not a woven technique like tapestry but decoration applied to a woven surface by means of a needle, which is embroidery. The term "tapestry work" applied to needlepoint is a misnomer.

In Europe prior to the sixteenth century tapestry was worked by hand upon close-woven cord canvas with colored worsteds, silks and gold thread and was really embroidery. Or it was made in a loom that was formed with a warp only, the cords being worked all over with short lengths of colored wools threaded upon needles (or later, pointed bobbins) which filled in the design without the use of cross threads or weft. This was neither true weaving nor embroidery, but a combination of both. In time tapestry was made without recourse to needlework and was woven upon a loom which created the pattern through the meshing or shuttling of varicolored wools. The needlework process was continued along separate lines in what was called "tapestry embroidery." The wool threads were applied with a needle to a ready-made canvas or linen of loose mesh, and worked in diagonal stitches across the even squares. This canvas material was not starched in olden times as it is at present, which made it far more difficult to work in needlepoint and achieve the even smooth-stitched surface which good craftsmanship requires.

This style of embroidery was later known as "canvas work," due to the type of material employed for the foundation. In Victorian days in America it became Berlin wool-work. The canvas foundations were imported from Germany and France, and some from England. Today canvas comes from these countries and also from Czechoslovakia and Austria. The imported French canvas has been generally conceded to be the best, due to the fine quality of the materials and the exceptional evenness with which the squares are made, which assures even results in the completed needlepoint as well as the lasting quality desired. There are some exceedingly cheap canvases of very poor quality upon the market which many people spend hours of wasted effort in covering. It is a pity to do so because the foundation material will not en-

Needlepoint four-fold screen; Chinoiserie design in golds, beige and germs. Worked by Mrs. William Warner Hoppin.

A needlepoint three-fold screen. Designed with monkeys swinging among trees in a jungle. One panel was completed in the Philippine Islands, one in Porto Rico, and the third in New York, from 1931 to 1934 by Mrs. Theodore Roosevelt, Jr., Long Island, New York.

dure any length of time and the work becomes lost. Only the best quality in wools and foundation canvas should be used. Canvases have many names and those described in the chapter on Berlin work are much the same today.

The needlepoint stitches have some new varieties, however. The main family is the tent stitch, used for all needlepoint. It resembles the half-cross-stitch and is always worked on an angle over the canvas from the lower left-hand square up to the right and across to the square on the row above. The stitches repeat on the diagonal and in the same direction until the entire area of canvas is completely covered. There are various methods of working the tent stitch. One style is named "bias tent stitch." The stitches are always worked in rows on the bias of the canvas and form a basket-weave of interlacing wools on the reverse side. Thus a webbing is formed which holds the canvas threads firmly together and helps to withstand hard usage. It is used on either single or double-mesh canvas and has become a very popular technique. Another style of work featured in the needlepoint shown in most department stores is termed "continental stitch." It is the tent stitch worked across the canvas in rows from left to right and back again until the covering is completed. The reverse side shows a repetition of the stitch on the front. Both stitch methods take exactly the same amount of wool and either may be worked on canvas stretched upon a frame or in the hand.

The French method of working is called *trammé*. A long thread of wool is laid on the surface of the canvas parallel to the canvas thread and then the tent stitches or needlepoint are worked over it. Some persons claim that this method provides a cushion or underlay for the surface of the needlepoint which is softer than the canvas and will not wear the threads which otherwise with hard usage would be cut by the hard canvas. There are two schools of thought upon this theory. It is a matter of individual preference which style is adopted since both seem to have endured remarkably well in antique examples.

There is also the half-cross-stitch method which was used in the days of Berlin wool-work but which, generally speaking, has been discarded by the informed who today prefer the first-mentioned methods.

The yarns employed in modern needlepoint are usually imported, with England, France and Austria taking the lead. The two last named countries have provided a heavy twist yarn for working gros point (large stitch) upon needlepoint canvases. With these have been sold designs with the center motifs already executed; the worker "fills in" the background only. This has been a popular diversion for many American women, but a larger percentage have been preferring designs which they develop themselves or in which they embroider all the pattern flowers, etc., filling backgrounds being to them a bore, a purely mechanical exercise devoid of creative expression. These women have worked their designs upon hand-painted or *trammé* designs either made by themselves or obtained from needlepoint designers. The yarns most generally used are crewel yarns worked in several strands to give the thread the desired weight, or regular needlepoint yarn obtained from abroad or at home.

Recently new American needlepoint yarns have been manufactured which are equal to the imported wools in both color permanence and fineness of quality. They are divisible in ply, making it possible to blend different shades of yarn together in one needleful or to use them for petit point (little stitch) in needlepoint, where fine strands of yarn are required. American craftsmen and technicians are gradually meeting the advanced needlework needs with the exception of the superior canvases and silk threads. In time we hope that all requirements will be fulfilled and with improvements.

In design contemporary needlework stands self-sufficient, confident of its capacity and its intentions. It is true that many traditional designs have been employed but even here there is evidence of the search for fine creative expression.

Zealously stitching their many canvases, American women of the twentieth century deliberately take time from their many active duties to embroider. They are highly intelligent women with various interests and occupations including the arts, social activities, housekeeping, and business administration. Numbers of them have discovered that needlepoint is a stimulating activity which provides an easy transition from the busy, active moments to the relaxation that follows. When time lags or the brain is fogged, a bit of needlework eases the tension pleasantly and amusingly, besides appeasing the desire for beauty by releasing creative and spiritual energies which exist in everyone to some degree.

In Europe such values in needlework were discovered ages ago. With most continental women needlework is not always thought of as a pastime or a hobby. It has been in the past and is today a necessary part of the daily routine, taken in hand as one cultivates an understanding of music or painting or seeks other worthwhile occupation for the mind and spirit. This is also true in America but not to the same extent.

It has become fashionable to ornament one's home with a touch of handwork, a needlepoint chair or a wall decoration. By the style of work exhibited in the home, one's guests and friends measure the understanding, ability and taste of the worker. Is the expression up-to-date and self-reliant or is the worker thinking back in the darker ages of design? By their needlework may you know what manner of person you are conversing with, what their awareness may be on the subject they are discussing. If they are conversant with the times it will show in their embroidery for there, as in any other art, it is necessary to understand techniques which are in current use and to take advantage of every new facet or idea which the contemporary mode has to offer. As surely as an antique costume would date one in clothes, so antique copies of needlework are equally out of tune in a sophisticated twentieth century scene, unless, of course, one wishes to recreate a definite period such as the Empire, the Jacobean or the late Victorian. Even productions of period designs must be simplified in order to remain in harmony with the present taste. The person who enters the eighteenth century room would not don the clothes worn in Queen Anne's reign, but might choose to wear a gown which would harmonize in color or texture.

Needlepoint rosebuds are still worked every day in the good old Berlin wool-work design fashionable a century ago. They are made from the same German and Viennese patterns and often used with a complete disregard for period or style and placement. These old-fashioned Victorian designs may even be applied to chairs in modern interiors, to Louis XIV or Early

American chairs with no concern as to the unrelated styles. Rosebuds as a subject are, of course, universal and perfectly permissible for use in any period; it is the manner or mode in which they are designed and interpreted on the canvas or drawing which indicates their place in design history. If they are not handled so as to harmonize with modern trends they are as much out of fashion as the old hat of a few years back.

Therefore needlepoint patterns and their application require intelligent consideration. Most contemporary embroiderers are aware of these requirements and in the majority of examples the canvas has been prepared by special designers. These artists are thoroughly conversant with this medium and are able to construct designs in proper period relationships and to select color harmonies to match the setting.

The use of color has altered considerably within the last twenty years. Recently air conditioning, which makes interiors practically dirt and dust proof, has had its share in revolutionizing taste and fashion in the use of color by allowing white and off-whites in decorative fabrics to appear. Many modern pieces of needlepoint which cover the chairs of today are filled in with off-white or ivory shades, permitting the colors in the main design to show up with charming effect against the clear, clean background. These off-whites should be selected with careful consideration of all the factors which enter into their use and here it is well to consult the needlepoint designer. This style in backgrounds is in direct contrast to the blacks of the Victorian era and the dark browns popular even today with those who prefer the dark tones because it harmonizes with the period of their furniture or with their interior decoration.

One of the chief attractions in modern needlepoint is its return to simple forms in both design and execution, a welcome change from the days when stitch technique was often more important than design. A thorough understanding of the various stitches is important and definitely necessary. A knowledge of good design and capable technique is also vitally essential. But these values need to be well balanced so that the observer will not at first be conscious of any one of them but will react immediately to the idea or mood expressed and then turn to an analysis of the technical methods employed.

2. *Courtesy of*: MRS. J. TEMPLEMAN COOLIDGE, Massachusetts.

Three-fold needlepoint screen, flowers in squares, worked by Mrs. J. Templeman Coolidge, Massachusetts, and designed by the Women's Educational and Industrial Union, Boston, Massachusetts.

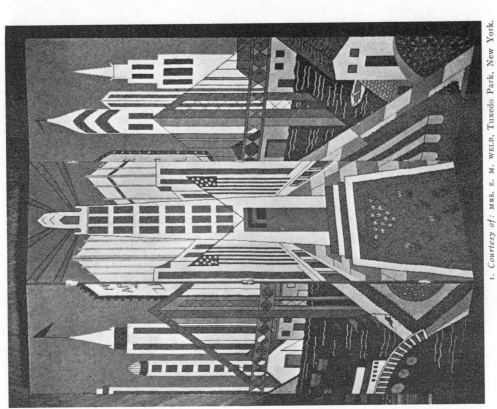

1. *Courtesy of*: MRS. E. M. WELD, Tuxedo Park, New York.

Three-fold needlepoint screen, ultra modern worked by Mrs. E. M. Weld, Tuxedo Park, New York and designed by Ann F. Hobdy, New York.

Needlepoint four-fold screen, "Deep South" 64" x 72" designed by Georgiana Brown Harbeson and worked 1936 by members of Minerva Yarn Industries, Pennsylvania.

Needlepoint Bench Top, ultra modern, interpreting a Jamaica Plantation scene. Designed and worked in petit point by Mr. Clement Hurd, New York.

New combinations of stitchery and newer arrangements of decorative forms are being developed. Qualities of discrimination, good taste and the harmonious use of color are being encouraged in needlepoint design. Future needlework in America may produce further interesting results. Solid foundations have been laid toward this accomplishment and the forward movement grows with greater momentum each day. This is evidenced by the great amount of brilliant contemporary work.

SCREENS

Among the most ambitious works of Mrs. William Warner Hoppin of New York City are the panels executed in fine needlepoint for a four-fold screen. Each panel measures five feet by eighteen inches. The background color is a soft beige. The chinoiserie design was painted on canvas professionally. A game of battledore and shuttlecock is being played on one panel, a scene with a water wheel occupies another, a Chinese youth flies a kite in a third, while the fourth panel depicts Chinese coolies sawing logs. These Chinese scenes and the scrolls, flowers and pheasants are all executed in four shades of jade green blending into blue green. All the shades have been matched to the paint and colorings used in the drawing room of Mrs. Hoppin's Long Island home, where the screen is the important feature. It is handsome without being obtrusive and has been worked with care and artistry. The panels were greatly admired when first exhibited in 1934 at the Needlework of Today showing of contemporary embroideries.

Mrs. Hoppin explains why she made such large pieces of painstaking needlepoint and also how she came to organize exhibitions of embroideries for charity benefits.

One day three years ago while working on the third panel of the four-fold five-foot high needlepoint screen, I stated that I had always hoped to finish such a piece and then I could die, satisfied that I had accomplished something worthwhile and of which my children could be proud. As I gave this reason, it suddenly dawned upon me that once in my grave, I became an Ancestor!

From that cheerful discovery originated the new Annual Exhibition of Needlework of Today. In counting up the various bags, cushions, stools, firescreens, etc. which I myself had worked, I mentally lined up the many women with whom I had compared stitches and designs and with whom I had exchanged wools. Astounded at the number which flashed through my mind, I then began to think over the various types of work which we all had been doing and how for years, I had unconsciously been studying the needlework exhibited in museums and palaces. If chairs embroidered by Marie Antoinette and Queen Anne and other ladies of by-gone years were of value today, why should not our work be of equal interest and value to our descendants.

With this thought in mind, Mrs. Hoppin organized the Amateur Needlework Group in 1934. The first exhibition attracted seven hundred and fifty entries of needlepoint, examples flowing in from various cities all over the country. For each piece of embroidery shown an entry fee was paid which was contributed to the Lighthouse Charity for the benefit of the blind.

This first dream of Mrs. Hoppin's has now resulted in the establishment of a national organization under her leadership, each unit contributing to a civic need of its community. For example, in Philadelphia for the past five years the annual Needlework of Today exhibition has been held for the two-fold purpose of encouraging interest in the fine artistry to be attained in needlework and to raise funds for the preservation of historical landmarks. The first to benefit is the Powell House Mansion in Philadelphia, a beautiful colonial mansion of the eighteenth century which is to be restored to its former charm and beauty with funds raised from the entry fees to this show. Part of its wall decoration is at present in the American Wing at the Metropolitan Museum of Art. When Boston, Chicago, San Francisco and other cities hold their exhibitions of Needlework of Today the women from various cities send on their embroideries not only for purposes of comparison but to return the compliment and aid sister philanthropies in other communities.

The jury of the first Needlework of Today exhibition held in New York in 1934 awarded Mrs. Theodore Roosevelt, Jr., its first prize of a Gold Star for her miniature table screen in needlepoint, which contained three panels of native American birds in a design adapted from old prints. In order to make certain that the coloring of the birds was accurate, Mrs. Roosevelt, who was spending a summer in Vermont, closely observed these little feathered friends. Her children were keenly interested in the needlework and kept watch for the different birds, contributing their bit to the enterprise while learning much birdlore. The general colorings of the screen are reds, yellows, and dark greens in the leaves, worked in small stitches which contrast gaily with the large stitches used for the cerulean blue sky effect of the background. These panels are initialed E. R. and dated 1926.

The high point in Mrs. Roosevelt's needle-point embroideries is a large three-fold monkey screen which is worked in gros point. Great vibration and rhythmic beauty is achieved through the graceful flow of the monkeys sweep-ing through the air from tree to tree. Jungle foliage is suggested through conventionalized tree branches sewn across the panels in diago-nals, emphasizing the movement of the monkeys as well as the density of the forest. In contrast or opposition to these curves and angles are up-right tropical plants which interrupt the swing with perpendicular lines. Curved leaves soften their straightness. These perpendicular forms also serve to "contain" the design within its own area so that the eye does not run away from the subject. This screen was adapted in part from the sketch of a well-known contem-porary American artist and it is beautifully designed and worked.

Mrs. Roosevelt embroidered the first panel in the Philippine Islands. Colored yarns had to be imported from England and were difficult to obtain. In one instance the particular robin's egg blue used in the sky effect in the back-ground was found to have turned to a yellowish tinge before the second half of the panel was completed. Being very sincere and conscientious about her craftsmanship, Mrs. Roosevelt unhesi-tatingly ripped out every stitch of the offending color and reworked the entire area with a sub-stitute blue which held its color. Such thor-oughness is essential in the perpetuation of the fine technical standards which good embroidery has held through the centuries.

The second panel was completed in Porto Rico while Theodore Roosevelt, Jr., was Gov-ernor of that Island and the third one was com-pleted in New York.

The general coloring is blue and green shaded in several tones rather simply. The monkeys are worked in black and white with accents of dark green. The embroidery is framed in flat silver and occupies one corner of the dining room of the home at Oyster Bay. The needlepoint is initialed E. R. and dated be-tween the years 1931 and 1934.

An ultramodern needlepoint screen with a skyscraper effect in the design combined with spans of bridges and steamboats in the river provides the decorative content of the three-fold screen executed by Mrs. E. M. Weld of Tuxedo Park, New York. It was designed on the canvas by Ann Hobdy and is interesting in its modern range of flat tones indicating triangles, squares and oblongs in the masses of stone and steel rising into the sky. A patriotic note has been introduced by placing two American flags in the composition.

Flowers are the subject of the three-fold screen recently worked in needlepoint by Mrs. J. Templeman Coolidge of Boston. It was de-signed by the Woman's Industrial Union. Vari-ous florals enclosed within blocks or square units fill the panels and suggest old flower prints. Worked in soft needlepoint crewel yarns the screen makes a beautiful decoration. The background has been filled in with a deep tan or beige color worked in Gobelin stitch. The contrasting needlepoint of the flowers has been very well done by Mrs. Coolidge, who is an ardent embroiderer.

A needlepoint screen designed by the author is composed of four panels which were worked in gros point by girls in the Minerva Yarn In-dustries. The panels are so arranged that when straightened out they create one large composi-tion. The subject is "Deep South," and the at-mosphere that of the thick, lush growth in jungle or swamp lands. The white herons stand-ing in the pool are surrounded by flowering plants of crimson and orchid tones. The trees are executed in shades of green ranging from pale yellow to deep blue green. The white swal-lows balance the herons in color, while contrast is introduced by a luscious, tropical butterfly. Drooping vines add a feeling of denseness and impenetrability to the scene. The background color is a deep boxwood green.

The screen was designed to provide contrast in an all-white room where one chair is up-holstered in crimson fabric. Lemon-yellow dra-peries and other off-white notes match the needlepoint decoration. The canvas is very coarse and is worked in fairly large stitches. It measures sixty-four inches by seventy-two, over all, and was made in 1936 in Pennsylvania as one of a group of sixty models based on designs created by the author. These designs introduced a series of needlepoint patterns, colored by a hand process, which for the first time allowed the worker herself to embroider the entire design.

POLE SCREENS

A delightful way to provide warm, colorful decoration for any room is through the introduction of the exquisite pole screen. These screens were used in former centuries to shield the face from the glare of the fire and were placed in front of fireplaces. The framed panel was raised or lowered to convenient heights. As heating systems changed the pole screen has been retained for its decorative value. Contemporary needlepoint has been placed upon some of these eighteenth and nineteenth century poles. Many persons have used family antiques, replacing earlier decorations with their own embroideries. Others have had pole screens made or designed to order to match the period of their furnishings.

Mrs. H. Bradley Martin of New York uses two techniques of embroidery in her pole-screen panels. One of the two screens she has made depicts on its front panel the coat of arms of the Chew family, beautifully worked in petit point. The light background very happily sets off the shield and the impaling Argent with the Griffin. On the reverse side Mrs. Martin has crewel-embroidered the family genealogy on linen to replace the usual brocade backing. A tree is stitched upon which the branches of her mother's family are indicated by the names worked in outline stitch on oblong spaces. The layout reads:

CORNELIA ANNE BRADLEY MARTIN B 1931

HELEN KATHARINE BRADLEY MARTIN B 1933

KATHARINE KENNEDY B 1907 TOD M H BRADLEY MARTIN

KATHARINE ALEXANDER B 1882 CHEW M ROBET ELLIOT TOD

BEVERLEY CHEW B 1773 D 1831 M MARIA THEODORA DUER

JOHN CHEW D 1799 M ANN FOX

LARKIN CHEW D 1728 M HANNAH ROY

JOHN CHEW BORN IN ENGLAND SETTLED IN VIRGINIA 1622 D 1668 M SARAH

PHINEAS PROUTY B 1854 D 1936 CHEW M MARGUERITE PISTOR

ALEXANDER LAFAYETTE B 1824 D 1911 CHEW M SARAH AUGUSTA PROUTY

LADY CATHERINE ALEXANDER DUER DAU OF WILLIAM ALEXANDER EARL OF STERLING

JOSEPH CHEW M RUTH LARKIN

A squirrel stands at the lower right-hand side of the tree looking at the names.

The lettering has been stitched in blue, the oak leaves are worked in greens and browns and the acorns are a "pinkish color" to use Mrs. Bradley's term. The stitches are varied, chain stitch on the squirrel and vines, long and short stitch on the acorns. The tree trunk is worked with different filling stitches, the y-stitch, star stitch, outline stitch, and lace or surface stitches are used in the shading and oak leaf fillings. These latter stitches are similar to those employed in making the lacework darning stitches on net in the 1800's. Other stitches are related to the early crewel embroideries of colonial days and yet the entire theme and style of the panel is distinctly contemporary in its novel simplicity.

The other screen panel is composed entirely of florals of Queen Anne style to match a chair of this period also worked by Mrs. Martin. The design was very well composed by Mrs. Lillian Barton-Wilson and worked in beautiful technique by Mrs. Martin. The background tone is a lovely wine-mulberry shade of yarn. The flowers are of soft brilliance, clear in their tones and not faded out or insipid. The poppies are a brilliant red. The wools to make them were a gift to Mrs. Martin from Lady Violet Crowley of England, whose family had inherited them from the days of Queen Anne. They were stiff and had to be softened by soaking in water in order to free the strands for use. They were braided for vitality. The color is typical of the brilliant tone all colors in this period possessed. This panel is mounted on the same type of pole-stand as the one first described and is a lovely decoration. The needlepoint is signed K. T. Martin and dated 1933.

Mrs. John W. Castles of Convent, New Jersey, worked a pole-screen panel on the single mesh canvas in fine needlepoint. She chose a "Map of Discovery" for her subject and it was designed by Ann Hobdy. The eastern hemisphere only is shown. Africa, Asia, Europe and Australia are indicated in simple flat colorings. A few sailing ships suggest the discoveries and a whale provides a decorative note. The top corners carry interpretations of the elements, the blowing winds, clouds, stars and lightning. In one of the lower corners are figures of explorers in fourteenth century costume. The opposite corner shows the scholars and scientists seated among their books making prophecies and deductions.

Mrs. Castles has embroidered many panels with splendid technique and is devoted to the art. This screen was made as a gift for her daughter-in-law, Mrs. John W. Castles, Jr., in 1933.

Mrs. Nicholas E. Brown has made use of an American scene for needlepoint interpretation in her gros point and petit point panel for a pole screen. The subject is "The Old Market, 1762," a famous Rhode Island shipping center in colonial days. The figures, the boy and the small pig, the lady and gentleman, and the outlines of the windows are all worked in petit point, while the buildings, ship and other details are in the larger stitch. Mrs. Brown worked the screen for her son, John Nicholas Brown, who has it in his colonial house on Benefit Street in Providence. This type of design makes a very appropriate subject for any colonial interior, since it represents that period in atmosphere and story.

Mrs. Reginald DeKoven has made an exquisite petit point panel in the eighteenth century manner showing a small urn holding flowers. In the foreground a bird is catching an insect. The group is daintily interpreted with colors of the Watteau palette. The design was suggested by a water-color study painted by a student at Cooper Union. The flowers, the pheasant and the entire foreground are worked in petit point and the background in gros point. It is a lovely decoration in a bedroom of eighteenth century furnishing.

A very delicate lovely flower panel has been worked in fine needlepoint for a pole screen by Mrs. Stewart S. Hathaway of Rye, New York. The design, made by Ann Hobdy, has a quality similar to primitive paintings of the early Italian school and the simplicity of a modern work as well. There is a very small vase in the center from which long sprays of flowers grow out over the panel. The stems are attenuated and the leaves give a sensitive character to the needlepoint. The colorings of the flowers are pastel, mauves, golds and yellows in faint tones, and the leaves are on a sage green. The background has been filled in with a cocoa brown on the mauve cast. It is a very attractive panel.

A charming needlepoint fire-screen panel worked in petit point by Mrs. Ambolena Hooker Cary is a genuinely modern work. It has an antique Jacobean background combined with contemporary motifs in the design. The horses, for example, are reminiscent of the form and feeling of the animals done by painters of the modern French school, yet this motif is enclosed in scroll outline-pattern quite characteristic of Elizabethan needlework found in England in the seventeenth century. Coloring in the tree, fruits, and flower groupings is definitely modern in tone. There is more brilliance in the reds and blues used for the stitchery than has been customary for some years.

Such strong or brilliant color used in any decorative scheme whether applied to costume, an interior or needlework, does not necessarily imply bad taste. It is only a bad keying of tones which is disturbing. When colors are in a harmonious scale and in keeping with the place or the event then discord is avoided. Mrs. Cary has softened the strong colors in her panel, to blend, no doubt, with antique furniture and a quiet interior, by filling the background in with a warm tannish beige. As in nature, the soft earth color offsets the bright oranges, reds, and yellow greens of trees in Autumn and the high, intense blues of the sky. Background and foreground colors are a most important consideration in keying the symphonic tones of one's needlework theme to one's personality.

1. *Courtesy of:* MRS. REGINALD DE KOVEN, New York.

Petit point pole-screen panel, "Vase of Flowers," by Mrs. Reginald de Koven, New York.

2. *Courtesy of:* MRS. LEWIS SHERRILL BIGELOW, New York.

Needlepoint fire screen panel, standing, partially adapted from a European design and worked in petit point and gros point by Mrs. Lewis Sherrill Bigelow, New York.

3. *Courtesy of:* MRS. REGINALD DE KOVEN, New York.

Needlepoint, large fire screen panel, "Adam and Eve" by Mrs. Reginald de Koven, New York.

4. *Courtesy of:* MRS. W. A. SEIFERT, Pennsylvania.

Needlepoint fire screen panel, standing "Friendship Hill," 1937 by Mrs. W. A. Seifert, Pennsylvania.

1. *Courtesy of:* MRS. H. BRADLEY MARTIN, New York.

Reverse side of Chew Family pole-screen panel with crewel embroidered genealogy by Mrs. H. Bradley Martin, New York.

2. *Courtesy of:* MRS. JOHN W. CASTLES, New Jersey.

"Map of Discovery," Eastern Hemisphere, Needlepoint pole-screen panel designed by Ann Hobdy and worked by Mrs. John W. Castles, New Jersey.

3. *Courtesy of:* MRS. AMBOLENA HOOKER CARY.

Petit point pole-screen panel by Mrs. Ambolena Hooker Cary.

4. *Courtesy of:* MRS. STUART HATHAWAY, Rye, New York.

Petit point pole-screen panel, floral, by Mrs. Stuart Hathaway, Rye, New York.

5. *Courtesy of:* MRS. H. BRADLEY MARTIN, New York.

Needlepoint pole-screen, The Chew Family Coat of Arms by Mrs. H. Bradley Martin, New York.

6. *Courtesy of:* MRS. NICHOLAS BROWN, Newport, Rhode Island.

Needlepoint pole-screen picture, "The Old Market," 1762, by Mrs. Nicholas Brown, Newport, Rhode Island, 1936.

The pole screen has become almost as important a feature in the room, decoratively, as the overmantel decoration and in some instances now functions as a substitute, particularly where the room is paneled or the place above the fire reserved for a portrait.

STANDING FIRE SCREENS

Made in larger size but also used in front of fireplaces are the decorative standing fire screens. Usually they are handsome examples of cabinet-work. The large space is ideal for needlepoint. Being an important feature in a living or drawing room, the design should be given much thought. Family crests are sometimes used but when applied to such a large panel, it is necessary to provide some other decoration to fill in the composition.

Mrs. W. A. Seifert of Pittsburgh has embroidered a very interesting panel in needlepoint which includes the coat of arms of the Nicholson and the Gallatin families in each lower corner. Between them is a scroll bearing the inscription "Friendship Hill." Below is the embroiderer's signature, Edith Seifert, and the date of completion, A.D. 1937. Above is a picture of the home of Albert Gallatin, who was the great-great-grandfather of Mrs. Mary Gallatin Hoppin of New York and served in important government positions both here and abroad. "Friendship Hill" was built as his quiet retreat from the world and is particularly notable for having housed General Lafayette, who was entertained there in May, 1825, while he was the nation's guest. At one end of the mansion is a balcony from which the famous General addressed the guests attending a lawn party given in his honor.

The buildings were painted on the canvas panel by Mrs. Lillian Barton-Wilson's studio. Mrs. Seifert explains that she replaced the vases of flowers on the drawing with the coats of arms worked on either side of her work. She says,

> It took me about seven months (fall of '37 and spring of '38). Much of the work I did on the way to and from Rio, the rest was worked in Pittsburgh, Pennsylvania.

This panel is the forty-eighth piece of needlepoint made by Mrs. Seifert.

Mrs. Lewis Bigelow of New York has made a large fire-screen panel in a combination of gros point and petit point stitches. The central figure is either an eighteenth century interpretation of Ceres, the goddess of agriculture, or a portrayal of a lady gardening. Bending branches meet over her head, while in the foreground large flowers are blooming profusely. A scroll border with branches of flowering vines frames the embroidery. The colorings in the border are a pale green accented with touches of French blue, while the foreground is worked in deeper greens and shades of rose yarns. Blue and gold ornament the rest of the design. The pattern was outlined in Paris to suit Mrs. Bigelow's individual taste and was developed in the United States with her own ideas of color shading and arrangement. It is initialed M. R. B., and dated 1935, and is a lovely, glowing bit of decoration in the living room it occupies.

The World War began Mrs. Reginald De-Koven's career in embroidery. Being marooned in Switzerland during that period, she found the long days tedious and sought solace in needlepoint. One design which she developed was adapted from an old piece of needlepoint which she found in Anjou. It was made into a standing fire-screen panel by Mrs. DeKoven, who builds her needlepoint by counting out her stitch patterns by the squares. The panel represents Adam and Eve costumed in the mode of the eighteenth century. The foreground represents the round earth with spots of sunshine upon it. The serpent has been changed to flowers, which twine around the tree. The background is worked in with rose; the rest of the decoration is carried out in soft eighteenth century tones.

Mrs. DeKoven spent all the spare money she had on wools in order to keep herself occupied during this period. The panel took three months to work and being executed entirely in petit point, it was evidently continuous work. The light in Switzerland was so bright that green glasses were worn to protect the eyes while working. When it was finished the colorings of the needlepoint seemed so bright to Mrs. DeKoven that a formula suggested by General Meigs' daughter made up of a large cup of black coffee into which a little ink had been added was thrown upon the bright colors to reduce their intensity.

The screen is a handsome addition to the beautiful eighteenth century drawing room in

Mrs. DeKoven's New York house and brings back many memories connected with its making. Mrs. DeKoven has made several standing fire screens for other rooms in her home which are equally lovely and well made in the difficult petit point.

STOOL-TOP COVERS

Mrs. Edward R. Warren of Boston, Massachusetts, has designed and worked a large and very attractive needlepoint footstool covering. The large flowers and the pheasant were suggested by some patterns on old Chippendale wallpaper. The design has been executed with spirited embroidery in simple stitches. The feathers on the bird are decoratively and effectively reproduced without too much detail. Mrs. Warren has caught the atmosphere of the period without becoming too elaborate in her expression.

Mrs. Harriet Griffin Baker, being a painter, works spontaneously upon her needlework just as she would paint upon a canvas. She finds delight and interesting diversion in doing needlepoint, working along at random and building in her floral forms as she goes. A particularly lovely large stool covering is engagingly worked in soft tones of beige gold and grayed reds laid on in the style of paint. The shadings on the flowers are worked without outlining. The leaves run into quite dark colors; the greens are considerably grayed. A lattice arrangement on the edge of the border is unusual in design and provides a break between the large floral pattern and the Provincial bench it covers very daintily. Mrs. Baker began the needlepoint in her New York studio and completed it in her home in Rome, Italy, working while traveling abroad. Her wools were carried in the shoe case of her trunk arranged in layers of shades and she chose her colors from this assortment at random, explaining that her needlepoint pieces "just grow, like Topsy." They are gay, unique examples and very personal because they are designed so spontaneously.

Mrs. Frederic C. Thomas of Cold Spring Harbor, Long Island, has designed and executed her "Greek Seahorses" in modern manner. This long stool covering is unusual in needlepoint since it is far away from the traditional themes frequently used. The design has a painting quality and really achieves atmosphere and movement in the long bands of sea colors in the background. The seahorses rise from the water in dawn rose shades which form a striking contrast to the blue greens of the background. Deep rose borders the panel which is mounted upon a long low stool, making an interesting decoration for the living room.

Mrs. Frank Rowell of New York combines petit point and gros point in her large stool cover. The design uses pomegranates and pineapple motifs on the Chippendale order, and has been worked beautifully with excellent color harmonies which are fresh in tone without being hard. The background coloring is turquoise blue. The small bird is stitched in rose red and deep turquoise blues. The butterfly has been worked in blue violet and gold. The general patterning is a reddish brown, gold and ochre tracery which is lovely in color placement. The design was painted by Mrs. Lillian Barton-Wilson. Mrs. Rowell's technique and color sense are excellent, due in a measure to her tireless effort and enthusiastic interest in the art.

Mrs. Harris Childs of New York enjoys her needlepoint almost as much as Mrs. Rowell. She has a great fondness for little animals and odd or unusual patternings. A low footstool has been covered with a design, also reminiscent of the Chippendale period, worked in simple masses. Instead of a pheasant or Chinese peacock, Mrs. Childs has featured with very decorative effect a dragon or salamander, chosen perhaps because he would be comfortably at home beside the fire. The design is well composed and nice in color. It is stitched upon a medium canvas which gives a rich surface.

Little footstools are exceedingly popular, useful and comparatively simple to work. Mrs. Francis Noble has made a needlepoint pussy-cat stretched out contentedly upon a square footstool of Victorian style. Around the white and black spotted kitty she has drawn an attractive wreath of morning-glories, worked in shades of rose. They are attractively placed against a colonial blue background. The piece is harmonious with the colonial furnishings in the apartment of Mrs. W. H. Leonard Edwards of New York, to whom it was given.

Mrs. Edwards also has made considerable needlepoint of her own. One example is a covering for a small curly maple footstool. The cover is worked in an allover pattern of flowers

1. *Courtesy of:* MRS. LOUIS B. MCCAGG, Newport, Rhode Island.

Needlepoint bench top, picturing "King Hall," St. Georges, Newport, Rhode Island, designed by Aquidneck Cottage Industries and worked by Mrs. Louis B. McCagg, Newport, Rhode Island.

2. *Courtesy of:* MRS. LEWIS ISELIN, Connecticut.

Needlepoint fireside bench top worked by Mrs. Lewis Iselin, Connecticut.

3. *Courtesy of:* MRS. REGINALD DE KOVEN, New York.

Needlepoint seat for boudoir bench designed and worked by Mrs. Reginald de Koven, New York.

4. *Courtesy of:* MRS. HELEN DAMROSCH TEE-VAN, New York.

Needlepoint bench top, Bermuda Fishes designed and worked by Mrs. Helen Damrosch Tee-Van, New York.

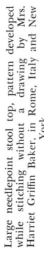

3. *Courtesy of:* MRS. FRANK B. ROWELL. New York.

Large needlepoint stool top by Mrs. Frank B. Rowell, New York.

2. *Courtesy of:* MRS. WILLIAM EDGAR BAKER, Rome, Italy and New York,

Large needlepoint stool top, pattern developed while stitching without a drawing by Mrs. Harriet Griffin Baker, in Rome, Italy and New York.

1. *Courtesy of:* MRS. EDWARD R. WARREN, Massachusetts.

Large needlepoint stool top, motif adapted from old Chippendale wallpaper, designed and worked by Mrs. Edward R. Warren, Massachusetts.

5. *Courtesy of:* MRS. ALFRED ROELKER, New York.

Long needlepoint footstool, "Sea Horses," designed and worked by Mrs. Frederick C. Thomas, Cold Spring Harbor, L. I.

4. *Courtesy of:* MRS. HARRIS CHILDS, New York.

Large needlepoint footstool top, by Mrs. Harris Childs, New York.

with wide branching leaves placed against a rose background. The design is very simple but well composed and admirably worked, in harmony with the room in which it is placed.

BENCH TOPS

Mrs. Lewis Iselin of New Rochelle, New York, has worked a particularly lovely needlepoint panel for a large English Regency fireside bench top. Attractive floral and pineapple motifs compose the design. Mrs. Iselin obtained the pattern, outlined in black and white, in Paris, but has created her own interpretation by readapting the design to suit her own ideas of color placement and arrangement of the large flower and leaf forms which cover the surface in a graceful manner. The background is a soft golden brown, obtained by mixing a needleful of two shades of wool. This is a modern and popular method of obtaining soft interesting tones for straight background fillings, and may be achieved only with the use of the needlepoint yarn which is made in fine divisible strands or ply. The golds, rose, blues, yellows and greens make a sparkling glow of color over the bench surface which is most appropriately placed in front of the fireplace in Mrs. Iselin's home.

A Queen Anne bench top made by Mrs. Louis B. McCagg of Newport, Rhode Island, has an architectural picture, King Hall of St. George's, for its principal decoration. It was designed by the Aquidneck Cottage Industries and effectively interpreted in needlepoint by Mrs. McCagg. The subject portrayed on the covering is in perfect harmony with the fairly severe, simple lines of the bench.

Mrs. Reginald DeKoven works needlepoint continuously and her home is filled with a quantity of chairs, stools, benches, table tops and screens executed by herself. A boudoir bench top was designed by her and worked with counted cross stitches, her invariable method, for an Empire period bench especially made in ebony with gold lacquer touches. The needlepoint was worked in a combination of black wools and gold-toned outlines. It is interesting as a departure from traditional patterns and Mrs. DeKoven found much pleasure and stimulus in creating something so unusual.

Miss Mary Madison Maguire of New York City has embroidered a very large bench top in needlepoint with a splendid design of interlaced leaves, flowers and fruits which are worked in fairly strong colors against a gold yellow background. The work is vital yet soft in general tone and makes a handsome covering for a long bench. Miss Maguire developed her pattern and coloring over a design foundation acquired in London, adding her own interpretation as Mrs. Iselin has done. Her technique is beautiful.

Helen Damrosch Tee-Van is another woman painter who enjoys needlepoint. Her embroidery design for a fireside bench top pictures under-sea life in the waters around the Bermuda Islands. Sketches and notes made while she was on the Beebe expedition with her husband, John Tee-Van, provided the pattern details. The background of this lovely panel is worked in blue greens in mountain effects; the ocean bed is worked in pale grays, white and violet. The sea coral, brain coral, sea plumes, sponges and sea fans are stitched most decoratively in purples, yellows, orange, red orange, peacock blue, corals and sandy pinks. The fish are a joy also. The little important-looking fish, worked in lemon-yellow, pale and deep, and cream and black colors, are sergeant majors, sometimes called cow-pilots or nuisances because they annoy fishermen by taking bait off their hooks very neatly. The long fish is a blue head and in Bermuda it is called king slippery dick because of its quick color changes. As they grow up, these fish alter their color considerably but Mrs. Tee-Van has chosen to make her king slippery dick permanently colored in peacock blue and a violet blue head, with black, yellow, chartreuse and green on top of his fishskin back and yellow green on the ventral surface and lower fins.

The entire decoration is fresh, clear and soft in color, the design refreshing and original in idea. It has been worked entirely in gros point and shows that Mrs. Tee-Van is as well acquainted with embroidery as she is with the fish which she renders so exquisitely in many mediums.

Mr. Clement Hurd is also an artist who finds it fun to design and execute his own needlepoint. He has made and exhibited a very interesting modern interpretation of a Jamaica plantation in the West Indies, worked in petit point for a bench top. The design has abstract qualities in its tonal gradations and shadings of color, and in the use of modern pictorial form which suggests the life of the natives, the spirit of the locale and the atmospheric coloring without exact reproduction of the actual scene. It is rather a composite of all the plantations one might visit in the West Indies, reduced in essence to one. Accent is given to the general scale of rose yarns worked in several shades by the use of powder blue and green, and vitality is added by the touches of Chinese vermillion appearing in the costumes of the natives. This is a splendid design for a modern interior and has been worked exceedingly well by Mr. Hurd.

TABLE TOPS

Tilt tables provide a splendid occasion for the display of needlepoint which is mounted in glass frames on their tops. They are not only an exceedingly decorative addition to a room, but are useful as well. Numerous contemporary examples have been worked, depicting many subjects.

Mrs. George M. Laughlin, Jr., of Pittsburgh has designed and worked her family coat of arms in fine needlepoint to decorate the tilt top of a coffee table. The crest is colorful and has the motif of the three leaves carried around the border of the arms for an interesting frame within which Mrs. Laughlin has worked her initials and the year of execution, H. S. L. 1933. This is but one example of the numerous needlepoint embroideries which have been made by this ardent and accomplished needlewoman.

Mrs. Edgar Felton, Jr., of Haverford, Pennsylvania, worked the Felton arms in needlepoint to be enclosed within the frame-top of a tilt table wrought in handsome proportions. The panel was designed for Mrs. Felton by Agnes C. Sims who explains that the original of the arms drawing came from the Garter Plate of Sir Thomas de Felton in St. George's Chapel of Windsor Castle in 1381. The crest with the lions rampant on the shield is attractive. The sprays of leaves, the crown and family name are finely rendered. The whole composition has been nicely balanced for the oval top. It makes a lovely panel for Mrs. Felton's home.

Mrs. Truxton Hare of Radnor, Pennsylvania,

has embroidered a coffee table top in a Chinese design arranged for her by Agnes Sims also. This needlepoint panel is a fairly elaborate scene filled with many Chinese figures splendidly worked. An old mandarin seated in a pagoda is attended by ladies bearing flowers and fruits, while a fan bearer is within call in the middle distance. Bamboo trees, garden flowers and shrubbery provide the rest of the ornament which is framed with a narrow latticed needlepoint border effect. It must be pleasant to catch glimpses of this delightful scene under the glass cover of the table top as coffee is being served by Mrs. Hare.

Mrs. William Whitehouse of Newport, Rhode Island, applies her needlepoint design to her tea table. Cups, saucers, tea caddy and teaspoons appear appropriately in the pattern which shows the Chinese influence in the decoration on the chinaware. It has been carefully executed in fine stitches by Mrs. Whitehouse for her home in Newport, and was designed by the Aquidneck Cottage Industries.

A perfectly delightful chessboard table top has been designed and worked by Mrs. Samuel Cabot of Massachusetts, after the manner of an old sampler. Florals are spotted in the light squares and the dark squares achieve character through the use of a different type of canvas stitch for each filling. The backgrounds of the lighter squares are confined to petit point, cross-stitch and Gobelin stitch, which is a wise arrangement since these stitches do not detract from the elaborate design employed in the other squares. The border has two sides worked in a conventional leaf motif; the top and bottom bands are spotted with a row of needlepoint chess motifs, castles, horses' heads, crowns and bishops' mitres worked in their proper sequence on the board. One square has been reserved for Mrs. Cabot's initials and the date, S. C. 1936. There is also a peacock in this table top which is an interesting repetition of this traditional motif.

Mrs. D. Oliver O'Donnell of Newport and New York has made a card table top in fine needlepoint which she roughly designed herself, over the Aquidneck Cottage Industries pattern of hunters, racing horses and dogs. She has added to the border the cards designed as a real poker hand, her monogram, money, chips, counters, dice, etc., all amusingly arranged. These

1. *Courtesy of:* MRS. WILLIAM WHITEHOUSE, Rhode Island.

Needlepoint tray top designed by Aquidneck Cottage Industries, and worked by Mrs. William Whitehouse, for her home in Newport, Rhode Island.

2. *Courtesy of:* MRS. TRUXTON HARE, Radnor, Pennsylvania.

Needlepoint coffee table top, worked by Mrs. Truxton Hare, Radnor, Pennsylvania and designed by Agnes C. Sims.

3. *Courtesy of:* MRS. GEORGE M. LAUGHLIN, JR., Pittsburgh, Pennsylvania.

Needlepoint coffee table top with Coat of Arms. Designed and worked by Mrs. George M. Laughlin, Jr., Pittsburgh, Pennsylvania.

4. *Courtesy of:* MRS. WILLIAM WHITEHOUSE.

Needlepoint panel on tea table top by Mrs. William Whitehouse, Newport, Rhode Island.

5. *Courtesy of:* MRS. EDGAR FELTON, JR., Haverford, Penn.

Tilt table top with the Felton Arms. Worked by Mrs. Edgar Felton, Jr., Haverford, Pennsylvania, and designed for needlepoint by Agnes C. Sims, Pennsylvania.

2. *Courtesy of:* MRS. GEORGE ANGUS GARRETT, Washington, D. C.

Needlepoint flower rug, contemporary, designed by Ann F. Hobdy, New York; worked in squares by Mrs. George Angus Garrett, Washington, D. C.

4. *Courtesy of:* MRS. REGINALD NORMAN, Newport, Rhode Island.

Needlepoint eight piece rug 88 x 46 inches, worked by Mrs. Reginald Norman for "Bellaire," Newport, Rhode Island, and designed by Aquidneck Cottage Industries.

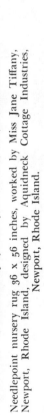

1. *Courtesy of:* MISS JANE TIFFANY, Newport, Rhode Island.

Needlepoint nursery rug 36 x 56 inches, worked by Miss Jane Tiffany, Newport, Rhode Island, designed by Aquidneck Cottage Industries, Newport, Rhode Island.

3. *Courtesy of:* MRS. FRANK C. MUNSON, New York and Nassau.

Needlepoint flower rug worked in one piece by Mrs. Frank C. Munson, New York and Nassau, and designed by Ann F. Hobdy, New York.

2. *Courtesy of:* MRS. WILLIAM GREENOUGH, Newport, Rhode Island.

Needlepoint four piece rug, "Empire Design" worked by Mrs. William Greenough for her home in Newport, Rhode Island.

4. *Courtesy of:* MRS. JOHN D. ROCKEFELLER.

Needlepoint rug nine squares, worked by Mrs. John D. Rockefeller. Used in their restored house at Williamsburg, Virginia.

1. *Courtesy of:* MARY GORDON PRATT, Newport, R. I.

Needlepoint six piece rug, 54 x 39 inches, worked 1932 by Mary Gordon Pratt, when 75 years old, Newport, Rhode Island.

3. *Courtesy of:* MRS. D. OLIVER O'DONNELL, New York.

Needlepoint rug describing animals hunted by Mr. O'Donnell in Africa. Designed after original paintings made by artist. at Museum of Natural History; worked 1934 by Mrs. D. Oliver O'Donnell, New York.

All Rugs Designed by Aquidneck Cottage Industries, Newport, Rhode Island.

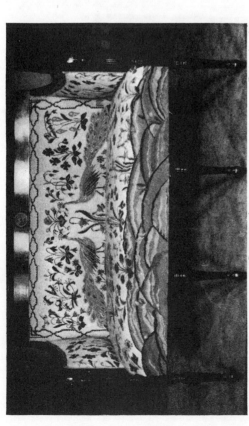

1. *Courtesy of:* MRS. WILLIAM H. MERCUR, Pennsylvania.
Needlepoint panels on settee, designed and worked by Margaret Speer Mercur, Pennsylvania.

2. *Courtesy of:* MRS. HARRIS CHILDS, New York
Settee, needlepoint coverings by Mrs. Harris Childs, New York.

4. *Courtesy of:* MRS. D. OLIVER O'DONNELL, New York.
Needlepoint card table top worked and designed by Mrs. D. Oliver O'Donnell, New York.

3. *Courtesy of:* MRS. RUFUS L. PATTERSON, New York.
"Alice in Wonderland," needlepoint covered settee for children's room with pair of pillows. Worked by Mrs. Rufus L. Patterson, New York, and designed by Aquidneck Cottage Industries.

motifs were carried out in petit point in gay colors while the rest of the table top is stitched in a quiet, deep blue. The horses and dogs are executed in simple, natural colors. It has been mounted on the top of a Queen Anne table and is used in Mrs. O'Donnell's New York apartment.

RUGS

Miss Jane Tiffany of Newport has made a nursery rug in needlepoint, measuring thirty-six by fifty-six inches. The panel is worked in one piece and shows children with their pets and toys and Mother Goose characters. The cow is jumping over the moon; Jack and Jill are going up the hill with their bucket in hand; the black sheep, made with plenty of black wool, is placed on one corner; on the opposite side is the shepherd. The boy is ringing his bell for the little black and white pussy who was in the well but who now has been rescued and is running toward him at his call. The border is gaily designed with a row of dolls worked in white like cut-out paper silhouettes, fastened hand in hand. They ring the entire rug amusingly. It was designed by the Aquidneck Cottage Industries.

Designed by the same group is the needlepoint rug executed by Mrs. Reginald Norman for her home, "Bellaire," in Newport. It is an eight-piece rug measuring eighty-eight by forty-six inches over all. The eight squares unite very successfully in the allover background design which gives an interesting setting for the different garden flowers embroidered in each square. The rug is delicately composed and finely worked by Mrs. Norman.

The same Industries have designed an Empire rug which was worked in needlepoint by Mrs. William Greenough for her new home in Newport. It was made in four sections which make one large unit or motif when combined. The patterning has been very well arranged and fits together evenly. Mrs. Greenough has worked the interesting florals in this lovely floor covering very simply and tellingly in eighteenth century colors.

Also designed by the Aquidneck Cottage Industries in one large composition is another needlepoint rug worked in six pieces which total fifty-four by thirty-nine inches. Its border is composed of florals and leaves. It was made in 1932 by Mary Gordon Pratt of Newport when she was seventy-five years old. It has been executed in gros point with taste and feeling in both technique and coloring, an heirloom which will be treasured.

A floral rug designed by Ann Hobdy on one long piece of canvas was worked in gros point by Mrs. Frank Munson of New York and Nassau. The borders show a very interesting design treatment. They have been worked in separate strips and added to the large central unit as a finish. The rug is soft in coloring and yet vital, since the colors are fairly clear in tone.

This artist also has designed a needlepoint flower rug which was made up in squares and worked in gros point on large single-meshed canvas by Mrs. George Angus Garrett of Washington, D. C. The design, contemporary in character, is a repeat motif of calla lilies which have been stitched in plain tones without shading, the outline coloring suggesting the form. A rug worked in this manner is entertaining since it can be arranged for any size by the addition of more squares, it is convenient to carry the work about and interested friends or relatives may work a square or two, thus hastening completion and giving added value to the rug.

Mrs. William H. Mercur of Pittsburgh has made a long gros point rug designed in one panel by the Misses Gebbetts of that city. It measures seven feet by four feet, four inches. This rug has one central unit composed of florals and two borders or bands containing sprays of flowers arranged in even spacing. The needlepoint has been exceedingly well done by Mrs. Mercur.

Nine separate squares compose the rug designed around American flowers by the Aquidneck Cottage Industries and worked in gros point by Mrs. John D. Rockefeller. It is used in the Rockefellers' restored house at Williamsburg, Virginia. The various lilies, tulips, morning-glories, iris and bleeding hearts have been chastely and charmingly arranged about a central square of dogwood blossoms. The dainty vine border and the colorings used for each square are pleasing and restrained while the ensemble is admirably suited for a room in the early colonial mansion of historic Williamsburg.

Mrs. Benjamin Tilton has worked a gros point rug composed of forty-eight squares in a very unique pattern which she designed from a section of a rug one hundred years old, which had been in an old church in England. It has been worked in yarns which reproduce the colors of stained glass, pigeon-blood red on the ruby tone, cerulean blue, clear yellow and bronze in the outlines. The symbolic geometric forms are highly decorative and warm in tone. The whole is almost like an Oriental rug in feeling and it is spread on top of the neutral living room carpet most effectively. Mrs. Tilton had the wools dyed to match the original colorings as nearly as possible.

Completely different in design and character from the preceding rugs is the delightful paneled rug worked in strips by Mrs. D. Oliver O'Donnell. The idea for a rug of this character developed from an impulse to record the hunting prowess of her husband upon his trip to Africa. Friends of the O'Donnells in the Museum of Natural History in New York made oil paintings of each animal in the rug. These were assembled and used for documents for the final grouping which was arranged and painted on the canvas by the Aquidneck Industries. Mrs. O'Donnell has worked each animal in its near colorings, the tiger in orange and the elephant in gray violet. The general tones of the background are pale green shades against which deeper greens in the trees and foreground foliage are shadowed. Brown African daisies provide variety, and monkeys have been worked in fine stitches in contrast to the gros point used for the rest of the rug. It measures three and a half by six feet and was worked in 1934 by Mrs. O'Donnell who has signed her initials and the date just inside the dark brown border. It is a splendid embroidery, a joy to her husband and all her friends.

SETTEES AND LOVE SEATS

Needlepoint panels for covering settees are another popular fashion in contemporary needlework. Numbers of love seats also are being upholstered in these handsome embroidered coverings.

Mrs. William H. Mercur, who is the chairman of Amateur Needlework of Today exhibitions in Pittsburgh, executes quantities of fine needlepoint. Her enthusiasm is boundless and among her accomplishments is a settee covered with needlepoint panels designed by Mrs. Robert H. Mercur. The panel at the back includes among the various flowering plants, two peacocks facing the center flower group. Their feathers extend to the ends of the settee and make a graceful line corresponding with the spread of the seat. The birds have been nicely simplified and are less ornate in rendering than earlier interpretations in embroideries of the nineteenth century. But here again we find this peacock motif emphasized as a symbol of protection. A conventionalized cord effect with two tassel ends provides a formal decorative finish for the top of this panel. The rest of the covering is designed with groups of flowering herbs and plants growing up and out from the hills of the foreground which extends to the front apron of the seat. This arrangement of mounds directs the eye to the birds which seem to walk on the ground quite properly. An effect is achieved in these panels similar to that of the fifteenth century tapestries. At the same time they are modern, particularly in the use of light backgrounds and clear, fresh color, indicating the preference in contemporary decoration for more vitality.

The settee is a fine piece of cabinetmaking of the Sheraton and Duncan Phyfe period, in the early nineteenth century American classic Empire style. Mrs. Mercur's needlepoint is effective and exceedingly appropriate for the furniture upon which it is mounted.

Mrs. Harris Childs of New York has made needlepoint coverings for a love seat in her living room designed with florals of the eighteenth century in the Queen Anne and Chippendale style. They are worked in an open pattern with interesting and graceful floral forms, birds, leaves and flowering vines. Upon the foreground hills on the seat rests a decorative bowl containing branches of flowers which reach to either end of the seat. At the base of the sides are mounds or hills from which grow sprays of flowers to match the patterning of the back of the settee. The colorings are softly clear in tone and a light cream gold is used for the background. The tulips, carnations, bells, narcissus and iris are delightfully embroidered by Mrs. Childs. She is a needlepoint devotee who has made a set of dining room chair seats and numbers of other pieces.

Mrs. Rufus L. Patterson of New York also

1. *Courtesy of:* MRS. H. BRADLEY MARTIN, New York.

Needlepoint coverings for Queen Anne chair worked by
Mrs. H. Bradley Martin, New York.

2. *Courtesy of:* MRS. WILLIAM WARNER HOPPIN, New York.

Needlepoint chair covering, design inspired by mother's
chair in "The Old Goelet Mansion" and worked in 1930
by Mrs. William Warner Hoppin, New York.

3. *Courtesy of:* MRS. GORDON K. BELL, New York.

Needlepoint chair coverings for French Eighteenth Century Bergere, designed and worked by Mrs. Gordon K.
Bell, New York.

4. *Courtesy of:* MRS. KENNETH BUDD, New York.

Needlepoint coverings for a Louis XIV Chair, designed
and worked by Mrs. Kenneth Budd, New York.

1. *Courtesy of:* MRS. CHARLES HOWE, Radnor, Pennsylvania.

Needlepoint Chair Seat, "Fable of La Fontaine"; one of a set of dining-room chairs. Worked by Mrs. Charles Howe, Radnor, Pennsylvania, and designed by Agnes C. Sims, Pennsylvania.

2. *Courtesy of:* THE COSMOPOLITAN CLUB, New York.

Needlepoint Chair Seat; one of 24 dining room chairs, made by members of the Cosmopolitan Club for their club house. Worked by Miss Agnes Miles Carpenter, New York.

3. *Courtesy of:* MRS. W. H. LEONARD EDWARDS, New York.

Needlepoint Seat for Side Chair; designed by Hiram Osborn, worked by Mrs. W. H. Leonard Edwards, New York.

4. *Courtesy of:* MRS. FRANK B. ROWELL, New York.

Needlepoint Chair Seat Design; adapted from an early American pattern; designed and worked by Mrs. Frank B. Rowell, New York.

is fired with an ambition to make fine needle-point. She has covered a small settee for a child's room with delightful Alice in Wonderland motifs. These figures, adapted from the famous Tenniel drawings, are embroidered in gay colors. The background is a colonial blue. Mrs. Patterson has worked this design on the fine, single-mesh canvas in what appears to be petit point in its smaller stitch but in reality is not as close as the petit point worked on double-mesh canvas. This single-mesh background is exceedingly fashionable today, covered with hand-painted designs matching the yarns with which the pattern is worked. The tea party on the back panel showing Alice, the Rabbit and the Mad Hatter, is excellent in its needlework rendering; likewise the matching pair of round pillows with two scenes showing Alice with the Duchess. The needlepoint design is perfectly adapted to the miniature Sheraton settee which it covers to the delight of the children who use it.

Many mothers are embroidering small bedroom chairs for children's rooms in the same fashion. Good period examples of furniture are selected for education in taste during impressionable years.

CHAIR COVERS

In the living room of Mrs. William Warner Hoppin's New York apartment, among many lovely examples of her needlepoint, is an occasional chair of the Queen Anne period. Its coverings were adapted from the design used for her mother's chair, which came from the old Goelet Mansion and is mentioned in an earlier chapter of this book. Mrs. Hoppin was inspired by its delicate traceries and herself created the lovely design based upon it. She has carried it out in shades of beige and green yarns to harmonize with the color scheme of the room. The needlepoint is fine, having been worked on medium meshed canvas. It has been initialed M. G. H. and dated 1930 on both back and seat. It is one of a group in the room which are very comfortable to use for a four-some at bridge.

Mrs. Hoppin has covered many chairs; in fact she always carries a piece of needlepoint with her, seizing every possible moment to add a stitch or two. A small tea table, shown in

one of Mrs. Hoppin's Amateur Needlework of Today exhibitions, had a petit-point panel of Alice in Wonderland framed under glass for the top, which had been made during a summer's travels. Her enthusiasm for needlework is inexhaustible, for she is eager to complete newer and better examples which her descendants in later centuries may be proud to own. Her enjoyment is contagious and numbers of her friends have become ardent supporters of the exhibitions of needlework held annually to provide funds for the benefit of the blind.

Mrs. H. Bradley Martin also enjoys needle-point and has accomplished a great amount of it. A very beautiful Queen Anne armchair is covered with finely stitched coverings designed by Mrs. Lillian Barton-Wilson in the typical florals of the Queen Anne period. The flowers are worked in fairly crisp, sparkling colors characteristic of the period, and the background has been worked by Mrs. Martin in a rich red mulberry shade of yarns providing color harmony for the coral pinks, rose blues, and yellow golds of the flowers and greens of the leaves; the tulips are particularly lovely against this background.

Mrs. Gordon Bell has made charming needle-point coverings for a French eighteenth century bergère. Her patterning has been arranged simply and has the daintiness in design associated with that period. To match the general color scheme in the drawing room of the New York house and the tone of the antique Portuguese brocade used in the decorations, Mrs. Bell has chosen soft terra cotta shades of wools which border between apricot, salmon and brick tones. The design, with very little shading, is carried out in a French or Nattier blue silhouette against this background color. The florals are gracefully arranged in a conventionalized basket very simply stitched in needlepoint. Scattered flowers are introduced in a faint resemblance to brocade effects, although not exactly copying that style of design. The entire composition is very handsome and highly appropriate to its setting.

Mrs. Charles Howe of Radnor, Pennsylvania, has executed in needlepoint a series of coverings for a set of lyre back Duncan Phyfe dining room chairs. Each canvas has in the center a different fable from La Fontaine. The borders are the same. They were hand painted and designed by Miss Agnes C. Sims. On one of them, within a circular panel, the fable of the wolf and the lamb has been illustrated in fine needlepoint. The little landscape and the animals have been delicately rendered by Mrs. Howe. A classic arrangement of laurel leaves, lyres and birds surrounds the center lunette. A ribbon scroll at the front of the chair seat bears the title of the fable in French script worked in needlepoint. The background colors are a pale green blue and the rest of the pattern colors are typical of those used in the period of Napoleon in France and the days of the classic revival in America.

Mrs. Francis McKnight of California has covered several large chairs with needlepoint upholstery of her own making. The one illustrated shows a large allover design of birds, with the Chinese pheasants and large flower motifs used in the fabrics of the Chippendale period. While the needlepoint itself is in the tradition of the period chairs and furnishings, the pattern has been adapted with broad technique and colorings suited to modern taste. Contemporary needlepoint designers control these opposites with that refined sense of balance and proportion which is necessary for meeting the requirements of decorators in their styling of present-day interiors.

Mrs. MacKnight is an exceptionally capable needleworker who is most enthusiastic about embroidery and encourages the development of this art in California, where she is the chairman of the Amateur Needlework of Today exhibitions originating under Mrs. Hoppin's leadership.

To make needlepoint upholstery coverings for large overstuffed chairs such as Mrs. MacKnight has made, a careful layout in muslin of the areas to be worked is usually made first and the pattern designed on the canvas accordingly. This is done by professional upholsterers and needlepoint experts when the chair is as intricate in design and as important as the one reproduced. Some embroiderers can make their own patterns but experience is necessary to insure satisfactory results in the finished work.

Mrs. Matthew Fleming of New York is another talented needleworker who has not only covered numerous chairs with fascinating needlepoint but also has embroidered cushions, benches, and many personal accessories in petit

point. Whenever Mrs. Fleming travels with her husband on long business trips, which he makes frequently, she takes a piece of needlepoint with her and thus the tedium of many hours on trains is diminished.

One of her largest works has been the complete coverage in needlepoint of a large eighteenth century wing chair for her living room. The Jacobean type of design usually styled for crewel embroidery has been delightfully adapted upon the fine imported French canvas by Ann Hobdy, who has combined her period design, using Jacobean styled flowers with a classic Greek fret motif placed around the cushion borders. A floral scroll and a vine ornament the band upon the lower front of the seat. The rich colorings against a background of linen shade have been simply worked with excellent feeling and technique by Mrs. Fleming. It is a highly effective piece of furniture and illustrates the careful professional layout and planning essential to the accomplishment of proper coverage on chairs of this type.

The Fleming coat of arms with the inscription "Pax Copia" has been used for needlepoint chair seats in the dining room of Mrs. Fleming's New York apartment. They have been worked on medium fine canvas of single mesh with a gray-green background. The crest makes a very interesting and stalwart pattern. The design is softened by the surrounding floral sprays of roses, carnations and thistles which ornament the rest of the panel. The colorings are deeply soft and make luxurious coverings which are appropriate in the richly toned wood paneled dining room.

A needlepoint chair seat worked by Mrs. Henry J. Fisher of Greenwich, Connecticut, is designed more in the American manner with grapes, the leaves and vines of which form a very graceful and simple pattern. The colorings have been chosen to harmonize with the room, the blue yarn background matching the walls and the rest of the colors picking up drapery notes. It is a refined and lovely example worked with skill and excellent taste for its setting.

Mrs. P. R. Mallory of Indianapolis, Indiana, has worked a set of twelve dining room chair seats which are delightfully unusual and original in design. Animals are placed among herbals and florals suggestive of the early Elizabethan embroideries in character and yet actu-

1. *Courtesy of:* MRS. REGINALD DE KOVEN, New York.

Needlepoint chair seat and back designed and worked by Mrs. Reginald de Koven, New York.

2. *Courtesy of:* MRS. FRANCIS MCKNIGHT, California.

Needlepoint arm chair covering worked by Mrs. Francis McKnight, California.

3. *Courtesy of:* MRS. MATTHEW FLEMING, New York.

Needlepoint covered wing chair, contemporary, worked by Mrs. Matthew Fleming, New York, and designed by Ann F. Hobdy.

4. *Courtesy of:* MRS. HARRIS CHILDS, New York.

Needlepoint for dining-room arm chair, set of six seats worked and designed by Mrs. Harris Childs, New York.

1. *Courtesy of:* THE COSMOPOLITAN CLUB, New York.

2. *Courtesy of:* MRS. THEODORE ROOSEVELT, JR., New York.

1. Pegasus, Seal of the Cosmopolitan Club; worked in needlepoint by Mrs. Robert Coleman Taylor, 1932, New York.

2. The Seal of Porto Rico; needlepoint detail of wall panel by Mrs. Theodore Roosevelt, Jr.

3. Needlepoint Chair Seat; worked by Mrs. Henry J. Fisher, Greenwich, Connecticut.

4. Needlepoint Chair Seat; one of a set of twelve made by Mrs. P. R. Mallory, Indianapolis, Indiana.

5. The Fleming Family Crest Needlepoint Chair Seat; one of dining room set by Mrs. Matthew Fleming, New York.

3. *Courtesy of:* MRS. HENRY J. FISHER, Greenwich, Connecticut.

4. *Courtesy of:* MRS. P. R. MALLORY, Indianapolis, Indiana.

5. *Courtesy of:* MRS. MATTHEW FLEMING, New York.

ally they were adapted from other and different sources. For example cactus plants are included in the decoration with thistles and drooping lily bells. An isolated small bird walks harmlessly along holding a small flower in its bill, a peace offering, perhaps, to the spotted lion rampant beneath it. There is a quality of fantasy in the design which is amusing and refreshing and Mrs. Mallory has executed her work with evident interest and skill.

Mrs. Kenneth Budd is a very accomplished needleworker. Her canvas embroideries, made before the use of silk regained its popularity, have been previously described. Her home in New York is filled with needlepoint wall pictures, table tops, small screens, stools, cushions and many chair covers of her making. A particularly handsome set of needlepoint coverings has a design adapted by Mrs. Budd from old brocades to suit the Louis XVI chair which they adorn. A lovely eighteenth century chair used in the drawing room has been chosen for illustration because of the particular appropriateness of the design and the charming composition, which is beautifully executed in fine needlepoint. Entwined ribbons, rosebuds, small roses and star flowers form the outside patterning of the chair seat and back. At the top center of the chair back is a ribbon bow and suspended from its ends is an oval plaque containing a cluster of roses and buds which is repeated on the seat. Small laurel wreaths encircle this motif, creating a dainty eighteenth century effect. These coverings are delicate and rich in design without being ornate like so many of the chairs of this period. The soft rose, beige, golden-yellow and cream notes are atmospheric and lovely. The small nail-heads are quite correct and smart for binding in the needlepoint decoration.

Mrs. Frank B. Rowell of New York, another indefatigable embroiderer, has adapted an Early American needlepoint pattern for a chair seat. The original is an antique cross-stitch chair seat covering owned by her sister, Mrs. Frank B. Kellogg. Mrs. Rowell counted out the stitches from the old design in transferring it to her canvas. The color scheme of the allover repeat is shades of mulberry tones, then shades of gold and deep turquoise blue violet. This charming design has been appropriately mounted upon a lovely Sheraton chair.

Another lovely set of chair coverings worked by Mrs. Rowell is executed in florals arranged in fairly large units in an allover effect. The colorings are yellows, golds, soft greens, coral rose shades and peach pinks against a colonial robin's egg blue background, selected in color tone to match the wall paint used in an eighteenth century room in the American Wing of the Metropolitan Museum of Art. These beautiful coverings combine well with the fine eighteenth century American chairs on which they are used.

Mrs. W. H. Leonard Edwards of New York has made a needlepoint chair covering for the slip seat of an antique American side chair which came from her family and belonged originally in the Governor Willis mansion in Hartford, Connecticut. The flowers arranged in the tole bowl are garden flowers in delicate shades. The background is a colonial blue. The design, adapted to suit eighteenth century American furniture, was painted by Hiram Osborn and ably worked by Mrs. Edwards.

The covering for an armchair seat worked by Mrs. Harris Childs of New York is one of a set of six needlepoint covers for dining room chairs. The interesting original patterns were composed for Mrs. Childs by Dorothy Harding, well known for her book plate designs. Each seat shows animals, flowers and tree arrangements somewhat related in theme and character to early Persian manuscript paintings. The cover for the armchair shown in the illustration depicts mountain deer grazing in a peaceful decorative paradise. The side chair covers show lions and tigers disporting themselves among luscious tropical florals and trees, or little monkeys having a glorious time chasing a butterfly which is almost as big as themselves. Graceful trees and little flowering plants add color and decorative pattern to the seats, which have been worked by Mrs. Childs in soft glowing colors against a light gold background in very fine needlepoint technique. The covers are very effective mounted upon shield back Sheraton chairs.

A very large Jacobean chair of the seventeenth century is one of a pair covered with needlepoint by Mrs. Reginald DeKoven. The cover in the illustration was adapted from an antique piece of needlepoint of the eighteenth century which Mrs. DeKoven admired so much that she painstakingly enlarged details of the design by counting out the color spaces of the original. This cover, which graces the long music hall in the New York house, has a Chinese Chippendale quality. A symbolic figure of a woman dressed in fantastic costume and wearing a Chinese hat kneels on a cloud, holding a bird cage. Placed on the opposite side of a quaint decorative tree is the figure of a hunter with his hawk. Pheasants, flowers, leaves and Chinese scroll motifs compose the rest of the decoration which Mrs. DeKoven has worked in both petit point and gros point. The colorings are rose vermillion, blue green, gray green, and yellow green arranged against a background of greenish brown.

Designed in ultramodern character are the needlepoint coverings used for the twenty-four chairs in the private members' dining room of the Cosmopolitan Club of New York. Miss Agnes Miles Carpenter is one of the twenty-four members who worked a chair seat for this room. The same design was hand painted on each canvas and yarns in the same colors were provided for each. The shades in the needlepoint match the general color scheme of the room which is entirely modernistic in decoration. The chairs are ivory color. The background of the seat covers is a shade of intense peach pink in deeper tone than the flesh-pink walls of the room. The abstract motif of the design is worked in pearl grays and blue gray with the tendrils in deep blue-gray lines almost a deep green metal color. Miss Carpenter added a touch of individuality by working in her initials A.M.C. with tendrils from them to match the motif on the chair. The needlepoint, worked on single-mesh canvas which is fairly fine, is quite handsome and a most interesting accomplishment.

1. *Courtesy of:* MRS. BREWSTER JENNINGS, New York.

5. PRIVATELY OWNED.

2. *Courtesy of:* MRS.
FRANCIS D. POT-
TER, New York.

3. *Courtesy of:* MRS. SAMUEL SEABURY,
New York.
4. *Courtesy of:* MRS. WILLIAM R.
NORTHROP.

1. Needlepoint strip, "Lilies" worked for over valance above windows, by Mrs. Brewster Jennings, New York.   2. Detailed section of fine needlepoint bell pull, garden, flowers, animals and birds by Mrs. Francis D. Potter, New York.   3. Needlepoint bell pull, flowers, "Old English Rings," by Mrs. Samuel Seabury, New York.   4. Needlepoint bell pull by Mrs. William B. Northrop.   5. Needlepoint bell pull, "Humming Bird," detail Georgiana Brown Haberson, New York, 1937.

Needlepoint pillow top "Young George Washington," worked and designed, 1938, by Georgiana Brown Harbeson, New York.

Needlepoint pillow top "Little Betsey Ross," designed and worked, 1938, by Georgiana Brown Harbeson, New York.

3. *Courtesy of:* MRS. JOHN BLAKELEY, Pennsylvania.

Needlepoint pillow top, Persian animal design by Agnes C. Sims, worked by Mrs. John Blakeley, Elkins Park, Pennsylvania.

4. *Courtesy of:* MRS. SAMUEL SLOAN, New York.

Needlepoint pillow worked, with silk floss on linen canvas, by Mrs. Samuel Sloan, New York.

5. *Courtesy of:* MRS. ABIGAIL VON SCHLEGELL, California.

Pillow in petit point; with native flowers, animals and birds. Designed and worked by Mrs. Abigail von Schlegell, California.

6. *Courtesy of:* MRS. EDWARD LAW, Haverford, Pennsylvania.

Needlepoint pillow top, "First Troop Philadelphia City Cavalry," worked by Mrs. Edward Law, Haverford, Pennsylvania, and designed by Agnes C. Sims.

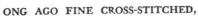

CHAPTER XXXII

CONTEMPORARY NEEDLEPOINT (CONTINUED)
MISCELLANEOUS FURNISHINGS, ACCESSORIES,
PETIT-POINT PICTURES

"Lives of great men all remind us
We can make our lives sublime,
And departing leave behind us,
Footprints on the sands of time."
HENRY WADSWORTH LONGFELLOW.

ONG AGO FINE CROSS-STITCHED, crewel-embroidered and needlepointed strips hung upon the walls. They served the purpose of handles and were attached to wires which, when pulled, called the servants to the living room, bedroom or other sections of the big mansion. Today they are hung upon walls purely as decorative reminders of an elegant past. Large numbers of these bell pulls are being worked in needlepoint.

Mrs. Samuel Seabury of New York has made a lovely pull which hangs in the combined music room and studio of Judge Seabury, built in the rear of their New York house. Mrs. Seabury is a garden enthusiast and has composed the design of her bell pull from old English rings. The background is executed in a deep brick red and the flowers are interpreted in light creams, greens and other light tones. The stitches are gros point and the pattern harmonizes very charmingly with the antique furniture used in the large room.

Mrs. Francis Potter of Rye, New York, has made a very long pull, designing it herself with numbers of little birds, animals and clusters of flowers. It is worked in petit point with colors that are delicate without being weak, backed with a lovely shade of clear gold yarn. It is a lovely decorative accomplishment.

Mrs. William B. Northrop of New York has made an equally lovely pull. The tiny lunettes, which show landscapes and ancient castles, are worked in petit point while for the florals and scroll motifs Mrs. Northrop uses gros point in soft colorings. The background is light cream.

The author has designed a bell pull which combines humming birds and trumpet vines and flowers. The ribbon leaf band entwined with the vines is worked in three shades of jade green and blue green with a deep spruce-green center vein. The leaves are in grass and sunlight yellow greens; the flowers in shades of cream, coral and vermillion red. The humming birds repeat these shades and add yellow to their feathered heads. The background is a pale cream or deep ivory shade. The border lines in needlepoint repeat the greens of the leaves. It was worked on fine single-mesh canvas.

Mrs. Brewster Jennings created a large needlepoint over-valance panel which covers the top of three large windows in her Long Island home. She chose large lilies suggested by those in her garden and has worked them in very large stitches on coarse canvas. The colorings are fairly strong and decidedly interesting in

209

the whites and violet-blue shadings on the lilies and the grass greens of the leaves. The background is a rich bright gold floss worked in needlepoint stitches. The side window draperies match the gold of this background in silk and the grass green of the embroidery is picked up in a matching green silk which binds the ensemble. This is a new and interesting use of needlepoint.

PILLOWS

In California some attractive needlepoint is being carried out in very fine "little stitches," or, as the French term it, petit point embroidery. Mrs. Abigail von Schlegell of Pasadena derives her inspiration for a pillow from American flowers, notably the tulip, wild rose, jonquils, violets, primrose and other favorites. Ferns are introduced as an innovation for the central motif. Squirrels, rabbits, snails, butterflies and native birds are scattered among the flowers much in the manner of the famous Arras tapestries of the fourteenth and fifteenth centuries. To further carry out the spirit of these magnificent hangings, Mrs. von Schlegell has used the Gobelin-blue wools for a background, a color frequently used in the tapestry originals made by these famous French weavers after whom the shade is named. The American design is simplified considerably over the tapestries referred to. There is a pleasant rhythm in the patterning of the grasses which meet or cross at the tip ends, thus tying in the composition. Mrs. von Schlegell has bound this pillow with heavy silk fringe, the usual fashion for binding needlepoint covers. Her own description of her work is interesting:

> The pillow is worked in Gobelin-blue background, flowers, birds and insects all in soft natural colors. The flowers are mostly in tones of rust, apricot, yellow and old ivory, some dull old blue. The leaves covering the background are in greens and bluish greens, which tone into the Gobelin-blue. They are strong enough not to be lost but neutral enough not to detract from the main figures. Again, my garden was the source of inspiration.
>
> It is an original design and not particularly "after" any period or school for two reasons. First, I do not know enough to design to period and second, I feel that if one is going to work out their own design, it's interesting to make it individually. Of course, this wouldn't be true if one were working for a period room. I've tried to make my design natural and simple, to balance design and colors so the effect would be pleasing, but in such a way that it would not force itself on your attention. All colors are naturally soft, not "antiqued" in any way; time will learn to take care of that.

Mrs. Charles Platt of Chestnut Hill, Pennsylvania, has designed and made beautiful needlepoint for many years. She has a great fondness for reproducing gardens and flowers, as well as other subjects. To decorate a pillow Mrs. Platt has chosen the night-blooming cereus. Explaining her color treatment and method, Mrs. Platt says:

> Naturally I do the diagonal stitch (tent stitch worked on the bias), but in this case, I had to do it the other way, as I started at the top with a light greeny blue and worked it down getting darker as I went till the bottom part was really deep. I wanted it to look like "night" and it really does. The flower is done in shades of white, both silk and wool. The anthers, pale yellow silk, and the leaf, bud, etc. in shaded gray silk. The background is wool.

In her own words, Mrs. Platt has explained her search to convey the atmosphere in which the flower is seen besides making a needlepoint rendering of the flower itself. This is a direct example of the modern approach to needlework. The Latin name of the plant has been written in needlepoint across the top of the pillow to balance in composition the straight line of the leaves at the base. The pillow has been bound with heavy closely-clipped silk fringe. It is a very recent and interesting work.

Mrs. Charles J. Rhoads of Bryn Mawr has made a needlepoint pillow, oblong in shape, which shows Chinese design influence in the composition painted on the coarse canvas by Miss Agnes Sims. Flowers in sprays rise from a Chinese bowl. They are simply arranged and worked in shades of Gothic red, yellow and brown. The vase at the right is Chinese blue. The entire theme is selectively decorative in the plain masses of color used to convey form. There is little of the shading so characteristic of the mid-Victorian techniques in Berlin woolwork.

Mrs. John Blakeley of Elkins Park, Pennsylvania, has made several pillows of intricate patterning. One, a Persian animal design, is covered with delicate stitch traceries of animals, trees, birds and leafy vines, all made in one shade of light yarn against a contrasting deep toned background. The use of two colors is very attractive. There is a complete omission of shading. Miss Agnes C. Sims designed this pillow in the modern manner, eliminating non-essentials by keeping the color simple and the masses elemental. The suggestion for the design came from the borders on old Persian manuscripts.

Mrs. Edward Law of Haverford, Pennsylvania, dedicates her needlepoint pillow top to the First Troop, Philadelphia City Cavalry. This title is stitched upon a scroll. In the oval above, the city trooper is shown in his strikingly handsome uniform charging ahead upon his horse, sword in hand, from the direction of Princeton, the name of which is stitched in the upper right-hand corner. In the left-hand corner is marked the name Trenton. The pillow records the date, November 17, 1774, when the troop was organized by the citizens of Schuylkill, Pennsylvania.

Designed in the Early American spirit, is a small box-pillow cover of "Little Betsy Ross," who stands upon a flowering branch dressed in her colonial costume and holding her pet bird upon her hand. This pillow cover was designed and worked by the author for a child's room. The colorings are, as may be expected, gay red for the background, white and blues for the stars and borders, with pale rose, pale peach, some tender green with touches of green blue, and brown to offset the stronger shades.

Pairing with this small boxed pillow is young "George Washington," who stands upon the cherry branch he has just chopped from the forbidden tree and is prepared to tell the truth and admit the error to his chiding parent.

For a needlepoint pillow, Mrs. Samuel Sloan of New York has adapted a design from a piece of French brocade. She has developed it in shades of henna red shading out to Indian pinks and peach tones in silk floss. Deep gold shading to pale gold in the smaller flowers is accented with deep brown centers. The stems and roots are in walnut browns and greens. The morning-glories are in French blues shaded from deep to pale blue colors surrounded with jade-green leaves, high lighted with touches of pale yellow green. This entire flower spray is offset with a soft fawn-tan background which has been finely worked on single-mesh canvas giving the entire piece the effect of petit point. Mrs. Sloan has embroidered a pair of these cushions for her home. While the adaptation has been made from a brocade, the design is delicately simplified and restrained so as not to give an over-elaborate effect in the room in which they are placed, a treatment typical of twentieth century needlework.

Mrs. Matthew Fleming of New York has worked many decorative pillows in needlepoint. A pair in her drawing room match each other in style, size and color, but the designs vary in arrangement. Both are squares of average size which are worked with large sprays of flowers. On one pillow the stems are clustered together at the base and tied with a small ribbon. On the other is an allover pattern of flowers scarcely discernible in the general effect, spread out much in the style of early Queen Anne needlepoint designs. They are original, however, having been designed by Ann Hobdy with her touch of modernism. The colorings are blue green on the leaves and on the flowers rose red blending into pink, henna reds with touches of lilac and violet and violet blues in the bluebells. The background is colonial yellow.

On the sofa between the large square pillows is a smaller one charmingly designed and worked by Mrs. Russell Wilson of Cincinnati, Ohio, who made it as a gift for Mrs. Fleming. A fox, a deer and a rabbit keep each other company on a green hill beneath a small decorative tree which bears little green and brown leaves. The cream background provides a delicate setting for the design and the pillow is artistically bound with green silk to match the shade of yarn used in the needlepoint. It is a gay little woodsy bit, and tucks itself amusingly among the florals of the neighboring cushions.

An Empire design with a classic vase worked in gold shades of yarn against a light off-white background provides a study in subtle color contrasts in the pillow made by Mrs. Robert Coleman Taylor for the Cosmopolitan Club of New York. She has surrounded this central motif with laurel leaves in pale green and berries in henna. The pillow, which is worked in fine needlepoint, was designed by Mrs. Taylor to match its setting and is interesting in style as well as technique.

Miss Mary Maguire of New York has designed

a pillow which is square in shape. She used florals in a single large spray or branch, much in the Jacobean spirit but employing familiar native flowers. It is tastefully arranged and finely worked. A needlepoint border on the edge of the pillow eliminates the necessity for a finish in fringe or braid.

Easter lilies decorate the top of a round pillow worked in petit point by Mrs. Benjamin Tilton of New York. The background is a beautiful clear canary yellow. The various shades of off-white which compose the lilies and the tender green used in the leaves are very beautiful placed against this glowing shade. This pillow has been finished with a silk fringe binding in a narrow uncut style. It is placed in a large upholstered chair in Mrs. Tilton's living room where it provides a lovely sunshiny note.

MIRROR FRAME

Mrs. Abigail von Schlegell of Pasadena, California, designs her own beautiful needlepoint and among her many embroideries is a mirror frame worked by her in petit point. The background is an old blue shade of wool. Garden and wild flowers are scattered around the frame in an allover patterning effect. These are alternated with butterflies, snails, dragon flies, and a busy bee. In the lower right-hand corner of the foreground a peacock stands with feathers proudly spread representing either vanity or good luck, the latter interpretation being that of the Pennsylvania Dutch who used this symbol in their needlework. The motifs are worked in excellent technique by Mrs. von Schlegell who obviously enjoys every stitch taken in her canvases.

BOOK COVERS

Also from California is an ultramodern design by Mrs. Francis H. McKnight. Among many examples which she has embroidered with evident pleasure is a telephone book cover adapted and executed in petit point. It is a very amusing work. Mrs. McKnight has stitched in needlepoint around the border of the book that it is "After Picasso, A Young Girl at the Mirror." It is initialed D.H.McK. 1938.

A petit-point book cover with a modern design of conventionalized flowers has been cleverly worked by Mrs. Kennard Winsor of

Massachusetts. These flowers are simply shaded and depend upon line arrangement in the composition for their very decorative effect. Plain rows of needlepoint establish the border outlines and the bands across the back simulate a binding. This and the small box covering finely worked in needlepoint by Mrs. Frederick S. Moseley, also of Massachusetts, were nicely designed by the Woman's Educational and Industrial Union of Boston. The box shows dainty scrolls ornamenting the top panel and enclosing an oval in which the owner's initials are centered in needlepoint stitches. Each is a lovely and distinctive accessory.

BAGS

Designed in the Chinese manner is a workbag painted by Agnes Sims from motifs on a Chinese lacquer screen. A bird among magnolia blossoms is the charming theme which has been worked against a Chinese yellow background with feeling and artistry by Miss Sims' mother, the late Mrs. Lancelot F. Sims.

An interesting design for a workbag employs the motif of a Russian sleigh. This design also is by Miss Sims and was worked in bright colors of red and yellows "that almost swear," by Mrs. Joseph B. Hutchinson of Pennsylvania. A Russian landscape is suggested by the mosque in the pattern, the entire scheme of which suggests the stage settings for the Chauve Souris fantasy. It is amusingly gay in character.

Having visited Alaska in 1933 with her mother, Mrs. Alfred Roelker of New York, Hildegard Roelker Slocum revived her impressions of these travels after her marriage by designing and working a needlepoint bag for her mother. An Alaskan thunderbird has been reproduced in the colorings and spirit of the paintings on the totem poles of the Alaskan Indians. The colors are reds, yellow, black, and creams against a green-blue background. This is an original and interesting example of contemporary needlepoint.

PURSES

The chinoiserie purse made by Mrs. Harold Randolph of Baltimore shows a gay little fisherman worked in two China blues on his blouse, two magenta pinks on his trousers and Chinese

1. *Courtesy of:* MISS MARY MAGUIRE, New York.

Needlepoint pillow top, original design, worked by Miss Mary Maguire, New York.

2. *Courtesy of:* MRS. CHARLES PLATT, Pennsylvania.

Needlepoint pillow top, "The Night Blooming Cereus," made by Miss Dorothy Falcon Platt, Pennsylvania.

3. *Courtesy of:* MRS. BENJAMIN TILTON, New York.

Needlepoint cushion top, "Easter Lilies" by Mrs. Benjamin Tilton, New York.

4. *Courtesy of:* MRS. MATTHEW C. FLEMING, New York.

Needlepoint pillow top designed by Ann F. Hobdy, New York, and worked by Mrs. Matthew C. Fleming, New York.

5. *Courtesy of* MRS. ROBERT COLEMAN TAYLOR.

Needlepoint pillow top for Cosmopolitan Club in New York. "Classic" design by Mrs. Robert Coleman Taylor, New York.

6. *Courtesy of:* MRS. CHARLES RHOADS, Bryn Mawr, Pennsylvania.

Needlepoint pillow top, Chinese design by Agnes C. Sims, worked by Mrs. Charles Rhoads, Bryn Mawr, Pennsylvania.

1. *Courtesy of:* MRS. JOSEPH B. HUTCHINSON, Pennsylvania.

"Russian Sleigh," needlepoint work bag made by Mrs. Joseph B. Hutchinson, Pennsylvania, and designed by Agnes C. Sims.

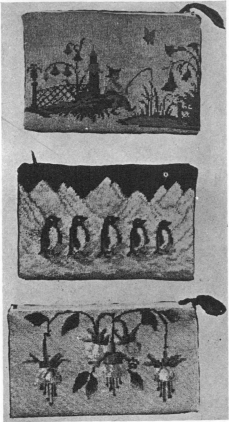

6. *Courtesy of:* MISS AGNES C. SIMS, Pennsylvania.

Needlepoint work bag, Chinese Bird design, by the late Mrs. Lancelot F. Sims, Pennsylvania.

2. *By* MRS. FRANCIS E. PEGRAM, Maryland.
Needlepoint zipper purse, "Equipoise," portrait, 1934.

3. *By* MRS. HAROLD RANDOLPH, Maryland.
Needlepoint zipper purse, "Chinese Fisherman."

4. *By* MRS. FRANCIS E. PEGRAM, Maryland.
Needlepoint purse, "Penguins."

5. *By* MRS. EUGENE LEGERING, JR., Maryland.
Needlepoint purse, "Fuchsias."

7. *Courtesy of:* MRS. ALFRED ROELKER, New York.

Needlepoint purse, "Alaskan Thunderbird" by Hildegard Roelker Slocum.

8. *Courtesy of:* MRS. LAWRENCE JACOBS, New York.

Petit point purse, "Chinese Scene."

coral for his hat and the little slippers on his swinging feet. These shades are repeated in the flower bells which rise out of varicolored green mounds. The left bank carries a golden fence and a decorative temple tower rising from a sage and pale green foundation. The opposite side shows nine brilliant colors in the florals and grasses. Deeper green-blue and emerald shades shadow the little pool of deeper China blue. The only note of purple appears in the orchid wing of the happy butterfly which surveys this peaceful scene from above. The entire background is worked in eggshell wools. Another little scene graces the opposite side of the purse which is made in eggshell taffeta with a little draw tab on the upper end made in coral taffeta to match the color of the Chinaman's hat.

Mrs. Frances E. Pegram, also of Baltimore, has enjoyed making "Five Little Penguins." They are marching along as if in search of food and are stitched in their characteristic dress suits in shades of black, off-white and pearl gray with the addition of pale cream and oyster gray. The icy background coloring is carried out in the same shades which are used on the little birds. The sky is worked in black which is a good background for the top of a bag since it will not soil quickly. The reverse side of the bag is also plain black with a narrow foreground on the bottom which repeats the ice shades. It is a smart and amusing accessory to use with many costumes.

Fuchsias grace a third purse, which was worked in shades of mulberry violet, deep and pale fuchsia shades, yellow green and a background of sand-pink threads by Mrs. Eugene Levering, Jr., also of Baltimore. It differs from the others in having its background worked in silk floss, an effective contrast to the wool of the flowers. It is lined and zipper-tabbed with taffeta in a deep fuchsia wine shade which is almost a deep magenta and which picks up the tones used on the needlework decoration outside.

Being fond of horses, Mrs. Pegram drew her own design on another purse which shows Equipoise, the famous racing horse who holds the world's record for the mile. The design is carried out in silhouette fashion, the horse being stitched entirely in black against a background filled in with silk floss in a pale pink beige. On the reverse side of the purse appears another well-known horse, Black Beauty, worked in the same manner.

All four purses have been worked on the single-mesh imported French canvas of medium fine weave, and in divisible needlepoint yarn of three threads or ply. All are amusingly original in design and are embroidered in excellent technique. The needlework ability displayed by the three sisters came, no doubt, directly from their mother, Mrs. W. L. Gary, who won prizes for her embroidery in the nineteenth century in Baltimore as previously described.

A small zipper purse, almost square in shape, was designed and made by Mrs. Frank Rowell of New York. A combination of needlepoint and cross stitch was employed for the embroidery. Mrs. Rowell owns a beautiful antique Spanish sampler from which she counted off some of the motifs used on the purse. These were worked in cross-stitch and the background of fine single-mesh canvas was filled in with needlepoint. Mrs. Rowell has made another purse, a little wider in shape, in Bargello stitches worked in a diagonal pattern with silk flosses. This design was adapted from an ancient Italian fabric in her possession. The colorings are very pale henna, creams, beige and gold. It is very beautifully worked in silk floss on canvas.

Mrs. Lawrence Jacob of New York has executed a handsome Chinese scene upon her purse with fine needlepoint. The little boats and figures are worked in Chinese blue and the background in a golden cream. It is a beautiful composition in color harmony.

Another Chinese scenic design was composed by Miss Agnes C. Sims to be worked by Mrs. Joseph B. Hutchinson of Bryn Mawr. Her fine needlepoint has ably interpreted the boats, temples and conventionalized waves.

MULES

The dainty petit-point slippers or mules made and worn by twentieth century ladies provide entertaining designs for posterity to enjoy. Their fine yet substantial woolen stitches are strong enough to last for many years to come.

Mrs. Matthew Fleming of New York has embroidered a lovely pair, designed by Alice Muir Baldwin of Boston, in a charming tiny chinoiserie pattern. On one of them a little fisherman sits upon the end of a miniature dock, probably philosophizing more than fishing, surrounded by dainty flowers which edge the toe of the slipper. A little pagoda is stitched on the opposite side and the make-believe temple bells must be ringing loudly to send the flock of small birds soaring into the pale, peach-pink sky near the top of the slipper. The mate has a different Chinese scene. A little mandarin sits meditatively in a miniature garden in which a tiny tea house rises from among the flowers and willow trees. The colorings are turquoise blue for the Chinese figures, gold and brown in the landscape and trees, with slightly shaded blue greens and jade greens in the foliage. Flowers in Chinese lacquer red are accented with touches of chartreuse which gives a sparkling note against the pale, peachy-pink background. The slippers are edged with a little strip of gold kid and lined with pink kid to match the wool.

Mrs. Frank B. Rowell of New York has a dainty pair of petit-point mules which are worked with silk floss and lined with satin. They were designed for her by the Aquidneck Cottage Industries of Newport. The needlework was begun by a friend, Mrs. Sinkler of Philadelphia, and later completed by Mrs. Rowell who made her own interpretation of the leaf pattern.

This readaptation of design often occurs in contemporary needlework. It is one of the chief delights in needlepoint that one does not need to follow the set arrangement of the painted canvas literally. Personal ideas have an opportunity to assert themselves in color preferences and alteration of the pattern while allowing enough of the original design to remain so that the main theme is not entirely lost.

PETIT-POINT PICTURES

Intimate and personal things such as pets, flowers and other interests are portrayed today in needlepoint pictures and samplers with as deep feeling and sentiment as that registered in preceding centuries by our grandmothers.

"Sir Galahad's Tuesday Dream" is just such a work of love, portraying in petit point the devotion of a little Scottie dog belonging to Mrs. Robert Coleman Taylor. "Galahad's" portrait was stitched with his own black hair couched onto the canvas to give him a natural Scottie look. He is pictured in a doggy heaven where he may frolic with inquisitive white rabbits in the wide pastures, free to run, bark and play to his heart's content. Sitting in the branches overhead are two Baltimore orioles which are, in "Galahad's" dream, Mr. and Mrs. Taylor watching over him.

He also has been portrayed, again in needlepoint, in a "Monday Dream" in which he is prancing along to play with little lambs which he may pursue in Scottie fashion over the hills. The orioles are again present in the tree, the bird on the top branch representing Mrs. Taylor busily noting where "Galahad" goes in his dreams.

It seems that they were called "Monday" and "Tuesday Dreams" because they were started on these days of the week. The idea for their composition came when little Sir Galahad was napping beside his mistress's chair. As she watched him twitch and start, sometimes making little gruff noises and half barks, she imagined him having the jolly times she has depicted. Now that "Galahad" has really found his happy hunting ground and is gone, his lonely mistress is happy to have these reminders of her loved pet.

Mrs. Taylor also has embroidered a small picture in petit point which shows the rotunda of the University of Virginia as seen from the lawn. It was made as a gift for her husband who attended that college, and is mounted in a round, antique gold frame.

Mrs. Benjamin Tilton's interpretation of "Nana's Night Out" is a petit-point picture which was stitched to amuse her little grandchildren, Helen, Archie, and Susan Alexander, when their nurse was off duty. To their intense delight she has depicted little dream girls and a boy dancing with all the small animals dear to children's hearts, bunnies, gazelles and a little white lamb, frisking as joyously as the rest. The woodsy pine needles spray out from their branches like bursting stars and a crescent moon adds a glow to the scene. This bit of fantasy is embroidered in eerie shades of blue, pearl whites and misty greens which suggest enchantment. It is entitled "For Helen, 1936. From Grandmother." Mrs. Tilton developed the theme from a newsprint reproduction of a drawing made by Dorothy Lathrop.

Equally magical in atmosphere is a petit-

1. *Courtesy of:* MRS. KENNARD WINSOR, Massachusetts.

Needlepoint book cover, modern design, worked by Mrs. Kennard Winsor, Massachusetts.

Courtesy of: MRS. FREDERICK S. MOSELEY, Massachusetts.

Needlepoint box worked by Mrs. Frederick S. Moseley, Massachusetts and designed by Women's Educational and Industrial Union, Boston.

2. *Courtesy of:* MRS. ABIGAIL VON SCHLEGELL, California.

Petit point frame for mirror, worked by Mrs. Abigail von Schlegell, California. Designed from native flowers.

3. *Courtesy of:* MRS. FRANCIS H. MCKNIGHT, California.

Needlepoint telephone book cover designed after a painting by Picasso and worked in petit point in 1938 by Mrs. Francis H. McKnight, California.

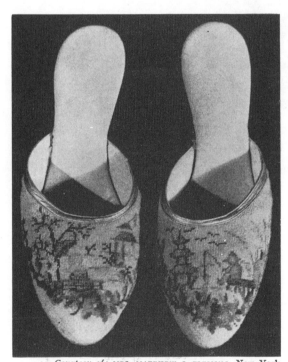

4. *Courtesy of:* MRS. MATTHEW C. FLEMING, New York.

Petit point pair of mules worked by Mrs. Matthew C. Fleming, New York, and designed by Alice Muir Baldwin.

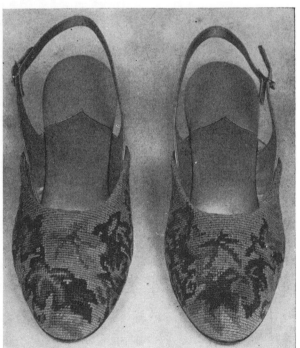

5. *Courtesy of:* MRS. FRANK B. ROWELL, New York.

Pair of mules worked by Mrs. Frank B. Rowell, New York.

1. *Courtesy of:* MRS. ROBERT COLEMAN TAYLOR, New York.

"Galahad's Tuesday Dream," Petit point picture describing the dream of the pet Scotty. The dog has been stitched in with its own hair. Designed and worked by its owner, Mrs. Robert Coleman Taylor, New York.

2. *Courtesy of:* MRS. ROBERT COLEMAN TAYLOR, New York.

Petit point picture of The Rotunda, University of Virginia, view from the lawn, designed and worked by Mrs. Robert Coleman Taylor, 1934, New York.

3. *Courtesy of:* MISS SARAH BARNARD. Massachusetts.

Petit point picture, French design from the Women's Educational and Industrial Union and worked by Miss Sarah Barnard, Massachusetts.

4. *Courtesy of:* MRS. BENJAMIN TILTON, New York.

Petit point picture, "Nana's Night Out," "For Helen, 1936, from Grandmother." Designed and worked by Mrs. Benjamin Tilton, New York.

5. *Courtesy of:* MRS. BENJAMIN TILTON, New York.

Petit point picture, "When Maud was Very Young," by her mother, Mrs. Benjamin Tilton, New York, 1930.

point picture of Mrs. Tilton's daughter, Maud. She is shown standing in the center of their garden at Black Point, Connecticut, in early Spring, surrounded by all her favorite flowers and pet dogs. Nearby and half-hidden among the garden plants are two rabbits, two wee lambs, and a deer. To the right in a dove cote are cooing doves. Ferns are at the lower left-hand corner of this tapestry embroidery, and to the right of them pond lilies are embroidered. These are followed across the picture by all of Maud's favorite Bermuda flowers. The pine tree above is a replica of one in the garden. Sitting on a limb are two affectionate parrakeets. In the sky are sea gulls from the Sound and another pair of birds are placed beneath the title of the picture which reads, "When Maud Was Very Young. By her mother. 1930."

Mrs. Tilton explains that this represents the history of one year and that she adapted the subjects as she went along without any particular plan. An atmosphere of fantasy and poetry manifests itself in this tender needlepoint rendering which is worked in hazy, misty, delicate shades of fine yarn.

Miss Sarah Barnard of Massachusetts made a pair of small oval pictures in petit point which are interesting in their light effects. Both are designed after the French classic period yet depart considerably in spirit from the formalized work of that time. The figures, in Empire costume, approach a lake where one of the group bends over to feed a swan. They are outlined with light as if the sun were just beyond the tree tops. There is an element of realism in the shadings and yet the hills and masses of foliage in the landscape are very simply and flatly rendered. The companion picture shows two blown figures in classic Greek draperies dancing with a gazelle upon a formal garden lawn. A summer house balances the Greek temple by the lake which appears in the companion picture. The pair were designed by the Woman's Educational and Industrial Union and have been very sensitively embroidered by Miss Barnard.

SHIP PICTURES

Clipper ships recall a romantic and vital period in American history which many American women are recording today in embroidered canvases for the decoration of their homes.

Mrs. Albert L. Mason, of Stonington, Connecticut, is directly descended from a famous family of owners and builders of clipper ships who conducted the industries at Mystic, Connecticut. She has made a needlepoint picture of "The Ana Eliza," a brig on which her grandmother, then a bride, made a voyage with her husband, Captain Charles H. Mallory. That was the period when the clippers sailed around the Horn to California, making their fastest records in the gold rush of '49. Captain Mallory ran a shipping line at the end of the clipper era. He would not go into the making of iron ships but became one of the founders of the Mallory Steamship Line then trading between Florida and Texas.

Mrs. Mason has stitched "The Ana Eliza" in tête-de-negre. The sails are in beige browns. The sky is carried out in shading from light pinkish yarns to pale blue blending into a deeper or royal-blue tone. These blues are reflected in the waves. The delightful panel is used as an overmantel decoration in the dining room of Mrs. Mason's home.

An interesting pair of small, oval pictures of shipping subjects has been finely embroidered in needlepoint by Mrs. Howard Pancoast of Philadelphia to decorate "a Victorian courting parlor." The first is sentimentally entitled "The Sailor's Sweetheart." The gallant ship's officer is greeting a romantic looking lady, dressed in Victorian costume. His ship may be seen in the distance. Matching this picture is "The Hopeless Vigil." The wife, dressed in a bouffant gown of the 80's, is shown standing upon a hilltop with her little son. They are looking out to sea for the loved one who will never return. Victorian atmosphere is further suggested by the tombstone introduced at the left of the scene. The pictures were designed by Miss Agnes C. Sims.

Mrs. Ethel M. Kremer of New York has made a needlepoint ship picture as an overmantel decoration for her salt-box house in Stonington. The design was drawn free-hand on the canvas by Mrs. Kremer who built it up from a newspaper advertisement. The yarns were selected at random from a large collection of wools accumulated during travels abroad. They are mostly French yarns. The landscape, Mrs. Kremer explains, is intended to look like Stonington, as seen from the harbor approach. It is rather delicately scaled in color and has been worked in both petit point and gros point.

A sailboat centers a composition designed by Miss Jane Kerr of Portland, Oregon, who describes her work in the following terms:

> This picture was stitched on canvas in quarter stitch, using French wools, and was made in 1934. The idea was inspired by the view of a small town and the hills beyond across the Willamette River from my home. Two years ago it won an award in the Junior League exhibition in Richmond, Virginia. The colors are rich and bright and it is an original design, stitched in as I went along, without using a preliminary design.

This is a decidedly entertaining picture. Various activities on the river are shown. Men are rowing in small boats or fishing; swans are swimming away from the swift sailing boat. Details of the bulrushes in the foreground and the many houses of the town which rises on the distant hill are stitched in decoratively. Fir trees add a tapestry effect to the interesting embroidery.

"The Clipper Ship Returns," designed by the author, is a gros-point wall panel which shows a vessel in full sail nearing the harbor. The period is 1868. A man and his wife are hailing the ship, the lady carrying a large bouquet from the garden which is intended for her sister who is returning home. An apple-woman is waiting to sell fruit to the sailors; a widow is joining the group of watchers to wait for her son, also a passenger. Ahead of her is the ship's owner on his way to the wharf, seriously concerned with the cargo and its value, while in the center a small orphan boy, with all his worldly belongings in the bag over his shoulder, is hailing the ship hoping to be taken on as cabin boy, thus to become a man and see the world.

FLOWER PICTURES

Flower studies reproduced from one's own garden or adapted from paintings always have been favorite subjects for embroidery. They are presented today in needlepoint panels large enough to place on the wall in living rooms, dining rooms or other parts of the home where soft, colorful decoration is desired. Many excellent flower pictures have been made in different sections of the country with a high degree of artistry and skill. Two are reproduced to record different styles of design. One was adapted from a painting and the other developed from flowers which appear in nineteenth century engravings widely used for interior decoration.

Mrs. Wharton Sinkler of Elkins Park, Pennsylvania, is a versatile embroiderer who is also tireless in working interesting designs in fine needlepoint. Keenly interested in gardening, Mrs. Sinkler admired an old Dutch oil painting of flowers done in 1736 by Jan Van Huysmans, and made a copy from the original in the National Gallery in London. The composition is reproduced in a "painty" way in stitches that richly blend the shadows and color tones of the numerous flowers clustered in the vase. Tulips, carnations, delphiniums, roses, morning-glories and poppies are all finely represented. Below on the pedestal base bunches of grapes in light green and deep mauve lend variety to the picture. A small bird's nest containing five eggs rests upon the lowest band at the base of the picture, providing further atmosphere. Mrs. Sinkler has stitched a frame in needlepoint around the group to emphasize the purely decorative quality of the panel, adding a very simple narrow frame for the final mounting. Her initials and the date of completion are placed in the lower corner, L. E. S. 1935.

Mrs. Benjamin Tilton, admiring the colored engravings of flowers made in America in the nineteenth century, decided to try reproducing her own garden flowers in a composition in petit point in the Victorian manner. She has accomplished admirable results considering the fact that she has not had any training in the fine arts and worked out her designs spontaneously. The bouquet has been embroidered upon the finest cream scrim similar to that used in the 1850's. The background is left uncovered, providing a soft tone against which to place in relief the many soft colorings of the roses, morning-glories, delphiniums, narcissi, tulips, lilies of the valley and freesias. The wall picture is signed and dated in petit point, Anna Tilton, 1937.

FAMILY PORTRAITS

Another petit-point tapestry picture made by Mrs. Benjamin Tilton is a family portrait of her daughter and son-in-law, Mr. and Mrs.

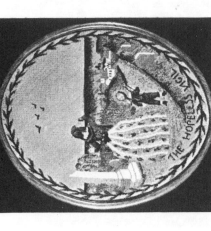

6. *Courtesy of:* MRS. HOWARD PANCOAST, Pennsylvania.

3. *Courtesy of:* MISS JANE KERR, Oregon.

5. *Courtesy of:* MRS. ALBERT L. MASON.

2. *Courtesy of:* THE MINERVA YARN INDUSTRIES.

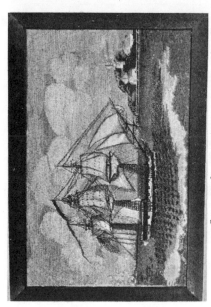

1. *Courtesy of:* MRS. ETHEL M. KREMER, New York.

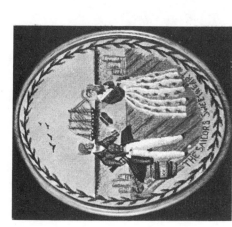

4. *Courtesy of:* MRS. HOWARD PANCOAST, Philadelphia, Pennsylvania.

1. Needlepoint Ship Picture with Stonington, Connecticut, landscape by Mrs. Ethel M. Kremer, New York. 2. Needlepoint picture, "The Clipper Ship" designed by Georgiana Brown Harbeson, 1937, New York. 3. Needlepoint picture of the Willamette River designed and made in quarter stitch by Miss Jane Kerr, Portland, Oregon. 4. Needlepoint Americana picture "Sailor's Sweetheart" worked by Mrs. Howard Pancoast, Philadelphia, Pennsylvania and designed by Agnes C. Sims. 5. Needlepoint Ship Picture, "The Brig, Ana Elisa of Mystic," by Mrs. Albert L. Mason, Stonington, Connecticut. 6. "Hopeless Vigil"; Needlepoint picture worked by Mrs. Howard Pancoast, Philadelphia, Pennsylvania.

1. *Courtesy of:* MRS. BREWSTER JENNINGS, Long Island, New York.

Needlepoint Picture; "The Shepherdess" by Mrs. Brewster Jennings, Long Island, New York.

2. *Courtesy of:* MRS. FRANK ROWELL, New York.

Needlepoint Chair Seat; in Floral Design by Mrs. Frank Rowell. Designed by Mrs. Lillian Barton-Wilson.

3. *Courtesy of:* MISS MARY MADISON MAGUIRE, New York.

Needlepoint Bench Top; designed and worked by Miss Mary Madison Maguire, New York.

4. *Courtesy of:* MRS. FRANK ROWELL, New York.

Chair Seat; one of set of six chairs worked in **Bargello** stitches by Mrs. Frank Rowell, New York.

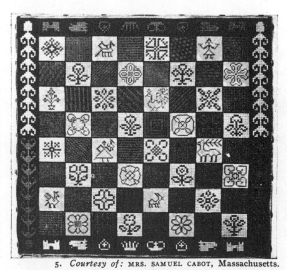

5. *Courtesy of:* MRS. SAMUEL CABOT, Massachusetts.

Needlepoint Chess Board. Designed and worked by Mrs. Samuel Cabot, Massachusetts.

James Jeremiah Wadsworth, and their small daughter, Alice Anne. Two pet Scotties and dignified German shepherds are pictured standing on a hillside which overlooks the Genesee Valley in upper New York State. The farm is in the distance and future dreams are envisioned on the imaginary mountains. The view includes the white house on top of the hill, the house which belongs to young James at the lower right surrounded with its gardens and trees, and at the left the home of James W. Wadsworth. Representative Wadsworth's home is shown at the upper right. E. B. Symington's children are stitched in, riding horseback to the lower right of the house, while above in the sky is an airplane representing the Wadsworths' interest in flying. The hunting costume which Mr. Wadsworth is wearing not only introduces gay color into the picture but indicates his love of that sport.

Mrs. Tilton has here created a soft-toned and atmospheric panel which carries a feeling of Spring in the soft greens of the landscape and in the flowering trees. Love's young desires, hopes and ambitions, and a delightful family unity are suggested in the composition. It is dedicated to "Hart Tilton Wadsworth from her Mother." Mrs. Tilton's initials are embroidered over the year in which it was made, 1931. Thus began a series of family records.

A second family portrait made the year following again displays Mrs. Tilton's prowess in petit point. It portrays another young daughter, Susanne Alexander, strolling in the garden with her husband, Archie Alexander. The landscape is romantic and symbolical. The twin apple trees in blossom indicate the united families; the doves, young love. The Stevens' castle in the background across the Hudson River represents the Alexander family home. The waters of the Hudson are stitched to flow around the foreground of the tapestry picture to meet the waters of Long Island Sound and idealize the tie to the home of the Tilton family at Black Point, Connecticut, which is embroidered at the left of the picture. Here also, Mrs. Tilton presents the pet Sealyham, the little bunnies, the pigeons, and numbers of dainty flowers worked in the mille fleurs manner of early fifteenth century French tapestries. Within a ribbon scroll is the legend, "1932 for Susanne Alexander from her Mother A. B. T."

SHEPHERDESS PORTRAIT

A needlepoint picture that is in a class by itself is the shepherdess panel made by Mrs. Brewster Jennings of Long Island, who loves such embroidery. It is, in a way, a reference panel of techniques on which many styles of canvas embroidery have been attempted very successfully. The design is adapted from an ancient seventeenth century English "tapestry embroidery" picture; Mrs. Jennings has made her own version of some of the details. The colorings are spontaneously fresh and crisp. It is framed with wood in an off-white tone. Being unglassed, the stitched surfaces give a true tapestry effect when it is placed upon the wall.

HOUSES AND GARDENS

Pictures of the home are a comparatively new fashion in needlepoint. They are increasingly popular for wall decorations.

A recently completed needlepoint panel worked by Mrs. Daniel Volkmann shows her home in San Francisco, with the panorama of San Francisco Bay and the Golden Gate with the new bridge spanning it. The view is that seen from the rear windows and was draughted onto the canvas by Mrs. Lillian Barton-Wilson. The flowers and shrubbery surrounding the house provide an attractive tapestry setting for the architecture. The family coat of arms has been worked in at the left of the foreground beside the panel bearing the inscription, "Beatrice Volkmann, San Francisco, Cal. 1937." The technique includes both petit point and gros point.

Crossing the continent to Mt. Desert in Maine, we find a residence depicted upon canvas by Mrs. Wharton Sinkler of Maine and Pennsylvania, who also executed it in needlepoint in 1937. The architecture and the landscaping is rendered on the whole in the romantic style. The naturalistic clouds and strong sunlight effects of light and shade are dramatic and typical of a breezy, summer day in Maine. Mrs. Sinkler paints with her needle in excellent stitch technique.

The approach to the country residence of Mrs. Rufus L. Patterson of New York has been charmingly rendered in soft, atmospheric tones. The design includes part of a formal garden and the terraces. It is a small panel and therefore was executed by Mrs. Patterson in fine needlepoint.

Mrs. John W. Castles of Convent, New Jersey, also has reproduced her country residence in needlepoint. The old-fashioned stone construction has been simply and amusingly rendered. It is backed by evergreens which have been treated somewhat in the spirit of a sampler. The decoration is also formalized in that fashion. Inclusion of the few garden flowers, tulips and dogwood, a bit of white fence and the large pet Scottie or Cairn is typical of the early personal records. Initials and the date are added, E. E. C. '33.

Mrs. Samuel Megargee Wright of Villa Nova, Pennsylvania, has pictured in needlepoint the house of an ancestor:

> The Residence of Nicasius de Sillé, First Councillor and Vice Director to Director General Stuyvesant, Commissioned as First Councillor July 24th, 1653. One of the original proprietors of New Utrecht, Long Island. In 1657 he built there the first stone house which remained standing there until 1850, when it was destroyed.

The design on canvas was adapted by Miss Agnes Sims from an old print. The quaint stone house of the seventeenth century is executed beautifully in both the landscape and architectural features. A lettered inscription gives the name of the ancestor and the date of his residence.

Stitch and color contrasts between the architecture in the background and the foreground of paths, urns, shrubs, and trees have been very ably handled by Mrs. Allston Jenkins of Pennsylvania in the panel showing the entrance to a garden on the estate of Mr. and Mrs. Fraser Harris in Chestnut Hill. A display of skillful technique is shown in the use of mixed wools in the grass of the foreground, which achieves the play of light and shadow in each tent stitch. The same principle is used in a three-tone blend of coral, orange and violet to render the coloring of the soft brick wall which is accented by the same general tone intensified in the steps. Shadows on the window panes are also adroitly suggested to give the feeling that they are glass and not merely wool. The general masses and drawing are worked in gros point; only the large urns are carefully and painstak-

ingly stitched in petit point. The light and shade in the details of the urns are dexterously indicated. The picture is bordered with a frame of trailing ivy leaves, a bit of formal design which conveys the true feeling of a garden, and reveals a sympathetic understanding of the subject on the part of the designer, Mrs. Charles Platt, also of Pennsylvania.

NEEDLEPOINT SEALS

The growing interest in all types of design to apply upon canvas to be worked in embroidery finds an entertaining outlet in seals of countries, organizations or clubs. These are often made in needlepoint and used as wall decorations.

Mrs. Theodore Roosevelt, Jr., has made a very large embroidery commemorating the family's residence in Porto Rico when Theodore Roosevelt, Jr., was the Governor there, 1929-1931. This notation is incorporated in the design and worked in outline stitch. The official seal of Porto Rico is worked in needlepoint. Its design comes directly from the days of King Ferdinand and Queen Isabella when Spain governed the Island. The central symbol represents the lamb of St. John for whom the city of San Juan was named. The large leaves back of the seal are worked in long and short stitch and the entire background is filled in with a fine Gobelin stitch in silk floss. The panel is inscribed "E. B. R. fecit." It was embroidered in 1936.

"Pegasus" is the official seal of the Cosmopolitan Club of New York which has been adapted and worked in petit point by Mrs. Robert Coleman Taylor of New York, a club member. It is executed in tones of off-white with canary-yellow shadows for the winged horse which prances on clouds of the same airy tones. Matching this is the ribbon band bearing the Club motto stitched in Latin, "Vivida Vis Animi," which translated is "Life, Strength, and Spirit." The decoration is silhouetted against a near turquoise-blue background. It has been mounted under a glass frame painted in black and gold. Hanging upon the wall in a small reception room of the Club, it repeats the color scheme employed for the decorations, at the same time providing a handsome note of interest for guests and members alike. It has been signed and dated, L. G. Taylor, 1932.

1. *Courtesy of:* MRS. BENJAMIN TILTON, *New York.*

Needlepoint Family Sampler of Mr. and Mrs. James Jeremiah Wadsworth, their daughter Alice Ann, Home and pets. By Mrs. Benjamin Tilton, New York, 1931.

2. *Courtesy of:* MRS. BENJAMIN TILTON, New York.

Petit point portrait sampler "For Susan Alexander" from her mother. A.C.T., 1932. By Mrs. Benjamin Tilton, New York.

3. *Courtesy of:* MRS. WHARTON SINKLER, Elkins Park, Pennsylvania.

Needlepoint Flower and Fruits Picture; after Old Dutch Flower painting by Huysmans, 1936, by Louise E. Sinkler, Elkins Park, Pennsylvania.

4. *Courtesy of:* MRS. BENJAMIN TILTON, New York.

Vase of Flowers; designed after old engraving and worked in petit point on fine scrim, 1934, by Anna Tilton, New York.

1. *Courtesy of:* MRS. SAMUEL MEGARGEE WRIGHT, Villa Nova, Penn.

Needlepoint portrait, residence of Nicasius de Sillé, in Long Island, 1653, from print, by Mrs. Samuel Megargee Wright, Villa Nova, Pennsylvania.

2. *Courtesy of:* MRS. DANIEL VOLKMAN, California.

Needlepoint portrait, residence of Beatrice Volkman, designed on canvas by Lillian Barton-Wilson and worked in 1937 by Mrs. Daniel Volkman, California.

3. *Courtesy of:* MRS. ALLSTON JENKINS, Pennsylvania.

House and Garden portrait, residence and garden of Mrs. Frazer Harris by Mrs. Allston Jenkins, Pennsylvania.

4. *Courtesy of:* MRS. RUFUS L. PATTERSON, New York.

Needlepoint residence portrait by Mrs. Rufus L. Patterson, New York.

5. *Courtesy of:* MRS. JOHN W. CASTLES, New Jersey.

Needlepoint residence portrait by Mrs. John W. Castles, New Jersey.

6. *Courtesy of:* MRS. WHARTON SINKLER, Pennsylvania.

Needlepoint portrait of residence, Mt. Desert Island, Maine, 1937 by Louise E. Sinkler, Pennsylvania.

To a certain extent patterns and design inspiration are still being derived from different European sources, but within recent years greater emphasis is being placed upon American design and creations which spring from the embroiderer's imagination. The general trend in today's needlepoint is toward a return to the simplicity of design of the pioneer period. It is the result of independent thinking on subject matter close at home. There is an indication of strength and vitality in this effort to develop individuality.

CHAPTER XXXIII

NEEDLEWORK OF THE FUTURE

"Far brighter scenes a future age,
The Muse predicts, these States will hail,
Whose genius may the world engage,
Whose deeds may over death prevail,
And happier systems bring to view,
Than all the eastern sages knew."

PHILIP FRENEAU.

 EQUALS THE UNKNOWN QUANtity and the Examplar of the future. All sorts of conjectures arise as to the designs which will evolve in newer needlework. Certain ideas and concepts will remain true to form. Familiar and natural elements, the symbols ingrained in racial expression as firmly as old folk tales, will appear in new styles and arrangements. Relating fundamentally to human experience, they recall older patterns of existence and for this reason will ever be thrown upon the white screen of future effort. Upon that same backdrop will be cast the shadows of personalities which, illumined by the past, are expressing themselves in needlework today. Thus the art of the present becomes a part of the living pattern which, like that cast by dancing figures spotlighted from below, constantly presents to the observer new concepts, new forms and new designs.

As long as human beings are human there will always be the urge to catch and preserve the hundred and one things we live by, things of the heart, the mind and the spirit. Needleworkers would fasten these elusive qualities with stitches upon canvas or gossamer. Whether the inspiration comes from the intimate joys of homelife, precious memories or deep experiences, they wish to give it visible expression so that it may be shared by others.

The examplar of the future may speak a new language through the medium of material as yet undiscovered. The essence of spun glass may be presented in a new thread with which to embroider upon transparent fabric, strongly fashioned yet giving the appearance of sheerest gauze. New color effects may be evolved, a strand of thread which is opalescent, for example. Instead of three threads of different shades to produce variety or depth in a background covering, one thread in the new order may achieve this effect by virtue of its composition. Materials heretofore unheard of may be developed from entirely new sources. A million possibilities rise before the mind's eye and seem as glitteringly magnificent as the treasure which Aladdin beheld when the Genii spread before him the jewels of an enchanted kingdom.

Designs inspired by new mediums may be indeed "such stuff as dreams are made of." More nearly approaching the heights where imagination and spirit roam, they may discard entirely the reproduction of familiar everyday things. Experiments with pure abstractions may become the rule, or rhythms expressive of the elements of harmony, the vibratory effects caused by the interplay of colors, with the emphasis not upon the recognition of form but on the effective interpretation of mood and transitory vision. Those who live, love and work at that time will perhaps find food for thoughtful new conceptions in looking upon the antiques produced in our time, even as we look back with appreciative pleasure and joy to find inspiration in the efforts of our ancestors.

We in our particular niche in history must express ourselves with whatever means we have at hand. The obvious requirements of solid accomplishment are sound materials and good craftsmanship. But more than this, needleworkers of today must develop their work in accordance with the newest, broadest and best conceptions of which they are capable. Otherwise expression through this medium will not grow in proportion to other accomplishments of our time. We have often overlooked the artistic possibilities to be found in this oldest outlet of personal creativeness in which women have been adept since the first fig leaf was sewn into a little apron by Eve. Heretofore much artistry has been diverted, and happily so, to utilitarian requirements. This also is true today, but not so much through necessity as was the case in earlier years. In this modern age more time might be directed toward poetic expression with the needle; then this twentieth century would be mirrored in as new and varied needlework as the minds of today are capable of creating.

With the rich supply of diversified materials at hand women of this period may expend their energies directly upon new conceptions in stitched composition. Modern textiles offer infinite scope for strikingly forceful and unique backgrounds along lines entirely different from those utilized before. We have the past examples of needlework made in America to inspire or amuse us, according to our disposition. Good or bad, they reflect a great effort to say something. They express a growth; continued growth means a pruning, the shearing off of odd conceptions and purely repetitive offshoots. Exact reproductions of outworn themes are wasteful of energy and impulse. Wherever an original idea looks gaily out at us from one of these older works we are immediately delighted and begin to inquire among ourselves how the needleworker came by it. Or when a work shows the new use of old, cast-off pieces of material, arranged, assembled and ingeniously patterned with amusing stitchery, we are pleasantly stimulated by the imagination shown. Many such examples remain from the sparse days of America's beginnings. This expenditure of creative effort is equally desirable today. Work so produced may suggest to other needleworkers in later years a new point of departure. They may see reflected in such needlework the fact that living has been courageously faced in this generation with the same pioneering zeal that was shown by the earliest settlers.

At the close of the twentieth century it may transpire that the art of embroidery and the art of painting will parallel the story of the hare and the tortoise; while painting goes through its convolutions of impressionism, futurism, realism, surrealism, abstractionism and the other "isms," needlepainting is quietly stitching its way toward greater things and may win its leadership eventually in the field of fine arts, a place which it once held in the earliest stages of the world's history.

~~~~~~

SPECIAL ACKNOWLEDGMENTS

~~~~~~

For the major photography special thanks are due Mr. Barron Callen of New York, whose artistry, patience and unfailing interest have been of tremendous value.

Also to Mr. A. D. Lindauer of New York and the many other photographers who have helped in the reproduction of the various items from different localities in the United States, the author offers her appreciation of their splendid craftsmanship and cooperation. Among them are:

J. H. Shaefer and Son, Maryland.
Drix Duryea, New York.
Peter Juley, New York.
Richard Averill Smith, New York.
Ed. N. Burdick, Rhode Island.
R. D. and M. E. Sniveley, Massachusetts.
Shapiro Studios, Massachusetts.

H. D. Barlow, New Jersey.
H. W. Reynolds, Massachusetts.
Ruth S. Baker, New York.
Walter R. Merryman, Massachusetts.
Mrs. Cora E. Wilson, New Jersey.
Studer, San Antonio, Texas.
E. P. McLaughlin, Massachusetts.

BIBLIOGRAPHY

ORCHARD, WILLIAM C., *Indian Porcupine-Quill and Beadwork* (New York: The Exposition of Indian Tribal Arts, Inc., 1931).

ORCHARD, WILLIAM C., *Beads and Beadwork of the American Indian* (New York: Museum of the American Indian, Heye Foundation, 1929).

WISSLER, CLARK, "Material Culture of the Blackfoot Indians," *Anthropological Papers, American Museum of Natural History* (New York, 1910), Vol. V., Part I.

WISSLER, CLARK, "North American Indians of the Plains," *American Museum of Natural History Handbook* (New York, 1927), Serial No. 1.

STEFANSSON, VILHJALMUR, "The Eskimo and Civilization," *The American Museum Journal* (New York, 1912), Vol. XII., No. 6.

NELSON, EDWARD WILLIAM, "The Eskimo About Bering Strait," *Bureau of American Ethnology Annual Report* (Washington, 1899), Vol. XVIII., Part I.

HODGE, F. W., ed., "Handbook of the American Indians North of Mexico," *Bureau of American Ethnology Bulletin* (Washington, 1907), No. 30, Vol. I.

CLARK, W. P., *The Indian Sign Language* (Philadelphia: L. R. Hamersly, 1885).

KROEBER, ALFRED L., "The Arapaho," *American Museum of Natural History Bulletin* (New York, 1902 & 1907), Vol. XVIII.

SPINDEN, HERBERT J., *Indian Symbolism* (New York: The Exposition of Indian Tribal Arts, Inc., 1931).

MORGAN, LEWIS H., "Report upon the Articles Furnished to the Indian Collection," *Regents of the University of the State of New York Annual Report* (Albany, 1850), Vol. III.

ADAM, RANDOLPH G., *The Gateway to American History* (Boston: Little, Brown & Co., 1930).

ADAM, RANDOLPH G., *Pilgrims, Indians and Patriots* (Boston: Little, Brown & Co., 1928).

GOODRICH, SAMUEL G. (Peter Parley), *The Manners, Customs and Antiquities of the Indians of North and South America* (New York: John Allen, 1844).

WINSLOW, OLA ELIZABETH, ed., *Harper's Literary Museum: Selected from Early American Writings* (New York: Harper & Bros., 1927).

DOW, GEORGE FRANCIS, *The Arts and Crafts in New England: 1704-1755* (Topsfield, Mass.: The Wayside Press, 1927).

DAY, SHERMAN, *Historical Collections of the State of Pennsylvania* (Philadelphia: George W. Gorton, 1843).

RICHARDSON, JOHN, *Thumbnail History of the Broad Silk Industry in the United States* (New York: Woodward Baldwin & Co., 1931).

LOSSING, BENSON J., ed., *Harper's Encyclopedia of United States History from 458 A.D. to 1912* (New York and London: Harper & Bros., c. 1912), Vol. VII.

BOWNE, ELIZA SOUTHGATE, *A Girl's Life Eighty Years Ago* (New York: Chas. Scribner's Sons, 1887).

LAMBERT, MISS, *The Handbook of Needlework* (New York: Wiley & Putnam, 1842).

HARRISON, CONSTANCE CARY, *Woman's Handwork in Modern Homes* (New York: Chas. Scribner's Sons, 1881).

SAWARD, BLANCHE C., *Dictionary of Needlework* (London: L. Upcut Gill, 1887).

PULLMAN, MRS., *The Ladies' Manual of Fancy-Work* (New York: Dick & Fitzgerald, 1858).

BLANC, CHARLES, *Art in Ornament and Dress* (New York: Scribner, Welford & Armstrong, 1877).

GLAISTER, ELIZABETH, *Needlework* (London: Macmillan & Co., 1881).

HALE, LUCRETIA PEABODY, ed., *Designs in Outline for Art Needlework* (Boston: S. W. Tilton & Co., 1879).

HARTLEY, MISS FLORENCE, *The Ladies' Handbook of Fancy and Ornamental Work* (Philadelphia: G. G. Evans, 1859).

FROST, SARAH ANNIE, *Ladies' Guide to Needlework, Embroidery, Etc.* (New York: H. T. Williams, 1877).

WEBSTER, N. D., *Quilts: Their Story and How to Make Them* (New York: Doubleday, Doran & Co., 1928).

FINLEY, RUTH E., *Old Patchwork Quilts and the Women Who Made Them* (Philadelphia & London: J. B. Lippincott Co., 1929).

KING, ELIZABETH, "Quilting," *Leisure League of America Little Books* (New York, 1934), No. 8.

BOWLES, ELLA SHANNON, *Homespun Handicrafts* (Philadelphia & London: J. B. Lippincott Co., 1931).

EARL, ALICE MORSE, *Homelife in Colonial Days* (New York: Macmillan Co., 1898).

GARRICK, ALICE VAN LEER, *Collector's Luck* (Boston: Atlantic Monthly Press, 1919).

EBERLEIN, HAROLD DONALDSON and McCLURE, ABBOTT, *The Practical Book of American Antiques*, revised edition (Garden City, N. Y.: Garden City Publishing Co., 1927).

LAWSON, MARIE A., *Hail Columbia: The Life of a Nation* (Garden City, N. Y.: Doubleday, Doran & Co., 1931).

McCLELLAN, ELIZABETH, *History of American Costume, 1607-1870* (New York: Tudor Publishing Co., 1929).

WARWICK, EDWARD and PITZ, HENRY C., *Early American Costume)* (New York: Century Co., 1929).

ABBOTT, KATHARINE M., *Old Paths and Legends of the New England Border* (New York & London: G. P. Putnam's Sons, 1909).

ROSSITER, WILLIAM S., *Days and Ways in Old Boston* (Boston: R. H. Stearns & Co., 1915).

MANCHESTER, HERBERT, *Four Centuries of Sport in America, 1490-1890* (New York: The Derrydale Press, 1931).

TATTERSALL, C. E. C., *A History of British Carpets* (London: F. Lewis, Ltd., 1934).

WALTON, PERRY, *The Story of Textiles* (New York: Tudor Publishing Co., 1925).

LITTLE, FRANCES, *Early American Textiles* (New York: Century Co., 1931).

BOLTON, ETHEL STANWOOD and COE, EVA JOHNSTON, *American Samplers* (Boston: privately printed by the Massachusetts Society of the Colonial Dames of America, 1921).

VANDERPOEL, EMILY NOYES, *American Lace and Lace Makers* (New Haven & London: Yale University Press, Oxford University Press, 1924).

WHITING, GERTRUDE, *Tools and Toys of Stitchery* (New York: Columbia University Press, 1928).

ASHTON, LEIGH, *Samplers* (Boston & London: The Medici Society, 1926).

HUISH, MARCUS B., *Samplers and Tapestry Embroideries* (London: The Fine Art Society & Longmans, Green & Co., 1900).

JOURDAIN, MARGARET, *The History of English Secular Embroidery* (London: K. Paul, Trench, Trübner & Co., Ltd., 1910).

SELIGMAN, G. SAVILLE and HUGHES, TALBOT, *Domestic Needlework* (London: Country Life, undated).

CHRISTIE, MRS. ARCHIBALD, *Samplers and Stitches: A Handbook of the Embroiderer's Art* (New York and London: E. P. Dutton & Co. and B. T. Bashford, Ltd., 1920).

CHRISTIE, MRS. ARCHIBALD, *Embroidery and Tapestry Weaving* (London: Sir Isaac Pitman & Sons, Ltd., 1920).

VAN DOREN, MARK, ed., *Masterpieces of American Poets* (New York: Garden City Publishing Co., 1936).

CHAMPLIN, J. D. and PERKINS, C. C., eds., *Cyclopedia of Painters and Paintings* (New York: Chas. Scribner's Sons, 1886-87), Vol. II.

Bryan's Dictionary of Painters and Engravers (London: George Bell & Sons, 1904), Vol. III.

CAFFIN, CHARLES H., *The Story of American Painting*, Garden City Publishing Co., N. Y., 1937.

INDEX